A Journey Of Words

A Journey of Words
Copyright © 2022 by Lin Stepp
Published by Mountain Hill Press
Email contact: steppcom@aol.com

Scripture used in this book, whether quoted or paraphrased by the characters, is taken from the King James Version of the Bible.

Cover design: Katherine E. Stepp
Interior design: J. L. Stepp, Mountain Hill Press
Editor: Elizabeth S. James

Library of Congress Cataloging-in-Publication Data

Stepp, Dr. Lin and James L.
A Journey of Words: A Christian Devotional

ISBN: 979-8-9853681-4-7
First Mountain Hill Press Trade Paperback Printing: April 2022

Library of Congress Control Number: 2022900700

DEDICATION

This book is dedicated to all our fans, friends,
and wonderful readers who kept asking and
urging us to write a devotional guidebook.
We listened.

ACKNOWLEDGEMENTS

A lovely quote reads: *"The one who blesses others is abundantly blessed"* … and truly as we worked on this devotional guide, praying over each daily devotion written, and asking for God's help about what to write, we ended up being the ones most blessed through our labors. So our most important acknowledgement is to the Lord for His gracious help with this book.

Thanks also to all those whose inspirational quotes we used throughout the book—some well-known, some lesser known, some still living, some gone on to glory long ago. Their words reminded us of the importance and impact of the words we speak and of the legacy we leave behind in everything we say and write.

Final thanks to all on our staff who worked to make this book a blessing:
- J.L. Stepp, production design, editing, and proofing
- Lin Stepp, research, editing, and proofing
- Elizabeth S. James, copy editor and editorial advisor
- Katherine Stepp, cover design and graphics

*"My heart is inditing a good matter: I speak of the things I have made
as touching the king: my tongue is the pen of a ready writer."*
- Judges 5:14

*"O Lord, that I may publish with the voice of thanksgiving
and tell of all thy wonderous works."*
- Psalm 26:7

INTRODUCTION
By Lin Stepp

How this devotional came to be is an interesting story …

In past, while writing one of my novels, DELIA'S PLACE, set in the Smoky Mountains, I found myself pausing in the midst of my story. Two of my fictional characters, cousins Delia and Hallie Walker, had recently met for the first time at the mountain home of Delia's aunt, Dee Walker Ward, in the Mynatt Park neighborhood behind Gatlinburg. Both young women were running from problems and troubles in their lives and had bonded quickly because of that.

After commiserating about their difficulties, and wishing for answers to the messes they both were in, the girls find themselves remembering how Aunt Dee's faith had always helped her in her day-to-day life. Hallie recalls Dee had a few favorite books she used in her prayer and study times and she suggests they look for one of those to read together to learn more of what Dee knew about walking in a deeper faith.

Needing an idea for one of Aunt Dee's books the girls could find and talk about in the story, I decided a devotional would be a good choice. I own several, that mean a lot to me, but for legal reasons I couldn't use an actual published devotional guide. I needed, for my storyline, to "think up" and design a book the girls could use, so after a little thought and prayer I created a fictional devotional. I imagined it would be fun if each day's devotion was built on a spiritual "Word for the Day"—like Zeal or Hope. Being a lover of quotes, I decided every devotion would begin with an inspirational quote, containing the word for the day, followed by a helpful life teaching with Bible references for further study. Then each devotion would close with a prayer and scripture, that contained the word for the day again. With my story idea in mind and needing a fictitious title, I chose *A Journey of Words* for the name of the book.

This became the devotional guide the cousins used each day in their morning Bible studies. At one point, over breakfast later in the story, when Hallie sees Delia at the kitchen table reading her Bible and the daily devotion, she asks, "*What's the Word for the Day? Read it to me while I cook.*" A scene follows with the girls reading and talking about the day's message and teaching built around the word "Walk". The girls use the book just as I envisioned, with the daily readings helping them both in their lives.

There were actually only a few references in the novel to this devotional guide, but to my surprise, after the book DELIA'S PLACE published, I began to get email requests wanting to know where to purchase the guidebook. Most readers seemed to assume it was a "real" devotional guide they might purchase and they wanted to know the book's author as they were having trouble locating the guidebook. Of course, I kindly replied to all these notes, telling readers the book was only a fictional title … but the requests continued for several years. Even after DELIA'S PLACE was reissued in a new format and cover, readers continued asking me for more information about this devotional guidebook. Many even encouraged me to write it!

At an author event, at an annual festival my husband J.L. and I attend yearly, a lady came up to our row of tables in the Authors Corner with several other regional authors. *"There you are,"* she said. *"I've read all your books but I came to get the name of that devotional guide you talked about in DELIA'S PLACE. I want to get several copies for friends and family for Christmas gifts. My bookstore said you must have written the name of the book down incorrectly, as they couldn't locate it in their system, so I want you to write down the name of the book and the author for me."* As she paused, my husband smiled at her and explained the devotional guide was a fictitious one I'd made up for the novel's storyline. She frowned at his words. *"Well, it sounded so good,"* the woman said, putting a hand on her hip. *"I think it's real mean-spirited it's not a real book. You need to write one."* And she all but stomped off in a huff. … One of our author friends sitting next to us laughed and said, *"Well, Lin, I guess I know what your next book needs to be."* I shook my head at him. *"Not unless J.L. Stepp writes half of the devotions,"* I answered. *"It takes a lot of time and prayer to write 365 devotions."* In the car later, driving home, we talked about the lady's visit and decided, due to the demand for the book we'd had for so many years, that we would write a devotional guide like the one in the novel. And that's how *A Journey of Words* came to be.

"Whatsoever ye do, do all to the glory of God."
-1 Corinthians 10:31

"Your potential is the sum of all the possibilities
God has for your life."
- Charles Stanley

"God will meet you where you are in order to
take you where He wants you to go."
- Tony Evans

January

JANUARY 1
The Word for the Day is "Year."

Quote for the Day:
"Enter the coming year with renewed hope in the power of God to do through you what you cannot." – John MacArthur

The New Year is often a time for self-evaluation and for making a list of New Year's Resolutions. These resolutions often focus on changes needed in our personal lives or in our habits to make our lives happier and better. We make our resolutions and then ask God to bless them and help us keep them. Perhaps a better route would be to ask God what resolutions He wants us to make first. Charles Stanley wrote: "Although our new year's resolutions may quickly crumble, God's plans never fail."

Our hearts should yearn to be closer to God, and every New Year brings a new opportunity to come to know God more intimately, to walk closer with Him, and to develop a deeper level of faith. Perhaps the wisest New Year's Resolution for any person of faith would be to seek a deeper relationship with God. You were created in His image, and you are meant to know Him deeply and to fellowship Him fully. Maybe you aren't in that place yet, but God can take you there if you will open your heart and time to Him. God can always bring change when we are truly open to receive it, and He can take what is weak, imperfect, or broken in our lives and change it into something new and amazing.

Keep in mind that a spiritual resolution needs as much heart, work, dedication, and effort as a natural one. Deeper spirituality and a greater closeness to God doesn't simply fall on us. We work to attain it; we reach out to God daily in prayer and study so He can take us forward and bring us into newness. He promises: "I will instruct thee and teach thee in the way which thou shalt go: I will guide thee with mine eye" [Psalm 32:8]. Do you want joy, peace, happiness, wisdom, and a more abundant life this year? Then let this be the year you seek, study, and find it. Make Jonathan Edwards' resolutions yours: "Resolution One: I will live for God. Resolution Two: If no one else does, I still will."

Prayer:
Lord, thank You for giving me a brand New Year ahead. Let me start it off right and keep it going in the right direction, ever growing in You and living each day after Your heart.

Scripture of the Day:
"This month shall be unto you the beginning of months: it shall be the first month of the year to you." - [Exodus 12:2]

The Word for the Day is "Newness"

Quote for the Day:
"I believe that an artist working for and representing the Kingdom of God should do the best of their ability to show and prove the depth, life, newness, creativity, truth and excitement of their Heavenly Father through the work that is set before them."
- Wildlife Artist Daniel Smith

One of the best thoughts concerning a new year is the idea that it can represent a new start, a fresh beginning, and a unique time for us. Sometimes we are relieved to just know that a new year can be different than the old one.

The Lord wants us to have a fresh and joyful outlook on this new beginning of time because it holds unique and original treasures for us in the Kingdom of God. We all can relate to the excitement and joy of things new. A new car in the driveway is an experience of newness we are familiar with. The new car has that bright, shiny, clean appearance that makes us feel good. And it has that fresh, clean smell and the satisfying, mechanical quality of running good!

God wants us to walk in newness of life every day [Rom 6:4]. Every day is a day of potential in the Lord for His compassions and mercies are new every morning [Lam 3:22-24]. Every day in the Lord holds the qualities of being new, original, novel, unique, fresh, and different from anything experienced before. God wants us to serve Him in newness of Spirit, and not in the oldness of the letter or the past [Romans 7:6].

Let us remember we are a new creature in Christ and that we should put off the old man (our old, carnal nature), which is corrupt, and put on the new man (the new creature in Christ) which, after God, is created in righteousness and true holiness [Eph 4:22-24]. Let's be excited about what new thing the Lord can do in us in this new day and time!

Prayer:
This is the day the Lord hath made; let us be glad and rejoice in it and walk in newness of life today, fresh and original, with new beginnings in Him.

Scripture of the Day:
"Therefore we are buried with him by baptism into death: that like as Christ was raised up from the dead by the glory of the Father, even so we also should walk in newness of life." - [Romans 6:4]

The Word for the Day is "Choose."

Quote for the Day:
"You have the ability to choose which way you want to go." – Benjamin Carson

Although God loves everyone in the world, not everyone in the world chooses to follow God, accept Jesus, and become a Christian. We often want to blanket everyone into Christianity, but no matter how well meaning non-Christians are, or whatever else they've got figured out for their personal belief systems, they have not truly chosen to seek rightful membership in God's organization.

Many people belong to a professional organization with specific requirements for entry. God's organization has requirements, too, but Jesus said: 'Come, the door is open to membership. Whosoever will believe and receive can enter' [Revelation 3:20]. Joining the Kingdom of God is simple and easy. Heartfelt belief and a repentance of erroneous ways is the single entry requirement. God's organization is less restrictive than most earthly organizations, the membership made by choice. The structure of God's organization is created to bring life, blessing, and joy to all who choose to enter in. Any bylaw is designed for the blessing of the members, for their health, their best, for their prosperity and happiness. However, belonging to the Kingdom of God, the organization of Christianity, is still a "choice." God doesn't force membership. In all things He gives choice.

A true trust in God means "trusting" that God knew what He was doing in setting up the Kingdom of God and the ordered organization of Christianity. We should always pray, work, witness, and hope that others we love and meet along life's journey, who are not in the faith or in the Lord, will "come in"—but we can't, out of a misguided compassion, blanket them in. We are each born into an earthly family by no special choice of our own, but it is "by choice" we can each enter into God's family, the Kingdom of God.

Prayer:
Dearest Lord, it is a blessed privilege to be in the Kingdom of God, to be built on the rock of Christ Jesus, to know we have abundant life here on the earth and eternal life in heaven. Help us to be truly grateful to be one with You.

Scripture of the Day:
"I have set before you life and death, blessing and cursing: therefore choose life, that both thou and thy seed may live." - [Deuteronomy 30:19]

The Word for the Day is "Instant."

Quote for the Day:
"Never walk away from an instant connection...it's happened for a reason."
- Unknown

We know the word instant has two meanings. As a noun it means 'a precise moment of time,' and 'a very short space of time.' As an adjective it can mean 'happening or coming immediately,' or 'urgent or pressing.' The apostle Paul exhorted the young minister Timothy to "Preach the word; be instant in season, out of season; reprove, rebuke, exhort with all long suffering and doctrine" (2 Tim 4:2). Paul used the word instant in the adjective sense to be ready to preach or minister the word under all circumstances. The Amplified Bible expands the meaning of this scripture as to the idea of keeping your sense of urgency to minister the word whether the opportunity seems to be favorable or unfavorable, convenient or inconvenient, whether it be welcome or unwelcome.

I think as Christians we sometimes lose our sense of being "instant" to share the good news of the gospel of Jesus. What causes this timidity in Christians? I think the two main reasons are a cold mediocrity in our own personal relationship with the Lord and the fear of man. It is nearly impossible to seem zealous about any topic if you are not genuinely enthusiastic about it yourself. You must have a close relationship with the Lord before you can have a readiness to share the Lord's goodness. Otherwise, you will be reluctant to witness for the Lord.

It seems to me the biggest taboo in our society today is "to offend" someone. We are reluctant to speak the truth because we might "offend" and be criticized as narrow-minded or rude. The Truth of God's Word is the only thing that can set a person free and we may only have an instant opportunity to share the love and grace of God. Our fear of man and selfish desire to be exempt from criticism negates our opportunity to share God's love to someone who needs the truth.

Prayer:
Lord, help us to be ready at any instant to share Jesus with the world.

Scripture of the Day:
"But sanctify the Lord God in your hearts: and be ready always (instantly) to give an answer to every man that asketh you a reason of the hope that is in you with meekness and fear." -[1 Peter 3:15]

The Word for the Day is "Gift."

Quote for the Day:
"Every day without exception is a gift from God, entrusted to us to use for His glory." – Billy Graham

How would you feel if you got a call tomorrow and someone said: "You know that Christmas gift I gave you? I need it back. I really regret even giving you that gift." It's hard to imagine what you would even say. They freely gave it, and you received it with joy.

If you're a Christian, you gave a gift to God, that I hope you don't regret, when you gave Him your heart and life, and made a decision to serve Him. In a sense, you are no longer your own now. You are His. You have been *gifted*. Madame Guyon wrote: "Dearly beloved, once you have given yourself to God, do not take yourself back again. Remember a gift once presented is no longer at the disposal of the giver."

In the Old Testament when a Hebrew servant was bought, he served six years, but in the seventh he could go out free for nothing. When brought before the master, he could walk away free or say: 'I don't want to go free. I want to stay and serve you because I love you' [Exodus 21:1-6, Deuteronomy 15:16]. If he made this choice, a little awl was put in his ear to denote his decision, much like a pierced earring, and he served his master all his days. As this story teaches, God does not bind us to Himself by force. But by love. With love we choose to receive God's love, to receive Jesus, to receive His Spirit…to become His beloved servants for all our days. Yet, too often we try to take ourselves back. We don't want to follow after His Ways. We don't want to give Him our time. We decide living the life God lays out is too hard. Don't take yourself back from God. Here at this new year remember you gave yourself freely. Like the old hymn, you 'decided to follow Jesus; no turning back.'

Prayer:
Lord, forgive us that we've let worldly ways and pursuits crowd You out of our lives, that we've taken ourselves back and forgotten to be submitted and surrendered to Your will. We gift ourselves back to You in repentance today.

Scripture of the Day:
"Even so by the righteousness of one the free gift came upon all men unto justification of life."- [Romans 5:18]

The Word for the Day is "Must"

Quote for the Day:
"Hold fast to the Bible. To the influence of this Book we are indebted for all the progress made in true civilization and to this we must look as our guide in the future." - Ulysses S. Grant

I once bought a gift of clothing at the local mall for a Christmas present for my wife. When it was discovered at the holiday that the item wasn't a good fit, I returned to the mall to exchange the item. As I approached the service counter I noticed a sign on the wall that read: "Must show receipt for all refunds and exchanges." I had lost my receipt but I thought since I had the item with me it would be ok. Wrong! I discovered "must" meant I had to have the receipt!

Jesus told Nicodemus that a man must be born again to even see the kingdom of God [John 3:3]. Nicodemus didn't understand the spiritual truth and asked if a man could enter his mother's womb a second time. Jesus explained that a man must be born of the Spirit to enter into the Kingdom of God [John 3:5]. Jesus was talking about a spiritual new birth of the spirit of man, or the hidden man of the heart [1 Peter 3:4]. Man is a three-part being: spirit (the inner man), soul (mental man), and body (physical man) [1 Thess 5:23]. Jesus taught that it was necessary to have the inner nature born again with His Spirit, and then to renew the mind by the Word of God [Eph 4:23], and to discipline the body which is the temple of the Holy Ghost [1 Cor 6:19-20].

Sadly, I have heard people, even ministers, trivialize and dismiss this essential experience. The term "born again" is condescendingly mocked as one of those outdated concepts of religious fanatics and "Bible-thumpers." Yet Jesus is the author of this term and declares it an essential necessity of the heart to be born again to enter and see the kingdom of God. Let every man believe in his heart the redemptive work of Jesus and make confession with his mouth [Romans 10:9-10] that he might be translated out of darkness into His marvelous light [1Peter 2:9].

Prayer:
Lord, we thank You that You are the door and the way into the Kingdom of God and life eternal.

Scripture of the Day:
"Marvel not that I said unto thee, Ye must be born again." - [John 3:7]

The Word for the Day is "Snow."

Quote for the Day:
"Snowflakes are kisses from heaven." - Unknown

Snow is beautiful when it first falls and covers everything in a delicious blanket of white —so pure, so perfect. Snow covers the dried up ground and bare branches. It even covers over dirty buildings and garbage dumps and the ugly things of the world. Perhaps that's why in the Word God says 'we shall be whiter than snow', changed, made white, clean, and pure when we come to know Him [Psalm 51:7].

Each snowflake is delicate, intricate, lacy, and totally unique. Not one snowflake is like any other—sort of like us. From afar, we may look somewhat similar but on closer observation we are all totally unique. Each of us is fashioned and designed like no other with a purpose no other can fulfill.

Our strengths in life are in our individuality, our ability to individually make a difference in our worlds and in our ability to collectively make a difference. One snowflake cannot create a glorious landscape to take our breath away but collectively, multitudes of snowflakes can. We have an "individual power" and a "collective power" in most all we do and are involved in—our families, work, churches, neighborhoods, groups, and organizations. Each of us can share our unique gifts, our personalities, talents, warmth and love, and we can individually make a difference. We can also work together in many efforts, to make a broader collective difference, a lovely blanketing effect. Both are important. However, it's always a "choice" what we give, what we share in life, and what we're willing to give and share.

Snow is beautiful—individually, in each flake, and in its collective beauty—but it can turn a little nasty, too. That is the aspect of all nature, having the ability to delight and to hurt, to be useful or problematic. So each day we need to choose to use the individual and collective gifts we've been given joyously and well. We need to choose to live a clean life—pure like snow—for a clean legacy.

Prayer:
Lord, help us use our gifts, so freely given, unselfishly in both individual and collective ways to make our world and the lives of others more beautiful.

Scripture of the Day:
"Come now, and let us reason together, saith the Lord; though your sins be as scarlet, they shall be as white as snow; though they be red like crimson, they shall be as wool." - [Isaiah 1:18]

The Word for the Day is "Lukewarm"

Quote for the Day:
"God doesn't do things halfway. He goes all out! When God does something, it's not just barely enough, mediocre or lukewarm." - Joyce Meyer

I discovered in my early marriage that when it comes to temperatures, my wife and I had some different preferences. I like my coffee hot and drink it quickly. My wife likes her coffee slightly warm and lingers over it. I like the room temperature in the house somewhat cool. Lin likes the temperature warmer and is always turning the heat up. These are just differences in our likes and preferences and can be easily tolerated.

But the state of lukewarmness as applied to the attitude is a different matter. The dictionary defines this attitude as indifferent, cool, halfhearted, apathetic, unenthusiastic, and noncommital. We can understand the indifferance of unbelievers toward the faith, but Jesus had something to say about this condition amongst his believers—the church. A halfhearted attitude in the church was replusive to Him. He said (to the church at Laodicea): "I know thy works, that they are neither cold nor hot; I would that they were cold or hot. So then because thou art lukewarm, and neither cold nor hot, I will spue thee out of my mouth" [Rev 3:15-16].

Why would Jesus prefer cold or hot to lukewarm? The hot condition is easy to understand. The Word says it is good to be zealously affected always with a good thing (seeking first the Kingdom of God and His righteousness) [Gal 4:18]. It is obvious who a "hot" believer serves. A cold-spirited person, whether he be an unbeliever or a backslider, knows in his heart he is not in a right place with God, but the light of the gospel truth can enlighten his darkened heart and he through repentance can be reconciled to God. The lukewarm heart, however, is comfortable in his halfhearted, apathetic state. He can "play church" and feel accepted both in the church and in the world—life's easy.

Prayer:
Lord, help us to shake off our tepid, halfhearted commitment and dedicate ourselves to walk with You and in Your ways whole-heartedly with a lively spirit.

Scripture for the Day:
"So then because thou art lukewarm, and neither cold nor hot, I will spue thee out of my mouth." - [Revelation 3:16]

The Word for the Day is "Singing."

Quote for the Day:
"As long as we live, there is never enough singing." – Martin Luther

From Old Testament to New Testament we read of God's people singing and praising. And we know 'God inhabits the praises of His people' (Psalm 22:3) and that He wants us to 'continually offer up a sacrifice of praise' (Hebrews 13:15). Even nature sings and praises God's name…and the pictures that God paints of nature rejoicing and singing are joyous ones to read and see. These show such a lovely picture of the ideal harmony that should exist between God, the heavens, the earth, and His people.

Isaiah 55:12 reads: "For ye shall go out with joy, and be led forth with peace: the mountains and the hills shall break forth before you into singing and all the trees of the field shall clap their hands." Envision that for a moment—the mountains singing and the trees clapping their hands when God's goodness and will prevail. It almost brings to mind a Disney movie scene like in *Fantasia* where all of nature sang and danced.

God's heart and desire is for goodness to prevail in our lives. He yearns to 'guide us continually and satisfy our soul in drought…to make us like a watered garden' [Isaiah 58:11]. The Word promises: "I will guide thee and teach thee in the way thou shalt go" [Psalm 32:8]. When we follow God's way as we should, success, joy, and comfort come to us—and a happy life. It makes it easier to "sing unto the Lord…to come before His Presence with thanksgiving and make a joyful noise unto Him" [Psalm 95: 1-2].

Prayer:
Your desire, O Lord, is for goodness and mercy to follow us and for Your joy to fill us as it fills the earth. Help us to look around in our world and to be more grateful, to have more joy, to sing more. To praise You for all that You are.

Scripture of the Day:
"I will make all my mountains a way, and my highways shall be exalted… be joyful O earth, and break forth into singing O mountains: for the Lord hath comforted his people, and will have mercy upon his afflicted." - [Isaiah 49:11,13]

The Word for the Day is "Quietness"

Quote for the Day:
"Coming before God in quietness and waiting upon Him in silence can accomplish more than days of feverish activity." - A.W. Tozer

Lin and I love to hike the trails in the Great Smoky Mountains. Besides the beauty of nature and the mountains, we love the quiet solitude of the hikes. We call the mountains our "green cathedral." It is easy to feel God's presence in the beauty and quietness of His creation. Sometimes we talk very little while we are hiking, but later we share thoughts of God that we received on the trail. We cherish these opportunities to exercise the body and refresh the soul in God's green world.

God tells us in His Word: "in returning and rest shall ye be saved; in quietness and in confidence shall be your strength" [Isaiah 30:15]. There is a strength and rest to be attained in quietness, but it is not always easy to find. The clamor and busyness of our life is always competing for our time and attention. There always seems to be something "that needs to be done." Then the noise and stimuli of the world assaults our senses with music, entertainments, news, communications, and all kinds of busy activities. Finding time to get alone with God can be a challenge. It requires a decision to make the time to get quiet before God. I found Matthew 6:6 a great help in this: "But thou, when thou prayest, enter into thy closet, and when thou hast shut thy door, pray to the Father which is in secret; and thy Father which seeth in secret shall reward thee openly." I found the shut closet to be an effective, quiet sanctuary against the outside, and communing with the Lord was easy in the darkness.

God always rewards seeking His righteousness and promises. "And the work of righteousness shall be peace; and the effect of righteousness quietness and assurance for ever" [Isaiah 32:17]. Someway, somehow, get alone and quiet with God; He will reward you as you draw nigh to Him [James 4:8].

Prayer:
Lord, help us to find more times of quietness that we might seek You better and hear from You more clearly.

Scripture of the Day:
"Better is an handful with quietness, than both the hands full with travail and vexation of spirit." - [Ecclesiastes 4:6]

The Word for the Day is "Good."

Quote for the Day:
"Whatever is good for your soul, do that." - Unknown

I love reading in Genesis of how God made the heavens and the earth—and everything in it—and how good and satisfied He felt while He worked and created. Genesis 1:31 says: "And God saw everything that He had made and behold it was very good."

God created a great beauty and diversity in the earth, vast numbers of different flowers, trees, birds, insects, all unique and individually fashioned and made—and all good. Likewise He created each of us as individuals, uniquely made, designed according to His purpose. Rather than comparing ourselves to others or striving to be like others, we should celebrate our unique individuality, knowing God made us to be as we are—and that he sees us as "very good."

Sometimes, as individuals and Christians, our individuality makes us feel a step apart from others and what appears to be the norm of the world around us. We may even feel separate and peculiar, but this is okay. God calls us a chosen and "a peculiar people" [1 Peter 2:9] and affirms that He wants us to "be a peculiar treasure unto Him" [Exodus 19:5]. Each of us is special and unique and has an individual purpose and design orchestrated by God for His pleasure. "Before I formed thee in the belly, I knew thee; and before thou camest forth out of the womb, I sanctified thee and I ordained thee" [Jeremiah 1:5]. We need to see ourselves more with the eyes of God—special and unique after His heart and in His sight.

I saw a sweet Facebook post earlier this week that inspired these thoughts. Emblazoned across a beautiful flower it said…"Each person is a unique expression of God's loving design."

Prayer:
Lord, help us to realize that You have made all things according to Your purpose and glory and to call them all good as You designed them—including us.

Scripture of the Day:
"For thou, Lord, art good, and ready to forgive; and plenteous in mercy unto all them that call upon thee." - [Psalm 86:5]

The Word for the Day is "Fervent"

Quote for the Day:
"Prayer—secret, fervent, believing prayer—lies at the root of all personal godliness."
- William Carey, missionary

I was at a prayer-group meeting with some fellow Christians once when a man in attendance requested prayer for an urgent need. One lady smiled and responded in a quiet voice: "Let us remember and keep this man's great need in our prayers." The group all nodded in silence. The man suddenly yelled: "No, I want you to PRAY!" The group was rendered speechless in shock at his loud demand, but I knew instinctively what he wanted. He didn't want some polite, rote, ritual prayer later—he wanted a prayer now that meant serious business with God!

The word fervent comes from a Latin root word "fervens," which means extremely hot, agitated, as boiling water. This man wanted a fervent prayer! Some believers are reluctant to embrace this kind of praying; it's too loud, too emotional, impolite. I'm sure Jesus didn't worry about being too fervent when He took a whip and drove the money changers out of the temple [John 2:15]! And He didn't consider politeness when He called the scribes and Pharisees hypocrites, blind guides, fools, serpents, a generation of vipers [Matthew 23:13-33].

The Bible tells us to be fervent in spirit, serving the Lord [Romans 12:11]. The scriptures give us an example of a certain Jew named Apollos who was fervent in spirit [Acts 18:24-26]. We learn that this man was "mighty in the scriptures"— he knew and reverenced the Word of God. This man was "instructed in the way of the Lord"—he sought the knowledge of God's ways. He spoke "boldly" and "taught diligently the things of the Lord." One cannot imagine someone as this man being timid, apathetic, or unemotional about the Lord. No, he was fervent in spirit, bold, and sometimes probably loud, to proclaim the truth and power of the holy scriptures and the ways of God. God wants all his people to boldly stand on their scriptural rights in faith to obtain the needs for themselves and others.

Prayer:
Lord, help us to know Your Word and to be mighty in the scriptures and faith that we might offer up fervent prayers.

Scripture of the Day:
"The effectual fervent prayer of a righteous man availeth much." - [James 5:16]

The Word for the Day is "Provides."

Quote for the Day:
"God provides the wind. Man must provide the sail." – Saint Augustine

Nature and God's creatures in the earth teach us many wise lessons. They teach us of beauty, growth, and industry. We read in the Word that laziness and slothfulness are not attributes God admires. Comparing the slothful to the righteous man, Proverbs teaches: "The way of the slothful man is as an hedge of thorns: but the way of the righteous is made plain" (Proverbs 15:19). A lazy and slothful life does not bring blessing. It makes getting through life like trying to work one's way through a hedge of thorns. Ouch. In Ecclesiastes more advice on this line is offered: "By much slothfulness the building decayeth; and through idleness of the hands the house droppeth through" (Ecclesiastes 10:18).

As a child I used to sit out on the grass in the yard and watch the ants work… climbing in and out of their anthill, struggling their way through the grass and over rocks, sticks, and other obstacles…never deterred in their course. If a big puddle or tree branch blocked their way, they just patiently went around it or climbed over it and kept on going. Their behavior and determination demonstrated such patience, diligence and persistence—all traits God admires. In our walk in life we need to be industrious…"steadfast and unmoveable, abounding in the work of the Lord" [1 Corinthians 15:58].

One of the Proverbs reads: "Seest thou a man diligent in his business? He shall stand before kings; he shall not stand before mean men" [Proverbs 22:29]. The way to success is through diligent work. Too often we wish success and provision would come to us without much effort but that is not God's way. 'The soul of the sluggard craves and gets nothing, while the soul of the diligent is rightly supplied' [Proverbs 13:4].

Prayer:
Father, as the ant presses on each day in diligence, may we press on without laziness or slothfulness in all that You want us to do and accomplish.

Scripture of the Day:
"Go to the ant, thou sluggard: consider her ways and be wise: which having no guide, overseer, or ruler, provideth her meat in the summer, and gathereth her food in the harvest." - [Proverbs 6:6-8]

The Word for the Day is "Meekness"

Quote for the Day:
"Meekness is not weakness, but spiritual strength harnessed for service."
- Joe Cothen

"Now the man Moses was very meek, above all the men which were upon the face of the earth" [Numbers 12:3]. This revelation is a shock to many believers. What did this meek man do? He encountered God personally in the burning bush; he confronted Pharoah to let the Hebrews go from Egypt; he pronounced the ten plagues upon Eygpt; he led the Hebrew children out of Egypt and parted the Red Sea with his staff; he destroyed Pharoah's army in the sea; he led his people to the wilderness and provided miracles from heaven for them; he received the laws and customs from God on the mount; he died at 120 years old, his natural force not abated, nor his eyes dimmed. This man Moses was totally submitted to the will of God and was strong in obedience to God, and described as the meekest man in the earth.

Another minister once used the famous race horse Secretariat as an icon of meekness. I remembered watching on TV this fabulous horse win the Triple Crown in 1973, winning the Belmont Stakes by 31 lengths! Secretariat was so impressive with his huge body and powerful muscles. Yet, Secretariat was meek—he was totally submitted and obedient to his jockey. The jockey could discern when to hold back this powerful beast and when to turn him loose to unleash his incredible power and speed.

There is a power and a blessing for Christians to walk in meekness (gentle and kind, not self abasing or servile) in submission and obedience to the Lord. The meek shall be satisfied [Psalm 22:26]; he shall delight himself in the abundance of peace [Psalm 37:11]; the Lord will lift up the meek [Psalm 147:6]; He will beautify the meek with salvation [Psalm 149:4]; the meek shall also increase their joy in the Lord [Isaiah 29:19]. This is a fruit of the Spirit [Galatians 5:23] we should try to nourish and grow.

Prayer:
Lord, help us to walk in meekness and righteousness that we might be strong in You.

Scripture of the Day:
"The meek will he guide in judgment; and the meek will he teach his way." -
[Psalm 25:9]

The Word for the Day is "Watchful."

Quote for the Day:
"More firm and sure the hand of courage strikes, when it obeys the watchful eye of caution." - James Thomson

My husband and I are avid hikers in the Smoky Mountains and love the beauty of the outdoors of East Tennessee. We have published a hiking guidebook and often speak to groups about trails and walks in our area. A question we inevitably are asked—with a shudder—is: "Do you see snakes?" Sometimes we do, although my husband says I 'pray them away' before we hike.

Most of us have a natural aversion to snakes, perhaps scripturally based, as the Word says there will be enmity between us because of the snake's part in Adam and Eve's fall [Gen 3:15]. Snakes can be dangerous and sometimes even deadly—as is our enemy satan 'who comes to kill, steal, and destroy' [John 10:10].

In the mountains we keep a careful eye out for snakes, to protect ourselves from possible harm. In the world, we need to keep a watchful eye out for satan's ways that can bring harm and hurt to us, too. The Bible cautions: "Be sober, be vigilant, because your adversary the devil, as a roaring lion, walketh about, seeking whom he may devour" [1 Peter 5:8]. We need to watch over our lives, living safely in righteousness, so satan won't get an advantage of us, but knowing, too, that God always causes us to 'triumph in Christ Jesus' [2 Corinthians 2:11,14]. Satan is a conquered enemy and God promises when we 'resist the devil he will flee from us' [James 4:7]. He may attack and break through even our best defenses now and then, but when we stay strong, we can rout him after an attack, run him out of our lives, and overcome the wicked one [1 John 2:14]. Living our lives in this world means we need to be watchful, like good soldiers, and be ever ready to "fight the good fight of faith" [1 Timothy 6:12].

Prayer:
Lord, help us to stay strong through your Word to resist evil, avoid temptation, and know that through Christ Jesus we have overcome the evil one.

Scripture of the Day:
"Be watchful, and strengthen the things which remain, that are ready to die: for I have not found thy works perfect before God." - [Revelation 3:2]

The Word for the Day is "Spoken"

Quote for the Day:
"To tell the truth is useful to those to whom it is spoken, but disadvantageous to those who tell it, because it makes them disliked." - Blaise Pascal

Pilate asked "What is truth?" [John 18:38]. The Word of God tells us that grace and truth came by Jesus [John 1:17]. "Jesus saith unto him. I am the way, the truth and the life; no man cometh unto the Father, but by me" [John 14:6]. He spoke the truth to him as He will to us. We also have the promise that when the Spirit of truth is come, he will guide us into all truth [John 16:13]. Jesus also prayed "Sanctify them through thy truth; thy word is truth" [John 17:17].

As believers we love the truth because we love Jesus, we love the Holy Spirit, we love the Father, and we love the Word of God. We desire to continue in the Word, to know the truth, and to be made free [John 8:32]. And every one that is of the truth heareth the voice of Jesus [John 18:37]. We are admonished to "study to show thyself approved unto God, a workman that needeth not to be ashamed, rightly dividing the word of truth" [2 Timothy 2:15]. So we as believers endeavor to have our "loins girt about with the truth" [Ephesians 6:14], that we walk in the "fruit of the Spirit in all goodness and righteousness and truth" [Epesians 5:9], "speaking the truth in love" [Ephesians 4:15].

But men without Jesus do not always seek or love the truth of God's Word. If you speak God's Word to those destitute of the truth, they may dislike you (as Pascal observed above). Why? Because the Word of God has a weighty quality when spoken, no matter who the audience. "For the word of God is quick and powerful, and sharper than any twoedged sword, and piercing even to the dividing asunder of soul and spirit, and of the joints and marrow, and is a discerner of the thoughts and intents of the heart" [Heb 4:12]. The Word of God is absolute truth and cuts right through to the true state of the heart. The unbeliever can offer his rationale for his rejection or unbelief in the Lord, but the truth of God's word discerns his heart and convicts his mind and heart. Pray that the Holy Spirit might break up the fallow ground of the sinner's heart that he might receive the truth.

Prayer:
Let us commit ourselves to the One who is truth and be guided by the Spirit of truth, that we may know the truth and hear the voice of truth, that we might always speak the truth.

Scripture ofthe Day:
"A word fitly spoken is like apples of gold in pictures of silver." - [Proverbs 25:11]

The Word for the Day is "Soar."

Quote for the Day:
"Refuse to be average. Let your heart soar as high as it will." -A. W. Tozer

The eagle, one of God's majestic creatures, is the national symbol of America. Occasionally, my husband and I see an eagle circling high above a mountain trail when we are hiking or spot an eagle's nest perched on a rocky ledge or lodged in the tops of a tall tree. Eagles can fly to great heights, some up to 33,000 feet above the earth. No other bird can go to the height of the eagle. When storms gather, eagles don't get concerned. They use the storm to rise above the winds and rain, to glide above the clouds, looking down on it all.

In the Lord, we can find protection in trouble and rise above the problems of life, too. In Exodus 19:4 God reminded Moses: "ye have seen…how I bare you on eagles' wings and brought you unto myself." God advised him further that if he would 'obey God's voice and keep His covenant that he would be a peculiar treasure unto God and always dwell in a sweet place' [Exodus 19:5]. What a wonderful protector our God is. As two of the Psalms remind us: 'For in the time of trouble…God shall set us upon a rock' [Psalm 27:5]…'He will cover us with his feathers and under his wings we will find refuge' [Psalm 91:4].

One of the ways the eagle stays safe is by living on the high cliffs and riding on the high places of the sky. In the Lord we can live in a high place In Him above the troubles and cares of the world. "He that dwelleth in the secret place of the most High shall abide under the shadow of the Almighty. I will say of the Lord, He is my refuge and my fortress: my God; in him will I trust" [Psalm 91:1-2].

Prayer:
Lord, we are grateful that when we lean to You, trust in You, and follow in Your ways that You will be our protection, that You will renew our strength…and lift us above our troubles in Your grace.

Scripture of the Day:
"But they that wait upon the Lord shall renew their strength; they shall mount up (soar) with wings as eagles; they shall run, and not be weary; and they shall walk, and not faint." - [Isaiah 40:31]

The Word for the Day is "Increase"

Quote for the Day:
"Believe God's promises more firmly than ever. Allow your faith to increase in its fullness, firmness, and simplicity." - Charles Spurgeon

It seems to me that increase was in God's will for His creation from the very beginning. His Word tells us that after God created all the creatures of the earth, both on the land, in the air and the sea, He blessed them and commanded them to be fruitful and multiply (increase). Likewise, after He created man in His image, He blessed and commanded man to be fruitful, multiply, and have dominion [Genesis 1:22-28]. And God called it all very good.

Nature shows us this natural order of increase everywhere. Things that are few increase into many—as a few seeds produce a crop. a few rabbits become many, a little kudzu soon covers the hillside. Things small increase into large. A small sapling becomes a giant oak, babies, whether animal or human, become grown adults, and a small sprig becomes a corn stalk. God wants this increase principle to apply to our spiritual man also. He wants us to increase in the likeness of Jesus and, as Jesus did, to "increase in wisdom and stature, and in favor with God and man" [Luke 2:52].

How do we increase in the Lord? The same way we increase in anything: we start where we are and add to it incrementally. A mathematician doesn't start out knowing calculus. He starts knowing nothing, but adds to his skills until he can handle advanced math. Our spiritual growth follows this principle also, 'increasing line upon line, precept upon precept, here a little, there a little' [Isaiah 28:10].

We increase in the Lord through prayer, devotion, obedience, and especially in the knowledge of God's Word. When the Word is sown and falls into a good heart (good ground), we can expect fruit with a multiplied yield [Mark 4:8]. We can expect an increase in knowledge, love, understanding, and wisdom with the added blessing of "thy days shall be multiplied, and the years of thy life shall be increased" [Proverbs 9:11]. So start increasing more in the Lord today!

Prayer:
Lord, thank You that no matter where we are today, we can still increase more and more into the image of Christ Jesus.

Scripture of the Day:
"The Lord shall increase you more and more, you and your children." -
[Psalm 115:14]

The Word for the Day is "Reverence."

Quote for the Day:
"Pursue some path, however narrow and crooked, in which you can walk with love and reverence." - Henry David Thoreau

Many scriptures suggest to us that the earth around us honors, reverences, and fears God more than humankind. At one point, when the Pharisees suggested to Jesus that He should rebuke His disciples for praising Him, He looked toward the rocks in the area around Him and then at his disciples, and said in reply: "If these (disciples) should hold their peace, the stones would immediately cry out" [Luke 19:40]. He cautioned that they didn't have the right knowledge or the eyes to see who He was. On an interesting note, shortly thereafter, Jesus 'went into the temple and began to cast out those that sold items there, rebuking them for not reverencing the house of God, and for making it a house of merchandise and thieves' [Luke 19:45-46]. Our lives should reverence God, and the worship—and actions—in our churches should reverence God.

Sometimes we forget to reverence and fear God as we should. We grow careless about staying righteous, start drifting along with the ways of the world. Second Corinthians 7:1 advises: "Dearly beloved, let us cleanse ourselves from all filthiness of the flesh and spirit, perfecting holiness in the fear of God." We are meant to have a righteous fear of God, to hunger and yearn to live clean and pure before Him every day. We are meant to sorrow if we do not always walk in a close place with God—because of our love for Him—and to understand that by living in righteousness and peace we have our safety and protection in the Lord. "In the fear of the Lord is strong confidence: and His children shall have a place of refuge" [Proverbs 14:26]. It is for our own good to fear and honor God. A reverent fear of God is a sign of love and respect.

Prayer:
Let a holy fear of God live always in us so we can walk safely and please the Lord in all we do.

Scripture of the Day:
"Wherefore we receiving a kingdom which cannot be moved, let us have grace, whereby we may serve God acceptably with reverence and godly fear." -
  [Hebrews 12:28]

The Word for the Day is "Touched"

Quote for the Day:
"There is nothing more glorious and more dangerous to the kingdom of hell than a man or woman touched by God." - David Wilkerson

What a profound consequence can result from a simple touch. In Mark 5:22-34, we read that Jesus was thronged with much people as he walked with Jairus to minister to his dying daughter. A woman in the press, who had an issue of blood twelve years, her condition only worsening, said to herself 'If I can just touch his clothes, I shall be whole.' She touched Jesus and He, immediately knowing that virtue (God's goodness) had gone out of Him, turned to see who touched Him. Jesus told the woman to be of good cheer, *her* faith had made her whole! Jesus can touch us, but we can also touch Him through our faith and receive His divine blessing as this woman did!

This is not the only way the blessings of touch can be ministered. We can use our physical touch to impart love and kindness. God can use natural means to impart His grace and power as He did when the mere shadow of Peter, as he passed by, healed the people [Acts 5:15]. God can use our words to minister grace to the hearers [Eph 4:29]. And God can use a kind act to bless. I was standing in the Kroger's self-checkout recently when a man standing in front of me turned to me and said "Why don't you go ahead of me, as you only have a couple of items." This simple act touched my heart, and I knew the Lord would reward him.

It is a blessing both to receive and to give a Spirit-inspired touch. Everyone desires the quiet, peaceful comfort of a loving touch. Some people can be blessed just to know that someone else knows they even exist, to know that somebody is aware of their deepest need, to know that somebody cares enough to connect with them in love. Let us never underestimate the value of that kind touch to someone hurting, the power of a word of encouragement or comfort to a troubled soul, or the sincere love of God toward another who needs to be touched. Touch someone today with the love of Jesus in you—the opportunities are everywhere.

Prayer:
Lord, prepare us to be ready in every day to somehow touch someone that You might touch them through us.

Scripture if the Day:
"And as many as touched him were made whole." - [Mark 6:56].

The Word for the Day is "Restore."

Quote for the Day:
"God is still a God of restoration and healing. No situation is too far gone for God *to restore."* - Pastor Brian Logue

Each day we should live our hours, even when problems and trials come along, with what the Word calls "a lively hope" [1 Peter 1:3], knowing that our God is a Restoring God. Throughout the Bible the Lord uses examples showing His Restoring power in nature. These examples help us envision restoration to areas where the enemy has come against our lives destructively, for a long time or only for a short season.

God uses natural pictures we can relate to so we will understand His restoring power. The extensive damage and destruction locusts and worms can do to plants is something we can relate to. But God says that is not the end of the story. God reminds us to always hold hope that He will restore loss to us. "And I will restore to you the years that the locust hath eaten, the cankerworm, and the caterpillar, and the palmerworm" [Joel 2:25]. In times of trial we need to hold fast and trust in God to turn wrongs around, to restore loss.

David's beautiful words in Psalm 18 reveal his trust in God to deliver him, to restore him, and to bless him. He was being cruelly pursued and without right cause by Saul, forced from his home, driven to hide in caves…but he did not become bitter. Instead he believed God would turn things around. Like David, we should always keep a lively hope and trust that God will deliver and restore us, 'draw us out of many waters and bring us into a large place' [Psalm 18:16-24].

Prayer:
Thank You, God, that You lift us up above those that rise up against us and that You are ever a restoring God.

Scripture of the Day:
"Be glad then, ye children of Zion, and rejoice in the Lord your God…and I will restore to you the years that the locust hath eaten, the cankerworm, and the palmerworm…and ye shall eat in plenty and be satisfied and praise the name of the Lord your God, that hath dealt wondrously with you." - [Joel 2:23-26]

The Word for the Day is "One"

Quote for the Day:
"As you walk down the fairway of life, you must smell the roses for you only get to play one round." - Ben Hogan

I love Ben Hogan's analogy of a round of golf to life. As a golfer myself, I can relate very easily to some of the comparisons. First of all, the golf course has 18 holes which played in sequence make a round—we live consecutive days in sequence for a lifespan. Each hole has a smooth fairway of turfgrass (a miracle in itself in my opinion) and penalty areas of rough and hazards outside the fairway. We hope each day of life is a smooth fairway, but in this life there are tribulations also, the rough and hazards [John 16:33]. Each hole has a different layout with different challenges, some easy and some difficult—life has challenges both easy and hard. In golf, we must play the ball "as it lies." And sometimes this rule isn't fair, we hit a good shot but still get a bad lie because of a "rub of the green"—an unlucky bounce or break. We get "bad lies" in life sometimes too, through no fault of our own, as time and chance happens to all [Ecclesiastes 9:11]. In golf, we try to get out of trouble and position our next shot to successfully continue our play. In life, we seek God's wisdom in trouble and His directions so that we can resume our life in His blessings, being assured that we 'always triumph in Christ' [2 Corinthians 2:14].

God wants us to enjoy this one life! "There is nothing better for a man, then that he should eat and drink, and that he should make his soul enjoy good in his labor. This also I saw, that it was from the hand of God" [Ecclesiastes 2:24]. Enjoy the delights of God's creation and all its beauty, and take pleasure in the Lord who "giveth us richly all things to enjoy" [1 Timothy 6:17]. 'And whatsoever ye do, do it heartily, as to the Lord, not unto men; Knowing that of the Lord ye shall receive the reward' [Colossians 3:23-24].

So, if you play a round of golf today, give it your best and enjoy the satisfactions and the challenges of the round. Let us give life our best this one day we have now, too, living it as unto the Lord, and enjoying both the delights and challenges.

Prayer:
This is the day the Lord hath made, this one day at a time the Lord hath given to enjoy our works and His creation. Let us rejoice in this day for all things, for we are the Lord's this day and forevermore.

Scripture of the Day:
"But, beloved, be not ignorant of this one thing, that one day is with the Lord as a thousand years, and a thousand years as one day." - [2 Peter 3:8]

The Word for the Day is "Stars."

Quote for the Day:
"Keep your eyes on the stars, and your feet on the ground." -Theodore Roosevelt

We may not clearly understand all the scriptures and promises given in Revelation—but it is clear that God promises blessing and reward to those who stay strong and true to Him. God often uses the concept of the stars in His teachings in the Word. A star in the east led the wise men to Jesus [Matthew 2:9], God promised Abraham and Sara their descendants would be as "the stars of the sky in multitude" [Hebrews 11:12], and at the end of Revelation Jesus spoke of himself as "the bright and morning star" [Revelation 22:16].

When we look into the night sky toward the heavens, at the stars and constellations, they remind us of the vastness of God's creation, the wonder of His power and might. Like the old hymn "How Great Thou Art" the stars remind us of the wonder of our God. Perhaps you have laid outdoors in the grass or on a quilt at night and looked up at the stars in heaven, finding the constellations, marveling at the beauty of heaven. It is humbling. "When I consider thy heavens, the work of thy fingers, the moon and the stars, which thou hast ordained; What is man, that thou art mindful of Him?" and yet "Thou madest him to have dominion over the works of thy hands" and "put all things under his feet" [Psalm 8:3,4, 6].

We are often counseled to keep our minds and eyes on the things of God and the things of heaven, rather than minding earthly things so much. Quotes suggest we 'reach for the stars' and tell us 'the stars are the limit,' encouraging us to pursue our dreams. We should pursue our dreams as led by the Lord and encourage others to do so also. "And they that be wise shall shine as the brightness of the firmament; and they that turn many to righteousness as the stars for ever and ever" [Daniel 12:3].

Prayer:
May the heavens and the stars on high ever remind us of God's glory and majesty and declare to us His righteousness [Psalm 97:6].

Scripture of the Day:
"And he that overcometh and keepeth my works unto the end, to him will I give power over the nations…and I will give him the morning star." -
[Revelation 2:26-28]

The Word for the Day is "Silence"

Quote for the Day:
"True silence is the rest of the mind, and is to the spirit what sleep is to the body, nourishment and refreshment." - William Penn

It doesn't occur often in East Tennessee, but sometimes in winter we do receive a snowfall. Snow can cause a disruption in travel and utilities, if deep enough, but our snows are usually moderate and short-lived. I love the beauty of seeing the earth covered in white, appearing clean and fresh. But I also love the silent tranquility of snowfall. Whereas rain is noisy, snowfall seems to have a quiet, serene quality when falling. For a short time at least, the world around us seems to quieten and feel more peaceful.

This condition of quietude seems harder to achieve in our day-to-day life when we want to be alone and communicate with God. The one word that to me best describes our world today is "noisy." Everything around us seems to be loud—the noise of vehicles and traffic, the shopping malls, the grocery store, the TV, the radio and more. Maybe that's why God admonishes us to get into our closet and shut the door [Matthew 6:6]. It may be the only quiet place we can find! This place of silence is a treasure for the man of God, a place to shut out the noise of the world and the distractions of our own busy thoughts. Since God speaks in the 'still, small voice' [1 Kings 19:12], we need this quietness to better hear the Spirit of God.

There are benefits and blessings to being quiet and silent before the Lord. "Then they cry unto the Lord in their trouble, and he bringeth them out of their distresses. He maketh the storm a calm, so that the waves thereof are still. Then are they glad because they be quiet: so he bringeth them into their desired haven"[Psalm 107:28-30]. The Word tells us to 'study to be quiet' [1 Thessalonians 4:11], to 'lead a quiet and peaceable life' [1 Timothy 2:2], and to wear the ornament of a 'meek and quiet spirit, which is in the sight of God of great price' [1 Peter 3:4]. We are promised the effect of righteousness is 'quietness and assurance for ever' [Isaiah 32:17]. Getting quiet alone with God is worth the time and effort!

Prayer:
Lord, help us put away the noise and clamor of the world, that we might be quiet before You, and hear more clearly the voice of Your Spirit.

Scripture of the Day:
"Be silent, O all flesh, before the Lord: for He is raised up out of His holy habitation." - [Zechariah 2:13]

The Word for the Day is "Rejoice."

Quote for the Day:
"All my life through, the new sights of nature made me rejoice like a child."
- Marie Curie

How joyous are the pictures God paints of nature rejoicing and singing when God blesses His people. It creates such a lovely picture of the ideal harmony that should exist between God and the heavens, the earth and His own people.

Ecclesiastes 3:11 reminds us that God "hath made everything beautiful in His time." In Genesis Chapter 1 we read the story of how God made the earth and the heavens in all their beauty—the day and the night, the waters, the heavens, the grass, the herbs and trees—and He called it all good. It's moving to read of the creation of our world. As one who loves to paint and write, the incredible creativity in these scenes touches me, and my mind imagines the wonder of creating and establishing all this glorious beauty.

My mother always took me on walks out in nature, teaching me the names of flowers and trees, opening my eyes to the beauty of the natural world. She always said she wondered how people could fail to believe in God and in His goodness when nature all around sang His praises. Even today, being in nature lifts my heart and spirit.

So many verses in the Word remind us of the beauty of God's creation. "The heavens declare the glory of God, and the firmament sheweth His handiwork" [Psalm 19:1]. All nature seems to speak of the work of the Lord and each of us are God's creations too. Always hold the wonder in your heart that you, too, were designed by God. And never be too busy to see the beauty of God's creation and to rejoice in the wonder of it.

Prayer:
Lord, open our eyes to see the beauty of the earth and Your creation all around us—and to rejoice in it, letting it always remind us of Your love.

Scripture of the Day:
"This is the day which the Lord hath made; we will rejoice and be glad in it." - [Psalm 118:24]

Quote for the Day:
"You might have to fight a battle more than once to win it." - Margaret Thatcher

Winning has a great value and high priority in American life. We value and reward winning in our society. It seems to be human nature to want to victor over opponents in a competition. Sports in our society place an emphasis upon winning; sports teams and individuals are rewarded with fame and fortune when they win. But we are intolerant of those that don't win enough. Coaches and players in this condition at season's end are often looking for a new job.

There are other arenas besides sports where winning is the goal. Another definition of *win* is to achieve success in an effort or venture. Another meaning is to struggle through to a desired place or condition. Both of these meanings imply an effort and a struggle against opposition to achieve a desired outcome.

But what is the struggle against to 'win Christ' Paul talked of in Philippians 3:8? I believe Paul was talking about the commitment of placing Jesus as highest priority in every area of his life. Paul counted all things loss 'for the excellency of the knowledge of Christ Jesus my Lord.' Paul wanted to know Jesus in a close relationship, not in just some shallow, half-committed way. This commitment was so strong in Paul that he counted all else 'as dung.' Paul struggled, as any man would, against opposition from without and within. He wrestled with the 'cares of this world,' trying to enter in and oppose him [Mark 4:19], and with opposition from his 'adversary the devil' always seeking to thwart him [1 Peter 5:8]. Paul saw clearly how 'his flesh fought against the Spirit', the two ever contrary to one another, making it difficult to do the things he knew he wanted to do [Galatians 5:17]. But Paul learned, despite all opposition, that God always caused him to triumph in Christ Jesus—as He will us too, if we stand firm in our faith and truly make Jesus our highest commitment [2 Corinthians 2:14].

Prayer:
Let us totally commit ourselves that we might 'press toward the mark for the prize of the high calling of God in Christ Jesus' [Philippians 3:14].

Scripture of the Day:
"Yea, doubtless, and I count all things but loss for the excellency of the knowledge of Christ Jesus our Lord: for whom I have suffered the loss of all things, and do count them but dung, that I may win Christ." - [Philippians 3:8]

The Word of the Day is "First."

Quote for the Day:
"Put God first and you'll never be last." - Unknown

God always wants to be first in our lives. He said "Thou shalt have no other gods before me" (Exodus 20:3] and there are many gods and things of this world clamoring and trying to outshout the quiet voice of God. A busy Pharisee and lawyer asked Jesus: "What's the greatest commandment?" Jesus answered: 'Thou shalt love the Lord thy God with all thy heart, and with all thy soul, and with all thy mind. This is the First and greatest commandment' [Matthew 22:37-38].

First means 'coming before all others, foremost…ranking above all in importance.' God wants to be first in our hearts, in our lives, in our time management schedules. He knows if we put Him first all will go well for us. Jesus taught us that we can't serve two masters—both God and earthly things. He said, "seek ye first the Kingdom of God, and his righteousness, and all these things shall be added unto you" [Matthew 6:33].

God gives you favor when you put Him "First." If we put Him first—the blessings come in, the favor comes in, the answers come in…but not when we waver or doubt or always look to the world first. The Bible cautions in several places that God's people 'have left their first love' [Rev 2:4]…'cast off their first faith' [1 Tim 5:12]. When we don't put God first, life grows harder then than it needs to. It seems more natural and easier to listen to and put our trust in the world, the voices of the world, the things we can hear, see, and touch—but, oh my, if we would step out and put God "First," as He asks, what marvelous things we might see—and how much more blessed life might be.

Prayer:
Lord, help us to re-order our priorities in life and to put You back in first place. Teach us through Your Word how trusting in You first and reaching out to You first in serious matters and in everyday ones, helps every aspect of our lives run more according to your best and perfect will.

Scripture of the Day:
"Seek ye first the kingdom of God, and his righteousness; and all these things shall be added unto you." - [Matthew 6:33]

The Word for the Day is "Walls"

Quote for the Day:
"It is possible for you to do all things through Christ strengthening you, even to overleap the highest walls." - Ralph Erskine

Most of us remember the song: 'Joshua fought the battle of Jericho, and the walls came tumbling down.' And we remember the Bible story of this event. Most acknowledge that God did a great miracle on that day, knocking down flat the walls of Jericho. But man had a part to play in this miracle, too. Without obedience to God's commands, it could not happen. God commanded Joshua to circle the city once for six days with the priests carrying the ark and sounding the horns. But on the seventh day, they were to circle seven times and then give a great, loud shout. When Joshua did his part obeying in faith, God did His part, and the walls fell down [Joshua 6:2-20].

Sometimes we face walls in our life. Walls that can keep us within or without God's best for us. Maybe our wall is a problem or situation keeping us outside the dreams, promises, and blessings we seek from God. Or, we may feel trapped inside a wall, a problem that binds us to our present condition or circumstances. In both cases, we need for the walls to come down. How do we tear down the walls that keep us from God's best for us? The same way Joshua did, by faith and obedience. We do our part by standing in faith on the promises in the Word of God that apply to our need and staying obedient. God then does His part by confirming His Word with signs following [Mark 16:20].

"The name of the Lord is a strong tower: the righteous runneth into it, and is safe" [Proverbs 18:10]. What a blessing to have the protection of the Lord about us by abiding under His covering. But we must still exercise faith and obedience to stay in that secret place with the Lord. We can jeopardize our position if we become lazy and void of understanding [Proverbs 24:30-31], if we fail to exercise judgment and fail to walk in righteousness [Isaiah 5:1-7], and if we fail to discipline our own spirit [Proverbs 25:28]. "But thou shall call thy walls Salvation, and thy gates Praise" [Isaiah 60:18]. Let us praise God for His great salvation to knock down the walls that hinder us!

Prayer:
Lord, thank You that You honor our faith and obedience by destroying the walls that hinder us from obtaining Your best.

Scripture of the Day:
"By faith the walls of Jericho fell down, after they were encompassed about seven days." - [Hebrews 11:30]

The Word for the Day is "Immortality."

Quote for the Day:
"Death, unanticipated, is death; death, anticipated, is immortality." - Saint
Vardapet Eghishe

Abraham Lincoln wrote: "Surely God would not have created such a being as
man to exist only for a day! No, no, man was made for immortality." Be assured,
human beings were created for immortality. Jesus said 'those who are His are
blessed because they have an inheritance, the kingdom prepared for them since
the creation of the world' [Matthew 25:34].

We were made to last forever, and if we are in the Lord in a right way, we will.
People often shy away from thoughts of death, forgetting our life on earth is just a
temporary assignment. Rick Warren calls our time on this earth "a practice work-
out before the actual game"... but I like to think of it as boot camp and preparation
for our work in heaven later. If you get your mind on all there will be for us to do
in eternity, it will start to change what you do here. It will change and color your
values.

Heaven is a busy, wonderful place. It's a vibrant, active kingdom...not a place
where people will sit around and play harps on a bunch of clouds. We will become eternal spiritual beings in that kingdom...not angels flitting about in white
robes with fluffy wings. What you will take with you to eternity is your inner
man. So the thought to often consider is: How well are you developing your inner man? How well are you developing your mind and talents to use better for
eternity? How well are you using your time and days productively?

God does have purpose for you every day here on earth...but He also has purpose
in mind for every day in eternity. What are you doing about that? How are you
preparing? Does God look down at you and see a worker or a shirker? Matthew
Henry wrote: "It ought to be the business of every day to prepare for our final
day." It's a quote worth thinking about.

Prayer:
Lord, help us to be more sensitive to see how we can better prepare for eternity.
Help us consider how You want us to use our talents and abilities for Your greater
purposes.

Scripture of the Day:
"For this corruptible must put on incorruption, and this mortal must put on immortality...then shall be brought to pass the saying that is written, death is swallowed up in victory." - [1 Corinthians 15:53-55]

The Word for the Day is "Cup"

Quote for the Day:
"You can't pour from an empty cup." - unknown

Have you ever noticed how many sports championship titles include the word cup? There's the World Cup, America's Cup, Ryder Cup, Stanley Cup, Davis Cup, Charles Schwab Cup, FedEx Cup, and many more. And individual champions are often presented a cup trophy of some sort in their sport. The championship "cup" symbolically represents holding the prestige, rewards, and benefits of the victory. It is not unusual to see the champion holding the cup or trophy and kissing it as news media snap photos of the victor for their media story.

One of my most pleasant images of cup, rather than a victory cup, is a fresh-brewed, steaming cup of coffee in the morning. I can enjoy the aroma and sight of the coffee cup, but the greatest pleasure is tasting it! You drink the coffee to enjoy and experience its goodness. The Lord wants us to 'taste and see' that He is good [Psalm 34:8]. His goodness is beyond description: life, joy, peace, wisdom, righteousness, health, blessings, and benefits that sound too good to be true.

When I walked in the world, before I knew the Lord, I had many misconceptions about "religion." I viewed it as a system of rules and dogmas—none seeming very joyous. But when I came to know the Person, Jesus Christ, the joy of relationship with Him became all. I 'tasted' and saw that the Lord was good! How did I 'taste and see that the Lord is good?" By having Him in my heart and learning of Him in His Word. God gives us free will, and we can look at the coffee cup, smell the coffee, talk about it, or even ignore it, but we have to drink it to experience its goodness. The Lord wants us to take the cup of salvation, drink it, know Him, and see that He is good!

Prayer:
Lord, let us drink full the cup of salvation and call upon Your name, that our cup may be full of You so we can give to those who thirst.

Scripture of the Day:
"What shall I render unto the Lord for all His benefits toward me? I will take the cup of salvation, and call upon the name of the Lord." - [Psalm 116:12-13]

The Word for the Day is "Beginning."

Quote for the Day:
"A good beginning makes a good end." – Louis L'Amour

"In the beginning God created the heaven and the earth" [Genesis 1:1]. Beginnings are always fresh times. God created all things in the beginning that we know on earth today. He made all of nature, the land and seas, the sun, moon and the stars of heaven. He created man and woman, giving us His creative ability, making us in His image, blessing us and giving us dominion over all things.

We were made by Him, for His love and His fellowship and for His purpose. Yet people have not always been grateful for all God has done, not chosen to walk close to Him, but have often 'rebelled against Him and vexed the Holy Spirit' [Isaiah 63:10].This was so from the earliest of times until today. "Since the beginning of the world men have not heard, nor perceived by the ear, neither hath the eye seen…what God hath prepared' [Isaiah 64:4]. Since God created us He wants to be close to us, for us to hear Him, to see His wonder and His love, and to appreciate all that He has done for us as the artist of the world.

Because we have the nature of God, we have the opportunity to create new beginnings for our lives, to make new choices, to begin new directions, to create marvelous works in the earth. Embued with God's creative wisdom, we are capable of so much more than we walk in. We were, after all, "made in his image" [Genesis 1:26], but we don't always draw on that spiritually inherited ability. Timothy wrote, regarding his work, "I thank Christ Jesus our Lord who hath enabled me …putting me into the ministry" [1 Timothy 1:12]. God enabled him to begin to do, and to complete, what he needed to do, what he was called to do.

God always enables us to do what we need to do and what He calls us to do. He has given us His wisdom and ability not only to begin but to finish all the works He gives us [John 4:34]. But only we can make a good beginning to start doing what He asks, to do the work ordained for us, and to make a good ending.

Prayer:
Lord, we are grateful for all You created in the earth from the beginning until now. And we are grateful for the opportunities You offer daily for new purpose and new beginnings.

Scripture of the Day:
"Thy word is true from the beginning: and every one of thy righteous judgments endureth forever." - [Psalm 119:160]

February

FEBRUARY 1
The Word for the Day is "Tree"

Quote for the Day:
"The apple never falls far from the tree." - old proverb

Heredity and environment play great roles in shaping our lives. Many characteristics of our physical looks and personality traits come from our parents or are inherited from family genetics. Many of our behaviors are shaped by the environments we grew up in, the teachings we are given. Inherited and taught traits can be both good and bad, positive or negative. But God promises when we come to Him, that we will be grafted into a new vine, a new tree of His nature [John 15:4-5]. He promises to make us a new creature [2 Corinthians 5:17]. He wants to change our old nature and to renew us to be changed and conformed to His image [Romans 8:29].

However life, heredity, upbringing, and experiences may have shaped or influenced us, God knows the purpose we were always intended to walk in, and the nature He always intended us to have. When we come to know Him and begin to grow in Him, He begins to change us into that image, to plant us in a new and better place.

The intent is that we will be a tree bearing His nature and His fruit—that our new nature and fruit never fall far from His, that we be perfected in Him. 'Even so every good tree bringeth forth good fruit...wherefore by their fruits ye shall know them' [Matthew 7:16-20]. "But the fruit of the Spirit is love, joy, peace, longsuffering, gentleness, goodness, faith, meekness, temperance: against such there is no law" [Galatians 5:22-23]. This is the nature of the tree and fruit God wants us to display. And as trees have their individual creation and purpose, so do we have our individual callings in God. We are meant to serve God, develop individually, and minister for God in His unique personal will and design for each.

Prayer:
Let us purpose to always abide in the true vine that we might grow the fruits of the Spirit, and the fruits of righteousness.

Scripture of the Day:
"And he shall be like a tree planted by the rivers of water, that bringeth forth fruit in his season; his leaf also shall not wither; and whatsoever he doeth shall prosper." - [Psalm 1:3]

The Word for the Day is "Foundation."

Quote for the Day:
"The foundation stones for a balanced success are honesty, character, integrity, faith, love and loyalty." - Zig Ziglar

From readings in science, we know the earth is built on a foundation of rock. Often when hiking in the Smoky Mountains near our home, I find a small shiny quartz rock alongside the trail. Occasionally, I carry it along in my hand for a time as I walk, marveling over it, thinking about the diversity and beauty of the rocks and geological wonders in our mountains here in East Tennessee. In the streams I see vast boulders, too, that although the stream surges and cascades around them, they hold fast and sure. There are such lessons in nature to see every day.

Our foundation in life is to be built on the rock of Jesus Christ [Matthew 16:18] so that we, too, can live sure, strong, tried lives and be precious in God's sight. If we build our lives on some foundation other than the rock of the Lord, our lives will be vulnerable to destruction. The parable Jesus taught of the Wise and Foolish Builders gives a good example of this in story form. Those who built their homes on the sand found their homes crumbling when the storms of life swept in but the house built on the rock was safe and held firm when the floods and winds came [Matthew 7:24-27]. When our lives are built on the strong and firm foundation of the Lord, we can withstand the problems and trials of life better, too.

Prayer:
Dear Lord, let each day be one in which we add to the good foundation of our lives by spending time in the Word and with You to ensure we can stand when the storms of life come.

Scripture of the Day:
"Behold, I lay in Zion for a foundation a stone, a tried stone, a precious corner stone, a sure foundation." - [Isaiah 28:16]

The Word for the Day is "Unbelief"

Quote for the Day:
"Turn your back on every sense of unbelief and believe God." - Smith Wigglesworth

To believe in something is to have confidence in it, and belief is a mental acceptance or conviction in the truth or actuality of something. Unbelief is therefore the opposite, a lack of belief or faith, or a lack of confidence. Belief builds with familiarity with a thing or person. The more we know of something, the more we can believe in it. It's hard to believe in or have confidence in something we know little of.

The beginning of a firm belief in God is in studying and coming to know God. A second factor in believing is making a decision to believe, as belief is a mental acceptance or conviction and also a developed habit. The Word is filled with examples of men and women full of faith and belief, and of those weak and unbelieving. The "faith hall of fame" found in Hebrews, Chapter 11, tells us of a few of the faithful: Abel, Enoch, Noah, Abraham, Isaac, Jacob, Joseph, and more. These were all of the mind that 'faith is being sure.'

It is easy to see that belief has reward and that God desires and wants belief in Him. "Without faith it is impossible to please him: for he that cometh to God must believe that he is, and that he is a rewarder of them that diligently seek him" [Hebrews 11:6]. Cultivate a strong, unwavering belief in God. Like adding chocolate topping to ice cream, believing makes faith better. "Jesus said unto him, If thou canst believe, all things are possible to him that believeth" [Mark: 9:23].

God wants you to make a mental, conscious decision to be a believer, and to be a person of unwavering belief in Him and in His Word. Decide today to turn your back on doubting, questioning, and unbelief, and determine to believe God as a daily habit. 'Jesus saith...Be not afraid, only believe' [Mark 5:36].

Prayer:
Lord, we vow to cast aside all unbelief and doubt, and determine to believe, living by faith, walking by faith, growing in faith, that we might give You glory.

Scripture of the Day:
"He [Abraham] staggered not at the promise of God through unbelief; but was strong in faith, giving glory to God." - [Romans 4:20]

The Word for the Day is "Love."

Quote for the Day:
"I want the love that cannot help but love; Loving, like God, for [the] very sake of love." - A. B. Simpson

We are meant to love as God loved us, and it is wired into our makeup. People pair in love and in marriage relationships that often last a lifetime. Many animals and creatures in God's natural world pair for life, too, including swans, wolves, penguins, voles, gibbons, and eagles. Ninety percent of birds mate for life and many creatures become very bonded in their habits and grieve when their mates die. Seahorses swim with their tails wrapped around each other to stay connected, otters hold hands when sleeping in the water so they won't drift apart, and wolves are known to be more loyal to their mates than humans.

In Eden, God saw that Adam had 'no helpmeet fit for him' [Genesis 2:20], and He took one of Adam's ribs and created woman. It is nice to realize, when we're in God's World of nature, that He designed most species of his creatures to live in pairs. So it is a natural hunger in our hearts to seek for and to want to link our lives to our right helpmeet. When we have not found this helpmeet, we can be prayerful and believe God will direct us to the right person at the right time—and if we have found that person, we should love and rightfully cherish them. "Being someone's first love may be great, but to be their last is beyond perfect" [unknown].

Prayer:
Thank you, Lord, that You designed us to hunger to live in pairs, to love and support one another, and we ask You to help us to be grateful for those you have linked our lives to.

Scripture of the Day:
"And we have known and believed the love that God hath to us. God is love and he that dwelleth in love dwelleth in God, and God in him." - [1 John 4:16]

The Word for the Day is "Prayer"

Quote for the Day:
"Daily prayers will diminish your cares." - Betty Mills

It would be unnatural to never talk to other people. Talk is how we relate the content of our heart and mind to others, and how we receive the communication of their heart and mind. Some talk little, others much, but it is still the means of giving to and receiving from others. Prayer is talking to God, communicating our heart to Him, and receiving the thoughts of His heart in return. Prayer nurtures our relationship with God, as talking to family and friends does in this life.

God wants us to pray. What kind of parents would not want their child to talk to them? A parent delights in talk with his child; God delights in the prayer of the upright [Proverbs 15:8]. Some feel they are not 'righteous' enough, or worthy enough to talk to God. But God does not despise or reject the prayer of even the troubled, the needy or destitute, the prisoner, or any who cry unto Him [Psalm 102:1-2,17-20]. We have God's promise that He will receive our prayers [Psalm 6:9], so why would we deny God what pleases Him and has such benefits for us?

God hears our prayers. We are seeking the Lord when we set our face to the Lord and pray [Daniel 9:3]. And when we seek in prayer, we have God's promise that He hears our prayers [Psalm 34:4]. Some men think God is too busy with the universe to hear their singular prayer. Some think they can work God up into a good mood to hear their prayer if they can get ten intercessors praying for them. No, God just wants to hear your prayer as His child, as you delight when your own child talks to you.

God also answers prayer. Obviously, we must not pray amiss by praying contrary to God's Word. But when we pray in agreement with God, we can be sure that in Jesus Christ 'all the promises of God in Him are yea, and in Him Amen, unto the glory of God by us' [2 Corinthians 1:20]. So, talk to God - Pray!

Prayer:
Lord, thank You that You want us to pray, that it delights You to receive our prayers, and that You save us out of all our troubles.

Scripture of the Day:
"But verily God hath heard me; he hath attended to the voice of my prayer." - [Psalm 66:19]

The Word for the Day is "Clean."

Quote for the Day:
"Live a clean life for a clean legacy." -Unknown.

When I was a child I asked my mother, "Why do we always have to get a bath, wash our hair, and wear pretty clean clothes on Sunday morning to church?" She looked at me with shock. "It would be disrespectful unto the Lord not to go to His House clean and looking our best. He deserves that, at the least, don't you think?" She straightened my dress and then looked at me directly with one of those serious expressions. "Always give God your best," she said. "Always look your best for God on the inside and on the outside." There was so much truth in that counsel.

In the natural, to be clean means to be free from filth or dirt. Metaphorically and spiritually, we know that to be clean means we've been washed clean and delivered from the power of sin through Christ Jesus [1 Corinthians 6:11] but that is just the beginning of our walk with the Lord and our new life in Him. God's desire is for us to keep putting away wrong ways and to keep being renewed. "Wash you, make you clean; put away the evil of your doings from before mine eyes; cease to do evil. Learn to do well." (Isaiah 1:16-17]. Becoming clean and staying clean in the Lord isn't accomplished wholly in one act—any more than taking one bath keeps us clean for a lifetime. This earth and its ways are full of filth and dirt, corruption and evil. We have to daily make an effort to stay clean and faith-filled, "unspotted from the world" [James 1:27].

In "The Faith Hall of Fame" in Hebrews Chapter 11, many of the men and women who lived by faith are applauded. Wouldn't we like our lives to be looked back on someday with admiration, too? Living what people term a good life is admirable, but leaving a legacy of worth and faith is even better.

Prayer:
Lord, help us to be more conscious in every day of the life we're choosing to live, of the potential memories and legacy we're leaving behind. Help that legacy to be a clean and worthy one—that it may be said of us: That was a person of great faith.

Scripture of the Day:
"Who shall ascend into the hill of the Lord? Or who shall stand in His holy place? He that hath clean hands and a pure heart." - [Psalm 24:3-4]

The Word for the Day is "Birds"

Quote for the Day:
"Everyone likes birds. What wild creature is more accessible to our eyes and ears, as close to us and everyone in the world, as universal as a bird." - David Attenborough

I enjoy putting out bird seed and water in a dish on my deck rail and watching the birds, especially in winter. I view the birds through my sliding glass doors in the kitchen as I drink my morning coffee. I marvel at God's creation of birds and their variety: different colors, shapes, and sizes. Bluejays, cardinals, doves, and small birds, like chickadees, sparrows, finches and others, crowd my deck rail at these feedings. It makes me feel good to think I have helped the birds with food and water during this tough season. But then I remember that the birds did quite well before I moved into this house, and would very well survive without me. The birds appreciate my seeds and water, but God provides for His creation and my help is not essential to their survival.

How can we imagine that if we care so much about the birds and our pets, that God does not lovingly care for us? Birds have needs, but they always appear to me as calm and confident, knowing instinctively their needs will be provided. Why can't we trust God like this? God assures us in His Word that we are much more valuable to Him than birds. Not a single bird falls to the ground without God knowing. God even knows the number of hairs on our head and declares we are of more value than many sparrows [Matthew 10:29-31]. If God knows us this well, why do we doubt that He knows all about our lives and what we want and need? If God provides the beasts and young ravens with food when they cry, will He not the more provide for us when we ask [Psalm 147:9]? Ravens neither sow nor reap, nor have storehouses nor barns, and they don't worry about it! Neither does God want us to worry. He can take care of us as easily as He does the ravens [Luke 12:24-26]. Let's decide today to trust the Lord and let the Lord 'renew our strength and cause us to mount up with wings as eagles' [Isaiah 40:31].

Prayer:
Lord, thank You that You provide for the fowls, thank You that You know everything in our lives, and thank You that we can trust You to provide for us.

Scripture of the Day:
"Consider the ravens: for they neither sow nor reap; which neither have storehouse nor barn; and God feedeth them: how much more are ye better than the fowls?" - [Luke 12:24]

The Word for the Day is "Rose."

Quote for the Day:
"We can complain because rose bushes have thorns, or rejoice because thorn bushes have roses." – Abraham Lincoln

The rose is perhaps one of the most beautiful of all flowers. It is thought of as "the flower of love" and roses are often sent to express love on anniversaries, birthdays, Valentine's and other special occasions. The rose is a perennial and there are hundreds of species of roses in a wide array of colors. The diversity of flowers God created, as well as the diversity among individual flowers among the same genus and species, teaches us a lot about God's nature and preferences. He loves diversity and individuality. Roses grow in cultivated gardens, wild in the countryside trailing over wood fences, climbing backyard arbors, and decorating everyday neighborhoods. All are beautiful and we know God called everything He made good.

Too often we try to be like others. We wish for a different appearance, a different life. But we each have worth and beauty in who we are, in what we look like, in where we live and how we spend our days—as long as those ways are pleasing to God. A glorious hybrid rose, a dainty tea rose, a scrambling shrub rose—all are lovely and all are beautiful in God's sight.

Our beauty and value, and our protection in life, is in the Lord. Roses have protective thorns and we should build a protective hedge around our lives to keep us safe from the enemy. When you walk through a garden of roses the next time, remember that God made every rose you see after His pattern and design. Be reminded, as in the love song in the Song of Solomon, that you are to the Lord like "the rose of Sharon" beloved in His sight [Song of Solomon 2:1-4].

Prayer:
Lord, thank You that You have made each of us unique and beautiful in Your sight. Thank You that as the rose, we come in many varieties and colors by Your design, but that each of us is beloved by You, created individually in Your love and purpose.

Scripture of the Day:
"And the desert shall rejoice and blossom as the rose. It shall blossom abundantly and rejoice even with joy and singing." [Isaiah 35:1,2]

The Word for the Day is "Storm"

Quote for the Day:
"It takes a real storm in the average person's life to make him realize how much worrying he has done over the squalls." - Bruce Barton

Most people engage in a great deal of unnecessary worry. They are overly anxious over the weather, over their health, over their children, over politics, over work, and over petty things people say and do. Although we may see worrying over imagined impending storms of life as natural, God views the matter differently. God tells us to be careful (anxious, worried) for nothing, to cast all our cares upon Him [Philippians 4:6; 1 Peter 5:7].

An old Mark Twain quote says: "I've had a lot of worries in life, most of which have never happened." Many of us treat our worries like the person who watches the weather forecast with a 20% chance of rain, and immediately cancels all plans for that day. We give the small percent of rain more weight than the overwhelming 80% chance that it will not rain! Another of my favorite quotes by Montaigne says: "As if there were not time enough to suffer evil when it shall come, we must anticipate it by fancy and run to meet it." How true this is. The Word tells us to "Take therefore no thought for the morrow: for the morrow shall take thought for the things of itself. Sufficient unto the day is the evil thereof" [Matthew 6:34]. Rather than worry over storms that haven't materialized yet, we should better use our time building faith and trust in God so that when the real storms in life come we will be prepared to face them with faith and fortitude.

Today in East Tennessee was a bright, cloudless day with beautiful blue skies and sunshine. If there had been storm clouds over the area today, with tempest and rain obscuring the blue sky and brilliant sunshine, it would not have changed the reality that the bright, blue serenity still existed in the firmament above the storm clouds. The storms pass away, but the beauty of God's goodness and Kingdom will always be there above to shine down on us.

Prayer:
Lord, we will be at peace knowing that though tribulations and storms may come, You will be our very present help and confidence from harm.

Scripture of the Day:
"For thou hast been a strength to the poor, a strength to the needy in his distress, a refuge from the storm, a shadow from the heat." -[Isaiah 25:4]

The Word for the Day is "Liar."

Quote for the Day:
"This is the punishment of a liar. He is not believed even when he speaks the truth."
– Rabbi Simeon

A favorite Aesop Fable of mine growing up was "The Little Boy Who Cried Wolf." In jest he alarmed the village and got everyone into a panic, calling "wolf" when no wolf was really coming to threaten the sheep. Sadly, when a wolf really came to threaten the herds, no one believed him when he sounded the alarm. The moral is not hard to see. When we lie often to others we are soon not believed anymore. We lose our honor and integrity of being a person of truth.

Why do people lie? In jest, from fear, to save face, because of greed or pride, to name but a few reasons. When Cain killed his brother, Abel, he tried to lie to God about it to cover up. Jacob lied to his blind father to steal his brother's birthright. For these lies both men soon met great sorrows. Lying often seems like a good idea at the time but it only creates more sorrow and a loss of respect when the lie is later revealed. Isaiah wrote: "a sword is upon the liars" [Jeremiah 50:36]. No good reward comes of lying or at least no lasting reward.

Our lives, our behaviors, are meant to emulate God's. "Every word of God is pure: he is a shield unto them that put their trust in him" [Proverbs 30:5] and it is "impossible for God to lie" [Heb 6:18]. In direct contrast, satan is termed 'the father of lies' and we know 'there is no truth in him' [John 8:44]. So when we lie we align ourselves with satan and not with God, with evil and not with good.

One of the six things God hates, called an abomination to Him, is lying, being "a false witness that speaketh lies" [Proverbs 6:19]. We are cautioned in the Bible to 'avoid even the company of liars' [Proverbs 14:5-7] and warmed that 'liars will not go unpunished' [Proverbs 19:5]. Lying is a serious matter before God. We may not always discern every lie we hear, but God always does [Is 59:1-4].

Prayer:
Lord, quicken us to the times when we are tempted to tell a lie, large or small. Teach us to walk in truth and to speak only truth.

Scripture of the Day:
"A wicked doer giveth heed to false lips; and a liar giveth ear to a naughty tongue."
- [Proverbs 17:4]

The Word for the Day is "Keep"

Quote for the Day:
"I do the very best I know how - the very best I can; and I mean to keep on doing so until the end." - Abraham Lincoln

Everyone knows the effort it takes when deciding to clean out the garage, the attic, the closets, the house, or any other space. It takes a lot of physical effort and, if you're like me, that alone tends to procrastinate the chore. But there's another effort in cleaning out—what to throw away and what to keep. This mental torture can be worse than the physical hardship. The decision is to determine what items no longer have use, benefit, or utility to us, and which do. We often, if reluctantly, trash or give away the items no longer useful (which usually seem to be the majority) and keep the rest. Due to ongoing changes in our lives, we give away things we no longer need to keep, as well, like clothes that no longer fit or an old tape player we used to take to the beach.

Likewise, when we become a new creation in Christ Jesus, we need to discard some old ways that God wants to remove, and keep the things God wants in our life. Proverbs 4:23 tells us to 'keep our heart.' We keep our heart by doing a "house cleaning"—letting the Lord break off and discard the old mold of the world, and transform us into His image and kingdom. God wants us to keep godly behavior that benefits us and to discard the ways of the world that war against the Spirit and hold us back from His best [Galatians 5:17].

As Christians, we are still in the world, but not of this world anymore. We clean our life up by casting off the mindset of this world, and taking on and keeping the mind of Christ—loving God, learning of God, obeying God, living in the love of God, and living by the Word of God. Sometimes it's a challenge to put off our old ways, but God promises He will keep us in perfect peace if we keep seeking His ways and trusting Him [Isaiah 26:3].

Prayer:
Lord, thank You that You help us root out the weeds and garbage of our old life when we commit to keep Your ways first. And that You change us into the image of the Lord from glory to glory by your Spirit according to your Word.

Scripture of the Day:
"Keep thy heart with all diligence; for out of it are the issues of life." -
[Proverbs 4:23]

The Word for the Day is "Aim."

Quote for the Day:
"If you aim at nothing, you will hit it every time." – Zig Ziglar

To "aim" means to strive to bring something to pass, to be ambitious and to aim for those ambitions. The aim of the believer is to be pleasing unto the Lord. A surprise to many is that God wants only the very best for us. He wants above all things for us to prosper and be in health' [3 John 2]. He 'wants to set us on high above all nations of the earth,' to send good our way to such a degree that the 'blessings overtake us' [Deuteronomy 28:1-2].

God has vision, purpose, and call for each life and He wants each person to pursue and to aim for that. Paul encourages his disciples to 'forget those things which are behind and to reach for those things which are before, to press toward the mark for the prize of the high calling of God in Christ Jesus' [Philippians 3:13-14]. We often aim too low in life, setting our sights and goals too mediocre, without realizing God desires us to move forward, push to our best, work hard, and achieve all we can.

If we were working for an employer, we know he'd expect our best. He'd expect us to be well informed about the company, to seek to grow in the profession, and to excel. The same would be true if we were athletes in training. We'd practice and hunger to be winners. God wants that for us in His work, too. "Know ye not that they which run in a race run all, but one receiveth the prize? So run, that ye may obtain," Paul wrote [1 Corinthians 9:24].

It should be because we're so thankful to God for saving us, for adding us to the wonder of the Kingdom of God, that we yearn to live for Him in all we do, to seek to do His will, and to give Him our best in everything. A quote says "If you do your best, God will do the rest." That's an important thought, because whatever effort we give, God will bless and multiply that effort. You simply can't out give God in your aims and work.

Prayer:
Lord, may we commit our work to You and aim to give our best in every effort every day.

Scripture of the Day:
"Seek ye first [and aim for] the kingdom of God, and His righteousness; and all these things shall be added unto you." - [Matthew 6:33]

The Word for the Day is "Sealed"

Quote for the Day:
"The Christian who will sit with sealed lips when his Master is assailed, when religion is attacked, when wickedness is broached and defended, when truth is denounced, is a denier of his Lord, as guilty as Simon Peter in Pilate's Hall."
- Theodore L. Cuyler

There are benefits to sealing certain things. My coffee stays fresh in the can because it comes with a plastic lid to seal the grounds after each use. We seal a package or box we are mailing by postal or UPS to protect and keep the inside content clean and undamaged. The idea is that something that is sealed is preserved and protected.

Ephesians 1:13 tells us we have been sealed by God when we believe on Him and receive salvation in Jesus. We receive a new spirit in our inner man when we receive Jesus and God seals that new spirit in us making it impervious to corruption or defilement. We are sealed in our spirit and made the righteousness of God in Christ Jesus [2 Corinthians 5:21].

Some believers may look at their faults and mistakes and feel like they have not been sealed unto righteousness. This is because that even though our born-again spirit is perfect in Him, we still have a mind to renew and a physical body to discipline. A child is born and "sealed" into his family. Children grow and learn, and sometimes make mistakes and misbehave. Because a child makes mistakes, he doesn't lose his family name or belonging. Christians start out as babes, and hopefully, grow, learn, and mature in the Lord as they follow His Spirit. A UPS box can get dirty or scuffed in shipping, but because it is sealed, the goods inside the box stay preserved. Likewise, our "outside" box of mind and body can get stained, but our inside good, our spirit, is sealed by God.

If you have made mistakes, repent, receive God's forgiveness, and rejoice that you are sealed in your inner man with the Holy Spirit of promise.

Prayer:
Lord, we have heard the truth of the gospel and trusted in Your salvation through Jesus our Lord. Thank You that You have sealed our new spirit to preservation by Your Holy Spirit.

Scripture of the Day:
"In whom ye also trusted, after that ye heard the word of truth, the gospel of your salvation: in whom also after that ye believed, ye were sealed with that Holy Spirit of promise." - [Ephesians 1:13]

The Word for the Day is "Word-of-God."

Quote for the Day:
"The soul can do without everything except the Word of God." – Martin Luther

The word Bible, derived from the Latin *biblia* and the Greek *biblios*, isn't used in any place within the Bible text. The term used instead is the "Word of God." "In the beginning was the Word, and the Word was with God, and the Word was God" [John 1:1]. The Bible is far more than a group of 66 books. It is authored by God through holy men of old [2 Peter 1:21], inspired by God [2 Timothy 3:16] and is a Living Word [Matthew 4:4]. Because of this we can go to the Word of God every time and find something new, some fresh understanding from God, some new revelation. The Bible also reveals God's love for us, how He has always reached out to us, and how He longs to relate to us. St. Augustine said: "The Holy Scriptures are our letters from home."

After we come to know the Lord, the Holy Spirit helps us to understand the Word of God, transcending our natural understanding and helping us 'spiritually discern the words' [1 Corinthians 2:14]. Through the Word of God we are instructed, taught, made clean, and helped forward in our walk in the Lord [John 15:3]. We are to receive it with humility as God's special word to us and be hearers and doers of it [James 1:21-23]. Developing your faith through studying the Word of God is critical to getting the needs and desires of your heart met. We don't have to be doubtful about the things we read and study in the Bible. The Word of God is pure [Proverbs 30:5] and true [Colossians 1:5]. Every word is established and the Lord confirms His Word [2 Cor 13:1; Mark 16:20].

However, no matter how anointed a book is, its benefits are not attained if the book is not read. A sorrow today is the Christian's neglect in reading and studying the Bible. Without feeding on the Word of God, people are weak in faith, just as someone who stops eating grows weak and sickly. R. C. Sproul wrote: "Here, then, is the real problem of our negligence. We fail in our duty to study God's Word not so much because it is difficult to understand, not so much because it is dull and boring, but because it is work. Our problem is not a lack of intelligence or a lack of passion. Our problem is that we are lazy."

Prayer:
Lord, help us to better discipline our time to cherish and read the Word more.

Scripture of the Day:
"Faith cometh by hearing and hearing by the Word of God." - [Romans 10:17]

The Word for the Day is "Endure"

Quote for the Day:
"Sure I am of this, that you have only to endure to conquer." - Winston Churchill

Everyone will face tough situations, trials of life, problems, and tribulations at some time. Neither are the saints of God excluded from these trials [John 16:33]. Sometimes these woes may last for a season, too, requiring endurance. I have heard it spoken from those going through a tough time that 'they are just trying to endure and hang on.' The implication is that they are defining endurance in the sense of patient suffering, and sometimes the expectation is that the problem has a long-term duration or even permanence. I discern that at times many may even imply they merit a badge of virtue to themselves because they are patiently suffering 'their cross to bear.'

I believe God wants us to have a different attitude in the face of adversity. I believe He would rather us endure by invoking its definition of 'to sustain without yielding.' I believe God does not want us to accept any adversity as permanent, but wants us to sustain our faith in Him, in His Word and promises without yielding. The Lord would have us endure all persecutions with patience and faith in God to glory over our trials with victory [2 Thessalonians 1:4]. The weapons of our warfare against adversity are mighty through God [2 Corinthians 10:4]. God wants us to endure, not yielding to the things that are seen, but believing His faithfulness to His Word, and believing in deliverance, not accepting the trial as permanent [2 Corinthians 4:17-18].

The Word tells us that men endure but for a time because they have 'no root in themselves' [Mark 4:16-17]. The decision to endure and believe God must be made in our heart by our own will and volition. Determine to have root in yourself so that you endure the trial without yielding your faith and the promised triumph in Jesus [2 Corinthians 2:14].

Prayer:
Lord, we determine to endure with patience and faith standing on the promises of Your Word.

Scripture of the Day:
"Behold, we count them happy which endure. Ye have heard of the patience of Job, and have seen the end of the Lord; that the Lord is very pitiful, and of tender mercy." - [James 5:11]

The Word for the Day is "Weapons."

Quote for the Day:
"I am proud of the fact that I never invented weapons to kill." – Thomas Edison

People are very concerned about security today. Airports, public buildings, schools, even churches have ramped up security measures. Individuals have purchased home security systems, outdoor spotlights, and weapons. Everyone wants to be prepared if there is an attack by a criminal, a terrorist, or some other enemy. Satan is all three—enemy, terrorist, and criminal—and his pervasive and destructive ways have been causing trouble since the dawn of time. The newspaper, television, and media are filled with reports of national and local threats, but satan's name is rarely mentioned—even in most churches. Yet, like a hidden enemy, a lion slinking and stalking in the bushes, eager to attack, he is there. And never up to any good.

The Bible warns, "Be sober, be vigilant; because your adversary the devil, as a roaring lion, walketh about, seeking whom he may devour" [1 Peter 5:8]. It's not a pretty picture, but few seem concerned. Yet the Bible teaches satan is our worst enemy in this life. Since all good comes from God, we know the source behind all bad is satan. Often in a movie, like a James Bond film, there is a brilliant mastermind behind a crime ring. Satan is like that mastermind, originally created by God for good, but choosing to turn his brilliance and his gifts to evil. What weapons can we use against a spiritual superpower we can't see? The answer is spiritual weapons. We fight "like with like," knowing God and his host war with us. "For though we walk in the flesh, we do not war after the flesh: (for the weapons of our warfare are not carnal, but mighty through God to the pulling down of strongholds)" [2 Corinthians 10:3-4].

You can learn to 'fight the good fight of faith' [1 Timothy 6:12] through prayer and study. You can 'resist steadfast in the faith' [1 Peter 5:9], 'not letting satan get an advantage' [2 Corinthians 2:11], remembering that 'greater is He that is in you than any evil in the world' [1 John 4:4]. But weapons sitting dusty on the shelf prosper no one. Will you learn to use your weapons or let your enemy ride roughshod over you, offering no offensive or defensive protection?

Prayer:
Lord, help me study and learn in Your Word how to gird myself for battle daily.

Scripture of the Day:
"No weapon that is formed against thee shall prosper…this is the heritage of the servants of the Lord." - [Isaiah 54:17]

The Word for the Day is "Testimony"

Quote for the Day:
"How you live your life is a testimony of what you believe about God." - Henry Blackaby

We are all familiar with the context of the word testimony as it applies to our legal court system. When someone testifies in a court of law he is giving a formal spoken or written statement pertaining to the case. The purpose of court testimony is to establish evidence or proof provided by the existence or appearing of something. The goal of court testimony is to establish evidence so that the case can be judged in truth and equity and render a verdict that is just and equitable.

A testimony in a spiritual context is a 'public recounting of a personal religious experience or conversion.' A believer's personal testimony can have great impact and benefits both for the individual and for others.

The Word of God tells us: "But sanctify the Lord God in your hearts: and be ready always to give an answer to every man that asketh you a reason of the hope that is in you with meekness and fear" [1Peter 3:15]. In this world of chaos, confusion, tumult, terror, and fear, the Lord's people should stand out as the salt and light of the world. "Why are you happy and optimistic when the world is such a mess?" "Why are you calm and at peace when there is such turmoil everywhere?" We should be ready to answer such questions with our personal testimony and share the evidence and truth of God's existence and goodness in our lives. He is the reason for the hope that is in us and our testimony gives us the opportunity to share His reality with another through our experience.

The Word gives us counsel on how to present our testimony. The scripture above tells us to give our answer with meekness and fear. The scripture also tells us to give our testimony with 'simplicity and godly sincerity, not with fleshly wisdom' [2 Corinthians 1:12]. So, an effective and sincere testimony should be simple and from the heart: sharing the difference that the reality of the Lord in our heart has made in our lives. Others need to hear the Spirit in you speaking.

Prayer:
Lord, help us to be always ready to shine the light of the gospel into men's hearts through our testimony.

Scripture of the Day:
"Blessed are they that keep his testimonies, and that seek him with the whole heart." - [Psalm 119:2]

The Word for the Day is "Backsliding."

Quote for the Day:
"You can blame circumstances, but backsliding always begins in the heart."
– A. W. Tozer

As I read through Jeremiah about Israel slipping away from the Lord, I couldn't help but see how this old picture applies to today. To backslide means to relapse into bad ways or error. In the Lord we're always meant to be growing and moving forward, but the people of Israel "went backward, and not forward...loved to wander, and did not refrain their feet from it" [Jeremiah 7:24, 14:10].

Proverbs 14:14 says: "The backslider in heart shall be filled with his own ways." God has a best plan and way for our lives, but often we have something else figured out. How had the people in Jeremiah's day backslid from a right life with God? They put other gods before the Lord, stopped delighting in the Word of God, started walking after vanity and greed, and became involved in sexual immorality without shame. They walked after the imaginations of their own heart, deciding for themselves right from wrong, and stubbornly refusing to acknowledge their sins or to repent and change. Even worse, their pastors backslid, too, didn't correct the people and no longer fed them with right knowledge and understanding. However, they all still prayed to God and expected Him to hear their prayers, honor them, and answer them. They were truly deceived.

When things began to go badly, they got mad at God, not seeing they had stepped out of a place of righteousness and blessing with the Lord. "Your sins have withholden good things from you" Jeremiah tried to tell them [Jeremiah 5:25]. He encouraged them to repent and to turn back again to a holy way of living. God, so loving and merciful, hated to see what they'd done to themselves. He said: "Return thou backsliding Israel...for I am merciful...acknowledge thine iniquity that thou hast transgressed against the Lord thy God" [Jeremiah 3:12-13]. 'Obey My voice, and I will be your God, and ye shall be My people: and walk ye in all the ways I have commanded you, that it may be well with you' [Jeremiah 7:23]. Then as today, falling away from God pulls people out of a right relationship with Him and into the enemy's net. But it is never too late to repent and to draw close to God again when we realize we've slid away.

Prayer:
Lord, examine our hearts and lives and help us back into a right place with You if we've backslid in our faith and relationship.

Scripture of the Day:
"And my people are bent to backsliding from Me." - [Hosea 11:7]

The Word for the Day is "Know."

Quote for the Day:
"Reputation is what men and women think of us; character is what God and angels know of us." - Thomas Paine

How many times have you heard "The Bible says the truth shall set you free"? I've heard it many times too, but that is not exactly what the Bible says. "Then said Jesus to those Jews who believed on him, If ye continue in my word, then are ye my disciples indeed; And ye shall know the truth, and the truth shall make you free" [John 8:31-32]. Jesus said it is the truth that you *know* of a surety that shall make you free. In other words, just hearing the truth doesn't equal knowing the truth.

Hearing is a vital element in knowing spiritual truth, for faith comes by hearing, and hearing by the Word of God [Romans 10:17]. But to know the truth means to be convinced and certain of, to be aware of the factuality of, to perceive directly, or have direct cognition of. In other words, to have the rock-solid assurance in your heart that you are certain, convinced, and settled upon a truth.

In John Chapter 14, Jesus also revealed two other keys to knowing spiritual truth. He said it came to those *who believed on Him*; and who *continued in His word*. Jesus is the way, and the truth [John 14:6], so the revelation of truth is for those who believe on Him. And the truth seeker must continue in His Word; the Bible must be read and studied as the guide to the knowledge of God and His truth.

As believers we have another great advantage in seeking to know truth in faith and life. The Holy Spirit has been given to help us: "Howbeit when he, the Spirit of truth, is come, he will guide you into all truth: for he shall not speak of himself; but whatsoever he shall hear, that shall he speak: and he will shew you things to come"[John 16:13]. So, as we pray, read the scriptures, study, meditate, and learn, the Holy Spirit will help to guide us into all truth. Then knowing the truth, we can believe the divine promises given to us to truly bless and make us free.

Prayer:
Lord, I commit to know Thy truth through prayer, meditation, and study of your Word. Thank You for the Holy Spirit to guide me into all truth so that I can be not a hearer only, but also a doer of Thy Word.

Scripture of the Day:
"And ye shall know the truth, and the truth shall make you free." - [John 8:32]

The Word for the Day is "Study."

Quote for the Day:
"No man ever reached to excellence in any one art or profession without having passed through the slow and painful process of study and preparation." – Horace

Everything worthwhile tends to come with study, practice, and work. As toddlers we struggled to stand and then walk. In sports, a budding athlete practices the basics again and again to move on to more mastery. In the arts, an artist observes the masters and then works day by day until talent is developed and grows. "There are no shortcuts to any place worth going" (Beverly Sills).

In the Christian walk, growth in faith also comes with study, practice, and work. Many years ago my husband and I taught a Sunday School class and marveled at the majority who showed up each week saying they'd been "too busy" to read a chapter or two in the Bible or to think about a few simple questions. In any work place, an employee who won't fulfill assignments is soon unemployed. In school, a student who is too busy to complete his work soon sadly fails the class. Most people sensibly apply themselves to needed tasks at work, school, and home yet will shirk their responsibility to grow in the Lord with little thought, guilt or remorse. It grieves the heart of God, though, when we don't find place for Him. Just as we'd get annoyed at a lazy, excuse-making student or employee, God is rightly displeased with us when we neglect growth in faith and time with Him. The Lord commanded "Thou shalt have none other gods before me" [Deuteronomy 5:7] and He expects to be first with us.

How can you study in the Lord? You purpose to make time for it. You pray, you read in the Word, you look up terms and concepts you want to clarify, you search out similar scriptures in your concordance to broaden your understanding. As you make time daily to spend with God—believing to learn, believing to grow in faith, believing to fellowship with God, He will meet you there and rich, sweet learning will occur. As we study in the Lord, it will become easier, more comfortable, and more a part of our lives and we will be blessed for it. 'In everything you do, put God first, and He will direct your paths and crown your efforts with success' [Proverbs 3:6].

Prayer:
Lord, may we begin to diligently study to grow more in You and learn more of You. Study in You will bring our lives blessing and enrich our days.

Scripture of the Day:
"Study to show thyself approved, a workman that needeth not to be ashamed."
- [2 Timothy 2:15]

The Word for the Day is "Fight."

Quote for the Day:
"Better to fight for something than to live for nothing." - George S. Patton

Mention the word "fight" and the average person envisions two boxers in a ring or a brawl-like physical confrontation. We are told to "fight the good fight of faith" [1 Timothy 6:12], but our fight as believers is not a physical combat, but a spiritual fight. We do not wrestle (fight) against flesh and blood, but we fight against spiritual wickedness, against those spirits of darkness that work against us in others and in the world [Ephesians 6:12].

Jesus was the Light of the world, yet He was rejected and hated by many. Why? The Word tells us: "And this is the condemnation, that light is come into the world, and men loved darkness rather than light, because their deeds were evil" [John 3:19]. Men reject God and His righteousness today just as they did when Jesus walked the earth. Think it not strange that some will reject, persecute, and hate your light as they did Jesus' light and truth [John 15:18-19].

I believe the best context of our fight of faith is remembering that fight means to attempt to prevent the success of. The devil wants to prevent our success in our walk of faith with the Lord. He does not want us to manifest the praises and works of God in our life to a lost world. Therefore he fights to sabotage our faith and power in the Lord. But we have to know that Jesus has already defeated the devil for us and given us everything we need to triumph over him. "Greater is he that is in you, than he that is in the world" [1 John 4:4]; 'I give you power...over all the works of the enemy' [Luke 10:19].

God has given us spiritual weapons to use [2 Corinthians 10:4] and the armor of God to stand against the wiles of the devil [Ephesians 6:11-18]. "Now thanks be unto God, which always causeth us to triumph in Christ" [2 Corinthians 2:14]. So let us exercise our authority and power in Jesus to always triumph in Him!

Prayer:
Lord, I purpose to fight the good fight of faith. Thank You for my spiritual armor and my mighty weapons that Jesus gives me for victory over my enemy.

Scripture of the Day:
"Fight the good fight of faith, lay hold on eternal life, whereunto thou art also called, and hast professed a good profession before many witnesses." -
[1 Timothy 6:12]

The Word for the Day is "Impossible."

Quote for the Day:
"God is looking for people through whom He can do the impossible; what a pity we plan to do only the things we can do by ourselves." – A.W. Tozer

A favorite phrase of many toddlers is "I can do it myself." A child feels developmentally compelled to begin breaking away from total dependence on his or her parents. In an odd twist, when we become Christians, God wants us to 'lean not to our own understanding' and abilities but to lean in dependence on Him and His ability [Proverbs 3:5]. Since we've spent much of our lives fiercely establishing our independence, this is not easy for us. But the truth is we are limited in what we can do and accomplish by ourselves but virtually unlimited in what we can accomplish and do if we allow God to work in and through us.

So often in the Bible we read where God's people tried to tell Him about their limitations or the obvious problems in tasks He set before them. Moses tried to tell God he didn't think he could go before Pharoah and had concerns about his ability to speak [Exodus 3:7-11]. After God led His people out of Egypt with signs and wonders, they argued that they couldn't go into the promised land because of giants [Numbers 13:30-33]. When God called Gideon to lead his people, he said 'I'm poor, the least in my father's house, and not the one to do this' [Judges 6:14-16].

With our eyes focused on the natural, and on what we perceive our personal limitations to be, situations can look impossible. But Jesus told his disciples 'with men many things are impossible; but with God all things are possible' [Matthew 19:26]. We need to fully trust in God for Him to do all He wants to do through us. Without stepping out on that limb of faith, we can't please God and be used of Him as He desires. "But without faith it is impossible to please Him" [Hebrews 11:6]. We may feel unable in many situations, but God is able. We may feel unqualified, but God is qualified. When we get out of the way and let God work through us, the impossible becomes the possible every day. "I can do all things through Christ who strengthens me" becomes our response instead of "I can't" [Philippians 4:13].

Prayer:
Lord, help us to see past our own abilities to see our possibilities in You.

Scripture of the Day:
"If ye have faith as a grain of mustard seed, ye shall say unto this mountain, remove hence to yonder place: and it shall remove; and nothing shall be impossible unto you." - [Matthew 17:20]

The Word for the Day is "Mountains."

Quote for the Day:
"The mountains are calling and I must go." – John Muir

One of the things I like most about living in East Tennessee are the mountains. Lin and I like to get away from the noise and business of life at times to hike the mountain trails in the nearby Smoky Mountains. We love the beauty of God's creation and the serenity and peace we experience there.

Jesus often retreated to the mountains to pray and to prepare for earthly ministry. On one occasion, His disciples came to him on a mountain and he taught them the principles of Kingdom living or what we now call the Sermon on the Mount [Matthew 5:1-2]. Another time when Jesus sent the multitudes away, he went to a mountain alone to pray at length. In the evening when he returned he found his disciples imperiled by a great storm and Jesus walked on the water, quieted the storm, and saved his disciples [Matthew 14:23]. Many times Jesus' time alone in the mountains, spending quiet time with God, strengthened and prepared Him for ministry ahead. Once, near the Sea of Galilee, after ministering at length among the people, Jesus went up into a nearby mountain again. A great multitude followed Him and He taught them with love and compassion and healed many who were lame, blind, dumb and maimed. Then later seeing they had gathered for so long a time and were hungry, he multiplied a few fishes and loaves of bread to feed them all, a total of four thousand people [John 15:29-39]. It was on a mountain, too, that Jesus was gloriously transfigured before Peter, John, and James [Luke 9:28]. So perhaps it should not surprise us if the mountains give us inspiration and make us feel closer to God.

Often in the mountains we get physically closer to the heavens, get away from the crowds, get into the beauty of nature and seem to touch the peace and wisdom of God more easily. John Muir, who spent much time in the mountains wrote these words: "Keep close to nature's heart and break clear away, once in a while, and climb a mountain or spend a week in the woods. Wash your spirit clean." Perhaps the mountains help us, too, to wash our own spirits clean of the daily clamor of our world. And perhaps that is why the mountains seem to call to us.

Prayer:
Lord, I will get to the mountains by walking, or figuratively by prayer, and I will let Jesus reveal to me His good tidings of great joy!

Scripture of the Day:
"The mountains shall bring peace to the people, and the little hills, by righteousness." - [Psalm 72:3]

The Word for the Day is "Blind."

Quote for the Day:
"The only thing worse than being blind is having sight but no vision." – Helen Keller

It hurts our hearts to see someone who is blind, to think of how much they miss not being able to see loved ones' faces and the beauty of the earth. Some individuals are blind from birth while others are blinded through accident or illness. Blindness can be partial as well as complete, but without a miracle, like Jesus touching the eyes of the blind man [Matthew 9:29], blindness is nearly always permanent.

God often talks about those who do not know Him, who have not received Jesus, or who have fallen away from Him in their faith as blind [Lamentations 4:14; John 9:40-41; Revelation 3:17]. We know God can 'open the eyes of the blind' and heal both spiritual and natural blindness and we know Jesus in His ministry healed the blind [Psalm 146: 8; Matthew 11:5]. Through His death and resurrection He passed on His glorious gifts to His disciples and to us so that healing, signs, and wonders could continue, touching lives and hearts [Luke 10:19-20; Philippians 1:6].

The percentage of individuals naturally blind is small, but the percentage of Christians spiritually blind is large. Spiritual blindness is a sorrow to the Lord and should be to us. We should hunger for people to be brought out of darkness into the light and to never thwart or discourage anyone's way as they seek to learn more of Him [1 Peter 2:9-10; Romans 2:19]. We often do not mean to lead others astray or down wrong paths. But satan, the god of this world, tries continually to blind the eyes to the truth of God and to corrupt our way [John 12:40; 2 Cor 4:4]. Knowing this, we should seek more truth daily and seek to always discover more spiritual light, so that like the blind man Jesus healed, we can always find new ways to say: 'I know one thing, I was blind but now I see' [John 9:25].

Prayer:
Lord, help us always yearn to see more every day, to never allow the god of the world or others to blind us to your truths.

Scripture of the Day:
"In whom the god of this world hath blinded the minds of them which believe not, lest the light of the glorious gospel of Christ, who is the image of God, should shine unto them." - [2 Corinthians 4:4]

The Word for the Day is "Preach."

Quote for the Day:
"Practice yourselves what you preach." - Flautus

We know that as believers we are to be the salt of the earth and the light of the world [Matthew 5:13-16]. And we are to be witnesses and "preach"—to impart the message of the good news of the gospel to all the world [Mark 16:15]. But how are we to most effectively preach this good news to the world? I think the scriptures instruct us best in 2 Corinthians 4:5-7:

1. "For we preach not ourselves, but Jesus Christ the Lord; and ourselves your servants for Jesus' sake" [2 Cor 4:5]. Jesus must always be first in priority in our witness, as we tell the good news of His love and salvation, that He is the hope of every man, and not us.

2. "For God, who commanded the light to shine out of darkness, hath shined in our hearts, to give the light of the knowledge of the glory of God in the face of Jesus Christ" [2 Cor 4:6]. The light of the knowledge of God must come from our heart knowing the Word of God and through personal fellowship with Him. The more truth we have of the Word, the more we can impart those truths, as the Spirit leads, to others.

3. "But we have this treasure in earthen vessels, that the excellency of the power may be of God, and not of us" [2 Cor 4:7]. When we witness about our Lord with words of Spirit and of Life, the world will know they are of the power of God and not of us.

We preach the gospel with our words and with our lives: "Let your light so shine before men, that they may see your good works, and glorify your Father which is in heaven" [Matthew 5:16]. So, for our words to 'shine before men', we should 'practice what we preach ourselves in our lives and ways.'

Prayer:
Lord, help us to always be preaching through our lives the good tidings to others of the great salvation through Jesus Christ.

Scripture of the Day:
"And he said unto them, Go ye into all the world, and preach the gospel to every creature." - [Mark 16:15]

The Word for the Day is "Breath of Life."

Quote for the Day:
"Freed are they who find their wings on a brand new breath of life." – Pepper Blair

'The world was framed by the Word of God so that things that are seen were not made out of things which are visible' [Hebrews 11:3]. God created the heavens and the earth and 'God created man in His own image, male and female' [Genesis 1:27]. We are made in God's likeness. God breathed life into us and spoke us into existence with His Words. With God's breath of life all the earth, the birds, the animals, the sky, the sea, the stars, and human beings, like us, came to be.

Through salvation in Jesus, and through the entry of New Life that occurs with receiving Him, Jesus enters into us. The Holy Spirit comes to dwell in us and we receive a greater measure of the life of God, the breath of life, than we had before. Like the clay from the dirt, that God formed into a man and then breathed the breath of life into, we receive the life and power of God, as well, when we come to know the Lord [1 Cor 15:45; Matt 28:18-20]. God crowned man with that same glory—His Glory—in creation, and though man lost that estate in the fall, in Jesus we get it back through salvation. We are made a new creature in Christ Jesus and a new, fresh breath of life comes into us and we are changed [2 Cor 5:17]. Jesus said 'the words I speak to you are spirit and life' [John 6:63] and now we, through Him, can speak with authority and power as Adam and Eve did. We can speak the breath of life, the words and will of God over our lives, over the world around us, and over the lives of others.

The breath of life has creative power. How do we use this great gift? Do we use it to speak good things, right words, and God's will, or do we use it to speak bad things, erroneous words, opposite to God's will? Just because we've been given the power to speak the breath of life doesn't mean we use it wisely and well.

Prayer:
Lord, may we evaluate how we use the great gift we've received of the breath of life, reverencing it and using it wisely and well.

Scripture of the Day:
"And the Lord God formed man from the dust of the ground, and breathed into his nostrils the breath of life, and man became a living soul." -[Genesis 2:7]

The Word for the Day is "Faithful."

Quote for the Day:
"A faithful friend is a strong defense; And he that hath found him hath found a treasure." - Louisa May Alcott

How good it is to know a faithful person. It is pleasant dealing with a faithful friend, someone who is loyal, constant, steadfast, reliable, and consistent. Faithful people create a tranquil ambience, not anxiety or worry.

We know that God is faithful, constant, and never lies. With God there is no 'variableness, neither shadow of turning' [Heb 13:8; James 1:17]. It is 'impossible for God to lie, and that which He speaks He shall do and shall make it good' [Numbers 23:19]. We can count on God's absolute goodness and faithfulness to His Word and count on Him to keep and fulfill his promises to us. God's Word is forever settled in heaven [Psalm 119:89] and He is faithful to the performance of His Word.

God is looking for a faithful people to serve Him [Psalm 101:6]. So what is required of us to be faithful? We must be a people of truth: "A faithful witness will not lie: but a false witness will utter lies" [Proverbs 14:5]. We must be faithful in the small things of life before we can be used for the big things: "He that is faithful in that which is least is faithful also in much: and he that is unjust in the least is unjust also in much" [Luke 16:10]. God expects us to be faithful in the things of mammon: our duties in the world such as getting to work on time, doing our job and obligations faithfully [v.11]. We must be faithful in our fiduciary trusts: "And if ye have not been faithful in that which is another man's, who shall give you that which is your own?"[v.12]. Above all, we must be faithful to hold fast to the Word without compromise [Titus 1:9].

The Lord preserves the faithful [Psalm 31:23] and we make ourselves useful for His service so that we can hear those precious words: "Well done, thou good and faithful servant" [Matthew 25:21].

Prayer:
We thank You, and praise You Lord, because You are Faithful and True. We seek to please You by being faithful stewards of the gospel and ambassadors for You.

Scripture of the Day:
"Mine eyes shall be upon the faithful of the land, that they may dwell with me: he that walketh in a perfect way, he shall serve me." - [Psalm 101:6]

The Word for the Day is "Charity."

Quote for the Day:
"If you haven't any charity in your heart, you have the worst kind of heart trouble."
– Bob Hope

Jesus was always very empowering in his leadership. He encouraged others to believe they could accomplish great things. He pushed his disciples out to work and minister in the world, even knowing they hadn't developed His skills or expertise yet. "Go ye therefore, and teach all nations" [Matthew 28:19]. He taught His disciples. "Ye shall receive power…and ye shall be witnesses unto…the uttermost part of the earth" [Acts 1:8]. Jesus was an encourager but never a micromanager, who overly controls the work and actions of those they manage or lead. We all know people who micromanage and seem to have a dysfunctional, excessive obsession with regulating others lives rather than empowering and encouraging them and allowing them to develop and grow in their own way. Studies say people try to micromanage others because of personal insecurity, arrogance, a lack of trust and belief in others, a perfectionist nature, and fear they won't have control. These characteristics are somewhat opposite of the Christian nature, which is secure in the Lord, not prideful—trusting and believing in others, realizing all are still learning and growing and not yet perfected, and knowing God is meant to be in control in all lives and actions. We are all meant to minister encouragement toward each other, to "increase and abound in love one toward another" [1 Thessalonians 3:12].

A true empowering leader helps others learn to lead and reach the potential God has imbued in them. Empowering leadership is loving and encourages people to feel safe and free to try new things, to learn and grow. As the people of God came into the Promised Land, God said to Joshua in encouragement: "Be strong and of a good courage, fear not, nor be afraid…for the Lord thy God, He it is that doth go with thee; He will not fail thee, nor forsake thee" [Deut 31:6]. Loving leadership always says, I will be here if you need me but I have confidence in your ability.

Prayer:
Lord, help us to remember to use our leadership as You did, to encourage and to empower others to be all they can be, to step past their limitations, knowing You will give the increase.

Scripture of the Day
"And above all these things put on charity, which is the bond of perfectness."
 - (Colossians 3:14]

March

The Word for the Day is "Green."

Quote for the Day:
"For in the nature of things, if we rightly consider, every green tree is far more glorious than if it were made of gold and silver." - Martin Luther

I always look forward to and welcome the arrival of March. For one thing, we have three birthdays in our family to celebrate this month: Lin's and mine at the middle of the month, and our son Max's at the end of the month. I will always cherish memories of Max's celebrations with his childhood friends and their laughter in the warm sunshine. With the arrival of March, we know the cold, dreary days of winter in Tennessee are almost past and the warm, greening season is here. Brown grass turns to lush green by the end of the month and the shrubs, flowers, and trees begin to put forth new buds and growth.

The delights of the spring season arrive this month. The earth is greening, the birds sing louder, and the days grow longer with more sunshine each day. It seems to be a time of refreshing anticipation of warmth, beauty, and new life as nature shakes off the brown dryness of winter and ushers in the delightful greenness of spring. God is always sure to bring the spring after the winter.

Sometimes in life we go through seasons that seem harsh and unpleasant, like winter can be. We can be enduring a season of hard natural cirmumstances, a time of financial hardships, family problems, job problems, health problems, or other sorrows that beset us. Maybe we are going through a trial of faith when answers to prayers have not manifested yet. These trials, natural or spiritual, can feel like a personal season of winter at times when life seems hurtful and cold.

But as God always brings about the new greenness of springtime to replace the bitterness of winter, if we stand fast in the promises of God's Word, and trust in His goodness, God is always faithful to turn our brown to green, full of life and beauty. Thank God that He is about to turn your winter into springtime!

Prayer:
Lord, we thank You for the fresh green and beautiful colors of a new season. And we thank You most of all for the newness of life we have in our Lord Jesus.

Scripture of the Day:
"He maketh me to lie down in green pastures: he leadeth me beside the still waters." - [Psalm 23:2]

The Word for the Day is "Sweet."

Quote for the Day:
"Love planted a rose, and the world turned sweet." - Katharine Lee Bates

It is always my joy on hikes or walks to come across wildflowers along the way or to find a neighbor's yard suddenly abloom with new spring flowers. Many of the flowers God designed, like the lily of the valley and certain varieties of roses, have a sweet and heavenly scent. God wants us to be 'a sweet savor unto Him' in our daily walk, too [Genesis 8:21].

God made all the wonders of the earth and called them good, and there are many passages in the Bible that use the beauty and sweetness of nature to teach us about God's love for us and about the way He wants us to live our lives. The Song of Solomon has many of these sweet passages, like "As the lily among thorns, so is my love among the daughters" [Song of Solomon 2:2]. This passage reminds us that we should be "a lily among thorns'—that in an often hurtful, negative world we should stand out differently, with a sweet savor, positive in a negative world, showing hope and the sweetness and goodness of God. Our lives should be uplifting to other Christians, to our friends and family, and to all we encounter in the world. "For we are unto God a sweet savor of Christ, in them that are saved, and in them that perish" [2 Corinthians 2:15]. The world talks about 'stopping to smell the roses.' We should be the sort of people others want to stop and spend time with—like flowers along the pathway.

Sometimes God's people are not sweet, acting like they've been weaned on a dill pickle, not drawing any to the Lord. But out of the same fountain should not come sweet and bitter water [James 3:11]. These things don't occur in nature and shouldn't occur in us. We should be like 'the rose of Sharon and the lily of the valley' [Song of Solomon 2:1].

Prayer:
Lord, may we show in a negative and often thorny world the beauty, goodness, and sweetness of Your nature in our lives.

Scripture of the Day:
"Pleasant words are as an honeycomb, sweet to the soul, and health to the bones."
- [Proverbs 16:24]

The Word for the Day is "Taste."

Quote for the Day:
"We are to introduce our people into the life of the Church, which is salvation, that they may grasp its meaning, its contents and purpose, to taste and see how good the Lord is." - Arthur Middleton

Not long after Lin and I married, she tried to expand my diet by getting me to taste foods (mostly vegetables) that I had not relished before (usually because I had never eaten them before). I loved cheeseburgers, chili, pizza, Milky Way bars, and ...what else could a person possibly want!? In time, she succeeded in getting me to eat a variety of vegetables. I learned to like broccoli and other vegetables over time but asparagus is still repugnant to me. In all honesty, I have to admit that my health benefitted from including more nutritious food in my diet (although I still think a man can subsist solely on cheeseburgers).

The Bible tells us to 'taste and see that the Lord is good' [Psalms 34:8]. What does this mean? Just as we taste foods to try them, to see if they are good or not to us, the Lord wants us to experience and try Him. He wants us to 'taste'—to take in, to experience, to *prove* that He is good!

We prove that the Lord is good by experiencing Him, by getting to know Him and His goodness! We do this by seeking Him with an honest, whole heart. "The young lions do lack, and suffer hunger: but they that seek the Lord shall not want any good thing" [Psalm 34:10]. We learn of the Lord and His goodness by 'tasting' or taking in His Word. We talk to God in prayer, and His wonderful Holy Spirit reveals His love and goodness to us. He proves His goodness to us through His loving fellowship with us, and His blessings and benefits to us: divine life, peace that passes all understanding, grace, knowledge, wisdom, health, and joy. O taste and see that the Lord is good!

Prayer:
Lord, let every man taste and prove to himself that You are good, that Your mercy and goodness endureth forever.

Scripture of the Day:
"O taste and see that the Lord is good: blessed is the man that trusteth in him." - [Psalm 34:8]

The Word for the Day is "Rooted."

Quote for the Day:
"The more rooted we are in the love of God, the more generously we will live our faith." -Brennan Manning

A tree, shrub, or plant grows strong and well if its roots are deep. Recently, we tried to uproot an undesirable shrub that had taken over one of our flowerbeds. My husband dug for an hour, hacking at that shrub's roots, but those roots were fierce and tough, extending deep into the earth, and were almost impossible to break up. Although we thought we'd gotten the shrub's roots out in the fall, this spring that bush popped up again. Its persistence and hardiness amazed us.

Our roots in the Lord need to be planted deep and strong like this, so when satan or the world hacks at them or when trouble comes, we will stand and endure, come back and flourish. We need to have 'Christ securely and strongly dwelling in our hearts by faith that we would be rooted and grounded' [Ephesians 3:17]. There is nothing more powerful than being rooted and grounded in the Lord. We should want to be like that shrub, 'steadfast, hardy, and un-moveable, always abounding in the work of the Lord' so we aren't easily dug up by the problems of the world, influenced by others not living for God, or swayed off course in our faith [1 Cor 15:58; 2 Thess 2:2-3]. We don't ever want to be shaken in mind or deceived but able to hold onto our faith firmly.

When we are not rooted deep in the Lord, built up in Him and established in the faith, the troubles, afflictions, and difficulties that come our way can uproot us. We may become discouraged, offended, fall away, and not endure [Hebrews 12:15; Mark 4:17]. When our roots are deep we are established, firm, and secure. We have depth and can hold steadfast.

Prayer:
According to your riches in glory, Lord, may we be strengthened by the Spirit in the inner man, staying rooted and grounded in You.

Scripture of the Day:
"A man shall not be established by wickedness: but the root of the righteous shall not be moved." - [Proverbs 12:3]

The Word for the Day is "Past."

Quote for the Day:
"Let the dead Past bury its dead! Act,—act in the living Present! Heart within, and God o'erhead!" - Longfellow

We live in the present, looking forward to things future, and back at things past. God wants us to have a proper perspective of every dimension of life, and above all, I think, He wants us to live in fullness of life today with an assured hope of the future, and to not let the past interfere with either of these first two desires.

I am reminded of the old Clint Eastwood movie *The Good, The Bad, And The Ugly* when considering the past. The past can contain each of these three elements. Let's consider the *Good.* All the happy and fun experiences that impacted us in a memorable, joyous way impress our mind in a positive way with rememberance of these good happenings. These delightful memories from the past we can cherish forever. Also, the past can be a teacher to show how we can use the lessons of history to grow in wisdom and understanding to 'avoid the mistakes of the past' as the old saying goes.

Now let's consider the *Bad* and the *Ugly.* I lump these two descriptors together because anything that is bad is also ugly. The enemy has no difficulty using the past to torment us when he reminds us of all our sins, mistakes, failures, and faults to laden us with guilt, regret, and shame. He also likes to weight our minds with thoughts of melancholy memories to sorrow the heart.

But God wants us only affected by the *Good* from the past and to be free from the *Bad* and *Ugly*. We must have the revelation that our past sins and mistakes are forgiven by our Lord Jesus when we repented and accepted Him as our Savior [Ephesians 1:7]. God does not remember our past sins, and neither should we [Hebrews 8:12]. If something is washed, it is clean, the stain is gone! God wants us to remember that we are cleansed from the past, and that we are to press on today toward the mark for the prize of the high calling of God in Christ Jesus [Philippians 3:14]!

Prayer:
Thank you, Lord, that our past is forgiven, we live in newness of life with You today, and our future is assured.

Scripture of the Day:
"Again, a new commandment I write unto you, which thing is true in him and in you: because the darkness is past, and the true light now shineth." - [1 John 2:8]

The Word for the Day is "Guard."

Quote for the Day:
"Guard your roving thoughts with a jealous care, for speech is but the dialer of thoughts, and every fool can plainly read in your words what is the hour of your thoughts." -Alfred Lord Tennyson

I well remember the grape vines that grew over a long garden fence at my childhood home place. My parents were consummate gardeners and I reaped the joy of their work without as much appreciation as I should have offered for all the work they did planting, tending, protecting, and harvesting. Instead, I simply picked the green grapes, warm in the summer sunshine, and popped them into my mouth! But looking back, I recall the wars my parents often waged over pestilence, bugs, and various blights that came to attack the grape vines and other growing things in our gardens.

It didn't take but one hungry little caterpillar or a sudden flock of black crows to eat up the new grapes and to spoil the vines—especially when tender and new. As Christians, we need to guard our hearts, minds, and lives against the subtle small things…the little sneaky foxes…that can so easily creep in and harm our faith [Song of Solomon 2:15]. These little foxes might be doubt, fear, or unbelief and can erode our faith. Other sneaky little foxes to guard against, that can weaken us, leaving us vulnerable to ill, are giving little time to prayer and neglecting to read and study God's Word.

We need to 'guard our hearts and minds through Christ Jesus' [Philippians 4:7]. God's words tell us the things to focus our mind and attention on and the things to avoid. An overdose of worldliness can begin to saturate and contaminate our thinking and soon creep into our actions and life. We were 'created to be like God in true righteousness and holiness' [Ephesians 4:24], to not be conformed to the pattern of the world. We have to keep our life as diligently tended—and more so—as we would keep a garden. We need to watch for 'the little foxes, the small things, that can so quickly spoil the vines' [Song of Solomon 2:15].

Prayer:
Lord, the little foxes of the enemy ever lurk hoping to weaken us and to keep us from abiding in the vine safely… so help us to be good gardeners of our souls and lives.

Scripture of the Day:
"Keep [guard] thy heart with all diligence; for out of it are the issues of life." - [Proverbs 4:23]

The Word for the Day is "Only."

Quote for the Day:
"All things are possible, only believe." - Smith Wigglesworth

What would happen if we *"only believed?"* If we took the Word of God and believed only in its Truth and infallability and in God's power and faithfulness? If we *"only believed"* and didn't let unbelief enter in to negate our faith? If we did not let our carnal mind and natural circumstances convince us to disbelieve, rather than holding fast in a solid conviction of faith? If we did not listen to fear and doubt tell us: 'This is impossible, you've got to be practical'; 'That stuff was for way back then, not now'; 'Our church doesn't believe that'; 'Who do you think you are? Get real!'

The Scriptures show us what can happen if we *"only believe"* as recorded in Mark 5:22-43. A ruler of the synagogue, Jairus by name, came to Jesus and besought Him that he would come and pray for his little daughter, who 'lieth at the point of death.' Jesus went with Jairus, but on the way they were thronged by much people, and a certain woman, who had an issue of blood, touched Jesus' clothes as he went and she received her healing. Just then, some came from Jairus' house and announced that his daughter had died. Jesus said to Jairus: 'Be not afraid, only believe.' Jesus then proceeded on to the ruler's house and found the people weeping and wailing greatly at the little girl's death. Jairus, still believing only, went in to the house with Jesus and received his twelve-year-old daughter back to life as Jesus took her by the hand and raised her from the dead.

What would happen if we *"only believed?"* We would see, as Jairus did, heaven open above and the light of the truth that 'with God nothing shall be impossible' [Luke 1:37] would shine down on us!

Prayer:
Thank You, Lord, that You are True and Faithful and that with You nothing is impossible if we only believe.

Scripture of the Day:
"As soon as Jesus heard the word that was spoken, he saith unto the ruler of the synagogue, Be not afraid, only believe."- [Mark 5:36]

The Word for the Day is "Light."

Quote of the Day:
"We are indeed the light of the world—but only if our switch is turned on."
- John Hagee

What a wonder it is when light is breaking through the darkness, lighting up our lives, shining its rays upon our path. A beautiful scripture in Isaiah says "And I will bring the blind by a way that they knew not; I will lead them in paths that they have not known: I will make darkness light before them, and crooked things straight" [Isaiah 42:16].

Often when hiking in the Smoky Mountains near our home, or walking on a woods trail, I will see a shaft of light streaming through the trees. It always makes me pause in my steps, seeing the light filtering through the deep shade of the forest—as if lighting the path ahead. It always touches my Spirit and seems to remind me of the scriptures that promise that 'Jesus came to be the light of the world for us' [John 8:12] and that He promised 'He would guide, light, and direct our paths' [Proverbs 3:6].

Whenever I stop in awe to look at the beams of light shining through the darkness of the forest, I am reminded, too, that 'I am to be a light in the world' [Matthew 5:14]. If I follow after Jesus I won't walk in darkness and I will have the light of life in me. Others can safely follow my example and my words can be a help to them when they walk through dark times or are not sure of their way. Jesus taught: "Let your light so shine before men, that they may see your good works, and glorify your Father which is in heaven" [Matthew 5:15-16].

Prayer:
Let us hold fast to the knowledge Jesus came to bring light to the world and that through us His light can continue to shine.

Scripture of the Day:
"I am the light of the world: he that followeth me shall not walk in darkness, but shall have the light of life." [John 8:12]

The Word for the Day is "Clouds"

Quote for the Day:
"Be still, sad heart! and cease repining; behind the clouds is the sun still shining." -
Longfellow

As a kid, in the summers I liked visiting my grandfather's farm near Tellico
Plains. I enjoyed exploring the hills, mountains, and streams around the farm.
Two things I remember about Granddad. First, he never got in a hurry. His life
moved always at a steady, easy pace no matter what needed to be done—and
he *always* got his work done! Secondly, Granddad had a subtle wisdom, and he
sometimes used unexpected humor to make his point.

Granddad could sometimes remind me of views I had never considered before. If
I complained that I couldn't go fishing in the creek because it was raining instead
of sunny, he might remind of the fact that above the rain clouds the sky was blue
and the sun always shining. I can hear him say: "Well, since the sun is shining
and the skies are blue above today, why don't you just go ahead and go fishing?"

The Lord has shown me that this is a good analogy of the Kingdom of God: it is
always there with beautiful blue skies and bright sunshine. We know God's Word
is the same forever [Psalm 119:89], we know His promises are always yea and
Amen [2 Corinthians 1:20], and we know that His kingdom endureth forever
[Psalm 89:36].

So if there seem to be storm clouds in your life and you can't see any sunshine,
remember that above the clouds God's Kingdom reigns supreme. Nature always
causes the times of clouds and bad weather to pass in time, and the blue skies and
sunshine return, and it is so in God's Kingdom, too. We know in life there will
be times of tribulation, but if we stand firm in our faith in Jesus [John16:33], and
the promises of God [2 Corinthians 1:20], the storm clouds will surely give way
to the beautiful firmament of God's Kingdom.

Prayer:
Lord, we praise You that Your Kingdom reigns constant and true, like the firmament of heaven above the clouds.

Scripture of the Day:
"For thy mercy is great above the heavens: and thy truth reacheth unto the
clouds." - [Psalm 108:4]

The Word for the Day is "Mercy."

Quote for the Day:
"Teach me to feel another's woe, To hide the fault I see; That mercy I to others show, That mercy show to me." – Alexander Pope

One thing Jesus was known for was his mercy and compassion for others. He reached out His hands to so many that others wanted to judge and condemn, drawing them in with love, showing them another way to live, bringing them healing, hope, and kindness. An old quote says "It costs nothing to be kind." It does cost nothing but it can mean everything to the person the kindness is bestowed on.

The Bible doesn't tell us how the woman caught in adultery got into that lifestyle. But according to law, she was to be stoned, and her accusers seemed eager to take on the task. "What do you say we should do?" they asked Jesus. In response, he waited a few minutes—calm, as though He hadn't heard them and then said, "He that is without sin among you, let him first cast a stone at her" [John 8:7]. Gradually, one by one, the men laid down their stones and left. When they had all gone, Jesus said to the woman, "Go, and sin no more."

God is a merciful God, again and again offering us second chances and pointing us in a better way. Exodus 34:6 says: "The Lord God is merciful and gracious." Aren't we glad for that? And shouldn't we live a little more on the side of mercy, too, rather than on the side of quick judgment?

After Jesus taught his disciples the Beatitudes, he counseled them, "Love your enemies, do good to them which hate you. Bless them that curse you and pray for them which despitefully use you…Be ye therefore merciful, as your Father also is merciful" [Luke 6:27-28, 36]. God wants us to be 'changed into his image, to give mercy as we have received mercy' [2 Corinthians 3:18; 4:1].

Prayer:
Lord, it always seems so easy to judge, to see the flaws in others while ignoring and excusing those in ourselves. Help us to be kinder and more merciful in our daily walk.

Scripture of the Day:
"Be merciful unto me, O Lord…for thou, Lord, art good and ready to forgive; and plenteous in mercy unto all them that call upon thee." - [Psalm 86:3,5]

The Word for the Day is "Continue"

Quote for the Day:
"Success is not final, failure is not fatal: it is the courage to continue that counts."
- Winston Churchill

There is a Law of Inertia that states: objects at rest, stay at rest, and objects in motion stay in motion (unless acted upon by an outside force). I read one paraphrase of this which simply stated: "objects keep on doing what they're doing."

This law is easy to observe in the natural world. For instance, my golf ball will stay at rest on the fairway and not move at all if I swing the golf club and whiff the stroke. I have to apply the club face to the ball to get it to move (hopefully in the right direction). An automobile will continue a long way even if we let it coast, and if it has some speed, we discover we need brakes to slow the motion.

I think this law also has a parallel application in the spiritual realm. God does not want us to stay at rest in our faith: unmoving, unchanging, staying the same, not growing in revelation and relationship with Him. We have to apply an outside force to get us to move from an inert state to a state in motion, just like the club has to contact the golf ball to move it. This force has to come from an act of our own free will; we have to *decide* that we are going to move on in the Lord.

Now we are in motion, seeking to grow and move on in God. There are forces now that can hinder or help us keep moving. Hindrances can be our own carnal mind which is at enmity against God, the opinions and unbelief of others, influences of the world, and our adversary the devil [Romans 8:7].

God wants us to stay in motion toward Him. How? By continuing. He wants us to continue in the Word of God [John 8:31], continue in the love of Jesus [John 15:9], continue in the grace of God [Acts 13:43], continue in His goodness [Romans 11:22], and continue in prayer and thanksgiving [Colossians 4:2]. Like keeping the gas pedal down, God will keep you moving close to Him if you continue in these things. It's the one who continues that arrives at the destination.

Prayer:
Lord, we will not be inert, but ever moving forward in You. Help us in this high calling to continue in faith grounded and settled [Colossians 1:23].

Scripture of the Day:
"Then said Jesus to those Jews which believed on Him, If ye continue in my word, then are ye my disciples indeed." - [John 8:31]

The Word for the Day is "Forget."

Quote for the Day:
"If we meet and you forget me, you have lost nothing, but if you meet Jesus Christ and forget Him you have lost everything" – Unknown

Adam and Eve got careless in the garden and lost their first estate. They lived in a beautiful, blessed relationship with God but lost it. I'm always amazed reading through the Old Testament at the different generations who forgot God and His instructions—as Adam and Eve did—and who started walking after some other way. You'll read one king was righteous and good but the next wicked, forgetting the Lord. These back and forth stories go on and on.

Is it so different from today? Don't we look around and see those who once loved and served God now drifting away? Why does this happen? In the same way we can forget other things, we can forget and drift away from God—through distance, lack of touch and communication, and neglect. We easily forget what we don't spend time with. We forget languages we learned in school but no longer use, old friends we once loved and talked with every day but now seldom see.

Truthfully, we must make effort daily to stay close to God, to not forget Him or His Ways. It doesn't happen naturally. The world competes too heavily for our time and heart. We make our excuses but God knows when we don't put Him first. James cautions about going off on your own way, 'forgetting what manner of man you were in the Lord' [James 1:23-25]. It's dangerous. We have an enemy stalking and just waiting for a chance to attack when we are careless and weak, when we don't keep the hedges around our lives strong.

God cautions: 'Take heed to yourself, remember and do not forget' [Deut 4:9], 'Walk after the Lord your God and fear Him and keep His Commandments, and obey His Voice' [Deut 13:4]. You can forget many things and it will not harm you, but to forget God is a sorrow.

Prayer:
Lord, help us to work daily to keep You first in our lives, to not forsake time with You, to not forget your Words, to love You as You love us.

Scripture of the Day:
"If we have forgotten the name of our God…shall not God search this out? For he knoweth the secrets of the heart." - [Psalm 44:20-21]

The Word for the Day is "Help"

Quote for the Day:
"God has chosen us to help one another." - Smith Wigglesworth

Everyone at some time gets into situations where they need help. Scripture [Pslam 46:1] shows us that God should always be the first we seek for help. There are many good-intentioned helps, but we need help that is effective and absolute in providing the remedy to our need. For instance, my neighbor may call me for help with an automotive or a plumbing problem, but I know well that I do not have the skills to provide her solution. However, I can recommend someone I know that is skilled and honest to remedy her problems. Like the old Beatles song *Help,* she needs 'somebody' (that can fix her problem), 'not just anybody' (not qualified to render the help needed). We can be confident the Lord will help us find the right person for effective help.

We also should always call on God first when our problems have to do with help needed for personal, mental, emotional, or spiritual situations. The Holy Spirit can provide our answers through God's Word and give us the guidance we need. Comfort, support, and compassion are not only needed, but also wisdom, discernment, and direction for life decisions. This is where we need to be very careful about where we seek our help. A carnal person, or person of little faith, will offer only helps according to the world's opinion, which can often lead to more hurt than help. Someone with a close relationship with God can help most, for he will give godly counsel according to the Holy Spirit's leading. We can also be that 'somebody' to help others most when we turn them to God first.

The Bible gives us assurance that God is always a present help to us, to deliver and save because we trust in Him [Psalm 37:40]. "Fear thou not; for I am with thee: be not dismayed; for I am thy God: I will strengthen thee; yea, I will help thee; yea, I will uphold thee with the right hand of my righteousness" [Isaiah 41:10]. The Lord wants us to "come boldly unto the throne of grace, that we may obtain mercy, and find grace to help in time of need" [Hebrews 4:16]. Call out to God for help now—He can fix anything!

Prayer:
Lord, when we need help we will call upon You because we trust in You, and because we know You are our help and our shield [Psalm 115:11].

Scripture of the Day:
"God is our refuge and strength, a very present help in trouble." - [Psalm 46:1]

The Word for the Day is "Seed."

Quote for the Day:
"The seed always has to lead." – Unknown.

Seeds always have to be planted before a harvest can come. Farmers know this. No crop of corn or beans comes up without a seed first being planted. This principle applies to all things if we would realize it—to all life conditions emotionally, financially, socially, and spiritually. "There is that scattereth, and yet increaseth; and there is that withholdeth more than is meet, but it tendeth to poverty" [Proverbs 11:24].

I was talking to one of my elderly aunts recently and she said, "Oh, I'm so glad you called me. No one ever calls me and I get so lonely." I laughed and said, "The phone works both ways. You can call me, too, if you're lonely. You can call others in our family, also. They tell me the same thing. I know they'd love a call from you." Isn't that something? Everyone is waiting for someone else to make the first move. But Biblically you should make the first move. You should reach out; that's how the blessing and the return comes. If you wish for friendship, fellowship, sharing—you call, you ask someone to lunch, you invite someone over to dinner. Why are we always waiting for someone else to initiate and then sitting home feeling sorry for ourselves and unloved when they don't? So many people tell me they're unhappy and depressed. Research has shown if you reach out to others depression will lift and you'll reap back a joyful spirit.

What do you want to harvest? Friendship, happiness, or caring? Go plant some and it will come back to you. Finances? Go plant into someone's life. Give some of your money or excess possessions and abundant blessings will come back to you. You have to seed to receive. "He which soweth sparingly shall reap also sparingly; and he which soweth bountifully shall reap also bountifully" [2 Corinthians 9:6].

Think today. What do you yearn for in your life? Seed it to reap it. God set up the principles of seedtime and harvest, but too often people want the harvest without doing any seeding. To reap you have to sow first.

Prayer:
Lord, may we diligently and generously sow good seed in all areas of our life so we will reap the harvest of blessing back.

Scripture of the Day:
"Whatsoever [seed] a man soweth, that shall he also reap." - [Galatians 6:7]

The Word for the Day is "Authority"

Quote for the Day:
"I have never changed my message. I preach the Bible, and I preach it with author-ity." - Billy Graham

We know that authority is the power or right to direct or control someone or something. Authority rightly applied is good [Proverbs 29:2], and we are com-manded to pray for those in authority to exercise power aright that we may lead a quiet and peaceable life [1 Timothy 2:1-2].

But authority can be harmful chiefly in two ways: misuse and nonuse. When the power of authority is misapplied arbitrarily to oppress, control, or deny rights, the result is tyranny and loss of freedom. Dictators and despots have shown the tragic results of this abuse throughout history.

Jesus gave us another example of misuse of authority when the focus is on the office of authority and not on the benevolence to others. Jesus taught that he who would be great must be your minister, and he that would be chief must become your servant [Matt 20:26-27]. Jesus had all authority, yet he 'came not to be min-istered unto, but to minister, and to give his life a ransom for many' [Matt 20:28].

Authority is also misused when not applied as it should. I recall the frustration of a friend who petitioned the authorities to stop another person from dump-ing garbage on his property. But the authorities took no action at all to stop this obvious violation of law. God has given us power and authority in the Word as believers in Jesus Christ [Luke 10:19], and He must be displeased when we do not exercise our rightful authority. We complain, whine, and petition God to do something for us, when He has already given us the authority to act, decree, and declare according to his Word. We should exercise God-given authority to meet the needs of our own and others, and not allow the enemy to prevail by our non-use of godly authority.

Prayer:
Lord, we purpose to learn of our righteous authority in Christ Jesus to better minister to others and to triumph over the devil.

Scripture of the Day:
"For the Son of Man is as a man taking a far journey, who left his house, and gave authority to his servants, and to every man his work, and commanded the porter to watch." - [Mark 13:34]

The Word for the Day is "Anger."

Quote for the Day:
"A moment of patience in a moment of anger saves you a hundred moments of regret." – Unknown

Jesus displayed a righteous anger when he chased the money changers out of the temple and when he rebuked the religious leaders for their hypocrisy. Yet in most every other aspect of his life, even when he had cause to be angry with the sin, unbelief, criticism, and betrayal around him, he walked in love and was patient and kind.

What causes us to be angry? Studies have found people react in anger mostly over small matters rather than the large important issues we might expect. The root behind anger is often selfishness and a lack of self-control. It can also be fear and disappointment over life's losses, illnesses, unfairness, hurts, and sorrows. People lash back in anger over situations in life instead of walking in love. But God expects to see the fruits of the Spirit always evident in our lives—"love, joy, peace, longsuffering, gentleness, goodness, faith, meekness, temperance" [Galatians 5:22-23].

Anger is a "reaction." Temperance is an "action." Anger lashes out without thought. Temperance thinks a situation through, prays a situation through, before responding. As we walk through life, and run the race of life, God wants us to run that race 'keeping our body, our flesh, our reactive side under subjection' [1 Corinthians 9:27]. The Word teaches that "every man that striveth for the mastery is temperate in all things" [1 Corinthians 9:25]. Temperate means showing moderation or self-restraint, not extreme in opinion or action, and disciplined.

Neurologists claim that every time you resist acting on your anger, you're actually rewiring your brain to be calmer and more loving. We need to work to cease from anger and to forsake wrath in our day to day walk, to 'walk after the spirit and not after the flesh' [2 Corinthians 10:3-5].

Prayer:
Lord, help us to learn to curb reactive anger in our words and deeds and to develop a temperate, disciplined life dominated by love and the Spirit of God.

Scripture of the Day:
"Wherefore, my beloved brethren, let every man be swift to hear, slow to speak, slow to wrath [and anger]: for the wrath of man worketh not the righteousness of God." - [James 1:19-20]

The Word for the Day is "Child"

Quote for the Day:
"The first happiness of a child is to know that he is loved." - Don Bosco

Lin and I attended a crafts festival as vendors in Kingsport, Tennessee, last November, and one of the crafters there had a most unique skill. She created infant and baby dolls that looked lifelike! Her dolls both looked and felt like real babies! She had propped up one doll in a small chair with a blanket around it, and I observed people passing by tiptoeing so as not to disturb the baby. They thought it was a real sleeping child. Almost everyone wanted to pick up and snuggle the dolls, they seemed so lifelike!

Jesus said we have to receive the kingdom of God as a little child. Not as a child in understanding, but with the pure heart of a child. We know children can be influenced by a malefic environment and by vile adults that can corrupt and pervert their pure nature. But let us consider the pure nature of children undefiled by environment. Children are innocent with no malice in their heart. Human nature understands this and we just want to embrace and cuddle them because we perceive we are holding a pure being, an innocent being that has no ill will at all. Little children are loving, accepting love and giving love so freely without selfishness.

Children are trusting and believing. They trust you have only good intentions toward them and they believe in your goodness. That's why we try so hard to never hurt or disappoint them in any way. And children love life! Their excitement about newness every day is contagious and makes us appreciate life better.

God wants our hearts to remain child-like toward Him: loving, trusting, believing, expecting, and being glad and joyful for every day. He wants us growing in wisdom and the knowledge of God, but keeping the heart of a child, "for of such is the kingdom of heaven" [Matthew 19:14].

Prayer:
Lord, help us to grow into the fullness of Christ Jesus our Lord while keeping the pure heart of a child.

Scripture of the Day:
"Verily I say unto you, Whosoever shall not receive the kingdom of God as a little child, he shall not enter therein." - [Mark 10:15]

The Word for the Day is "Blessed."

Quote for the Day:
"Being blessed is more important than being lucky." – Unknown

When I was a girl, my friends and I often searched for lucky four-leaf clovers. In mid March around St. Patrick's Day, they seemed easier to find. If we found one, we showed it off to our friends and often pressed it in a book to keep. I don't think we ever really believed finding the clover would bring us luck, but it was fun to believe in the idea. One of my uncles kept a horseshoe over his barn door for luck and I remember getting a lucky rabbit's key chain for a birthday gift one year. People do all sorts of things to attract luck—blow on dice before throwing them, wish upon a star, carry a lucky penny.

Luck is something that happens to a person by chance, bringing good fortune, prosperity, or success. As I grew older I soon learned that most of the luck people find in life comes from hard work and not chance. Yet many people today still buy lottery tickets hoping to win a jackpot of money or enter contests for homes, cars, vacations, or other luxuries generally out of their reach financially. Instances of luck do sometimes occur in life, but it is somewhat foolish to count on them as the route to happiness and well-being.

At one point in my early life as a Christian, I believed that receiving anything from God was like luck, too. Sometimes He was in the mood, sometimes He wasn't. Sometimes He might look down and decide to zap me with favor, sometimes He might not. Gradually I learned that being in the Lord, living close to Him and following in His ways brought me into the best and luckiest situation of all—full-time, all-the-time blessing and favor. It was a revelation to learn that those who 'trust and hope in the Lord would be blessed' [Jeremiah 17:7-8]. God set up a system for His people that if they walked in His ways and trusted in Him that 'He would set them on high and that an abundance of blessings would come on them and overtake them' [Deuteronomy 28:1-2]. The continuing verses in Deuteronomy 28 detail the blessings God gives—blessings in the city, in the field, in all works, in health, in favor, in goods, in peace and comfort, and in protection from the enemy. These are wonderful promises and much better than sheer luck.

Prayer:
Lord, we stop to thank You today for our many blessings. They are indeed far better than mere luck.

Scripture of the Day:
"Blessed is that man that maketh the Lord his trust." - [Psalm 40:4]

The Word for the Day is "Visit"

Quote for the Day:
"As a Christian, you forgive, and you feed the hungry and clothe the naked, and you visit the sick and comfort the lonely. If I'm a true follower of my Lord and Saviour Jesus Christ, [I've] got to do the things you're supposed to be doing."
- Lawrence Tureaud (Mr. T)

When we visit others, it is our decision as to whom we visit. But the Word of God gives us some direction even in this decision. The apostle Paul visited every city where he had preached to see how the brethren were doing [Acts 15:36]. So it would seem appropriate to visit others, and especially brethren in the Lord, to inquire of their general welfare. Concern for their well being is appreciated.

Of course it is more obvious to visit those with more urgent afflictions. The Word tells us we should visit the fatherless, widows, and the afflicted [James 1:27]. And we are to visit the sick and hurting [Matthew 25:36]. In all our visits, we are to go as the ambassadors for Christ [2 Corinthians 5:20]. We are to be the salt and light of the earth and ready vessels to be used by Christ to minister His grace and power to any afflicted or in need. Then, any grace bestowed by Him, through us, may cause the people to say 'that God hath visited his people' [Luke 7:16].

As the visited, we welcome those who come in love, peace, goodwill, and benevolence. Those that visit us with other motives are not so welcome. Our adversary the devil likes to visit, too, seeking whom he may devour [1 Peter 5:8]. Our best defense against unwanted or harmful visitors is to stay in a right relationship with God: "The fear of the Lord tendeth to life: and he that hath it shall abide satisfied; he shall not be visited with evil" [Proverbs 19:23]. Our protection is dwelling in the secret place of the most High and abiding under the shadow of the Almighty. We then walk in God's protection from evil and He gives His angels charge to protect us [Psalm 91:1-11]. If we visit God through prayer, praise, and studying His Word, and invite Him to constantly visit us by His Spirit, then all our visitations will be blessed.

Prayer:
Lord, we purpose whether as visitors, or as the visited, to always be ambassadors for Christ that His grace, power, and Light may touch others.

Scripture of the Day:
"Pure religion and undefiled before God and the Father is this, To visit the fatherless, and widows in their affliction, and to keep himself unspotted from the world." - [James 1:27]

The Word for the Day is "Ashes."

Quote for the Day:
"Life always comes out of death. The present rises from the ashes of the past. The future is always possible for those who are willing to re-create it."
– Joan D. Chittister

Often when we see a sealed urn today we wonder if it holds ashes. It is a new burial method now. A friend recently scattered the ashes of a loved one, by request, in a beautiful spot in the mountains. Some people scatter ashes in favorite places outdoors, old home sites or cemeteries, while others keep an urn containing ashes in their home.

Sometimes we have ashes in our lives of what might have been, should have been. We hold on to the memories and often to the bitterness of unfair things that have happened to us, broken dreams, disappointments, failures, hurts. But God says He wants to give us 'beauty for ashes, joy for our mourning' [Isaiah 61:1-3]. In Psalm 30:11 the Word promises 'He'll turn our mourning into dancing, put off our sadness and sackcloth, and gird us with gladness'—if we will let Him. That's the key: if we will let Him. We have to let go of the ashes before God can give us the beauty. We can't hold on to those ashes and disappointments. If you keep dwelling on the ashes of the past you will block God's blessings in your life today. You can't keep carrying that hurt and pain year after year. There's 'a season for mourning and then a time to move on' [Ecclesiastes 3:4]. Walking into newness and restoration depends on your willingness to let go of the past.

This spring dig around in the closets of your life to look for any urns of ashes you've kept. Shake yourself out of "should-have-been, might-have-been, could-have-been" thinking and regrets. Take those ashes out somewhere in nature— perhaps symbolically—and let them go. Don't let your ashes become your identity. God 'wants to make all things new' [Revelation 21:5]. Let Him turn your disappointments into reappointments and move you into the new things He wants to do in your life.

Prayer:
Lord, help me move past any sorrows, hurts, and disappointments I've been holding on to for too long, and help me to release the ashes of my life so You can bring in restoration and newness.

Scripture of the Day:
"The Lord hath anointed [Jesus] to preach good tidings unto the meek…to bind up the brokenhearted…to comfort all that mourn…to give unto them beauty for ashes, the oil of joy for mourning," - [Isaiah 61:1-3]

The Word for the Day is "Affected"

Quote for the Day:
"The least movement is of importance to all nature. The entire ocean is affected by a pebble." - Blaise Pascal

To be affected generally means to be influenced, impacted, or touched by an external factor or force. In today's high-tech, informational society, there are many things that can influence and affect our thinking. Anyone can now voice an opinion and make it available to the masses with no requirement that it be truthful, factual, or even sensible. Galatians 4:18 tells us that "it is good to be zealously affected always with a good thing." God wants us to only be influenced and impacted by good things, and He wants this at all times.

So what are some of the good things God wants to always impact and influence our lives with? Jesus said "And ye shall know the truth, and the truth shall make you free" [John 8:32]. Many will ask, though, as did Pilot: 'What is truth?' [John 18:38]. Jesus speaking to his disciples answered this: "thy word is truth" [John 17:17]. So the truth of the Word of God should be the first priority in affecting our thinking and our believing. We increase our faith by increasing our knowledge of the Word: "So then faith cometh by hearing, and hearing by the Word of God" [Romans 10:17]. God's Truth must be our anchor and foundation against all the voices, deceits, clamor, and unbelief of the world.

Believers should be zealously affected by the Holy Spirit. God gives the Holy Spirit as the Comforter: who is with us and in us to comfort, aid, and help us through all trials and troubles [John 14:16]. The Comforter is the Spirit of Truth [John 14:17] and He will guide us into all truth [John 16:13]. What a great advantage to truth when we have someone who will teach us all things, and bring all things to our rememberance [John 14:26]. The Holy Spirit will also show us things to come as we seek God's guidance, wisdom, and direction for our lives [John 16:13]. God's Word and his Spirit will guide us with His absolutes of truth as we shine out in this world of confusion.

Prayer:
Lord, help us to cast off the influences of this world, and to be affected only by the Truth of God.

Scripture of the Day:
"But it is good to be zealously affected always in a good thing, and not only when I am present with you." - [Galatians 4:18]

The Word for the Day is "Friend."

Quote for the Day:
"A friend is what your heart needs all the time." – Henry Van Dyke

I'm grateful for so many special friends in my life. Perhaps you are, too. One of the first hymns I learned to play on the piano was "What A Friend We Have in Jesus," a favorite hymn both then and now. It is a blessing to have friends.

When growing up, I always loved the Bible story of Jonathan and David's friendship and how Jonathan dared to help David when his own father was trying to kill him. We often speak of close friends as soulmates, as the Word did of Jonathan and David's friendship—"the soul of Jonathan was knit to the soul of David, and Jonathan loved him as his own soul" [1 Samuel 18:1]. Friends can help us, love us, and enrich our lives or they can turn on us as Jonathan's father Saul did to David [1 Samuel 18:8-12]. Friends can try to cheat us as Jacob did his brother Esau [Genesis 27:1-35] or even plot to kill us as Judas did Jesus [Matthew 26:47-49]. Those times hurt, as Psalm 41:9 says: "Yea, mine own familiar friend, in whom I trusted, which did eat of my bread, hath lifted up his heel against me." We expect enmity from the world to come our way at times but it's always harder when it comes from someone we love.

Gratefully, our friendship with the Lord is always something we can rely on. We know we'll always 'have a friend in Jesus', the loyalty of the love of God in our lives. And when we live close to God, He is able to be an even closer friend to us. I always loved that not only did Abraham see God as his friend but God called Abraham His friend [James 2:23].

Just as we like a loyal friend, God does too. He wants no other gods before Him [Exodus 20:3] and He wants us to strive to live a righteous life, to grow in Him and be close to Him [Deuteronomy 6:25; Isaiah 33:15-17]. Then we can know and cherish that 'friend who sticketh closer than a brother' [Proverbs 18:24], who 'loveth at all times' [Proverbs 17:17] both here and forevermore.

Prayer:
Lord, thank You for being not only our God but our friend; we are blessed that we can know and hear your voice, and have close fellowship with You.

Scripture of the Day:
"Ye are my friends if ye do whatsoever I command you. Henceforth I call you not servants; for the servant knoweth not what his lord doeth: but I have called you friends; for all things that I have heard of my Father I have made known unto you." -[John 15:14-15]

The Word for the Day is "Sky."

Quote for the Day:
"Red sky at night, sailor's delight. Red sky in the morning, sailor's take warning." -
Ancient Proverb

A few years ago, I began taking pictures of beautiful sunsets from my deck at evening. I saved these colorful photos just for my own collection and enjoyment. I noticed over the years that late winter and pre-spring provided some of the most gorgeous scenes of all, perhaps because of the low humidity and clear air at that time. The quote of the day above has been proven to generally be true because of the way weather fronts move west to east in our latitude. Anyway, it is always nice to enjoy a red sunset and think of nice weather the next day.

Some Pharisees and Sadducees came temping Jesus to show them a sign from heaven [Matthew 16:1]. They had seen and heard of all the miracles and works Jesus had done, and they had heard of His teachings about heaven. But they were carnal and could not receive spiritual truth; they wanted a physical sign of some kind. Jesus, as in the saying above, declared to them that they could discern the face of the sky: 'red sky at night, fair weather; red sky in the morning, foul weather.' But they could not discern spiritually: "Ye hypocrites, ye can discern the face of the sky and of the earth; but how is it that ye do not discern this time?" [Luke 12:56].

God wants us to be aware of our natural and physical surroundings, but He wants us to be spiritually discerning above all. The natural and carnal observations can sometimes be true, but sometimes wrong and deceitful. God wants us to have the truth of His Word and His Spirit in our hearts to lead and guide us. His truth, promises, wisdom, and knowledge will always prevail over the natural. So enjoy that beautiful sunset with your eyes, but always let God's Spirit direct your days.

Prayer:
Lord, help us to be wise and discerning of the natural signs, but more so of the things that are of the Spirit, that we might walk in truth, wisdom, discernment, and direction by your Holy Spirit.

Scripture of the Day:
"O ye hypocrites, ye can discern the face of the sky; but can ye not discern the signs of the times?" - [Matthew 16:2-3]

The Word for the Day is "Fire."

Quote for the Day:
"In everyone's life, at some time, our inner fire goes out. It is then burst into flame by an encounter with another human being. We should all be thankful for those people who rekindle the inner spirit." - Albert Schweitzer

Life sometimes holds difficult seasons and difficult times. Inwardly, in those times it feels like our inner fire grows dim. Our hope and faith, and even our bedrock beliefs, are challenged and attacked by the circumstances of life. In those times we struggle to hold fast to our beliefs, to the promises of God we know are true. In those times, too, right words and encouragement from another can turn the tide. How sweet and uplifting those words can be. Proverbs 25:11 reminds us beautifully: "A word fitly spoken is like apples of gold in pictures of silver." Right words spoken in the right timing can help us; they can lift us up. They speak to our inner spirit and rekindle the fire growing dim. We each can speak to and encourage ourselves and God wants us to. Ahead of battles, "the men of Israel encouraged themselves" (Judges 20:22), and we often read of David 'encouraging himself in the Lord' when he was 'greatly distressed' or in a grievous or difficult situation (1 Samuel 30:6).

But God also meant for us to encourage and exhort one another. We are advised to: 'Harden not our hearts…to exhort one another daily," (Hebrews 3:8, 13), and we are told to "Comfort…and edify one another" (1 Thessalonians 5:11). We all need encouragement, like flowers need sunshine and rain, and we all need love and comfort. And we need it in person. All scientific research has found how touch is needed to people of all ages, how important a pat on the back or an embrace can be in a time of trial, how ministering prayer can be when we hold another's hands or lay our hands on them in prayer. Timothy admonished that 'we stir up the gift of God in others by the laying on of hands' (2 Timothy 1:6), but we too often hold ourselves distant from others. We are meant to reach out to share that love with others. We need to reach out with encouraging words, with prayers and loving gestures to encourage and comfort others' hearts. It may well be your stronger fire that rekindles the waning fire in another's life, rekindling their hope, their faith, and their inner spirit.

Prayer:
Lord, stir up the fire in us and make us sensitive to reach out to encourage others in their time of need, to be Your servants in a world hungry for a touch of Your presence.

Scripture of the Day:
'Who maketh his angels spirits, and his ministers a flame of fire.'– [Hebrews 1:7]

The Word for the Day is "Delight."

Quote for the Day:
"From heav'nly thoughts all true delight doth spring." - Thomas Campion

There are many things in this world we can delight in, things to take pleasure in. Like the beauty of the earth and nature. Man can delight in things of beauty, accomplishment, recreation, friendships, love, and pleasures innumerable. God has given us 'richly all things to enjoy' [1 Timothy 6:17], but as children of God, He wants us above all to delight and take pleasure in Him and He will give us the desires of our heart [Psalm 37:4].

How do we delight ourselves in the Lord? Just as we can hear from others about delightful things, if we never see or experience those things ourselves, we cannot truly delight in them. We must know and experience God to delight in Him. "Thy word is a lamp unto my feet, and a light unto my path" [Psalm 119:105]. Knowing God through His Word is a sure way to come to delight in the Lord. For in the Word we learn the knowledge of God, that God is love [1 John 4:7-10]. The Lord gives us wisdom to direct our ways: "For the Lord giveth wisdom: out of his mouth cometh knowledge and understanding" [Prov 2:6]. We learn of His promises: "Whereby are given unto us exceeding great and precious promises: that by these ye might be partakers of the divine nature" [2 Peter 1:4]. Through His Word we learn who we are in Jesus and the authority we have in His name [Luke 10:19].

The Word of God also instructs us to delight in His commandments, His testimonies, and His law, and to do His will [Ps 119:47,24,70; 40:8]. Just meditating and thinking on God's Word brings delight to our soul: "In the multitude of my thoughts within me thy comforts delight my soul" [Psalm 94:19]. When we know God's love and goodness, His power and promises to us, His awesome benefits He gives us, and His wisdom and guidance by His Holy Spirit, it is impossible not to take pleasure in the Lord!

Prayer:
Lord, let our chief desire be to delight, and to take pleasure in You and Your ways, so that we may receive the righteous desires of our heart.

Scripture of the Day:
"Trust in the Lord, and do good; so shalt thou dwell in the land, and verily thou shalt be fed. Delight thyself also in the Lord; and he shall give thee the desires of thine heart." - [Psalm 37:3-4]

The Word for the Day is "Truth."

Quote for the Day:
"Truth is powerful and it prevails." – Sojourner Truth

What is truth?…It is one of the central subjects in philosophy and has been a topic of debate for thousands of years. People have sought throughout time to know what real truths are and what (if anything) makes them true. In our daily lives we are also interested in truth. We need to constantly determine the accuracy or veracity of most everything we hear, read, or even think every day. It can be a little overwhelming to know what is right and authentic or what is false in our present world.

As you might imagine extensive research has been done to determine how people define truth or "ways of knowing." Studies found fifty percent of people are basically Authoritative Knowers who believe "someone else" always has the truth they need, some external authority. Generally, if faced with any life problem they will act and advise…*Go see your doctor…Check the Internet …Ask your mother… Talk to your minister.* They don't perceive reliable truth can come from "within"— or from "that which *is* within." I hope you're beginning to see where this can be a problem for Christians. God lives within us. Jesus and the Holy Spirit live within us. We should look first to God within. He wants us to seek Him first. But most of us lean to something in the world first before seeking Him. We're taught that way; perhaps we're even wired that way. Without thinking, we tend to seek everywhere else for truth—to authorities, opinions of others, TV, social media—when we need help or answers and then finally to God when nothing else works out. Yet God said "Thou shalt have no other gods before me" (Exodus 20:3), no other authorities before Me. Jesus said…*"I am the way, the truth, and the life"* (John 14:6). As Christians we already hold the truth—but we don't always draw from it. We don't always seek it.

We need to purpose to see more clearly that we hold the truth within we each need daily, because God is within. We need to seek more for His truth through prayer and in the Word of God. If we truly reach to God first and put Him first, His truth will guide us to all the answers we need. And set us free from leaning to the world.

Prayer:
Lord, help us to reach to You first for the answers we need day to day. Wean us from seeking first to others and teach us to always come first to You.

Scripture of the Day:
"And ye shall know the truth, and the truth shall make you free." - (John 8:32)

The Word for the Day is "Harden."

Quote for the Day:
"If you see most people neglect the Bible, and many that can read never look into it, let it not harden you and make you think lightly of it, and that it is a book of no worth." - Jupiter Hammon

Any farmer knows that if he throws seed on top of hard ground, he isn't going to grow a crop. The birds and squirrels may think they've won the lottery, but the farmer will reap nothing. He knows he has to break up the fallow, hard ground for the seed to go down into the soil to receive the nourishment it needs to grow. The Word tells us that God is the potter in our lives, and we are the clay [Isaiah 64:8]. God wants our hearts to be malleable, not hardened, so He can fashion, mold, and shape us to be vessels suited for His purposes.

What is a hardened heart? It is a heart that hinders or stops the Spirit from penetrating. It is like putting up a shield or wall around our heart to block out God. A hardened heart hears the voice of the world, but not God's [Hebrews 4:7].

What are the causes of a hardened heart? The Word gives us several answers. First, when we get angry and resentful at God for present circumstances or begin to doubt His provision and guidance, our hearts can become hardened, like the hearts of the children of Israel in the wilderness [Heb 3:8-12; Mark 6:52]. Doubt and unbelief is always opposite of faith, and, if entertained, will begin to harden the heart [Heb 11:6]. The deceitfulness of sin can harden the heart, too. Sin, whether small or big, always separates us from God [Heb 3:13]. Pride can also harden the heart and mind when we elevate self and lean to our own knowledge, strength, and understanding, celebrating ourselves above God [Daniel 5:20].

God gives us counsel to avoid hardness of heart: "For we are made partakers of Christ, if we hold the beginning of our confidence steadfast to the end" [Hebrews 3:14]. Notice "we" are to hold the beginning of our confidence, God doesn't do it for us. It's an act of our will and decision to stand "steadfast to the end," no matter what happens. Keep your confidence that God is good, He is faithful, and all things are possible with God—keep your heart malleable, not hardened!

Prayer:
Lord, we determine to resist the forces that harden us, and to keep a heart that can hear Your voice and follow the Holy Spirit's leading.

Scripture of the Day:
"Today if ye will hear his voice, harden not your hearts." - [Hebrews 4:7]

The Word for the Day is "Foolishly."

Quote for the Day:
"It is always sinful to foolishly charge God for anything, at any time, for any reason. Our Creator is a good God and everything that He does is right." – David J. Stewart

As I write this devotional, the world is experiencing a pandemic, or a global outbreak of the corona virus, infecting and sickening many around the world. When serious trouble happens in our lives and world, there is a tendency to look for someone to blame. Blame is a quick defense mechanism and an unconscious protective measure all people tend to use when facing trauma or disaster. When things happen that we don't understand, we want someone or something to blame for it. Even in day-to-day matters we tend to fall victim to blaming someone or something without ever stopping to examine our own lives. Yet, in many small personal matters, whether we want to acknowledge it or not, we are often to blame for the trouble that comes our way. We're repeatedly late for work and get fired. We don't study for a test or exam and fail. The culprit behind our daily problems in many areas is ourself, a fact we don't want to well examine. But in a world crisis, the answers are less simple.

A lot of people are falsely blaming God right now for the problems going on in our world—an unrighteous response. But God is always good, righteous, faithful, loving, loyal and the author of all Good Things [James 1:17; Nahum 1:7]. I believe of a certainty, above anything others might say, in the integrity of God—and that God wants above all things for us to prosper and be in health [3 John 2]. If there is an author of bad to name for the ills and sorrows of the world I'd like to clearly state that it is Not God. The author of Bad Things is actually well known, or should be, although few churches seem to mention his name today. But the devil is still very much alive and well on planet earth and he is Not a friend to humankind. The devil comes whenever he can get access to steal, kill, and destroy and he is the enemy of God and of our soul [John 10:10; 1 Peter 5:8; Ephesians 6:12]. We need to rightfully discern who brings sorrow to the world and to not cast blame wrongly to God when we encounter problems in life we don't understand. Whatever comes, be counted as one who stands up for the excellent character, goodness, and love of God.

Prayer:
Lord, let us look wisely within and without when things go wrong in our lives, not erroneously and foolishly attaching blame where it doesn't belong.

Scripture of the Day:
"In all this Job sinned not, nor charged God foolishly." – [Job 1:22]

The Word for the Day is "Commit."

Quote for the Day:
"The more we resign and commit ourselves to God, and the more we renounce our-selves, of the greater value are we." - Montaigne

The Word tells us that we are to commit our spirit into God's hand, for He is the Lord God of truth. Our first priority should be to settle this eternal issue. We commit our spirit, which is eternal, into God's hand by accepting the salvation of Jesus Christ. We know of a certainty that we are redeemed through Jesus because we have God's eternal Word on it, and He is the God of truth for it is impossible for Him to lie [Hebrews 6:18].

Having our eternal spiritual destiny settled through trust in Jesus Christ, God then wants us to commit our ways, our life's direction, to Him. "Commit thy way unto the Lord; trust also in Him; and he shall bring it to pass"[Psalm 37:5]. We trust in the Lord's goodness, faithfulness, and eternal promises that He will always bring all His blessings and promises to pass.

We also commit our works unto the Lord: "Commit thy works unto the Lord, and thy thoughts shall be established" [Proverbs 16:3]. Have you ever known some-one distressed or anxious about decisions concerning their work, relationships, or any other life choices before them? They search for answers from people; they search the internet and find a thousand different opinions, only to end up more confused and stressed than they were before. But God promises that if we com-mit our works unto Him, He will establish our thoughts. He will guide us where to look and get the answers we need for our directions and decisions. And when we let His Spirit direct our mind and thoughts, He will lead us into the right way with peace, instead of confusion [Philippians 4:7]. Commit all unto the Lord, and let Him restore your soul and lead you into paths of righteousness for His name's sake [Psalm 23:3].

Prayer:
Lord, let us commit our spirit into Your hands to establish our eternity, and let us commit our ways and works unto You that our thoughts and directions in this life might be established in righteous paths by Your Spirit.

Scripture of the Day:
"Into thine hand I commit my spirit: thou hast redeemed me, O Lord God of truth." - [Psalm 31:5]

The Word for the Day is "Blossom."

Quote for the Day:
"Nothing great is created suddenly … let it first blossom, then bear fruit, then ripen."
–Epictetus

With the spring we look forward to wildflowers blooming in the Smokies. J.L. and I love to hike the trails looking for them popping out of the dead growth and dried brown leaves of winter. Each wildflower has its own special beauty, its own history and purpose. Each flower is unique, too, and by the hand of God, blooms each year where planted. A thought for us to consider also is to "bloom where we are planted"[Mary Engelbreit].

We need to lean to God and ask, "How can I bloom more this spring with beauty and surprise?" I use the word "surprise" because there is always more hidden in each of us in the Lord, because He is within us. We may be ordinary but He is not, and through Him, we can blossom out to do extraordinary things we could not do on our own. God surely shows us in the spring how he loves variety and individuality...from early pink Spring Beauty and white Bloodroot, to sweet purple Violets and yellow Buttercups spreading over the fields and trailside. Each wildflower is so unique and handsome, just as you are.

God never disappoints, either. The flowers always bloom. Yes, sometimes there is a freeze or frost, a drought, or the trampling of feet...but undeterred, each plant resurrects and flowers again with new beauty. We can, too, even after hardship and difficulties. Jeremiah 31:25 says: "I have satisfied the weary soul, and I have replenished every sorrowful soul." Don't give up even when you have passed through a harsh winter season. God will help you bloom out again.

I encourage you to believe to blossom out in new ways this spring, to bloom where you are planted in fresh ways, to let your seed, your special gifts, fly on the wind into new places and new endeavors. And each time you see a wildflower, or even a garden flower, blooming this spring...say a small prayer asking God to draw the best from within you to bloom out—just as the flowers rise from out of the ground to delight all who see them.

Prayer:
Lord, let me blossom forth this spring with new life, new purpose, and new beauty so others will see the glory of God in my life.

Scripture of the Day:
'The wilderness and the solitary place shall be glad...the desert shall rejoice, and blossom as the rose...even with joy and singing.' - [Isaiah 35:1-2]

The Word for the Day is "Savour."

Quote for the Day:
"A wise man ought always to follow the path beaten by great men, and to imitate those who have been supreme, so that if his ability does not equal theirs, at least it will savour of it." - Machiavelli

Everyone delights in the pleasing smell, or savour, of good things. I savour fresh-brewed coffee, just-baked pecan pie, fresh cinammon rolls and many other delicious treats. There is a spiritual savour to delight in as well as a natural. The Word tells us that we are the salt, or seasoning, of the earth. We are to delight the earth with the savour of Christ that is in us as believers. The Bible tells us that Jesus gave himself for us as "an offering and a sacrifice to God for a sweetsmelling savour" [Eph 5:2]. God wanted us in Jesus to be a delightful savour to the world.

The Word of God tells us how to be the salt, or savour, of the earth. First, we are to walk in love as Christ loved us. We are to 'triumph in Christ, and make manifest the savour of His knowledge by us in every place' [2 Cor 2:14]. Nothing is more delightful and sweet to a believer than someone sharing the knowledge of Jesus to reveal the truth of the victory He always brings. Likewise, nothing can be better to an unbeliever than to hear the revelation of salvation that is offered by Christ Jesus, sharing the good news that there is a promise of life, and that more abundantly [John 10:10].

The Word also warns us of losing our saltiness, or sweet savour, so we then become 'good for nothing'[Matthew 5:13]. We lose our savour if we lose our love and kindness, if we practice sin [Ephesians 5:1-5]. Many corrupt (compromise) the word of God [2 Corinthians 2:17], and men can deceive with vain words, perverting the gospel of truth [Ephesians 5:6]. If we follow Machiavelli's advice in the quote for the day and follow the path of Jesus and imitate Him, we will be a sweet savour of hope in this world of God's truth, righteousness, and deliverance.

Prayer:
Lord, help us to be the salt of the earth and a sweet savour by manifesting the knowledge of Jesus to the world by walking in His love, His Word, and His Spirit.

Scripture of the Day:
"And walk in love, as Christ also hath loved us, and hath given himself for us an offering and a sacrifice to God for a sweetsmelling savour." - [Ephesians 5:2]

April

The Word for the Day is "Shower."

Quote for the Day:
"God made us for one reason: so He could have fellowship with us. It wasn't that He was lonely or needed us but He made us so He could shower His love upon us."
-Billy Graham

All of us, at one time or another in our lives, have been caught out in a shower. Generally when this happens we hustle to get in out of the rain. Yet it is often joyous to watch a shower out the window, especially a needed one. It seems as though the branches of the trees seem to reach up to welcome the rain and one can almost hear the grass sigh as it is soaked deeply with the rich, needed rain.

Showers of blessing fall in our lives, in big and small ways, not just occasionally but every day. Sometimes we are mindfully grateful of them and stop to thank God and give Him praise. Other times we run on along our way, almost seeming to take God's rich blessings for granted. When Jesus healed the ten lepers, only one returned to thank Him [Luke 17:11-18]. Although we get busy and often forget, we know we should thank God daily for His blessings. He is so good to us. The Word reminds us that 'a faithful man abounds with blessings' [Proverbs 28:20]. Every day we should always be grateful to God for His love and goodness.

I love the concept in the Bible that 'God will cause the showers to come down in season on us and that there will be showers of blessing' [Ezekiel 34:26]. As the rain showers come to bless the earth, God's showers of blessing and love come to enrich and bless us. "O give thanks unto the Lord, for he is good; for his mercy endureth forever" [1 Chronicles 16:34].

Prayer:
With thankful hearts we offer gratitude today for the showers of blessings that come to us from God our Father.

Scripture of the Day:
"I will cause the shower to come down in his season; there shall be showers of blessing." - [Ezekiel 34:26]

The Word for the day is "Fishers"

Quote for the Day:
"Some go to church and think about fishing, others go fishing and think about God."
- Tony Blake

As springtime arrives, we all look forward to outdoor activities we enjoy. One activity I especially enjoy, when time allows, is fishing, and particularly trout fishing in the streams around Tellico Plains. My mom lived there, and she always appreciated me sharing my catch with her so she could prepare her delicious lemon-seasoned trout recipe.

I learned over the years a few basic techniques for successful trout fishing. The most basic was to use bait that was natural or artificial lures that closely resembled the natural food in the stream. Trout can instinctively discern that which is natural to their stream and that which is alien, and they will not bite anything that isn't natural to the stream. Trout will also reject anything that isn't naturally presented, so I learned to work my baits in a natural manner with the stream flow.

Jesus' disciples were fishermen, and He told them to follow Him, and He would make them fishers of men, a concept they could understand. And we know from the scriptures the impact the disciples had on the world. They "caught" many men with the gospel truth and "reeled" them into the Kingdom of God.

Likewise, Jesus wants us to be fishers of men. The first requirement is to be a follower of Jesus: to know Him, to be like Him, to know His truth and His gospel. His Truth is analagous to the bait we use in fishing for fish. "And I, if I be lifted up from the earth, will draw all men unto me" [John 12:32]. Jesus is the One we are trying to catch men to, but the lure must be true to Him. When fishing for men, it is the Spirit of Truth that draws them. We must present Jesus in Truth, as He truly is according to His eternal Word. Any other gospel is false, much like unnatural fish lures in the stream; the fish sense this is not real—'I'm not biting!' Let's be fishers of men with the real Jesus and the true Word of God.

Prayer:
Lord, help us to be true followers of You in truth and spirit, that we might be more effective fishers of men.

Scripture of the Day:
"And he saith unto them, Follow me, and I will make you fishers of men." -
[Matthew 4:19]

The Word for the Day is "Plant."

"Don't judge each day by the harvest you reap, but by the seeds you plant."
-Robert Louis Stevenson

So many scriptures and teachings in the Bible talk to us about planting good seed and planting righteousness as we go through our days. God wants us to be known as His in our walk in life, like 'trees of righteousness, that the planting of the Lord might be glorified' [Isaiah 61:3]. In a symbolic sense we are God's plants, God's seed through Jesus Christ in the earth [Galatians 3:16]. We are meant to be healthy, strong, and mighty [Psalm 112:2] and we are meant to multiply and be fruitful in the earth [Genesis 26:24]. God sows His Good seed into us through His Word, through His Spirit, and through good teachers and books of faith so we can grow in Him, put down strong roots, flourish and be fruitful….So we can become sowers of His Word.

God uses a process to bring people to Him and then to grow them into Him. As His workers we play different parts in the planting, watering, and harvest, and we're taught that each part of the labor is valuable and has reward as God gives the increase [1Cor 3:6-8; John 4:36]. But there are cautions, too, about what we should sow in our walk with others. "Thou shalt <u>not</u> sow thy vineyard with divers seeds: lest the fruit of thy seed which thou hast sown, and the fruit of thy vineyard, be defiled" [Deut 22:9]. God wants us to sow true, right seed—good seed, spiritual seed, not worldly and erroneous seed. God wants us to stay pure and in a right place in Him. "Ye shall keep my statutes, Thou shalt not let thy cattle gender with a diverse kind: thou shalt not sow thy field with mingled seed" [Lev19:19]. People who plant grass seed and sprinkle straw over it often wonder where the weeds come from later when the grass germinates. They don't realize there was mingled seed, weeds, in the straw they added. It's wise to remember we will each be judged by the seeds—or weeds—we plant every day, a reason to be prayerful and conscious that what we teach and speak to others is good and righteous and not tainted by worldliness.

Prayer:
Lord, let the seed we sow in the world be true and right and not mingled and defiled with weeds and worldly unrighteousness. We want You to rejoice over us for good with Your whole heart each day and to not need to come behind us to root out the weeds we plant erroneously.

Scripture of the Day:
"Yea, I will rejoice over them to do them good, and I will plant them in this land assuredly with my whole heart and with my whole soul." - [Jeremiah 32:41]

The Word for the Day is "Lean."

Quote for the Day:
"We suffer to lean and rely so strongly upon the arm of another, that we destroy our own strength and vigor." - Montaigne

When you lean on something, you better make sure what you're leaning on is solid and secure. I learned this lesson early in life visiting my grandfather's farm as a boy. We were in a field with a row of fence posts around the perimeter when I decided to take a break and lean up against one of the posts. As soon as my weight pressed against the post, it broke, and I fell to the ground scratched and embarrassed. I can hear my granddad say "Son, don't ever lean against rotten wood."

This principle has application both in the natural and spiritual realms. Proverbs 3:5 tells us to 'Trust in the Lord, and lean not on our own understanding.' This doesn't mean God wants us lacking knowledge or wisdom, but it must be built on the solid truth of God, and not on man's wisdom. Many today lean on what they hear, see, and read of others, and never check to see if the opinions they are hearing are based on truth or Godly wisdom. It is a lazy way to form your judgments according to the world and be with the 'in-crowd.' This requires nothing more than the ape-like quality of merely imitating others and having no conviction of your own.

When we trust in the Lord, we can be assured that we are leaning on knowledge that is solid. God's word is a "lamp unto my feet, and a light unto my path" [Psalm 119:105]. Just reading the Proverbs would strengthen anyone in wisdom: "To know wisdom and instruction; to perceive the words of understanding; To receive the instruction of wisdom, justice, and judgment, and equity; To give subtilty to the simple, to the young man knowledge and discretion" [Prov1:1-4].

Let God's Word teach you truth, knowledge, and wisdom; then you can be strong in yourself and rightly judge all things, not leaning on the "rotten wood" of the world.

Prayer:
Lord, thank You that by trusting in You we establish our thoughts on the solid Rock of truth, and not on the sinking sand of mammon.

Scripture of the Day:
"Trust in the Lord with all thine heart; and lean not unto thine own understanding." - [Proverbs 3:5]

The Word for the Day is "Beauty."

Quote for the Day:
"Everything has its beauty, but not everyone sees it." -Confucius

An old hymn titled "For the Beauty of the Earth" reminds us to seek and praise God for all that is beautiful. There is so much beauty in our earth, in nature, in the trees, in the skies, and in the goodness of all that God has created. We should never grow careless and forget to behold God's beauty around us. Neither should we grow careless and forget to seek for more of God's beauty and goodness to abound in our hearts. We should always yearn to 'grow in more beauty, grace, and knowledge of God' [2 Peter 3:18], to be continually 'renewed day by day' [2 Corinthians 4:16].

The earth renews itself in an ongoing way. The changing of the seasons, and the beauty in each one, help to show us a picture of God's ongoing method of renewal. Ecclesiastes 3:11 says: "He hath made everything beautiful in his time." The seasons come, the seasons go, on the earth and in our lives, and there is beauty in each. We need to be grateful for each season, for the simple, good things—the sweetness of a baby's face, the joy of a child's laughter, the blessing of good work and purpose, the memories of the beauty we have seen and enjoyed of God's good earth year to year.

All too often we are short on gratitude, focusing on the negative and not the positive in life. But Jesus taught us to think on the things that are positive and good. "Finally brethren, whatsoever things are true, whatsoever things are honest, whatsoever things are just, whatsoever things are pure, whatsoever things are lovely, whatsoever things are of good report…think on these things" [Philippians 4:8]. We should appreciate what is beautiful and good in this earth and seek to be a person who exemplifies that which is beautiful and good.

Prayer:
Lord, help me focus on that which is good each day, remembering to be grateful to You for life's beauty and blessings—and believing to be changed more and more daily into His Likeness.

Scripture of the Day:
"One thing have I desired of the Lord, that will I seek after; that I may dwell in the House of the Lord all the days of my life, to behold the beauty of the Lord."
- [Psalm 27:4]

The Word for the Day is "Beast"

Quote for the Day:
"There is no religion without love, and people may talk as much as they like about their religion, but if it does not teach them to be good and kind to man and beast, it is all a sham." - Anna Sewell

Okay. I admit it. I am a big wuss when it comes to kitty cats. And cats know it. Lin and I pulled into a rest area once to take a trip break, and I sat down on a long bench with other travelers to relax. A kitty from the other side of the street saw me and came running straight to me, wide-eyed and meowing. I knew then God had given these little beasts a special inward discernment and it was futile to resist. I have accepted my fate.

Proverbs 12:10 tells us that 'a righteous man regardeth the life of his beast.' God expects us to consider and think on our beasts, whether they be pets or not, with special concern. He wants us to give them care, love, and attention. This seems so natural and easy to me, but God says this is a trait of a righteous man, one whose heart is right with God.

Regrettably, I have known people that did not regard the life of their beast. Even worse, some of these people professed to be Christians. I always felt that something was wrong with the heart of any person who would not care for his or her pet. There is something amiss, in my opinion, when one mistreats an animal. I would never take advice, counsel, or ministry from such a person. God cares for His creatures: 'O Lord, thou preservest man and beast' [Psalm 36:6], and we should too. Proverbs 12:10 also tells us: 'but the tender mercies of the wicked are cruel.' They may show kindness when someone is watching, but their heart is not in it. When alone they willfully cause pain or suffering to others, man or beast, and have no feeling of concern about it. So don't mistreat that kitty cat, and then tell me about your religion—I don't want to hear it!

Prayer:
Lord, thank You for all Your creation and for all the beasts of the earth. Teach us to regard the life of both man and beast as righteous guardians of your domain.

Scripture of the Day:
"A righteous man regardeth the life of his beast: but the tender mercies of the wicked are cruel." - [Proverbs 12:10]

The Word for the Day is "Anxious."

Quote for the Day:
"True happiness is to enjoy the present, without anxious dependence upon the future." - Seneca

Many people are interested in genealogy and bloodlines passed down in families. Sometimes personality traits get passed down, too—and not always good ones. I come from a long line of "worriers." I've had to work hard, with God's help, to change that aspect of my life, to be more positive versus negative, to expect the best and not the worst. It took effort to learn to lighten up and enjoy life more and to keep on the sunny side of life. Leo Buscaglia wrote: "Worry never robs tomorrow of its sorrow, it only saps today of its joy."

Nature doesn't worry—a fine reason to go out into the natural world often to observe and enjoy its calm and peace. My husband and I like feeding the birds that come to our deck every morning, and at breakfast we watch them out the window. In sunshine, rain, or cold they come…and although they may puff their feathers out against the rain or cold…they never look anxious or unhappy. And even in the chilly spring rain they sing. Jesus taught his disciples when the crowd gathered on the mountain hillside: "Behold the fowls of the air: for they sow not, neither do they reap, nor gather into barns; yet your heavenly Father feedeth them. Are ye not much better than they? "[Matthew 6:26-27]. Jesus used the example of birds to teach us not be anxious about our lives.

We all fret and worry over entirely too many things. Even research has found eighty-five percent of what people worry about never happens. A humorous quote, written five hundred years ago, by the philosopher Montaigne said: "My life has been filled with terrible misfortune; most of which never happened." Norman Vincent Peale wrote that of all the thousands of letters he received, the problem of worry was the most frequently presented. In his book *Stop Worrying and Start Living*, he said people become worriers by "practicing worry" and become free of worry by "consciously practicing the opposite." That has been true for me, and now I consciously look for the best and not the worst…and like the birds I'm happier and I sing more.

Prayer:
Lord, help us to rest in You more each day, to take no anxious thought for tomorrow and to trust in You for all we need.

Scripture of the Day:
"Be careful (anxious) for nothing; but in everything by prayer and supplication with thanksgiving let your requests be known unto God." - [Philippians 4:6]

The Word for the Day is "Purge."

Quote for the Day:
"God is purifying me in every meeting. I can surely say that unless the power of the Spirit purges me through and through, I cannot help you. First of all, before I can give any life to you, the life must be in me." - Smith Wigglesworth

Health experts tell us it is advantageous for for us to purge (clean out) our natural bodies of toxins and other harmful chemicals in our blood. They usually advise to abstain from particular harmful foods or substances and to take in more beneficial things. Drinking more water and fasting have been proven to rid the body of unhealthy elements in the blood.

God wants us to have clean, healthy bodies, but He also wants us to purge our mind and soul of impurities. There are toxic influences to our soul both internally, like our thoughts and desires, and externally, like people. Rebels and those that transgress against God have no communion with the righteous [Ezekiel 20:38]. Their evil conversation and words can infect thinking like a virus: "Be not deceived: evil communications corrupt good manners" [1 Cor 15:33].

The Word describes the righteous as unleavened (unspoiled) bread, and we are to avoid the leaven (toxin) of malice and wickedness. We are to be the unleavened bread of sincerity and truth [1 Cor 5:6-8]. We are to purge ourselves from vessels of dishonor, that we might be vessels of honor, prepared for every good work for the Master's use [2 Timothy 2:20-21].

The Bible tells us to purge our own conscience from impurity by striving to increase in faith, virtue, kindness, temperance, patience, godliness, brotherly kindness, and charity, never forgetting that we were purged from our old sins by the blood of Christ [2 Peter 1:5-9]. Proverbs 16:6 gives us wise counsel: "By mercy and truth iniquity is purged; and by fear of the Lord men depart from evil."

Prayer:
Lord, let us purpose to keep our body and soul purged and clean that we might be vessels of honor, prepared for every good work for You.

Scripture of the Day:
"How much more shall the blood of Christ, who through the eternal Spirit offered himself without spot to God, purge your conscience from dead works to serve the living God?" - [Hebrews 9:14]

The Word for the Day is "Fruit"

Quote for the Day:
"A tree is known by its fruit; a man by his deeds." - Saint Basil

The Dogwood Arts Festival is ongoing here in Knoxville, Tennessee. Whenever we are out, we see the lovely white and pink flowering trees in the yards and fields and along the way as we travel. Many legends have grown up around the dogwood. One says Jesus' cross was made from the wood of a dogwood tree; others say the dogwood petals represent the cross, and the center the thorny crown. These are lovely legends, but dogwoods can't be found in Israel or the surrounding areas, so these stories are only folklore, even if sweet and inspirational.

Dogwood trees do speak, though, of God's incredible creative ability and they whisper of hope, reminding us that after cold winters and hard seasons or difficult times, that spring and beauty come once again. Every spring, we look forward to and can count on the dogwoods blooming out once more. It might make a cute children's storybook for a dogwood tree on one of Knoxville's Dogwood Trails to refuse to bloom one year. But in reality we know God designed the trees to bloom and flourish in their right season. We're expected to flower and bloom to show forth God's love, to use all our gifts wisely and well, to live according to His commandments and truths. Psalm 1:3 reminds us "And he shall be like a tree planted by the rivers of water, that bringeth forth his fruit in his season; his leaf also shall not wither; and whatsoever he doeth shall prosper."

We can learn a lot from trees about how to wisely live our lives. We need deep roots in God. We need to keep growing—trying to learn more of God and to yearn to be all He wants us to be. We need to be hardy and resilient. Despite hardships and life attacks, trees recover and in time bring forth new life, leaf and blossom, and so should we. It might be well if we check our own "trees," our own lives, during this season to see if we're growing, flowering, and blooming as we should. Jeremiah 17:8 reminds us that our leaf is supposed to stay green and that we're not to 'cease from yielding fruit.' Trees are rightly expected to yield their blossoms and their fruit and so are we.

Prayer:
Lord, let us check our branches and leaves in this season to be sure we are doing all we can to bear blossom and fruit that others can see and smile over. Help us to flower so that our lives reflect You.

Scripture of the Day:
"The fruit of the righteous is a tree of life; and he that winneth souls is wise." - [Proverbs 11:30]

The Word for the Day is "Price."

Quote for the Day:
"Men know not the gold which lies in the mine of Christ Jesus, or surely they would dig in it night and day. They have not discovered the pearl of great price, or they would have sold their all to buy the field wherein it lies." - Charles Spurgeon

Price is the amount we pay to buy something. Generally, the more value that is placed on an object, the more it is priced. In this season of Easter we often observe many traditions: special sunrise services, special Easter services at our churches, fellowship with family and friends, and colorful Easter egg hunts for kids. We are celebrating the salvation gained through the death, burial, and resurrection of our Lord Jesus, but do we take time to consider the great price that God paid for our salvation?

I think the parable of the pearl of great price that Jesus gave is a great teaching as to the value of the Easter event. Jesus taught: "Again, the kingdom of heaven is like unto a merchant man, seeking goodly pearls: Who, when he had found one pearl of great price, went and sold all that he had, and bought it" [Matthew 13:45-46]. The merchant man valued the pearl of great price so much, that he gave up all he had to possess it. Do we consider the great price of Jesus? He was the Son of God, with God from the beginning, creator of all things, having the Name above all names [1 John 5:20; John 1:1,3; Philippians 2:9]. This same Jesus, who came as flesh, the Son of Man, lived and experienced life as a man in the flesh, yet without sin. This sinless sacrifice offered Himself on the cross, shed His blood, and gave His life for our sins, that we might obtain salvation and eternal life by faith in Him. Do we value life in Him enough to give up all to obtain the pearl of great price as the merchant man did?

We are purchased in our salvation with a great price in Jesus, and we should commit all to Him, as He did unto us. Turning away from the darkness of this world and it's ways, God wants us to walk in His Light, glorifying God in body and spirit since we are His in Jesus. Jesus paid the price we couldn't pay, that we might have the free gift of Life in Him. Let us value Him above all this Easter.

Prayer:
Lord, we praise and thank You for salvation bought with the precious blood of Jesus; we will give our all and serve Him with our all today and evermore.

Scripture of the Day:
"For ye are bought with a price: therefore glorify God in your body, and in your spirit, which are God's." - [1 Corinthians 6:20]

The Word for the Day is "Captivity."

Quote for the Day:
The resurrection power of Jesus Christ broke satan's captive power. When he led the Old Testament saints from paradise to heaven he led captivity captive." – Leon Morris

One of the most overlooked stories related to Easter is that period of time between Jesus death and resurrection when He descended into hell. There Jesus triumphed over satan and his kingdom, not only conquering death, but putting satan in his new place as a defeated enemy [Colossians 2:13-15]. In early times and in ancient Rome, when a military leader defeated an enemy, a triumphal parade and procession was held to celebrate the victory. A spectacle of chained captives, princes, and leaders were displayed in the procession to demonstrate clearly their defeat. This is what Jesus did in hell. Satan and his fallen angels thought they'd won, killed and defeated Jesus. Imagine their surprise when the power and anointing rolled through Jesus, the glory of God shining about Him. And satan realized he'd made a critical mistake.

"Jesus triumphed over all of hell right at the time all of hell was thinking it had triumphed over him" [Pastor Chas Stevenson]. In his rightful power and authority Jesus preached to the captives held in Paradise, proclaiming liberty and salvation [Isaiah 61:1, 42:6-7; 1 Peter 3:18-21]. Can't you just imagine how they loved parading through hell in the processional and celebration held that day? "Oh death where is thy sting" [1 Cor 15:55]? They were gloriously liberated and given gifts when Jesus ascended up on high [Ephesians 4:8].

At Easter we escaped death and hell in more ways than one. Jesus took back what satan had stolen from Adam in the beginning [Psalm 53:6, 68:18; Matthew 16:19; Revelation 1:18]. He not only attained eternal life for us but he triumphed over evil in hell for us once and for all. He brought about freedom and a restored relationship with God for us and rent the veil [Matthew 27:51]. How gladly we should purge away any unrighteousness in our lives to walk in love and obedience to Jesus for all He did for us.

Prayer:
Lord, help us to keep the enemy under our feet, remembering all You did to defeat him and to take captivity captive.

Scripture of the Day:
"Casting down imaginations, and every high thing that exalteth itself against the knowledge of God and bringing into captivity every thought to the obedience of Christ." –[2 Corinthians 10:5]

The Word for the Day is "Practice."

Quote for the Day:
"Practice does not perfect. Only perfect practice makes perfect." - Vince Lombardi

I love this Spring season when I get a few opportunities to play golf. Sometimes my game is in good shape early in the season, but most times I have some faults to correct. I know the only way to get my golf game back in shape is to practice, and practice the right way, as Vince Lombardi implies above. You can practice wrong moves and make your game worse, or you concentrate on the right fundamentals to improve. Sometimes just a small adjustment can make a big difference, like standing just a few inches closer to the ball.

The Lord wants us to always strive to conform more and more to the image of Jesus [Romans 8:29]. If our spiritual walk needs improvement, we can "practice" to get better, to improve our walk with the Lord. But we must not practice the wrong things. Psalm 141:4 tells us not to 'practice wicked works with workers of iniquity, or any evil thing.' The world and the enemy will try to get us off the good track by listening to the voice of the world with it's error, deceit, and ungodly behavior. Conforming to this world will render our practice imperfect with even more imperfect results in our spiritual walk [Romans 12:2].

We must practice aright to cure a faulty golf swing or a faulty relationship with the Lord. First, we get our hearts right with the Lord by confession, by repentance, and by prayer to receive His forgiveness and grace: "If we confess our sins, he is faithful and just to forgive us our sins, and to cleanse us from all unrighteousness" [I John 1:9]. We read God's Word, the Bible, with discipline and purpose, to renew our minds to righteousness and build up our faith: "The entrance of thy words giveth light; it giveth understanding unto the simple" [Psalm 119:130].

We then practice to cure our relationship with our neighbor by loving him as ourselves [Matthew 22:39]. We show kindness, mercies, and charity to our neighbor. Sometimes a small thing like talking to God more, by being a little more polite and patient with our fellow man, can help get our "A" game back.

Prayer:
Lord, we commit ourselves to practice truth and righteousness that we may be conformed more and more to Your image.

Scripture of the Day:
"Incline not my heart to any evil thing, to practice wicked works with men that work iniquity: and let me not eat of their dainties." - [Psalm 141:4]

The Word for the Day is "Obedience."

Quote for the Day:
"The whole duty of man is summed up in obedience to God's will."
– George Washington

Our often fiercely independent natures chaff a little at the concept of obedience and yet obedience is an essential part of faith. Obedience is being submissive to or complying to one in authority and following the rules laid out by that authority. As children we learned to be obedient to parents, teachers, and to moral guidelines laid out for us.

When we became Christians we chose to submit ourselves to God's authority. We made a personal decision to yield our lives and our wills to Him. It isn't just a matter of duty in our faith walk like in the world, it's a matter of love. Jesus said, 'If you love Me, keep My commandments' [John 14:15] We show our love to God daily by keeping his commandments. And because of that love 'His Commandments are not burdensome' [1 John 5:3].

The responsibility for obedience in God, however, lies within us. We have to seek to know what God's will is. We have to study God's Word to learn of Him, to come to know Him and His rules and commandments. Unlike an earthly parent God doesn't make us obey. He doesn't make us read His Word and learn His commandments and laws. He doesn't make us draw close to Him or make us pray. But He yearns for us to. He wants our willing love, our willing devotion, and our willing obedience. And when we give that and begin to follow in his Ways, we become transformed. We grow more like Him. We act like and sound like our Father. And people see Him in us.

Prayer:
Lord, so often we go our own way. We forget that we are yours. We forget that we gave You our lives and promised to serve and obey You. We forget that the way to peace, joy, true happiness, and fulfillment is in yielding ourselves to You, in following after You, and in living our lives as You want and desire us to. We forget that obedience is really a joy and no burden at all when our hearts are right. Help us to a right heart and mind today. Help us to yearn to be your obedient children not because we have to but because we Love You and want to serve You. Because we want to glorify You and because we want people to see You in our lives so they will be drawn to You through us.

Scripture of the Day:
"For your obedience is come abroad unto all men. (*It shows!*) I am glad therefore on your behalf." - [Romans 16:19]

The Word for the Day is "Masters."

Quote for the Day:
"A dog barks when his master is attacked. I would be a coward if I saw that God's truth is attacked and yet would remain silent." - John Calvin

I always look forward to watching The Masters golf tournament on TV at this time of year. I think my zeal for this particular tournament was sparked by the excitement of watching Arnold Palmer back in the 60's. His aggressive passion in this tournament made it special for millions of fans. I loved the tournament concept: a field of "masters" of golf competing to be the Masters Champion of all the golf masters in this unique tournament.

There is a "masters" competition going on in life, too. Who will be our master, God or mammon? Whether we know it or not, mammon is our master by default before we receive the salvation of God. We accept the world's ways when we serve mammon. We think like the world, talk like the world, believe like the world, and act like the world. Like the old Peggy Lee song we think 'that's all there is,' so we are trapped in a worldly mindset.

But if the Holy Spirit is able to open our eyes and hearts to a new life offered in Christ Jesus and we accept Him as saviour, we change our master, the one we serve. Our heart, or nature, gets changed to a new creation, and we walk in a new life in Him. We seek to grow in Him by learning of Him and His Word, and we follow a different Spirit than the world.

It grieves me today to see so many in the church seemingly trying to serve two masters. But we cannot serve both God and mammon. Yet many, it seems to me, are trying to operate in both kingdoms. If people hate it when scripture is used as the authority for all matters pertaining to life and godliness, and when they despise you for taking a view different than the current fad of the world, they are serving only mammon as master. "If any man love the world, the love of the Father is not in him" [1 John 2:15]. Let men choose: it's either God or mammon, not both.

Prayer:
Lord, let every one that names Jesus as Lord serve Him as Master, being in the world, but not of the world.

Scripture of the Day:
"No man can serve two masters: for either he will hate the one, and love the other; or else he will hold fast to the one and despise the other. Ye cannot serve God and mammon." - [Matthew 6:24]

The Word for the Day is "Finish."

Quote for the Day:
"Stopping at third adds no more to the score than striking out. It doesn't matter how well you start if you fail to finish." – Billy Sunday

In one of those anonymous Facebook posts I saw at Easter Time, the words said: *"Jesus didn't say 'I am finished.' He said, 'It is finished.' He was just getting started.'* Isn't that a great thought? Jesus finished His Father's Work so that we, through Him, could finish His Work and keep finishing His work. "For if the Spirit of him that raised up Christ from the dead dwell in you, he shall… quicken your mortal bodies by his Spirit that dwelleth in you" [Rom 8:11-12]. We are not bound to the old restrictions of the world and the flesh anymore but we're made new through Him and changed. He paid a debt He did not owe for us, and I believe we owe a debt back to Him to finish His work. He didn't only want to raise us up to be able to go to heaven one day, He wanted us to finish all that He started and more.

Jesus said to His disciples "Ye have not chosen me but I have chosen you, and ordained you, that ye should go and bring forth fruit, and that your fruit should remain" [John 15:16]. He later prayed to His Father 'I send them into the world now as you sent me and the glory You gave me I give them so they can finish my work' [John 17:18, 22]. Whether you realize it or not, you have work to do for Him, work to finish. No, we're not all meant to be pastors or missionaries, but we are each meant to find what He has for us to do in the earth and do it with all our will and heart. "Now therefore perform the doing of it, that as there was a readiness to will, so there may be a performance also out of what which ye have" [2 Corinthians 8:11]. Be also 'confident of this very thing, that He which hath begun a good work in you will perform it' [Philippians 1:6].

Sadly many of us never seek to find the work that God wants us to do. We get caught up in the day-to-day life of the world instead. If we occasionally get a glimpse of what God is calling us to do, we don't follow up on it with heart, passion, and diligence or with a firm belief that Jesus will enable us to do whatever He asks. We fail to start, or finish, as we should and decide it doesn't matter.

Prayer:
Lord, help us to see the works You have for us to do for You, to have the courage to start them, and the heart to finish them.

Scripture of the Day:
"My meat is to do the will of him that sent me, and to finish his work." - [John 4:34]

The Word for the Day is "Trials."

Quote for the Day:
"A gem cannot be polished without friction, nor a man perfected without trials."
 - Lucius Annaeus Seneca

There are various types of trials in this life. Most readily we think of a trial at law before judge and jury. The purpose is to bring forth a just and fair verdict. There are also trials pertaining to testing something, or someone, as to the performance, qualities, or suitability of the subject. Products are often tested with pre-marketing trials to see if consumers will like the item enough to purchase it. Athletes are subjected to trials, often called tryouts, to see if they have the skills to compete at a high level. Job applicants may have a trial period of performance before being offered full-time employment. Military personnel can have trials to test performance and physical abilities before being assigned a special branch of service. We can think of many other trials of this type in society.

We can have trials of our faith when God is trying to prepare us for growth or greater ministry. Just as a young student is mentally tried while learning math, English, and other new subjects to grow mentally, God wants us to grow in faith and purity to be of greater service in the Kingdom. Sometimes these trials require exercise of patience, growth in the fruits and gifts of the Spirit, revelation, boldness and confidence in the Word, but God intends all these trials for our good that we may grow in Christ Jesus and in service to Him by being ministers of the gospel.

Some trials come because our enemy, satan, is always trying to find a way to steal, kill, and destroy [John 10:10]. If he can find a way to afflict us with any trial, whether it be bodily ills, attacks, or vexations by people that he can control, he will try to sabotage our faith to discourage us. These are evil trials to destroy our walk with God, rather than increase our walk as God wills. The good news is that Jesus always causes us to triumph in Him [2 Corinthians 2:14], and greater is He that is in us, than he that is in the world [1 John 4:4]. So don't fear any trial, you're going to come out the victor and increased in the Lord!

Prayer:
Lord, we patiently endure our trials of every kind knowing that our faith is being perfected and we are assured the victory we always have in Christ Jesus.

Scripture of the Day:
"That the trial of your faith, being much more precious than of gold that perisheth, though it be tried with fire, might be found unto praise and honour and glory at the appearing of Jesus Christ." - [1 Peter 1:7]

The Word for the Day is "Abide.

Quote for the Day:
"To be occupied with Christ is to abide in Christ." – Andrew Murray

A friend of mine is a Master Gardener. Attaining this gardening distinction implies completing classes and training in a Master Gardener Program. Where I live in Tennessee that program is provided through the University of Tennessee's Cooperative Extension specialists. It's about an eleven-week program consisting of forty hours of coursework. After attaining the Master Gardener credentials all graduates are required to do horticultural and community volunteer work. They share their expertise with others.

I do not have a Master Gardener's green thumb or their extensive knowledge. My parents were both excellent gardeners, though, and I miss their knowledge when I encounter problems in my yard. However, as Christians we each have a Master Gardener of life we can call on. Jesus said "I am the true vine and my father is the husbandman," a term meaning the Master Gardener [John 15:1] He added, "Abide in me, and I in you. As the branch cannot bear fruit of itself, except it abide in the vine; no more can ye, except ye abide in me" [John 15:4]. John 15 is a very instructive scripture on how to live well under God's good care.

To abide in God means we need to stay grafted in to the vine, keeping a daily personal relationship with the Father, characterized by study, trust, obedience, and prayer. All plants draw life and strength from the sun and pull through their roots the nourishment they need to thrive, to grow, and to bear fruit. In God's Garden, we draw from Him as our source. We live for Him a productive, pleasing life and bear good fruit like "love, joy, peace, long-suffering, gentleness, goodness, faith, meekness and temperance" [Galatians 5:22-23]. We are promised, too, that if we 'live in the Spirit, we will also walk in the Spirit,' [Galatians 5:25]. If we stay grafted into God, our roots entwined with His, He will shine through us. A good gardener loves his plants and plants love a good gardener. In a sweet way, for those of us who live close to the Master Gardener, it's like living each day in a secret garden.

Prayer:
Lord, we all love to walk in a beautiful garden. Help us to lean to You as our Master Gardener, to abide in You, to be occupied and entwined with You fully, so You can live and work in us freely and so we can bear good fruit.

Scripture of the Day:
"He that dwelleth in the secret place of the Most High shall abide under the shadow of the Almighty." - [Psalm 91:1]

The Word for the Day is "Old."

Quote for the Day:
"Old is authentic. Old is genuine. Old is valuable." - Billy Graham

When I was growing up, I loved and enjoyed rock & roll music. To me it was so delightful and diverse. Even today I still listen to the "oldies" for enjoyment. The Holy Spirit even improves some songs for me by giving me His enhancements. For instance, google the song "Since I Met You Baby" by Ivory Joe Hunter, and substitute the word "Jesus" for "baby" in the lyrics and your heart will be blessed by this new "hymn." If you're in a funk, try this 10-minute "oldies" remedy: google in order these songs: "Peggy Sue" by Buddy Holly; "Suzie Darlin" by Robin Luke; "Love You So" by Ron Holden; "I've Had It" by the Bell Notes; and "Pipeline" by the Chantays. Try it, your mood will be uplifted and happier.

God also gives us blessings from the past. As Billy Graham noted 'old is authentic, genuine, and valuable.' Psalm 77:11-12 reads: "I will remember the works of the Lord: surely I will remember thy wonders of old. I will meditate also of all thy work, and talk of thy doings." The Bible tells us of God's wonders from Genesis to Revelation. These works seem too miraculous to be true, but we know God's Word is truth. What a blessing to meditate, to think on, the miracles that God has performed and His faithfulness to His people. No matter what the obstacles or trials we may face, we have a God that we can call on and trust in, "For with God nothing shall be impossible" [Luke 1:37]. We also need to 'talk of God's doings' according to Psalm 77:12. When we think on God's wonders of old, and also speak of them, our words help to confirm and strengthen these revelations and our faith. Some think on God's wonders, but don't speak to confirm His Truth to themselves and others. So let us remember God's wonders and judgments of old and comfort ourselves, and others, in such an awesome God [Psalm 119:52].

Prayer:
O Lord, we remember Your great and mighty works and wonders of old, Your steadfast faithfulness to Your servants, and Your wisdom and counsel preserved for all ages. We thank You for Your Spirit that guides us in today's present, leading us toward our assured future.

Scripture of the Day:
"O Lord, thou art my God; I will exalt thee, I will praise thy name; for thou hast done wonderful things; thy counsels of old are faithfulness and truth." -
[Isaiah 25:1]

The Word for the Day is "Fortress."

Quote for the Day:
"Prayer is a strong wall and fortress of the church: it is a goodly Christian weapon."
 - Martin Luther

We have a new term today in America during the corona virus pandemic—
"Social Distancing"—but spiritually the concept is an old one. When we walk in
a strong place in the Lord there is always a protective hedge around us [Job 1:10].
It is visible to the enemy and he has to keep his distance from it. Over time many
have talked of seeing the halo, the aura, the protective radiation of the Spirit of
God around those who walk close to the Lord. John Lake wrote: "When the Spirit
of God radiated from the man Jesus, I wonder how close it was possible for the
evil spirit to come to Him? Do you not see that the Spirit of God is as destructive
of evil as it is creative of good? It was impossible for the evil one to come near
Him, and I feel sure Satan talked to Jesus from a safe distance."

Jesus came, died, and was resurrected to destroy the works of the devil [1 John
3:8] so that we might walk in a place of safety and protection, with the hedge
of God around us keeping evil and the works of the devil away. That hedge and
fortress around us keeps the devil and his works—at a distance—and we are safe.

Martin Luther wrote the words to the wonderful hymn "A Mighty Fortress is
Our God," reminding us of God's protective care. In times past when enemies
attacked, the people ran into the established forts and fortresses of their time
for safety. Those impenetrable walls and the numbers of strong defenders within
them kept the people safe from harm. Beloved, we live in the fortress of God. We
live in His protective care, within His walls and protective hedges. Who should
we fear when we know we have God's help and shield, when he is 'our rock, our
fortress, and our deliverer?' [Psalm 118:6, 115:11, 18:2]. Be assured that God will
always keep you "socially distanced" from the enemy and from all harm.

Prayer:
Father, help us to know that You guard and protect our lives and that no deadly
thing can hurt us.

Scripture of the Day:
"I will say of the Lord, He is my refuge and my fortress: my God; in him will I
trust…A thousand shall fall at thy side, and ten thousand at thy right hand; but it
shall not come nigh thee." – [Psalm 91:2, 7]

The Word for the Day is "Prune."

Quote for the Day:
"The purpose of pruning is to improve the quality of the roses, not to hurt the bush."
- Florence Littauer

I love the springtime with the flowers blooming, the trees in full growth of leaves, the birds singing, and especially with the smell of fresh-cut grass. But some chores, like pruning the shrubs and trees, I have not been so eager to perform. In the past, I looked at pruning only as a cosmetic motive, just to make the shrubs look neater. But after I understood that pruning was essential for the shrubs' health and long-term growth, I took the job more seriously.

John 15:2 shows us that God prunes us for the same purpose: for our health and growth, that we may bring forth good fruit. Just as we prune shrubs to cut off any branches that may be unwanted, undesirable, or superfluous to ensure the plant's best long term health, God wants to take the things out of our life that might hinder our spiritual or even natural growth. Galatians 5:12 says "I would they were even cut off which trouble you." Things that trouble us can be physical, like not taking care of our bodies. The Word says our body is the temple of the Holy Ghost which is in us, and that we are to glorify God in our body [1 Corinthians 6:19-20]. So we prune out any harmful effects by decision, patience, persistence, and prayer.

God wants us to prune out bad behaviors that are undesirable. I sometimes used to utter oaths at rude fellow drivers, but the Lord corrected my impatience. He showed me my job was to stay calm, focus on driving, and discipline my tongue: "And the servant of the Lord must not strive" [2 Timothy 2:24]. We must prune all behavior that does not show the fruits of the Spirit. We must also guard our spirits by pruning anything that is not of God's truth. Doubt, unbelief, heresy, ignorance of scripture, and opinions hostile to God can damage growth. Pruning is not easy, but we must be diligent to cut out anything contrary to God's uprightness that we may stay healthy and strong in the Lord.

Prayer:
Lord, help us to prune ourselves of hindrances to growth in You whether they be in the flesh, in the mind, or in the spirit, that we may bring forth much fruit.

Scripture of the Day:
"Every branch in me that beareth not fruit he taketh away: and every branch that beareth fruit, he purgeth (prunes) it, that it may bring forth more fruit." -
 [John 15:2]

The Word for the Day is "Forward."

Quote for the Day:
"I will go anywhere as long as its forward." - David Livingstone

Life is a forward journey. We can change and grow as we go, both positive and negative experiences impacting us. We damage ourselves and interrupt the process of growth if we don't keep looking forward and moving on. We shouldn't overly focus on the past, good or bad, nor should we yearn to return to the past. We're not going that way. This is true when we are young; this is true when we are old. Martin Luther King said it so beautifully: "If you can't fly then run. If you can't run then walk. If you can't walk then crawl. But whatever you do you have to keep moving forward."

Many people look down through the years, wistfully thinking about retiring. "I can't wait until I don't have to do anything, 'til I can sit back and do nothing." All scientific research has found this 'rocking chair' concept is unhealthy. The happiest and healthiest individuals are busy and doing. For many, idle un-production is the beginning of a downward spiral in health and well-being.

Philippians 3:13 reminds us to be always "reaching forth unto those things which are before." Faith looks to the future. "Successful men and women keep moving. They make mistakes but they don't quit" [Conrad Hilton]. Your question every day as a person of faith should be: "What are we going to do today God?" The concept of un-productivity, of sitting around and doing nothing on a regular daily basis, did not originate from God. You will not find the word "retirement" in the Bible. And any mention of sloth, laziness, un-productivity, or being stagnant is always admonished against.

As long as you are here, God has work for you. "I must work the works of Him that sent me, while it is day" [John 9:4]. We're not meant to look back longingly, seeing the past with rose-colored glasses. Nor are we meant to sit stagnant and idle, whiling away God's time.

Prayer:
Lord, may we keep our eyes, our vision, set forward and may we keep moving forward—remembering that the past can't be changed or returned to, but the future is in our power.

Scripture of the Day:
"Say not thou, what is the cause that the former days were better than these? for thou dost not inquire wisely concerning this." - [Ecclesiastes 7:10]

The Word for the Day is "Proof."

Quote for the Day:
"In the absence of any other proof, the thumb alone would convince me of God's existence." - Isaac Newton

One definition of proof is a trial impression of a page used to make any changes before a final copy or printing. Until recently, I published a monthly local magazine, and in Spring I also market advertising on wall-size UT football schedules. I have learned over the years it always benefits to provide customers initial proofs of their ads before printing. This keeps customers happy and saves me costs.

In this sense, we continually present ourselves as "proofs" to God, as if He is looking at a page impression of our lives, our hearts, our thoughts, and our behavior. We should gladly desire for God to make corrections to our life "proof" page, to correct errors and make revisions to enhance the quality of our lives. We should eagerly accept these "proof" revisions as we seek to be more and more conformed to the image of Christ Jesus.

Another definition of proof is to provide evidence or argument to establish a fact or truth of a statement. We should always be ready to offer proofs of the validity of our faith and experience in Jesus. After His passion Jesus showed Himself alive by many infallable proofs, by being seen and by speaking of the kingdom [Acts 1:3]. We can present proofs of God's kingdom by speaking the word of our testimony [Revelation 12:11]. Every grace Jesus has done for us in our lives is a reality. We can testify of His works in our lives because they are real. Man can still reject or refuse to believe us, but our testimony is fact. We can keep speaking the truth of God's Word without compromise. God's Word is truth [John 17:17] and it is established forever [Psalm 119:89]. God will provide proof of His Truth by confirming His Word to us [Mark 16:20]. He does not establish those who turn their ears away from God's truth or invent fables after their own lusts [2 Timothy 4:1-5]. Let God keep "proofing" you, conforming you more and more unto Jesus, and keep sharing your testimony with boldness.

Prayer:
Lord, like a Divine Editor, please keep making corrections, edits, revisions, and enhancements to our life page that we might be more and more perfected.

Scripture of the Day:
"For to this end did I write, that I might know the proof of you, whether ye be obedient in all things." - [2 Corinthians 2:9]

The Word for the Day is "Profess."

Quote for the Day:
"Looking back, I am ashamed that I have not always upheld the values that I profess and believe in." – Cardinal Sean Brady

When I was growing up, my mother and my aunts were fond of life proverbs, and one I often heard was: "Actions speak louder than words." In many ways your words mean nothing if your actions are the complete opposite. We tell people everyday "who we are" more by our actions than by our words. But our words reflect our hearts and actions, too.

I spend my life now writing words in books but I believe those words speak deeply about who I am and what I believe and value. The Word teaches in Matthew that 'out of the abundance of the heart the mouth speaks' [Matthew 12:34] and in Luke 'that a good man out of the good treasure of his heart brings forth that which is good' [Luke 6:45]. Another scripture I like reminds us that 'both sweet and bitter water shouldn't spring forth out of the same fountain' [James 3:11]. This scripture paints a vivid picture. When we stop by a water fountain to get a drink, we expect pure, clean water to come out of it. We'd be a little shocked, or as my kids used to say grossed-out, if dirty water spewed out instead.

In our somewhat compromised spiritual world today, we see more and more crossover gray areas and often hear we shouldn't judge, but none of us are so naïve that we don't recognize when something is vile or nasty. We expect Christians to exemplify goodness, kindness, and righteousness in their lives, and deep in our hearts we know how we should act as God's children.

Prayer:
Lord, help us to lead uncompromised lives in the world, to show through our actions and words Your truth and Your love and to stay constant in our faith.

Scripture of the Day:
"They profess to know God, but in works they deny Him." [Titus 1:16].

The Word for the Day is "Promises."

Quote for the Day:
"I build on Christ, the rock of ages; on his sure mercies described in his word, and on his promises, all which I know are yea and amen." - John Wesley

Remember how exciting it was to receive a promise as a child? As a little boy my Mom promised to take me to a real restaurant, and eat steak! I'll never forget that day when I ate steak for the first time in a real restaurant, even if it was hamburger steak at a small diner in Etowah, Tennessee. I felt like a king! And remember how disappointing it was to expect a promise, but not have it materialize? It's always sad when you learn some people do not keep or perform their promises.

We have awesome promises from God in His Word, and all the promises of God in Christ are yea and amen [2 Corinthians 1:20]. God gives us 'exceeding great and precious promises; that by these ye might be partakers of the divine nature' [2 Peter 1:4]. How awesome! But sometimes when we haven't yet received an expected promise of God, we are deceived by the enemy into thinking God isn't faithful to His promises. What is the cause of this doubt?

One of the primary causes is unbelief. Abraham is a prime example of being strong in faith toward God. The Bible tells us Abraham was promised a son when he was long past the age. But Abraham 'considered not his own age, about an hundred years, nor aged Sarah's infertility, but against hope he believed and staggered not at the promise of God, but was strong in faith' [Rom 4:19-20]. Abraham believed more in God's promise than his natural circumstances, "being fully persuaded that, what he had promised, he was able also to perform" [Romans 4:21]. Abraham was 100% persuaded that God was true to His word.

The enemy wants us to divert our eyes off the promises of God and onto the circumstances around us. He wants to dissuade us from the spiritual truth by trying to persuade us that the obstacles are too big for God to perform the promises to us. The enemy is a liar, but God cannot lie, and like Abraham, we must be fully persuaded that what God has promised, He will perform.

Prayer:
Lord, we will not be dissuaded, but will believe Your great and precious promises to us that we might partake of the divine nature now and give You the glory.

Scripture of the Day:
"For all the promises of God in him are yea, and in him Amen, unto the glory of God by us." - [2 Corinthians 1:20]

The Word for the Day is "Flourish."

Quote for the Day:
"God's intent for His Creation was for it to flourish." – Hugh Whelchel

To flourish means to grow and develop in a healthy, vigorous way. As people of faith we are meant to flourish and prosper. God formed and made us and created us for His Glory [Isaiah 43:7]. We are meant to be a "crown of glory in the hand of the Lord" [Isaiah 62:3].

Although God wants us to flourish and prosper in our lives, works, health, and all we do, He needs our belief and cooperation for this to happen. Our souls and inner man can't be forced to grow. Just as flowers need sun, water, and a positive environment in which to produce, we need spiritual nourishment in order to blossom, flourish, and produce. And as we grow in God, we flourish more and more. Like an equation, our continuing growth in God yields more and more positive results and blessings to our lives.

In the natural world, what you feed will flourish and what you neglect will wilt and eventually die. It is our responsibility to feed our souls and our lives so that God's best will keeps developing in us. We flourish and grow from studying the Word of God, from seeking and learning about God, from prayer and quiet times with Him. These times with God nourish our souls and bring us into a close place with Him. Jesus promised when we seek the 'kingdom of God, and his righteousness that all these things we want and desire shall be added unto us' [Matthew 6:33]. "The righteous shall flourish like the palm tree; he shall grow like a cedar in Lebanon…to show that the Lord is upright" [Psalm 92:12-15].

Do you wish to see your life flourish and prosper? Then do the things you know to do to bring these blessings to pass in your life. We are promised to be blessed and filled when we "hunger and thirst for righteousness" [Matthew 5:6]. God's best won't simply fall on you because you define yourself as a Christian. You have to do your part to bring God's best and blessings to pass in your life.

Prayer:
Lord, help us to realize how much You want us to prosper and flourish but that we often stop the flow of those rich blessings toward us by our indifference to You, our neglect of quality time with You, and by our heart and loyalties planted more in the things of the world than in You.

Scripture of the Day:
"Those that be planted in the house of the Lord shall flourish in the courts of our God." - [Psalm 92:13]

The Word for the Day is "Conformed."

Quote for the Day:
"Every possible pressure is being brought to bear upon Christians to make them conform to the standards of the present world." - Billy Graham

For a Christian, the concept of conformity is a two-sided coin: both positive and negative. Conformity can be a positive force when taken in the concept of complying with certain rules or standards. For instance, we want everyone to conform to upholding the laws; we want drivers to conform to traffic laws and not run that red light! The military and other agencies expect conformity to their rules of appearance and conduct when performing required duties. You buy a product expecting it to conform to certain standards. I want my jug of Weigel's milk to conform to the taste standard I expect.

But the trial for a Christian is the temptation to conform to worldly behavior. The world has had its own ideas of what is acceptable and conventional since the beginning. The world easily changes their norms of right or wrong behavior by simply labeling new concepts as 'progressive.' The pull of the world is always "follow the crowd, don't be different."

Jesus came to earth and walked amidst the crowds of the world; He was in the world, but not of the world [John 15:18-19]. He declared God's Truth as to right and wrong, sin and righteousness. John 3:17 says "For God sent not his Son into the world to condemn the world: but that the world through him might be saved." Jesus knew it was only the truth of God's Word that could set a man free, not conforming to the world's ways [John 8:32].

We are not to be conformed to this world, but to be transformed by the renewing of our mind. We must have the revelation of God's Truth by knowing His Word, and have the courage and commitment to live and speak the truth before the world, so that the world might be saved.

Prayer:
Lord, we will not compromise Your Truth or be conformed to this world. But in love we will shine the light of truth to the world, that men can be delivered out of darkness into Your marvelous light.

Scripture of the Day:
"And be not conformed to this world: but be ye transformed by the renewing of your mind, that ye may prove what is that good, and acceptable, and perfect, will of God." - [Romans 12:2]

The Word for the Day is "Doubt."

Quote for the Day:
"The habit of doubt is a hindrance to prayer." – A. B. Simpson

Doubt is an insidious hindrance to the success of any Christian's life. By definition doubt implies a feeling of uncertainty, mistrust, and a lack of conviction. Doubt is a sin of unbelief, an opposing force to faith. A. B. Simpson wrote that the enemy of God wants to introduce doubt into the mind and heart of a Christian because it destroys contact of the soul with God and interrupts God's intervention.

Faith without doubt is powerful. The woman with the issue of blood who sought out Jesus in the crowds said within herself 'if I can just touch his garment I shall be whole' [Matthew 9:21]. She held a positive non-doubting stance pushing and pursuing after Jesus in the throngs and crowds around Him. Jesus turned when he saw her, connecting with her faith and said "Daughter, be of good comfort; thy faith hath made the whole. And the woman was made whole from that hour" [Matthew 9:22].

Many people would say, 'Well, everyone has doubts; it's only natural." But that's a careless, dangerous attitude and opposite of God's teachings. The Word says: "But let him ask in faith, nothing wavering. For he that wavereth is like a wave of the sea driven with the wind and tossed. For let not that man think that he shall receive any thing of the Lord. A double minded man is unstable in all his ways" [James 1:6-8]. God wants faith without doubt and seeing strong faith pleases Him. God called Abraham His friend, praised and blessed him because "he staggered not at the promise of God through unbelief, but was strong in faith" [Romans 4:20-21]. He did not doubt about the promises of God.

In your life you need to root out doubt. Daily. When the enemy sends doubts to your mind, opposite of what you know to be God's truth, fight those thoughts. You cannot entertain both doubt and faith at the same time. One counters the other.

Prayer:
Lord, help us to be keen to recognize doubt when it knocks on the door of our minds and to not let it in, nor make it comfortable, but to see it as the enemy of faith that it is.

Scripture of the Day:
"O thou of little faith, whereforth didst thou doubt?" - [Matthew 14:31]

The Word for the Day is "Intercession."

Quote for the Day:
"Jesus Christ carries on intercession for us in heaven; the Holy Ghost carries on intercession in us on earth; and we the saints have to carry on intercession for all men." - Oswald Chambers

We know the prayer of intercession is the act of intervening on behalf of another. It is like we become a mediator or go-between to help solve the problem in someone else's life. We come between the person prayed for and God, to get a desired righteous result for that person.

We have a heavenly intercessor on our behalf. Jesus was prophesied to be an intercessor for us: "because he hath poured out His soul unto death....and he bare the sin of many, and made intercession for the transgressors" [Is 53:12]. One of our benefits of salvation in Jesus is that He 'ever liveth' to make intercession for the saved [Heb 7:25]. What a blessing to know our Savior ever intercedes to the Father on our behalf [Rom 8:34]. We also enjoy the blessing of having a helper when we don't know exactly what we should pray. The Holy Spirit helps our infirmities in prayer and prays in intercession for us according to the will of God, [Rom 8:26-27], what a benefit!

We are to be intercessors on earth for others, for intercessors are too few in the kingdom of God. The Word tells us that when His nation departed from His ways, He 'saw that there was no man, and wondered that there was no intercessor' [Is 59:16]. The Lord also looked for a man among His people to make up the hedge and stand in the gap before Him, but He laments: 'I found none' [Ezek 22:30]. As God's children we are instructed to offer up prayers and intercessions for all men, including those in authority [1 Tim 2:1-2]. We intercede by putting ourselves, spiritually, in the place of another, to be between that person and God. We 'make up the hedge' or stand to provide a shield of protection. We 'stand in the gap,' in the separation of that person from God, to invoke God's grace and mercy to spare, heal, or rescue. We stand on the Word of God for others as if we were praying for ourselves. Exercise your God-given authority, and intercede to rescue and save those in need.

Prayer:
Lord, thank You for the benefits we enjoy by having heavenly intercessions on our behalf by Jesus. We will then also obey and offer intercessions for all men.

Scripture of the Day:
"I exhort therefore, that, first of all, prayers, intercessions, and giving of thanks, be made for all men." -[1 Timothy 2:1]

The Word for the Day is "Whale."

Quote for the Day:
"Never attempt to catch a whale with a minnow." – P.T. Barnum

I sometimes think about the time when God was creating all the animals…and wonder what was on His mind when He envisioned the whale [Genesis 1:21]. Whales are huge creatures of the sea, the blue whale the largest creature that ever lived, up to 100 feet in length, weighing 200 tons. Whales have keen hearing, can dive to great depths and stay submerged for long periods, and when they roar up out of the water it is a sight to see. "He maketh the deep to boil like a pot…upon earth there is not his like" [Job 41:31,33]

Early societies used whale oil in oil lamps and other products creating a whaling industry that nearly killed off the whale. Recent archeologists found bones of large whales, now extinct in the Mediterranean, showing whales once lived in that area where Jonah would have been swallowed up by a giant whale. In the natural it might be unlikely for a person to survive being swallowed by a whale without divine intervention, but God wasn't finished with Jonah yet. So divine intervention was called for in order for Jonah to go to Ninevah as ordained to try to turn the hearts of the people around. I enjoyed rereading this story where it said, "Then Jonah prayed unto the Lord his God out of the fish's belly…and it vomited out Jonah upon the dry land" [Jonah 2:1,10]. I imagine after three days "out of the belly of hell" [vs 2] Jonah was glad indeed to have a second chance to be obedient to God.

Later in Matthew in the New Testament, a comparison is made that as Jonah spent those three horrible days and nights in the whale's belly, so would Jesus spend three days and nights in hell in the heart of the earth. And as Jonah rose from that watery grave, Jesus conquered sin and death and rose from hell triumphant. In Jonah's story he willingly allowed himself to be thrown overboard to his death to save the mariners. And Jesus willingly allowed himself to be crucified to save each of us.

Prayer:
Lord, may we realize how wonderful and miraculous Your creations are…and may we see the lessons You provide through them, knowing all things on earth are in Your Hands.

Scripture of the Day:
"For as Jonah was three days and three nights in the whale's belly; so shall the Son of man be three days and three nights in the heart of the earth." -
[Matthew 12:40]

The Word for the Day is "Confidence."

Quote for the Day:
"Faith is a living, daring confidence in God's grace, so sure and certain that a man could stake his life on it a thousand times." - Martin Luther

Having played several sports in my youth, I always admired those athletes that performed with the highest skills in their sport. I also noticed another factor beyond physical talent that made a huge difference in performance: some athletes possessed a confidence that caused them to outperform others with greater natural talents. I am convinced they obtained confidence the same way anyone does in any endeavor. First, they learned the truth of the correct way to play their sport, then they practiced those mechanics until they played at a high level, which inspired confidence in themselves.

As Christians we should always possess confidence. But many believers seem wishy-washy and timid about their faith when confronting the world. They almost seem apologetic instead of witnessing with bold confidence. How does the Christian walk in confidence? First, we must feel certain about the truth of God. It is impossible to be confident in your faith if you are ignorant of God's Word. We must read the Bible to have the light of God's Truth to penetrate our hearts and minds [Romans 10:17, 12:2]. By knowing God more through His Word, we come to the firm trust that we can rely on God, and our confidence in Him grows.

With the Truth of God and the Trust of God acquired, we then practice our faith. If we live upright, striving to keep sin and worldly pollutions out of our life, our heart does not condemn us, and we have confidence toward God. "And whatsoever we ask, we receive of him, because we keep his commandments, and do those things that are pleasing in his sight" [1 John 3:21-22]. As God confirms and manifests His eternal promises to us, we grow in our self-assurance and confidence that we can live by faith and demonstrate our faith to the world.

Prayer:
Lord, we put our confidence not in man, but in You. We learn of Your Truth from the scriptures, and we grow in confidence exercising our faith and trust in You, that we might boldly witness and shine the light of the Gospel to the world.

Scripture of the Day:
"Cast not away therefore your confidence, which hath great recompense of reward." - [Hebrews 10:35]

May

The Word for the Day is "Born-Again."

Quote for the Day:
"A born-again Christian is someone who has repented of their sins and turned to Christ for their salvation." – Billy Graham

If someone asked you: "What is a Christian?" what would you answer? Most people today seem rather uncertain about what a Christian is. Billy Graham simply defines a Christian as "a person who has made a personal connection with Jesus Christ." Being a Christian is totally different from being religious or just believing in God. You can choose whatever religion or set of beliefs you wish to follow, but being a Christian means to follow in the steps of Jesus. Franklin Graham wrote: "People often use the term Christian as simply a category for describing someone's cultural, religious or family heritage. Other people believe a person is a Christian because he or she attends church or was raised in a godly home. But a Christian is someone who has been 'born again' by the Spirit of God." When this change is vital and real, a person's life will change. They want to follow God's commands, to know His Word, to grow closer to God and to Jesus every day.

If a person does not become "different" and a "new creation" when he or she becomes a Christian, I wonder about the depth and reality of their salvation. Oswald Chambers explained: 'It is impossible for a man to become a Christian by natural reasoning effort, which is simply the working of his own mind; a man becomes a Christian by there being wrought in him 'a new creation,' and that new creation is the forming of the Son of God in him.' 'The old things are passed away; behold they are become new'[2 Corinthians 5:17].

Becoming a Christian begins with a spiritual experience resulting in a changed nature and a new relationship with God. "Being a Christian isn't a physical thing, like which church one attends, or what good deeds or religious practices one does. Being a Christian is experiencing a new birth that fundamentally transforms who you are, from the inside out" [Donna Jones]. The gift of salvation is available to anyone who chooses to accept it. A wise evangelist once said, 'If you are not sure if you are born again, you are probably not.'

Prayer:
Lord, may we come to know You if we have not been truly saved and may we not be deceived in buying into some "religious generality" defining what a Christian is with limited truth.

Scripture of the Day:
"Except a man be born again…he cannot see the Kingdom of God." - [John 3:3]

The Word for the Day is "Faith."

Quote for the Day:
"Grow in the root of all grace, which is faith. Believe God's promises more firmly than ever. Allow your faith to increase in its fullness, firmness, and simplicity."
- Charles Spurgeon

What is faith? I like to think of faith as an absolute conviction, confidence, assurance, and reliance in something. I have heard others simply define it as "totally believing something is so." The Bible tells us "Now faith is the substance of things hoped for, the evidence of things not seen" [Hebrews 11:1]. It is a real, tangible thing, even before we see it. Faith is total trust in God, and every believer should desire for his faith to always increase and grow.

Spurgeon exhorts us to increase our faith in fullness, firmness, and simplicity. First, how do we grow in fullness of faith? The same way you increase an empty water pitcher from empty to full: you pour more water into it. So then if 'faith cometh by hearing, and hearing by the Word of God' [Romans 10:17], we increase fullness of faith by pouring more of the Word of God into ourselves. By reading, learning, and meditating upon the scriptures, we increase in fullness of faith. How does faith increase in firmness? The same way our bodies do, by exercise. It is a natural law that by disuse the muscles become weak. By disuse faith becomes weak, ineffective. At some point a believer must exercise his faith by daring to believe God. God is eager to confirm His word to those who trust in Him by believing [Mark 16:20].

How does faith increase in simplicity? I think the key is to ignore all the voices that try to dissuade us by carnal reasoning, doubt, and unbelief. We must become as an innocent child in simple trust, and believe God just because He said it [Matthew 19:14]!

Prayer:
Lord, we will increase our faith by increasing our knowledge of Your Word, that we might be vessels of greater power to show and demonstrate the Gospel to a lost world.

Scripture of the Day:
"But without faith it is impossible to please him: for he that cometh to God must believe that he is, and that he is a rewarder of them that diligently seek him."
- [Hebrews 11:6]

The Word for the Day is "Creation."

Quote for the Day:
"When we look at the order of creation we form in our mind an image, not of the essence, but of the wisdom of Him who made all things wisely." – St. Gregory of Nyssa

We learn a lot about a photographer, an artist, or even an author by looking at their work. Photos by George Masa or Ansel Adams show the glory of U.S. National Parks—and reflect the photographers' love for them, as artist Jim Gray's paintings reveal the beauty of the Smoky Mountains. Authors portray the beauty of places in words, too, as Zane Gray's books depict the western frontier and author L.M. Montgomery's Anne of Green Gables stories show her love for St. Edward Island in Canada.

God's Word paints a picture of His nature. We see His infinite creativity in all the natural wonders, large and small, in the world. We are awe inspired at vistas across the mountains, sweeping fields of flowers, and the wonder of birth. Nature inspired the psalmist David to write many beautiful lines like: 'The heavens declare the glory of God and the firmament shows His handiwork' [Psalm 19:1].

God's creations reflect Him and they confirm His being and His nature. God's world and His creation live on far beyond an artist's paintings, a photographer's pictures, or an author's stories, showing His creativity through all time. 'In His hand is the soul of every creature and the breath of all mankind' [Job 12:10]. I find it hard to see how anyone could walk in the beauty of God's world and not believe in Him, with His glory all around at every turn.

As God's world and its beauty live on, so does His Word to guide us and show us the way to live. It can ever remind us of God's infinite glory and his love. To look upon the beauty of God's Word is to look into His heart. "O how I love thy law," David wrote, "It is my meditation all the day…How sweet are thy words unto my taste! Yea, sweeter than honey to my mouth…Thy word is a lamp unto my feet, and a light unto my path" [Psalm 119:97-105].

Prayer:
Lord, help us every day to learn of You through the beauty of Your world and its creation and through the beauty and wisdom of Your Word.

Scripture of the Day:
"For the invisible things of him from the creation of the world are clearly seen, being understood by the things that are made, even his eternal power and Godhead; so that they are without excuse." - [Romans 1:20].

The Word for the Day is "Sin."

Quote for the Day:
"The first step in a person's salvation is knowledge of their sin." - Seneca

If I were an oddsmaker, I would give you odds that you would not hear a sermon this next Sunday in your church on "sin." I would almost give the same odds that you would not even hear the word "sin" uttered at all. It seems to be a taboo in the compromised churches today to even mention sin. This is a travesty since the whole point of Jesus coming was to put away sin and free man from satan's hold [Hebrews 9:26; 1 John 3:8].

Sadly, many today do whatever is right in their own eyes because they have not been told the truth about sin [Prov 21:2]. But if a person comes to the revelation of his sin, what is the cure? Only the shed blood of Jesus cleanses away sin: "But if we walk in the light, as he is in the light, we have fellowship one with another, and the blood of Jesus Christ his Son cleanseth us from all sin" [1 John 1:7]. Jesus came to 'put away sin by the sacrifice of himself' [Heb 9:26]. 'Without the shedding of blood there is no remission of sin.' Good works and good intentions are not sufficient; to God they are as 'filthy rags' [Heb 9:22; Isaiah 64:6].

The good news is that every man can be set free from the sin nature by the blood of Jesus and receiving Him as Lord. A man must repent and trust in the sacrifice of Jesus for his salvation. He can then become a new creature in his spirit man and walk in a newness of life [2 Cor 5:17, Rom 6:4]. God then gives us a new spirit whereby we cry 'Abba, Father' [Rom 8:15], for now through Jesus we are a son of God [1 John 3:2]. The old 1876 Robert Lowry hymn will rise up in our hearts to sing: "What can wash away my sin? Nothing but the blood of Jesus; What can make me whole again? Nothing but the blood of Jesus. Oh! precious is the flow, That makes me white as snow; No other fount I know, Nothing but the blood of Jesus."

Prayer:
Lord Jesus, thank You for washing away the sins of this 'good ole boy' and setting me free to serve the living God!

Scripture of the Day:
"And He is the propitiation for our sins: and not for ours only, but also for the sins of the whole world." - [1 John 2:2]

The Word for the Day is "Lead."

Quote for the Day:
"A man who wants to lead the orchestra must turn his back on the crowd."
-Max Lucado

I love walking down a quiet pathway in a garden filled with beauty or following pathways tucked away in pretty parks. J.L. and I love hiking the trails and paths in the Smoky Mountains near our home, too—but sometimes a pathway we're following leads to an intersection and we're not sure which way to go. We want to follow the safe path, the path that will lead to the right destination, but we're sometimes uncertain which to take.

Throughout our lives we come to turns and intersections in our pathway. If we are wise, we stop to pray that 'God will teach and show us the right way, lead us in a plain and clear path' [Psalm 27:11]. Occasionally we barrel on down a path of our choice, following and leaning to our own understanding and then run into trouble. We often remember at that point the counsel in Proverbs 3:5 to 'lean not to our own understanding'…and realize we should have sought God more, before moving ahead, and waited on His counsel and direction. God did promise us that if we acknowledge Him that 'he would direct our paths' [Proverbs 3:6] and make our paths plain, straight and right [Psalm 32:8]. The key is to remember to ask God for the right directions in life so you can hear the words you yearn to hear: "This is the way, walk ye in it" [Isaiah 30:21].

All life pathways are best when they are God's best pathways for our lives. Psalm 32:8 says: "I will instruct thee and teach thee in the way which thou shalt go: I will guide thee with mine eye." If we ask of God and wait on God, He will lead us in the right way.

Prayer:
Teach us the right way and the paths we need to take today, Lord…and show us to the right or to the left after Your will.

Scripture of the Day:
"Teach me thy way O Lord and lead me in a plain path." - [Psalm 27:11]

The Word for the Day is "Trust"

Quote for the Day:
"If people like you, they'll listen to you, but if they trust you, they'll do business with you." - Zig Ziglar

I picked up my vehicle, I use in my business, from the repair shop early this morning, and tonight, after a long day with 300 miles travel, I was just thanking God for the excellent service and repairs I received. I thank God that many years ago I discovered this shop which I can totally trust when I need my car repaired. I trust this business because over many years it has proved trustworthy. Jim, the owner, has always been candid and honest. When I take my vehicle in, he tells me exactly what is wrong, what it will require to fix it, and gives me an accurate figure of how much it will cost for repairs. The work is always reliable, and the problem gets fixed. I have recommended this shop to many of my friends and they also have enjoyed excellent service. It is good to know someone you can trust when you need them.

I think learning to trust the Lord follows this pattern. First, we cannot trust someone we don't know. I trust Jim with my vehicle because I know him. God is easy to trust when we take the time and effort to learn of Him through fellowship, in prayer, and in learning His Word. The study of the Bible is key, and says 'In whom ye also trusted, *after* that ye heard the word of truth' [Ephesians 1:13]. We tell God our problem that needs fixing, we find the promise of God that applies to our problem in the Word, and then we pray and trust knowing that God is reliable to confirm His Word [Mark 16:20]. Trust in God grows as we are blessed with experiences of His faithfulness.

It can be a challenge to trust in the spiritual before we see the manifestation of answers in the natural. But faith is 'the substance of things hoped for, the evidence of things *not* seen' [Hebrews 11:1]. We must trust that the thing we hope for is already a substance (reality) before we see it, and then stand fast in believing that God will affirm His Word and prove Himself totally trustworthy.

Prayer:
Lord, we resolve to trust You at all times and You have promised "Blessed is he that maketh the Lord his trust" [Psalm 40:4].

Scripture of the Day:
"Trust in the Lord with all thine heart; and lean not unto thine own understanding. In all thy ways acknowledge Him, and He shall direct thy paths." -
[Proverbs 3:5-6].

The Word for the Day is" Garden."

Quote for the Day:
"A garden is a grand teacher." – Gertrude Jekyll

Man began in a garden and one of Adam and Eve's first tasks was to tend and keep the garden. In Tennessee, where I live, this is the time of year when many begin to plow up and put in their gardens. Many spiritual truths and wise understandings for life can be linked to the practice of gardening, and God often used understandings about them in His Word in the Old and New Testaments.

Gardens need to be planted with the right plants and seed and they need to be well tended. Neglect in a garden, and in a life, spoils it, making it less satisfying and fruitful. After God created man 'He took him and put him into the Garden of Eden He had created to dress it and keep it' [Genesis 2:15]. The Lord expects us to care for the garden of our lives, to take good care of all we're blessed with and given by Him. We are to be 'like a watered garden' [Jeremiah 31:12], not defiled with mingled weed and seed [Leviticus 19:19]. We're to be rich with growth bringing forth good fruit and a rich harvest [Matthew 7:17].

Poor traits of a natural gardener are the same poor traits we should not cultivate in the garden of our lives—laziness, inattentiveness, carelessness, apathy, ingratitude, ignorance, disrespect, planting and acting out of timing and out of season. We should be a fruitful garden 'planted by the rivers of water, bringing forth fruit' in our lives [Psalm 1:3] like "love, joy, peace, long suffering, goodness, gentleness, faith, meekness, temperance" [Galatians 5:22].

Like a gardener, we know, too, that 'what we sow we will reap,' [Galatians 6:7]. If we sow our lives, our gardens, full of wrong and un-virtuous things, these things will spring up and crowd and hinder the growth of that which is good. Our job is to grow in the Lord, to grow in grace and in His knowledge [Ephesians 4:15; 2 Peter 3:18]. Our gardens and our lives should 'be established in righteousness' [Isaiah 54:14]. When we tend the gardens of our lives as we should, we are promised a rich harvest, blessings and reward.

Prayer:
Lord, we thank You for all the lessons we can learn about life from the garden. We yearn to be good gardeners of our lives so that You will look upon us and be pleased at what you see.

Scripture of the Day:
"And the Lord shall guide thee continually...and thou shalt be like a watered garden, and like a spring of water, whose waters fail not." - [Isaiah 58:11]

The Word for the Day is "Sow."

Quote for the Day:
"Look around for a place to sow a few seeds." - Henry Van Dyke

My grandfather farmed his land in Tellico Plains. In the Spring he worked his fields preparing the soil and making ready for planting. He then planted his crops, waited for a time, then reaped the harvest. I know this for sure: he *never* reaped a single crop without planting seeds first.

Living things in the natural world work according to this seed principle; everything living comes from a seed, even humans. The Kingdom of God operates according to this seed principle of planting and reaping. The Word tells us the Kingdom of God is as if a man plants seed into the ground. He waits until the seed should spring up in stages to full growth, and then he harvests the fruit. He doesn't know how the seed grows up, but it happens [Mark 4:26-29].

So, how do we sow spiritual seed to get a harvest of our need, whether it be a spiritual or material need? The seed we sow must be the incorruptible seed, the Word of God [1 Peter 1:23]. We find the promise in the Word that applies to our need, then in faith plant that spiritual seed into our heart. We keep our hearts as good ground for the seed to produce by continuing in faith and patience. Then, as the scripture in Mark 4 above explains, the incorruptible seed produces in due time the intended fruit, letting us reap the harvest we desired.

Sow the promise of God into your heart, keep your heart (the soil) good, wait patiently for the seed to grow [Hebrews 10:36-38], and let God bring forth an abundant harvest of the desired fruit (promise).

Prayer:
Thank you Lord, that we sow the Word of God into our hearts and with patience receive the promises.

Scripture of the Day:
"And he said, So is the kingdom of God, as if a man should cast seed (sow) into the ground." - [Mark 4:26]

The Word for the Day is "Praise."

Quote for the Day:
"It is thrilling to know we can give God something He does not have—the praise of our hearts." – Rex Humbard

God is surely "worthy of praise" [Psalm 18:3]. He saves us, loves us, keeps us, and comforts us. God guides, blesses, and provides for us. When the Lord has done so much for us, and when He does so much for us every day, we should always be eager to be thankful—as we would to anyone who was overly good to us. David asked: "What shall I render unto God for all His benefits toward me?" and then answered: "I will offer to Thee the sacrifice of thanksgiving" [Psalm 116:12, 17].

Praise is a vital part of a life truly surrendered to God. To praise means to express our love, admiration, and thanks to God in words and song…not to just think about it. Without gratefulness, we become a little self-centered, like a child who takes everything for granted they are given. Giving praise helps to keep our hearts right and our relationship loving, close, and strong with God.

Praising God is beneficial to us, too. Praising the Lord releases His power, brings help to defeat the enemy, ushers in miracles, lifts our spirits, draws us closer to God, and brings us directly into God's presence. Hebrews 13:15 says "let us offer up the sacrifice of praise." Taking the time in our busy lives to praise God and to pray may seem a sacrifice when we first begin but praising quickly becomes a joy and a blessing. It moves our focus from ourselves to God. Evil seldom hangs around when you're praising God, either, nor does a dark or discouraged mood. We always come away renewed when we praise.

I've often found the best time to praise God is when you least feel like it, when the enemy has sent problems, when hopes have been shattered by some worldly event or happening, when you are facing a serious trial or sorrow. But because God "inhabits the praises of His people," I always feel His presence come and my Spirit lift when I begin to praise [Psalm 22:3].

Prayer:
Lord, help us always to remember to praise You, knowing that praise is the path that will always bring us closer to Your power, Your grace, and Your love.

Scripture of the Day:
"I will praise thee O Lord with my whole heart…I will be glad and rejoice in thee." - [Psalm 9:1-2]

The Word for the Day is "Inheritance."

Quote for the Day:
"This is all the inheritance I give to my dear family. The religion of Christ will give them one which will make them rich indeed." - Patrick Henry

Anyone who receives an inheritance counts it a joy and a benefit, whether the inheritance be large or small. However, if a benefactor is unaware, uninformed, or ignorant of his inheritance, it does no good for him if he does not possess it. God wants the understanding of His people to be enlightened to the riches of His glory in their inheritance, and to know His exceeding greatness of power to us who believe [Ephesians 1:18-20].

When we are delivered from the power of darkness and translated into the Kingdom of God through salvation in Jesus Christ, we are made partakers of the inheritance of the saints in light [Colossians 1:12]. We are given an awesome and glorious inheritance that is incorruptible, not subject to decay or death, undefiled, pure and holy, and that is eternal and 'fadeth not away,' [1 Peter 1:4]. Since our inheritance is eternal, starting at salvation and lasting forever, God wants us to believe for our benefits in Him *now*.

Here are just some of the blessings we inherit now: we inherit the earth and delight ourselves in the abundance of peace [Psalm 37:11]; the wise shall inherit glory [Proverbs 3:35]; God's wisdom shall cause us to inherit substance and fill our treasures [Proverbs 8:21]; the kingdom of God is prepared forever for our occupation [Matthew 25:34]; through faith and patience we inherit the promises of God [Hebrews 6:12]; we inherit the blessings of God [1 Peter 3:9].

Having obtained Eternal Life through our salvation in Jesus and being sealed with the Holy Spirit of promise, let us *now* believe God for His blessings in our inheritance and manifest the praise of His glory and power, both now and forever [Ephesians 1:11-14].

Prayer:
Lord, help us manifest the reality and benefits of our eternal inheritance in You, that we might bring praise and glory to Your name.

Scripture of the Day:
"Knowing that of the Lord ye shall receive the reward of the inheritance: for ye serve the Lord Christ." - [Colossians 3:24]

The Word for the Day is "The Way."

Quote for the Day:
"I will love the light because it shows me the way." – Og Mandino

Jesus Christ is called "the way" because it is by and through Him we obtain eternal life [John 14:6]. In the Old and New Testament God has laid out the pattern our lives should follow as His children. In our walk and life in the Lord there is always one better way, one right way to follow in all things. Daily the choice emerges to take it or not. Often the "broad" way, the world's way, is more appealing than the narrow way and the pathway God desires [Matthew 7:13-14]. But to not follow in God's way leads to negative consequences in our lives and often brings sorrows and troubles.

Every day we have a choice to go the way of the Lord or not. When there is a choice, a turning or a crossroads, you should always want to take the good way, the right way, the way where there is light, the way of truth. One day driving home with my young children in the car, I felt the Spirit speak to me to turn off to the right and go home a different way. My son said, "Mom, this isn't the right way." Even he knew this route home was a longer one. Not understanding why God wanted me to take this other route, I obeyed. Later when watching the news that night my husband and I learned there had been a massive wreck, with many injured, just a little further down the main road we would have traveled on. How grateful I was I had listened to God's counsel. In all things God knows the best way for us to travel in our lives, wanting to watch over and keep us safe.

The Word advises "teach me O Lord the way…and I shall keep it unto the end. Give me understanding…I shall observe it with my whole heart…make me to go in the path of thy commandments" [Psalm 119:33-35]. We should pray not to choose the way of lying, the false way, the way of the wicked, and the way of the fool. We should try not to follow the way of the slothful man, the way of the disobedient and froward, and the way of the heathen. If we lean only to our own understanding and intelligence, that will not be enough either. But in all things we need to trust God and let Him direct our paths [Proverbs 3:5-6].

Prayer:
Lord, help us to lean to You to show us the way for each day in our lives, knowing You want to lead us to truth, life, happiness, and safety.

Scripture of the Day:
"I am the way, the truth, and the life." - [John 14:6]

The Word for the Day is "Peculiar."

Quote for the Day:
"The plot for all of those who are in the real life drama of Christianity is to remember that we are a 'peculiar' people, a purchased possesion with a purpose, and duty to serve, and a future." - Pastor John Williams

It seems to be human nature to want to fit in with the crowd. Even from our youth we want to feel like we "belong" with the crowd we associate with. A 1964 oldies tune "The 'In' Crowd," written by Billy Page and originally performed by Dobie Gray, expresses the desire to be "in" with the in crowd, to go where they go and know what they know, to follow their way of walking and talking to be cool. The urge to conform is strong.

Most people just want to settle into the "norm;" they don't want to be too different or stand out in any way for fear of being peculiar, unusual, strange, or an "odd-ball." The biggest insult for them is for someone to say "You're weird!" So, the safety net is to conform, go along with the crowd, embrace the conventional norms so that you're not perceived as different or "weird."

But God wants His people to be peculiar in a different way. He wants us to be special, distinctive, distinguished, and unique, different from the usual or normal. God called Israel to be His peculiar people, high above all other nations in praise, in name, in honor, and to be a holy people unto the Lord [Deuteronomy 26:18-19].

Likewise, Jesus has called us out of darkness into His marvelous light to be a peculiar people to show forth His praises [1 Peter 2:9]. To follow Jesus and be like Him is to have the supernatural peace, joy, and blessings of God, and to do the supernatural works that Jesus did. We may still be in the world, but definitely not of the world, when we follow the One that makes us His peculiar treasure [John 15:19, Exodus 19:5]. Dare to be peculiar in Jesus Christ and you will show forth His praises as men are drawn to this divine escape from the unhappy norm and darkness of this world into His marvelous light.

Prayer:
Lord, thank You that You have given us the privilege of being peculiar people of God that we might partake of the divine nature.

Scripture of the Day:
"Who gave himself for us, that he might redeem us from all iniquity, and purify unto himself a peculiar people, zealous of good works." - [Titus 2:14]

The Word for the Day is "River."

Quote for the Day:
"He who does not know his way... should take a river for his guide." - Blaise Pascal

I saw a wise sign at a craft festival we visited titled: "Advice from a River" and decided rivers have a lot to teach us. It read: "Go with the flow. Immerse yourself in nature. Slow down and meander. Go around the obstacles. Be thoughtful of those downstream. Stay current. The beauty is in the journey" [L. Shamir].

These are some good thoughts for us as Christians, too. We often forget to enjoy the journey of life or to see the beauty of the journey. We get so busy, so caught up in so many things, so focused on the problems and the obstacles. We each need to slow down more, to trust God more, and to let God show us the way around the obstacles. The river always flows on. So constant—that's one of its attributes. We should flow on constant and true, too, following the leadership of the Holy Spirit, leaning to God, trusting in Jesus. A way for us to stay current, as Christians, is by spending quality time in the Word and in prayer. That's our place of strength, of peace, of guidance. Psalm 46:1 says: 'God is *our* refuge and strength, a very present help in time of trouble.'

We need to slow down and meander more—taking time for the beauty of life, savoring it, living it—flowing with purpose and meaning, not just rushing on. And not looking back on our days and weeks either and seeing we've accomplished little to nothing, grown stagnant and stale. Like the river, we always need to flow on with beauty and meaning—following God's unique purpose and plan every day. God *has* a plan and purpose for you individually and for me, just as He does for every single river and stream. Jeremiah 29:11 says: 'I know the plans I have for you, declares the Lord, plans to prosper you and not to harm you, plans to give you hope and a future.'

The river is beautiful and wise and we can learn from it. So slow down, meander, find that purpose God has for you in each day, each week—and then, like the river "go with the flow," constant and true to the One who guides you and gives you life.

Prayer:
Lord, may we each stop, listen to the river, and think on its lessons and become more "river-like," more constant, true, directed, and aware in our lives.

Scripture of the Day:
"And he showed me a pure river of water of life, clear as crystal, proceeding out of the throne of God and of the Lamb." - [Revelations 22:1].

The Word for the Day is "Looking."

Quote for the Day:
"People are looking for something a little more stable; people are feeling they need to get closer to God." - Dolly Parton

A song by The Valentinos in the early 1960's, "Lookin' For A Love," sang about looking here and there, searching everywhere for a love 'to call my own.' In life it seems we sometimes have to do a lot of looking for things we seek for ourselves. We search every clothing shop in the mall to find the new clothing that fits and suits us just right. I can look through my whole garage to find that one tool I need to fix the lawn mower. We often have to do a lot of looking in our natural life to find the things we need or want.

In like manner, the things we want to obtain in our spiritual life require looking and seeking. Regretfully, many people look to the natural, carnal things to seek spiritual truth and answers. They look to the ways and opinions of the world to try to find spiritual guidance. But this looking will not profit. Jesus said 'no man having set his hand to the plow or committed to follow God and looking back, seeking mammon instead of God, is fit for the kingdom of God' [Luke 9:62].

The Word of God tells us we are to look 'unto Jesus the author and finisher of our faith' [Heb 12:2]. If He's the author, He has left something for us to read: the Word of God. We look for all our answers, for the wisdom, guidance and instruction we need, in the Bible He authored. Our faith and knowledge of God grows as we know His Word [Romans 10:17].

Jesus is also the finisher of our faith. When I played baseball, I was a pitcher and sometimes I was called on to be a "closer" or finisher of a game. I would relieve the starting pitcher and finish the game, hopefully with a win. Jesus wants us to apply our knowledge of God by standing in faith, and then He is the finisher of our faith. He brings the fulfillment of His Word to us, and Jesus is a *sure* finisher [2 Corinthians 2:14]. He always wins!

Prayer:
Lord, we purpose to keep ourselves in the love of God, looking for Thy mercy unto eternal life [Jude 21].

Scripture of the Day:
"Looking unto Jesus the author and finisher of our faith; who for the joy that was set before him endured the cross, despising the shame, and is set down at the right hand of the throne of God." - [Hebrews 12:2]

The Word for the Day is "Angels."

Quote for the Day:
"One of the ways God carries out your protection, His covenant and your deliverance is through angels." -Kenneth Copeland

There is no area possibly more mistaught than that of angels. Many people persist in believing they will become angels when they die, versus saints in heaven who will help to judge and govern the angels [1 Cor 6:3; Col 1:12). Books and movies have helped to popularize the idea that angels pop down to earth on assignment to meddle in the affairs of men and women, fall in love with mortals, and often wish they could return to live on earth again—a preposterous idea if anyone thinks about it clearly for a minute.

God created all the heavens and the host of heaven [Genesis 2:1]. Just as God gave man free will to love and serve Him, He gave the same free will to the angels of heaven. Unfortunately Lucifer, or satan, an angel of high order, became rebellious, wanting to raise his throne above God [Isaiah 14:14]. No longer content to serve under God and greedy for self aggrandizement and power, he led other angels into sin and rebellion, causing them to lose their first, precious estate under God's love and protection and to be cast into darkness and hell [Jude 6; 2 Peter 2:4]. So we now have two host factions, the good serving God and the evil opposing Him.

Many classifications of the angels of heaven are mentioned in the Bible such as cherubim and seraphim, and there are doubtless more beyond our knowledge. God's angels have personality, identity, and names, and some are mentioned like Lucifer and Gabriel. Many Bible stories talk about the intervention of angels in the lives of men and women, and we are assured there are specific ministering angels, like guardian angels, who minister and aid in the lives of God's people in the earth [Heb1:14; Ps 34:7; Matt 18:10]. For our comfort we know that God's angels dwell in the heavens with Him, carrying out His Will on the earth, and that our own citizenship, too, will one day be in heaven [Phil 3:20]. We will be the saints of God, ever with the Lord and His angels, helping God to rule over His universe [Eph 2:19; 1 Thess 4:16-17].

Prayer:
Lord, thank You for the angels of Heaven who serve You and for those who give us aid and protection here on the earth.

Scripture of the Day:
"For he shall give his angels charge over thee, to keep thee in all thy ways." -
  [Psalm 91:11]

The Word for the Day is "Set."

Quote for the Day:
"Growing older with grace is possible for all who set their hearts and minds on the Giver of grace, the Lord Jesus Christ." - Billy Graham

I have a fond childhood memory of visiting my grandmother's farm in the summer and remembering her mealtime ritual. When preparing the family meal, she made everyone leave the kitchen except for one or two helpers. We all scattered outside or to the porch and waited. When the meal was ready, grandmother would come outside and announce: "The table's set, now come on!" That meant all was ready for the family to come to the kitchen to enjoy a delicious meal.

The Lord has set some special blessings before His people to enjoy, too. In Genesis 1:17, we are reminded that God made the sun and moon and set the stars in the firmament, a delight for us to look up and see in the night sky. God also set before us a blessing if we obey His commandments and walk in His ways, promising He would set us on high if we would hearken to His voice in obedience [Deut 11:26-27; 28:1]. We are promised He has set before us life and good and that He will always hear when we call unto Him [Deut 30:15; Psalm 4:3]. God sets safety and protection for us, setting us in the way of His own steps and assuring us He will bring us out of any pits or problems that come our way, setting our feet on a rock [Psalm 12:5; 40:2; 85:13]. So many scriptures confirm that the Lord sets before us a banquet of blessings!

The Lord expects us to set some things too. Colossians 3:2 tells us to set our affections on things above, not on things on the earth. God wants our heart to love and be devoted to the things of heaven and not on things of the world. We should 'seek first the kingdom of God, and His righteousness' [Matthew 6:33] by devotion to God first in all our ways, and we are to set our hope in God first before all others [Psalm 78:7].

Just as a football player gets "set" before the snap to be prepared to perform his position, we set our affections on things above to perform God's will and put us in position to receive the blessings God has set before us.

Prayer:
Lord, we set our affections on You and things above and we thank You for the awesome blessings that You have set for Your obedient people.

Scripture of the Day:
"Set your affection on things above, not on things on the earth." [Colossians 3:2]

The Word for the Day is "According To."

Quote for the Day:
"We have to understand that the Lord is only going to move according to our faith."
– Tamara Anderson

During Jesus ministry, when fame went out that God healed through His hands, two blind men began to follow him crying out for his healing mercy. Jesus said to them, "Believe ye that I am able to do this? They said unto him, Yea, Lord. Then touched he their eyes, saying, According to your faith be it unto you. And their eyes were opened" [Matthew 9:27-30]. As this story shows it was "according to" their faith that healing came to them. If they'd responded, "Well, I don't know" or "I heard you heal people so I thought I'd give it a shot" the end of this story might have been different. Often God wants to act, yearns to act and to help on our behalf but our unbelief holds Him back. He, in general, cannot step past our faith or trample over our entrenched unbelief to get to us. We must come to Him in a receptive state, believing God can provide and wants to provide what we need. Of what purpose would it be for God to push past our limited belief only to have our words of unbelief and doubt rise up afterward and disannul what God had done? No, the key is always to come in a believing state of mind.

All things operate according to God's Word and like the blind men, we need to know God's Word on a matter, align our faith with that Word, and then speak and stand in that Word to receive our greatest blessing. This is one of the main reasons the enemy fights to keep you from reading the Bible, studying it and establishing it in your heart. He knows how powerful The Word is and how your faith is built and strengthened every time you read and study it [Psalm 119:105]. Out in the world, people know their legal rights and stand in them but all too often people are unsure and wishy-washy about their spiritual rights. If you don't know your rights, either in the natural or spiritual, you can't stand in them in confidence when attacked wrongfully in any area of your life. In a sense it's not 'the truth that sets you free,' it's the truth you know that sets you free and the confidence you have in that truth [John 8:32].

Prayer:
Lord, help me to strengthen my knowledge of the Word of God so I can rightly say, "Yea, Lord, I believe" in complete faith and confidence so Your Best can come to me.

Scripture of the Day:
"Strengthen thou me according unto thy word." - [Psalm 119:28]

The Word for the Day is "Afar."

Quote for the Day:
"Seek not for fresher founts afar, just drop your bucket where you are." - Sam Walter
Foss

Isn't it a blessing when something we seek or delight in, but seems afar to us, is
brought near? Both my son and daughter have jobs in states that are far from
Tennessee and I don't get to see them very often. But when they call unexpectedly and say they are coming for a visit, what a joy it is. I hold fond thoughts of
my children in my heart all the time, but it's always good to see them when their
work schedule allows.

Lin and I take hikes in the Great Smoky Mountains and sometimes we hike a trail
to a destination that seems far off on a mountain ridge we see in the distance. But,
we continue walking and eventually reach our goal that now seems near and not
far. In life we are sometimes faced with problems or situations we need answers
to now, but the answers seem inaccessible and afar to us.

We know that in this life we will have tribulations [John 16:33] and in our trials
of faith God can seem far away. This is a device of the enemy to try to discourage
us and sabotage our faith. The trial can be of a personal nature involving family,
friends, work relationships, or personal relationships that need repair and restor-
aton. The trial can be a financial or a job need. Sometimes it can be a personal
health problem we are enduring. God may seem far away when our answers to
these trials have not manifested yet.

But the Lord is near us, not afar, as Psalm 145:18-19 says: "The Lord is nigh unto
all them that call upon Him, to all that call upon Him in truth. He will fulfill the
desire of them that fear Him: He also will hear their cry, and will save them." Jesus has promised that He is always with us [Matthew 28:20]. Draw nigh to God,
and He will draw nigh to you [James 4:8]. He will come with awesome things to
answer your prayers as you stand in faith and confidence.

Prayer:
Lord, we thank You that You will never leave us or foresake us, but that You are
always near to be our ever present help in times of trouble.

Scripture of the Day:
"By terrible things in righteousness wilt thou answer us, O God of our salvation;
who art the confidence of all the ends of the earth, and of them that are afar off
upon the sea." - [Psalm 65:5]

The Word for the Day is "Discipline."

Quote for the Day:
"With self-discipline most anything is possible." - Theodore Roosevelt

Discipline isn't always a word we like to think about too much. The word hints of self-restraints and demands we often try to avoid in life. But the level of discipline in a person's life tells a lot about his or her life, character, success, and faith. Tertullian, in his early Christian writings, insisted you could judge the quality of a person's faith from the way they behaved and he claimed discipline was an index to a person's doctrine or beliefs.

When we were children discipline was imposed on us in most areas of our lives, but as we became adults we began creating our own guidelines, self-control, and discipline. In life, we soon learned the bridge to accomplishing most things of worth and value seemed to demand self-discipline and perserverance. In all arenas we also learned that self-disciplined people are more successful, healthier, and happier in their lives than those undisciplined, unfocused, and disorganized.

God wants our lives to be disciplined spiritually, patterned after His Nature, and for the disciplined fruits of the spirit to be evident in us [Galatians 5:22-23]. None of this comes easily without development of the spiritual man because only the discipline of spiritual growth helps an individual renew and change inwardly to become someone sold out to God [Colossians 4:12; 2 Peter 3:18]. The only route to a changed, disciplined spiritual life is through the surrender of self and through giving disciplined time to the growth of faith every day, through prayer for guidance and understanding, and through studying God's Word with diligence [Ephesians 4:13-15].

Prayer:
Lord, help us to develop the reliance in You we need to live an ordered spiritual life, pleasing to You in every way.

Scripture of the Day:
"He who refuseth instruction [and discipline] despiseth his own soul: but he that heareth reproof getteth understanding." - [Proverbs 15:32]

The Word for the Day is "Calling."

Quote for the Day:
"When you have a sense of calling, whether it's to be a musician, soloist, artist, in one of the technical fields, or a plumber, there is something deep and enriching when you realize it isn't just a casual choice, it's a divine calling. It's not limited to vocational Christian service by any means." - Charles R. Swindoll

We all admire those people who seem to have known and achieved the individual calling for their lives. We respect and maybe envy somewhat those lucky individuals who are convinced they are performing their life's calling. Sometimes we make the mistake of thinking that God's callings are only in the various Christian ministries. But as Swindoll points out in the quote of the day, God's callings are not limited to just vocational Christian service. God's callings can be in other vocations which are needed in this world. What would we do without plumbers, teachers, laborers, parents and all the other workers that fulfill society's needs?

We can also make the mistake of thinking that just because we are not presently involved in some special work or vocation, that we have no calling of God for our lives. This is a lie of the enemy. God has a high calling for each believer [Philippians 3:14]. God has a holy calling for each of us, sometimes more than one in a lifetime, that is not based on anything we offer in the natural, but according to His own purpose and grace [2 Timothy 1:9]. We should press toward this calling of God for us, always seeking to grow in Him.

What is this calling in Christ Jesus? The Word tells us that God wishes to give us wisdom and revelation that our understanding might be enlightened to know what is the hope of His calling [Ephesians 1:17-18]. We are called so "we might come into a perfect man, unto the measure of the stature of the fullness of Christ"[Ephesians 4:13]. We are to grow more and more into the image and fullness of Christ Jesus that God may fulfill all the good pleasure of His goodness, and the work of faith with power [2 Thess 1:11]. Our job is to be at peace and conform more and more to the image of Jesus, and God will show us His will for our lives and bless us with the special callings that He chooses for us.

Prayer:
Lord, thank you that we have a High and Holy calling in Christ Jesus to be partakers of all your goodness and to perform our faith with power.

Scripture of the Day:
"I press toward the mark for the prize of the high calling of God in Christ Jesus." - [Philippians 3:14]

The Word for the Day is "Stone."

Quote for the Day:
"Every block of stone has a statue inside it and it is the task of the sculptor to discover it." – Michelangelo

The great artist and sculptor Michelangelo wrote that he could see the sculpture in the stone and felt it was the 'sculptor's hand that could break the spell to free the figures slumbering in the stone.' Similarly God sees the potential in every life. He yearns to help to bring the best in each person's life to its full potential. Often life is filled with stumbling stones that get in the way of individuals reaching their best, that block the way. God can raise each of us up, if we believe that He can and believe that He will. "Nothing is impossible to God" and there is nothing God can't do if we believe and let Him work through us [Luke 1:37].

We are meant to be 'lively stones, full of life, built up into a spiritual house, acceptable to God.' Jesus was the chief corner stone, made the head, and God wants to fashion each of us in His image to bring us "out of darkness into His marvelous light" [1 Peter 2:5-9]. There is no stone, no problem in your life that God can't help you overcome or miraculously move out of your life. The miracles of the Bible show us how often God opened the waters to lead His people through them, brought water out of hard rock, made the walls of a fortress fall to the ground. He can move any stone, any obstacle, any problem out of your life if you have faith to believe He can and if you want Him to. Some people like to cling to the stones and problems in their lives. The stones become excuses for not growing in some way, for not working, for not being willing to discipline the life to change. There are some who hold to their burdens, their illnesses, their problems, because they provide an excuse not to allow God to bring change, which might require a discipline and a personal effort they want to avoid.

A huge stone, rolled in front of the grave where Jesus lay after death, did not keep Him there. God supernaturally rolled the stone away and Jesus rose from the dead [Luke 24:2-4]. When Jesus' friend Lazarus died, the stone rolled in front of his grave did not keep Lazarus from being raised from the dead either. Martha worried the problem too great to resolve but said to Jesus in faith, "But I know, that even now, whatsoever though wilt ask of God, God will give it thee" [John 11:22]. And Lazarus walked out of the tomb in his grave clothes.

Prayer:
Lord, let no stone keep us from all You have for us in this life and beyond.

Scripture of the Day:
"Take ye away the stone." - [John 11:39]

The Word for the Day is "Yea."

Quote for the Day:
"I build on Christ, the rock of ages; on his sure mercies described in his word, and on his promises, all which I know are yea and amen." - John Wesley

The word for the day, yea, means "yes" in today's language. How pleasing it is to hear the word "yes" to our wants and desires that are good and upright. Sometimes, of course, wisdom and prudence require the answer to be "no" to things that would be negative to our lives. Unfortunately, some Christians have a hard time believing that God's answer to all His good and precious promises to us is "yes." Some believe God would say no when we would say yes to those same requests from those we love. For instance, assuming you are a loving parent, you would agree with the following between child and parent:
"Daddy, do you love me?"
"Of course I do, I will always love you."
"Daddy, will you protect me from harm and keep me safe?"
"I will always be your protector."
"Daddy, will you always tell me what is the right thing to do?"
"Yes, I will always give you the best advice."
"Daddy, will you still love me if I mess up sometimes?"
"Yes, I will help you get fixed, and I will still love you always."

Why do we easily believe we would always be good and loving to our own kids, but doubt that God would be equally good and loving to us? Some Christians even believe God would put something bad on them or their kids to teach them a lesson of some kind. Yet we would never contemplate such an evil thought against our own! The Word tells us that *all,* not some, of the promises of God are yea (yes) and amen (so be it) in Christ Jesus. Jeremiah 29:11-13 says: "For I know the thoughts that I think toward you, saith the Lord, thoughts of peace, and not of evil, to give you an expected end. Then shall ye call upon me, and ye shall go and pray unto me, and I will hearken unto you. And ye shall seek me, and find me, when ye shall search for me with all your heart." What do you need from God? Search with all your heart the Word and find the promise you need, then believe and trust God for His answer is "Yes!"

Prayer:
Thank you Heavenly Father that your promises to us in Jesus are always yes.

Scripture of the Day:
"For all the promises of God in him are yea, and in him Amen, unto the glory of God by us." - [2 Corinthians 1:20]

The Word for the Day is "Stumble."

Quote for the Day:
"Nobody trips over mountains. It is the small pebble that causes you to stumble."
- Ralph Waldo Emerson

As a girl at summer camp, one of the scariest times was walking alone from my tent to the latrine in the middle of the night. Even with a flashlight, it was easy to trip and stumble and my imagination ran wild about what the sounds and noises I heard might be. Later, when J.L. and I were hiking in the mountains once, we underestimated our return time and got caught on the trail after dark, with no flashlight with us. Believe me, there is nothing darker than a trail in the Smoky Mountains once dark falls. I don't think any of us likes to get caught in total darkness anywhere. It's frightening. We can't see or find our way.

In areas of faith, we often stumble and fall when we hold little light or truth in us. John 11:10 says: "But if a man walk in the night, he stumbleth, because there is no light in him." The world is often a dark place, full of pitfalls and difficulties, but with the Lord guiding our path and way, we can avoid most of life's problems and walk safely through our days. Two things help to guide and direct our paths: (1) the guidance we gain from the Word of God, and (2) the inner witness, direction, and guidance we receive directly from God through His Holy Spirit. Psalm 119:105 promises "Thy Word is a lamp unto my feet, and a light unto my path" assuring us the Bible will teach us how to walk through life as we should, showing us the way to walk, even in difficult times, like a lantern might light a dark path. God lovingly promises to be with us through all our days and nights, guiding and leading us, even in the dark times. Jesus promised "I am the light of the world: he that followeth me shall not walk in darkness, but shall have the light of life" [John 8:12].

Sadly, many do not know God well or study His Word diligently to gain the Light they need to keep them from stumbling in dark places. They often bewail when they fall. Personally I'm going to seek to gain all the Light I can for my life because walking in darkness, tripping and stumbling, is not fun.

Prayer:
Lord, help me build myself up on my most Holy Faith every day, ever gaining more light, staying close to You, so my paths by day and night will be right ones.

Scripture of the Day:
"Then shalt thou walk in thy way safely, and thy foot shall not stumble." -
[Proverbs 3:23]

The Word for the Day is "Image."

Quote for the Day:
"This perfection is the restoration of man to the state of holiness from which he fell, by creating him anew in Christ Jesus, and restoring to him that image and likeness to God which he lost." - Adam Clarke

You look in a mirror—you see your image. That is, you see your outward appearance. You may be pleased with your appearance, or you may thank God that He looks on the heart, not the outward appearance [1 Sam 16:7]. Every believer should strive to take care of his body, for the Word tells us to 'glorify God in your body' [1 Cor 6:20]. We are not all "10s," but we should respect and care for our body as God's creation [Psalm 139:14], and not abuse or misuse it.

Most people in the world obsess over their image; they want to impress with both the physical and personal image. There is nothing wrong with comely looks and personal success, unless it becomes the main focus and obsession and leads to pride [Proverbs 6:16-17]. Some have good looks and success, but still have a negative image of themselves. Maybe they were criticized as a child, or negative words planted a poor image in their minds. Rejection can also damage self-image, as everyone wants to "fit in" and be accepted.

God does not want us to have a negative image of ourselves. People attend behavior-modification classes, listen to motivational speakers, and other programs to cure a negative self-image. But the key to change is not in the mind, but in the heart. The Word tells us that as a man 'thinketh in his heart, so is he' [Proverbs 23:7].The mind must be renewed so that we can perceive ourselves as God sees us [Romans 12:2]. God sees the beauty of holiness and righeousness in the born-again spirit [2 Cor 5:21]. He sees us as sons of God and as joint-heirs with Jesus [1 John 3:2, Rom 8:17]. God sees that we can 'do all things through Christ which strengtheneth us' [Phil 4:13]. And God sees this potential as limitless because with God all things are possible [Matt 19:26]. So each of us should see ourself as God sees us: beloved, special, precious, and strong in Him. Look in that mirror again and see the new creature in Jesus - you look g-o-o-d!

Prayer:
Lord, thank You that we are bearing about the image of our Lord Jesus Christ.

Scripture of the Day:
"But we all, with open face beholding as in a glass the glory of the Lord, are changed into the same image from glory to glory, even as by the Spirit of the Lord." - [2 Corinthians 3:18]

The Word for the Day is "Everlasting."

Quote for the Day:
"The most important gift you receive as a believer in Christ is everlasting life."
- Jesse Duplantis

In our world today we find that many things do not last long. Products we buy seem less well made. Everything seems more disposable and less durable.

Relationships also seem less enduring. Employers are less loyal to their employees and employees to their employers. People change jobs and careers often and many times with hurt and disappointment. Friendships, too, seem less lasting and enduring. Divorce has increased. Disloyalty in relationships seems to hold less stigma. Selfishness reigns more than selflessness. The underlying guideline seems more about "what's in it for me" in all that people do. With these ongoing changes in all arenas, perhaps it is not surprising people have grown less trustful. They wonder if true loyalty and honorable, unconditional affection even exist anymore.

Yet in the midst of these changing times and changing feelings God remains the same. C.S. Lewis wrote: "Though our feelings come and go, God's love does not." God's unconditional, everlasting love remains the same. His Word assures us over and over that 'with His everlasting love He will have compassion and care for us' [Isaiah 54:8]. He promises that 'nothing can separate us from His love' [Romans 8:39] and that "He is and will be with us always to the end' [Matthew 28:20]. What wonderful assurances!

In an unstable world, we have a stable God. In a world where affections are often unreliable, we have a reliable love available from the Lord. In our lives on earth where not everyone we give our hearts and loyalty to in love is faithful, God's love is always faithful and everlasting. Psalm 136:1 promises us that "His mercy (love) endureth for ever." What a comfort, like the old hymn, to know we can rely and lean on His Everlasting arms to abide with Him forever.

Prayer:
Thank you, Lord, that we can hold in our hearts the knowledge that Your Love for us is everlasting and that nothing can separate us from Your love. Ever.

Scripture of the Day:
"But the mercy of the Lord is from everlasting to everlasting upon them that fear him, and his righteousness unto children's children." - [Psalm 103:17]

The Word for the Day is "Hope."

Quote for the Day:
"If you do not hope you will not find what is beyond your hope." - St. Clement of
Alexandria

When I was growing up it was common for someone with a serious concern
when asked about it, to reply: "Oh, I'm just wishin', hopin', and prayin' it will work
out." It sounded like the right thing to say, but I seldom perceived that there was
any confidence or conviction that the outcome desired was going to be positive.
To me, the person seemed to have resigned themselves to accept whatever might
be. In my mind I could hear Doris Day singing *"Que Sera, Sera (Whatever Will
Be, Will Be)."* I got the impression that hope was just wishful thinking after you
had given up faith in believing for something.

But after I came to the Lord, He corrected my thinking by showing me that hope
was an integral part of faith and that He wanted believers to have high hopes.
The Word of God tells us that through the learning of the scriptures we have
hope [Romans 15:4]. When we find the scripture that promises the answer we
want, Jesus wants us to trust Him by faith and to hope in the promise. We hope
by imagining or seeing the answer we want: "Now faith is the substance of things
hoped for, the evidence of things not seen" [Hebrews 11:1]. If we want healing,
we must see ourselves healed; if we want prosperity, we must see the abundance
in our mind. By keeping this hope as the anchor of our souls [Hebrews 6:19], we
keep our faith alive in God's Word by seeing the answer in our heart even before
it manifests. Jesus then confirms His Word and fills us with all joy and peace in
believing through the power of the Holy Ghost [Romans 15:13].

Jesus in us is our hope of glory [Colossians 1:27]. We are promised that the hope
of the righteous shall be gladness [Proverbs 10:28]. "Blessed is the man that trusteth in the Lord, and whose hope the Lord is" [Jeremiah 17:7]. We can share these
truths to any that ask us a reason of the hope that is in us [1 Peter 3:15].

Prayer:
Lord Jesus, thank You that You want us to pray big, to believe big, to hope big,
and to receive big!

Scripture of the Day:
"Happy is he that hath the God of Jacob as his help, whose hope is in the Lord his
God." - [Psalm 146:5]

The Word for the Day is "Back."

Quote for the Day:
"It's good to know that God's got your back." – Bishop Kirk Devine

Often in watching a movie, one of the characters will tell the other, "Don't worry, buddy. I've got your back." In essence he's saying 'If those bad guys come after you, I'm here. I'll fight for you and defend you if you need it.' Basically, when someone has got your back, you're safer and more protected. It's comforting also to know that someone cares enough about you to put their own well being ahead of yours. It is rarely a stranger who makes this kind of offer. Usually it's someone you know well, like a good friend, colleague, or family member.

It's popular to say today "God's got your back" to someone. We want them to feel God is on their side in trouble, that God will strengthen them and work on their behalf. He does and He will. But just as in the earth, that care extends most to those God knows well, to His own. Not that this is always the case, but it is the more usual scenario in all the Biblical stories. God has the back of His own because He promised it in His Word and because they, knowing this, have the confidence and belief that God is there for them as He promised. To His own, God said: "Fear thou not, for I am with thee: be not dismayed; for I am thy God: I will strengthen thee; yea, I will help thee; yea, I will uphold thee with the right hand of my righteousness" [Isaiah 41:10]. When God is on your side you are strengthened, because then 'the battle is not yours but God's' [2 Chronicles 20:15]. 'Is anything too hard for the Lord?' [Gen 18:14; Jer 32:27]. No, nothing, because 'nothing is impossible to the Lord. With men many things are impossible but with God all things are possible' [Luke 1:37; Matthew 19:26].

When God is walking with You, when you know Him and walk in His ways, and trust Him to guide you, direct you, work things for your highest good, your back is well protected. 'The glory of the Lord shall be your rear guard' [Is 58:8]. Even when people intend evil against you, God turns things around [Ps 21:11]. Even at death, He will roll away the stone of death and take you home to Himself just as He did Jesus, giving victory even over death [1 Cor 15:57].

Prayer:
Lord, we are happy and blessed to say You have our back, to know You protect and care for us, even in death. Help us walk after Your will and close to Your heart, so You will always be our rear guard.

Scripture of the Day:
"Behold…the angel of the Lord descended from heaven, and came and rolled back the stone from the door, and sat upon it." - [Matthew 28:2]

The Word for the Day is "Creature."

Quote for the Day:
"The happiness of the creature consists in rejoicing in God, by which also God is magnified and exalted." - Jonathan Edwards

We know that *creature* means something that is created, and the mind can form different images to this concept. We can think of humans as creatures and sometimes use the phrase "he's a creature of habit" to refer to someone whose behavior is predictable and repetitive. Creature can also refer to animals. We see fuzzy puppy dogs and say "Oh, aren't they cute little creatures." We also associate the word to beings of sci-fi creation such as super-heroes or monsters. One of my first exposures to this concept was the 1954 movie *The Creature From The Black Lagoon.* The monster looked like an ugly lizard to me, but was still scary to an eight-year old.

The Bible tells us that in Christ Jesus we each have become a new creature, a being that did not exist before [2 Cor 5:17]. The Word tells us that God Himself is the Creator of this new being, and that it is created for good works—works of blessing and peace to the creature, and praise, glory and honor to the Creator [Ephesians 2:10]. Ephesians 4:24 tells us that this new man (creature) is created in righteousness and true holiness after God, no more under condemnation of sin, but made the righteousness of God by Christ Jesus [2 Corinthians 5:21].

'In Christ old things are passed away, all things are become new' [2 Cor 5:17]. But we look in the mirror and see the same person, with the same face and body as before, and we think "how can this be new?" We must realize that we are a three-part being: spirit, soul, and body [1 Thess 5:23]. We have a physical body that houses the soul, the mental, intellectual, emotional being, and the spirit, which is the inner man or eternal part. God wants us to put on the new man which is created in the image of God [Col 3:10], renew the mind by the Word of God [Rom 12:2], and control and discipline the body [1 Cor 9:27]. Pray that all would become this new man in spirit in Christ Jesus.

Prayer:
Father, thank You that when we receive Jesus as Lord and Savior in our hearts, we are made a new creature created unto righteousness, blessing, praise and glory unto our God.

Scripture of the Day:
"Therefore if any man be in Christ, he is a new creature: old things are passed away; behold, all things are become new." - [2 Corinthians 5:17]

The Word for the Day is "Yoke"

Quote for the Day:
"The yoke you wear determines the burden you bear." – Edwin Louis Cole

It is easy, all too easy, to become a "Martha, Martha," busy about many things that seem very important and imperative things to do, but are not the right things. "Martha, Martha," Jesus said, "thou art careful and troubled about many things but one thing is needful" [Luke 10:38-42]. So often our minds, our intellect, our own understandings set us off on a course or directive that seems so important. We read this or that, hear this or that—and suddenly feel compelled to follow that idea or advice we've heard or read—but there is no underlying rest and peace in it, but instead a discontent that even spreads to criticism and judgment. Martha complained to Jesus, "Lord dost thou not care that…"

There is always a way that seems right unto a man, and the enemy wants to lead us in that way. Taking us off course. Into busy works not led and directed of God. The enemy's greatest concern is that we will fulfill the definitive will of God, so he works tirelessly to distract us, to pull us from the right focus, to keep us busy about unneedful things. He wants to keep us from following after and from 'choosing that good part' which will not be taken away from us. What is the answer? To not be so cumbered by doing unneedful tasks, that seem to be important, but to come to Jesus' feet. To listen. To tune in to His quiet voice, His quiet will. And to follow that only.

When you are tuned in to God and following his leadings and directions there is a deep peace and satisfaction not found in any other course. 'Jesus' yoke is easy,' not a yoke without work, but easy to walk in, not pulling and chaffing as when you are yoked into labors and works not of the Lord [Matthew 11:30]. There is always a true and right path to be found and Jesus promised, 'when you know the truth, the truth will set you free' [John 8:32]. When we find and know God's best will and are yoked into that will and way, there will be joy. For then we are in the middle of the will of the Father.

Prayer:
Lord, help us to take time with You daily to hear Your voice and know Your will and to not be distracted and pulled away from Your best purpose by the clamor and demands of the world and our own understanding.

Scripture of the Day:
"Take My yoke upon you and learn of me;…and ye shall find rest unto your souls." - [Matthew 11:29]

The Word for the Day is "Give."

Quote for the Day:
"We should give as we would receive, cheerfully, quickly, and without hesitation; for there is no grace in a benefit that sticks to the fingers." - Seneca

The Word tells us that it is more blessed to give than to receive [Acts 20:35]. But to most people this seems contrary to good reason. Carnal man, being naturally selfish, wants to keep all he has, and to get even more for himself. He sees giving from his own goods as a net decrease instead of a benefit or blessing. The carnal man without the Lord wants to take rather than give, and to give as little as possible when he does give.

But when we are born-again into Jesus, our nature is changed and we become more desirous of giving, instead of always taking. God's Holy Spirit works in our hearts to love others more perfectly and to give unto others.

Some believers, however, still struggle with being givers. I think the reason is we feel forced and compelled to give out of obligation. But God wants us to give, not grudgingly, reluctantly, or resentfully, or out of necessity, 'for God loves a cheerful, willing giver' [2 Corinthians 9:7]. We start where we are and grow into cheerful givers by the Spirit. God does not condemn us for the amount we give, but He does want our hearts to grow and to give in the right spirit, and He wants us to grow in the revelation of the blessings and benefits that are promised to givers.

God's kingdom principle tells us we are given back according to the measure we give. If we give love, kindness, compassion, or our time to any Godly work or ministry, or if we give money or material benefits, we are given back in kind, plus a lot more! Think of all the things the Lord freely gives us: eternal life [John 10:28], the Comforter [John 14:16], peace [John 14:27], good things that you ask [Matt 7:11], beauty for ashes [Is 61:3], the water of life [John 4:14], and so much more! We can never out-give God, and we can become more conformed to the image of Jesus as we grow into cheerful givers.

Prayer:
O Lord, giver of life, it is a good thing to give thanks unto You, and to sing praises unto thy name, O Most High [Psalm 92:1].

Scripture of the Day:
"Give, and it shall be given unto you; good measure, pressed down, and shaken together, and running over, shall men give unto your bosom. For with the same measure that ye mete withal it shall be measured to you again." - [Luke 6:38]

The Word for the Day is "Always."

Quote for the Day:
"No matter the season of life we face, we can always count on the love of God."
- Bryan Taylor

There's an old sweet love song titled "Always on my Mind," first recorded by B.J. Thomas in 1970. Did you know you're always on God's mind? You are, whether you realize it or not, and God wants you to draw close to Him so you'll know what's on His mind, too. How can you do that? By submitting to Him daily—not always an easy thing to do with cross purposes pushing us to please ourselves or others ahead of God.

Jesus gave up self-desires and people pleasing to submit to God and to God's Will and Purpose [John 6:38]. How was He able to do that? Because He put God first every day. He looked to God, at what God thought and wanted, ahead of what the world pressured Him to think or do [John 5:30]. Jesus made a conscious, determined decision to follow God as He hopes we will do [Matt 4:19]. An old hymn sums up the spirit of this well: "I have decided to follow Jesus, no turning back, no turning back."

When your eyes are on Jesus, your heart tuned to God's mind and God's leading —God gets bigger and bigger in you every day. People start seeing God in your life and it draws them. Jesus said "I will draw all men unto me' [John 12:32]. He came to earth—submitted to God, lived, taught, and died so you could carry on that mission, too. Why would you settle for less? "Draw nigh unto God and He will draw nigh to you" [James 4:8].

Prayer:
Lord, we thank You that we are always on Your Mind. What a privilege and an honor. Help us to direct our hearts and minds to seek to know Your mind and Your heart for how we are to live each day and be our best for You.

Scripture of the Day:
"I was daily His delight, rejoicing always before him." - [Proverbs 8:30]

June

The Word for the Day is "Steps."

Quote for the Day:
"Life is a series of steps. Things are done gradually. Once in a while there is a giant step, but most of the time we are taking small, seemingly insignificant steps on the stairway of life." - Ralph Ransom

One could think of our life's journey as a series of steps, the movement of our feet that has carried us to all our life experiences and to an untold number of various destinations. We can also think of the literal definition of step as simply placing one's foot to move forward. Many years ago when my younger brother Steve was still a young kid, he invited me to look at some of his drawings in a folder. Among his nice drawings I noticed he had also written some sayings of his own, one of which caught my attention: "Step where there is land." I have appreciated the wisdom of little brother's quote for it is true if you plant your foot on ground, you have a firm foundation. But if you step on something else like water, mud, or quicksand, you might have trouble. Worse yet, step on air and you might be falling into a hole or off a cliff!

Our wisest counsel for life is to let God direct our steps. The Word promises that 'the steps of a good man are ordered by the Lord' [Ps 37:23]. This means our life's way will be directed by the Lord to keep us on a firm, secure path in His will. God wants our steps to be directed by Him to lead us to all the good He has for us: the achievement, success, peace, blessing, and abundant life He has promised. "In the way of righteousness is life" [Proverbs 12:28] and our goal is to keep our steps on this way of righteousness. If we acknowledge the Lord in all our ways, He shall direct our paths [Proverbs 3:6]. We can then be sure we will always step on firm footing 'where there is land,' and not step into muck or off a cliff!

Prayer:
Lord, thank You that when we seek You first in all our ways, You direct our steps, our direction, our life, to keep us in the way of righteousness and life abundant.

Scripture of the Day:
"The steps of a good man are ordered by the Lord: and he delighteth in his way."
-[Psalm 37:23]

The Word for the Day is "Diligence."

Quote for the Day:
"Learning is not attained by chance, it must be sought for with ardor and diligence."
– Abigail Adams

To move forward effectively in anything is not to race forward heedlessly in haste, nor to drag along sluggishly with little to no effort, but to continue on a course with persistence. It is the steady effort in any endeavor that eventually leads to accomplishment and success. Diligence tends to be a slow and steady process like the old proverb: "Slow and steady wins the race." All too often, however, we start well but finish poorly or quit altogether when the going gets rough or the way grows hard. Yet seldom is anything of great value attained without diligence and without ardor, passion, and belief. Think back on all the years we each stayed in school because we valued education and learning. We knew it's importance; we believed in it and we stuck to it for the rewards we knew it would bring.

In the things of God we need to apply diligence, too. To grow spiritually, we also need to learn, read, study, seek, and pray. We need to become devoted to finding God's best will in all things, to yearn to please Him in all we do, and to dedicate ourselves with diligence to do His Will every day of our lives [Rom 12:1]. This means we need to 'study to show ourselves approved' [2 Tim 2:15], 'to not deal with a slack hand' as we grow spiritually and work for God [Prov 10:4], and to 'not weary in well doing' or give up just because results don't come quickly in any area [Gal 6:9].

Prayer:
Lord, we live in an impatient world in which people expect quick results, not wanting to give patient time and diligent effort to much of anything. We confess we are often impatient if we don't see quick answers to our prayers, quick results to our efforts, and quick, eager praise from others for it. We repent of this today. Help us to learn to live with more diligence, being willing to give ongoing, dutiful effort, ardor, and steadfast work to become the person You want us to be.

Scripture of the Day:
"Wherefore the rather, brethren, give diligence to make your calling and election sure: for if ye do these things, ye shall never fall." - [2 Peter 1:10]

The Word for the Day is "Compassion."

Quote for the Day:
"If you have men who will exclude any of God's creatures from the shelter of compassion and pity, you will have men who will deal likewise with their fellow men."
- Francis of Assisi

It is likely that every believer has experienced the sorrow when a loved one, who once was in the faith, wanders away from the Lord and returns to the rudiments of this world. How do we pray for such a person to come back to fellowship with the Lord? I think we must continue to love the wayward soul and be consistent in our compassion toward them. We must continue to have a heart of love, gentleness, mercy, warmth, and tender-heartedness toward the loved one gone astray.

The story of the prodigal son [Luke 15:11-24] gives us insight and wisdom in this matter. I think the son represents the wayward soul, and the father represents the Heavenly Father. The story tells us the younger son demanded his portion of the goods, then departed the father to a far country. There he wasted his substance on riotous (sinful) living. A famine then forced him to feed swine in his dire condition. Then the turning point came: 'he came to himself' [v.17]; he came to his good senses. He then came back to the father, repenting, expecting rejection, just hoping to survive as a servant.

But what did the father do? He had compassion and ran to welcome his lost son back. The Lord never rejects any that come to Him [John 6:37]. Next, the father put a robe on his son and a ring on his finger. The Lord restores the right standing in righteousness to all who repent and turn to Him [1John 1:9]. The father then prepared a feast for his returned son. The Lord restores the covenant blessings to those who come back to Him. Let us be compassionate like our Heavenly Father, and ready to receive the prodigal soul again in love when 'he comes to himself.'

Prayer:
Father God, we cover with prayer and compassion our loved ones who have wandered astray. We pray to break the darkness that has blinded their minds and that they might 'come to themselves', and come back to You.

Scripture of the Day:
"And he arose, and came to his father. But when he was yet a great way off, his father saw him, and had compassion, and ran, and fell on his neck, and kissed him." - [Luke 15:20]

The Word for the Day is "Beautiful."

Quote for the Day:
"I think we can block beautiful events by refusing to expect them to happen."
–Eugenia Price

As Christians, we know God is omnipotent and all powerful. We know God can do all things and yet we sometimes forget our role of expectancy and belief in seeing that God's best comes to pass in our lives. It's important to live in faith, confidence, and prayerful expectancy that God will fulfill His Word and the promises in His Word toward us.

In ignorance we can block beautiful events God wants for us by refusing to expect them to happen for us. Why in the world would we do this? Here are the main reasons and the scriptures to support the right view on each:
  1. We don't know God and we don't know His Word [1 John 2:2-5; 2 Tim 3:16].
  2. We don't really believe God is a good God and wants only good for us [Psalm 119: 68].
  3. We get confused about where evil and trouble in the earth come from [John 10:10].
  4. We have been falsely taught God brings sorrows to teach us something [James 1:17].
  5. We don't understand our part in seeing God's will and best come to pass (John 15:7].
  6. We don't ask to receive or keep an expectant heart when we do [Matt 7:8].

To be expectant means we have an excited, eager, hopeful belief that something good is about to happen, something pleasant and beautiful. We are meant to live with an expectant, confident heart toward God, all the time, every day. Expectancy—an aspect of faith—opens the heart to hear from and to receive from the Lord. The question is: Will you decide to live with an expectant heart or block beautiful things from happening in your life?

Prayer:
Lord, too often we have lived below Your best, not believed in Your Goodness. We've lived double-minded not knowing Your Word or Your Will for our lives. Help us to build ourselves up on our most Holy Faith so that we can live a life of expectancy, expecting all the good and beauty You want for us and not blocking it with our unbelief.

Scripture of the Day:
"How beautiful upon the mountains are the feet of Him that bringeth good tidings, that publisheth peace, that bringeth good tidings of good." - [Isaiah 52:7]

The Word for the Day is "Seek."

Quote for the Day:
"Finally, let them recognize that there are two kinds of people one can call reasonable: those who serve God with all their heart because they know Him, and those who seek Him with all their heart because they do not know Him." - Pascal

Effective seeking sometimes takes effort and diligence. While working in my downstairs office recently, I received a phone call with a message for Lin. She was gone at the time, so I wrote the return phone number on a piece of paper and placed it on my desk. But when Lin returned, I could not find the note for her. I went through all my papers over and over, but to no avail. Finally, I got down on my knees and searched, and found the note on the floor under a chair skirt—what a relief! Finding things sometimes takes a lot of looking and seeking.

God wants us to seek Him with our whole heart: "Blessed are they that keep his testimonies, and that seek him with the whole heart" [Psalm 119:2]. God also wants us to seek Him, and seek Him first before other things. God wants our seeking Him to be a dedicated, fervent first priority in our lives. We know Jesus does not accept a half-hearted, lukewarm effort [Rev 3:16]. And with our seeking, God promises blessings, that if we seek we will find what we need [Matt 7:7], and that God is a rewarder of all who diligently seek Him [Heb 11:6]. We are also promised that when we seek the Lord with all our hearts we will prosper and all things we need and desire will be added to us [2 Chron 31:21; Matt 6:33].

What other ways can we seek God? We seek God by prayer, knowing that 'the effectual fervent prayer of a righteous man availeth much' (gets a lot done) [Dan 9:3; James 5:16]. We also seek God when we study and grow our faith in His Word [Heb 11:6; Rom 10:17]. Praise and thanksgiving, too, are means of seeking God. As Psalm 69:30 says: "I will praise the name of God with a song, and will magnify Him with thanksgiving." We can seek to know and serve Him better in so many ways.

Prayer:
Lord, we will seek You in all our ways. We will seek You diligently with our whole heart and soul to grow in You, to learn of You, and to be blessed in You.

Scripture of the Day:
"And ye shall seek me, and find me, when ye shall search for me with all your heart." - [Jeremiah 29:13]

The Word for the Day is: "Doers."

Quote for the Day:
"The kingdom of God does not consist in talk, but in power, that is, in works and practice. God loves the 'doers of the Word' in faith and love, and not the 'mere hearers,' who, like parrots, have learned to utter certain expressions with readiness." – Martin Luther

My mother used to tell me: "You're known by the company you keep." Another favorite of hers was: "Bad company corrupteth good morals." I understood what she meant but I learned the wisdom of her words more as the years went by. Countless studies confirm the reality mother taught that people do tend to start acting like the people they surround themselves with. Spending time with negative people who make poor choices increases your likelihood of doing the same, and spending time with positive people who inspire you to reach higher and live better increases your chances of being happier and more positive and of reaching your goals.

Not surprisingly, many scriptures warn about keeping bad company with the worldly, with fools, with the corrupt and immoral [1 Cor 5:11-13; Proverbs 13:20; Psalm 26:4-5]. The counsel for choosing companions and marriage partners wisely cautions 'to be not unequally yoked together with unbelievers' because dark and light never mix happily and well for long [2 Cor 6:14; 1 John 2:15-17].

People who live close to God are different in a positively impacting way. God called himself a consuming fire [Heb 12:29]. He said He wanted His people and His ministers to be a flaming fire, too, always fervent in spirit and never lethargic and lukewarm in faith [Romans 12:11; Psalm 104:4; Rev 3:16]. Why? Because fire is contagious. Fire begets fire. Those strong in the Lord ignite a fire within others to be more, do more, and to walk higher and leave the world a better place than they found it.

Prayer:
Lord, help us to have a zealous, contagious, positive faith that ignites the spirits of others to reach higher, to impact the world and change lives for the better.

Scripture of the Day:
"But be ye doers of the Word, and not hearers only." - [James 1:22]

The Word for the Day is "Understand."

Quote for the Day:
"I understand God by His Word. I cannot understand God by impressions or feelings. I cannot get to know God by sentiments." - Smith Wigglesworth

The mighty evangelist Smith Wigglesworth proclaimed that one cannot understand God by impressions, thoughts, and opinions formed without conscious thought or on the basis of little evidence. Nor can he understand God by feelings: emotions which can be vague, irrational, and subject to the vicissitudes of the carnal nature. He cannot get to know God by sentiments, either, those judgments prompted by feelings.

Yet it seems that most of the world today utilizes these touchy-feely concepts to form their opinions and judgments. The most irrational, illogical ideas are promoted with loud displays of emotion for effect, more so than facts, proofs, and evidence. This can be observed in churches today, too, where affected emotion substitutes for the sound wisdom and knowledge of God's Word. "My people are destroyed for a lack of knowledge" [Hosea 4:6], 'walking in the imagination of their own heart' [Jeremiah 9:12-14].

We can only understand God by His Word. Jesus said, "Hear, and understand" [Matthew 15:10]. "The entrance of thy word giveth light, it giveth understanding unto the simple" [Psalm 119:130]. We grow in knowledge, wisdom, understanding, and faith, as we make prayer unto the Lord and receive the Word of God into our hearts. Men can have many fleshly feelings, impressions, and sentiments, but the only Truth that stands is what the Bible says. I think Proverbs 2 gives us good counsel to seek and find understanding of God. It instructs that if we will receive God's Word, seek God's knowledge, and search for God's wisdom as we would treasure, 'then shalt thou understand the fear (reverence) of the Lord, and find the knowledge of God' [Proverbs 2:1-5]. What a blessing to know we have the promise: "but they that seek the Lord understand all things" [Proverbs 28:5].

Prayer:
Lord, thank You that as we open our hearts to receive and seek Your Word as we would treasures of gold and silver, that You, by the Holy Spirit, open our eyes and mind to understand the scriptures.

Scripture of the Day:
"Then opened he their understanding, that they might understand the scriptures." - [Luke 24:45]

The Word for the Day is "Shine."

"This little light of mine; I'm gonna let it shine." –Harry Dixon Loes

In June the lightning bugs begin to pop out as darkness falls in Tennessee. I loved watching the miracle of their lights flashing in the backyard as a child and I still delight in the small summer miracle of watching the lightning bugs every year. In certain places in the Smoky Mountains of Tennessee, lightning bugs even flash in unison or synchrony—a rare sight in the world today. Sadly, fireflies are disappearing from backyards, forests, and fields around the world. No one is totally sure why but the guesses are that it is because of development, pesticides, and light pollution. Natural habitats are being destroyed and too many manmade night lights are disrupting fireflies' natural cycles and patterns. Many firefly species are now endangered.

Because fireflies "light" at night they have always exemplified the symbolic meaning of an exceptional human being—shining in the dark of the world, making a difference, illuminating sorrow and darkness, bringing hope. Even though the firefly is tiny, it's welcome light is seen. The old children's song "This Little Light of Mine" is built around a concept similar to what we see with the lightning bugs, that no matter our size or age, no matter who or where we are, we can let the light of God shine from within us—and that it will make a difference. Matthew 5:16 says, "Let your light so shine before men that they may see your good works and glorify your Father which is in heaven." When we let the love and light of God shine through us, it can help others see their way when in a dark and hard time in their lives. Our light and example can help others find their way to the Lord or to a deeper faith, too. We're meant to be 'the light of the world' [Matthew 5:14]. Our light points people to Jesus and to God.

There's no darkness in the Lord [1 John 1:5] and there shouldn't be any darkness in us. Jesus said 'as long as he was in the world, he was the light of the world' [John 9:5] and admonished us to carry on His work after He was gone. 'He called us out of darkness into His marvelous light' [1 Peter 2:9] and He wants us to keep the light shining.

Prayer:
Lord, we are meant to receive the love and light of God and to carry it forth into a dark world. Help us, like the old children's song, to let our lights shine.

Scripture for the Day:
"Arise, shine; for thy light is come, and the glory of the Lord is risen upon thee."
–[Isaiah 60:1]

The Word for the Day is "Wind."

Quote for the Day:
"The swift wind of compromise is a lot more devastating than the sudden jolt of misfortune." - Charles R. Swindoll

We can't see the wind, but we can feel it's effects. I was mowing my lawn a few days ago on one of those muggy, sticky, East Tennessee summer days. As I finished, a wind suddenly whipped up, and though warm, it felt refreshing against my hot, sweaty skin. Anyone guiding a sailboat knows the wind can be favorable, or contrary. Yet sailors can angle the sail against the wind and still keep their intended direction. People, like sailboats, are sometimes affected by certain types of "winds," figuratively speaking. The opinions of others or the mindset of the world can "blow" our lives in certain directions. Listening to the wind of worldly opinion will blow our boat into the mold of the world.

The Bible tells us not to be 'carried about (influenced), tossed to and fro (unstable and unsure) with every wind of doctrine (carnal unbelief and reasoning); by the sleight (cunning deceit) of men, by cunning craftiness (deception) whereby they lie in wait to deceive (to lure you into their ungodly ways)' [Eph 4:14].

Sometimes adverse cirmumstances can blow our life off course like a contrary wind. Financial problems, health problems, personal relationship and other life problems can blow like a storm against us. But we have an anchor of the soul against the storms of life. As redeemed, born-again believers, Jesus has become our high priest. We come to Him presenting and resting on the promises of His Word. We have the blessed assurance that God cannot lie, and that all the promises of God in Jesus are yea and Amen [Heb 6:18-20; 2 Cor 1:20]. So let the wind of the Holy Spirit direct your heart and mind to lead you to God's destination for you: havens of peace, joy, and comfort.

Prayer:
Lord, thank You that the Holy Spirit, like a wind, moves to revive our hearts toward God, giving guidance, wisdom, and direction.

Scripture of the Day:
"The wind bloweth where it listeth, and thou hearest the sound thereof, but canst not tell whence it cometh, and whither it goeth: so is every one that is born of the Spirit." - [John 3:8]

The Word for the Day is "Soul."

Quote for the Day:
"The immortality of the soul is a matter which is of so great consequence to us and which touches us so profoundly that we must have lost all feeling to be indifferent about it." – Blaise Pascal

The soul is the part of humans that survives death. Each soul is created by God and infused into the body by God at conception. Genesis 2:7 says: 'And God formed man of the dust and he became a living soul.' Unfortunately man lost the designed connection to God with the fall. The soul became a hidden un-awakened part of man after satan's intervention. We became satan's servants without the understanding of it, destined to live eternally with him instead of with God. But God in His Grace made a way to bring us back into fellowship and union with Him through Jesus Christ.

Despite whatever you may hear or read no individual can keep alive his or her own soul and keep it from spiritual death [Ps 22:29]. We need the spiritual component only God can provide to be changed. Through salvation the nature and destiny of the soul is changed (John 3:16). Rebirth changes the soul, filling it with the life, purpose, and destiny of God again. Rebirth ushers the Spirit of God back into our beings, as originally intended, renewing soul, mind, and body. It is indeed a "freedom song" for the soul—out of bondage and into liberty. David prayed "O Lord deliver my soul; oh save me for thy mercies' sake" [Ps 6:4]. God yearns to restore our souls [Ps 23:3], for our souls to dwell at ease [Ps 25:13], blessed and joyful [Ps 35:9], healed and at peace [Ps 41:4; 55:18]. The enemy wants to torment and persecute the soul [Ps 7:1-2] while God hungers to convert the soul and to deliver the soul from the wicked [Ps 19:7;17:13]. But it's a choice. God doesn't force us to become His but through Jesus and the sacrifice of His death, we have that choice. Will we take it or think we can master our own soul, our own fate? God is the lover of your soul. Satan is the hater of your soul. One will someday have your soul. The choice of whom is yours.

Prayer:
Lord, we are grateful You have provided freedom and deliverance of our souls and a way back into Your love, grace, and Kingdom forever.

Scripture of the Day:
"He restoreth my soul." - [Psalm 23:3]

The Word for the Day is "Smitten."

Quote for the Day:
"They were rotted from within before they were smitten from without." - Winston Churchill

In the quote above, Churchill was referring to a European nation that was quickly overrun and conquered by Germany at the start of World War II. He was saying the nation had "rotted" from within, that is, they had lost their moral vigor by rejecting long-held standards of morality and had compromised into secular thinking and pursuits of pleasures and immorality. This loss of moral vigor also caused the loss of martial vigor as they lost the will and strength to fight and they were smitten by their enemy. We should be praying that our nation does not become rotted from within by forsaking God's laws of morality.

How does a nation become 'rotted from within'? By its people becoming 'rotted from within'. All men have sinned and come short of the glory of God before redemption in Christ Jesus [Romans 3:23]. But believers can fail to renew their minds and get polluted in their thinking. The Word gives two main ways the enemy gets access [Deut 28:14-15]. The first is by going aside from the Word of God, by not hearkening unto the Voice of God. When we listen to the voice and opinion of the world and deny God's Word as the authority to absolutes of truth, the conscience becomes defiled. Secondly, problems come when we go after other gods to serve them. The gods of self, secularism, and worldly mammon turn the heart away from the righteousness of God.

The Lord does not want us 'rotted from within' so that we are in danger of being 'smitten without' by the enemy. God wants us strong within by His Spirit. God translates us out of darkness into His marvelous Light and Life by salvation in Christ Jesus [Col 1:13]. Jesus gives abundant life and God intends for us to be a living tree bringing forth His righteous fruit [John 10:10, Psalm 1:3]. Keep your heart alive and whole 'with all diligence,' and in Jesus rejoice that we are 'more than conquerers in Him that loved us' [Prov 4:23; Rom 8:37], then our enemy will be the one smitten.

Prayer:
Lord, we vow to keep our heart with all diligence, rooted and grounded in Your Word and love, that our enemy might be smitten every time he attacks us.

Scripture of the Day:
"The Lord shall cause thine enemies that rise up against thee to be smitten before thine face: they shall come out against thee one way, and flee before thee seven ways." - [Deuteronomy 28:7]

The Word for the Day is "Discouraged."

Quotes for the Day:
"God would never discourage me. He would always point me to Himself to trust Him. Therefore, my discouragement is from satan." – Charles Stanley

No one goes through life without facing times when they are tired, worn out, beaten down, disheartened, and discouraged. Discouragement comes from many sources with the enemy behind the bulk of those sources, but they are faced by all of us—job losses, betrayals, tragedies, personal hurt. So what should we do when discouragement comes knocking on our doors?

A story in the Old Testamant in Numbers 20-21 is a good reminder of where most discouragements originate—from life events and people. The Israelites, journeying from Egypt had to detour at great length around Edom after being barred from passing through it. The way through the wilderness was harsh and the 'souls of the people were much discouraged because of the way'[Num 21:4]. Instead of keeping their focus on God and the vision of the Promised Land, they started whining, wishing they were back in Egypt in slavery, forgetting all God had done. An important note here is that when discouraging times come, we need to always view them as times we're only "passing through" temporarily, keeping our eyes focused ahead and on God. Never settle in and welcome setbacks and discouragement. Keep your eyes on God's promises.

People in our lives cause discouragement, too. In two situations 'other brethren discouraged the hearts of the Israelite people' as they sought to follow God, discouraging them from following the path God had laid out [Num 32:9; Deut 1:28]. Friends, family, and church friends can sometimes discourage our hearts. For whatever reason they don't see the direction God is leading and subtly or directly discourage the way. Your answer then is to always reach to God, to not be swayed and give in to false counsel or direction, to not let these discourage your heart [Deut 1:28]. Whenever people or life events discourage you, take it to God. "Wait on the Lord, be of good courage, and He shall strengthen thine heart" [Ps 27:14]. God always advises: "The cause that is too hard for you, bring it unto me, and I will hear it" [Deut 1:17].

Prayer:
Lord, help us to remember that life's discouragements are only temporary, to never see them as permanent, and to reach to You to refresh and renew us in those times.

Scripture of the Day:
"Fear thou not... be not [discouraged or] dismayed." – [Isaiah 41:10]

The Word for the Day is "House."

Quote for the Day:
"A house is made of walls and beams; a home is built with love and dreams." -
William Arthur Ward

In the South, we are familiar with the phrase: "Well, I guess it's time to go back
to the house." We know house here refers to one's home or dwelling. The word
can also refer to those dwelling in that place or family kindred. God always wants
our house to be built by hearing and doing the Word of the Lord upon the Rock
Christ Jesus, and not upon sand (the loose and shifting mores of the world). We
are then promised our house shall stand against the storms of life [Matthew 7:24-
27]. God gives us instruction in His Word for building our house with some wise
do's and don'ts.

The first thing to do is always trust in the Lord for all things and for a house of
defense [Psalm 31:2]. Seek God's wisdom for any matter concerning your house
and get knowledge and understanding by His Word [Prov 9:1, 24:3-5]. Purge
yourself and house from vessels to dishonor, anything contrary to righteous purpose [2 Tim 2:20-21]. We are the Lord's house if we "hold fast the confidence and
the rejoicing of the hope firm unto the end" [Heb 3:6]. And thank God we have a
new heart in Jesus Christ and in Him we can walk with a perfect heart [Ps 101:2].

God also instructs with some don'ts concerning our house. Don't covet thy neighbor's house [Ex 20:17], and don't wear out your welcome by spending too much
time at your neighbor's lest he grow weary of you and come to hate you [Prov
25:17]. Slothfulness, idleness, thievery, and swearing falsely by the Lord's name
cause the house to drop through and be defiled [Eccl 10:18; Zach 5:4]. A house
divided against itself, in strife and quarrelsome oppositions, shall not stand [Matt
12:25]. Don't open your home and life readily to those spreading false doctrines
[2 John 10]. Never reward evil for good, or trouble your house by being greedy of
gain [Prov 17:13, 11:29, 15:27].

Praise God that the house of the righteous is blessed and shall stand [Prov 3:33,
12:7], and we will dwell in the house of the Lord forever [Psalm 23:6]!

Prayer:
Lord, we stand against the storms of life because our house is built upon the solid
Rock Christ Jesus, who is our hope and salvation.

Scripture of the Day:
"But Christ as a son over his own house; whose house are we, if we hold fast the
confidence and the rejoicing of the hope firm unto the end." - [Hebrews 3:6]

The Word for the Day is "Home."

Quote for the Day: *"There is no place like home."* - L. Frank Baum

Most of us best know the phrase "There's no place like home" from the 1939 film *The Wizard of Oz* and we remember Dorothy clicking her ruby red slippers together and returning from Oz to her Kansas home. The phrase is a sentiment most people can relate to as there is usually some place everyone thinks of as "home." It might be the house where they grew up, the city they've spent most of their lives in, or even a place that "feels" like home and calls to their heart like no other.

J.L. and I feel at home in Tennessee, where we were both born and raised. Our ancestors came from this area, many trekking down the Appalachian Trail to settle in the valleys and mountains of Tennessee in its earliest days. We have roots here, a sense of belonging, a love for our state and the mountains around us. Even our house is one we have lived in for over forty years full of rich memories. We both carry remembrances of being away for a long time and yearning to come home, glad to see the mountain ranges as we drove into East Tennessee again, smiling to see familiar sights, streets, and our house waiting for us, welcoming us.

The prodigal son felt that call toward home when he realized he'd foolishly left his family and all who loved him, squandered his inheritance and fallen into unrighteous living. His heart must have filled with joy when he saw his father running out to meet him with loving welcome [Luke 15:11-32]. The parable is a parallel to show us how God rejoices when we come home to Him and how even the angels in heaven rejoice when one on earth is saved and comes into the Kingdom of God [Luke 15:10]. Although we love the things of earth, our home, our family, and the beauty of nature around us, as we grow closer and closer to God we begin to also hunger for our home in heaven. Paul acknowledged it saying, 'For I am in a strait betwixt the two, having a desire to depart, to go home to be with Christ or to stay here on earth with you' [Philippians 1:23]. Our home here on earth may be sweet but it can't compare to the eternal and everlasting home prepared for us in heaven.

Prayer:
Lord, we thank You that You have created a home for us in heaven more beautiful than anything we can imagine.

Scripture of the Day:
'For here we have no continuing city (home), but we seek one (heavenly home) to come.' – [Hebrews 13:14]

The Word for the Day is "Stand."

Quote for the Day:
"Be sure to put your feet in the right place, then stand firm." - Abraham Lincoln

The dictionary tells us the definition of stand is: 'to be placed or situated in a certain position, to be and stay erect, not overthrown or demolished, to remain upright, steady, to maintain a posture of resistance or defense, to continue unchanged.' The Bible tells us we are to stand fast in the Lord, the One who is Holy, has all authority, and is the same forever [Phil 4:1]. The Lord does not want His people to be shaky, unsure, weak, compromised and entangled again with the yoke of bondage to the ways of this world [Gal 5:1]. We are to be overcomers in the law of liberty which we have in Christ [James 1:25].

We stand fast in the Lord when we stand fast in the gospel: the good news that in Jesus we have forgiveness and salvation, being made a new creature in our spirit and being made the righteouness of God in Him [1 Cor 15:1; 2 Cor 5:17, 21]. This awesome salvation, this awesome grace wherein we stand, is accessed by faith through Jesus [Rom 5:2]. We stand firm in faith which comes by hearing and believing the Word of God, not standing on the wisdom of men, but in the power of God [2 Cor 1:24; Rom 10:17; 1 Cor 2:5].

A quote by Thomas Kinkade says: "You have to expect spiritual warfare when you stand up for righteousness or call attention to basic values. It's just a matter of light battling the darkness. But the light wins every time. You can't throw enough darkness on light and put it out." We stand against the wiles of the devil by putting on the whole armour of God: "Stand therefore, having your loins girt about with truth, and having on the breastplate of righteousness; And your feet shod with the preparation of the gospel of peace; Above all, taking the shield of faith, wherewith we shall be able to quench all the fiery darts of the wicked. And take the helmet of salvation, and the sword of the Spirit, which is the word of God: Praying always with all prayer and supplication in the Spirit, and watching thereunto with all perserverance and supplication for all saints" [Eph 6:14-18]. Praise be to God, who causes us always to triumph in Christ Jesus [2 Cor 2:14]!

Prayer:
Lord, we stand in You strong, steady, constant forever in your mercy, grace, love, victory, and blessings we enjoy through the gospel of your salvation.

Scripture of the Day:
"For now we live, if we stand fast in the Lord." - [1 Thessalonians 3:8]

The Word for the Day is "Simple."

Quote for the Day:
"Sometimes the questions are complicated and the answers are simple." – Dr. Seuss

As the Seuss quote above suggests, the world is full of endless questions that frequently complicate simple matters. We all know or have met those who love to debate and argue most any subject endlessly. My mother used to say, "He loves to argue so much he'd argue the tail off a rooster." The Bible warns to avoid those prone to argument and to not to get into debate with them, to 'not cast your pearls before swine lest they trample them under their feet or turn and rend you' [Matt 7:6] and to avoid 'foolish and unlearned questions, knowing they generally gender strife and more argument' [2 Tim 2:23]. This means we shouldn't waste good words or get into debate with stubborn, unreceptive people. We always need to follow the leading of the Lord in sharing our faith, knowing some people don't want to come out from their holes of ignorance.

Did you ever look for doodlebugs outdoors as a child…singing a rhyme and poking a piece of grass down into their hole to lure them out? The game seldom profited. Doodlebugs are small bugs that live down in funnel shaped holes in the soil. Somewhat lazy creatures by nature, they wait for insects to fall in their holes so they can eat them. From that lazy habit, the term "doodlebug" came to imply a simple person who wastes their time and can waste your time. People who endlessly argue are like that. Even when there is an easy answer to find, they aren't open to find it. Often they don't want to 'know the truth that can set them free' about anything, including faith [John 8:32].

Jesus taught his truths in such a simple way that all could understand them. He made the concept of salvation so easy even a child—or a simpleton doodlebug—could receive it. It isn't hard for us to share faith, or for someone to receive our words, if they are receptive. But we need to be discerning of how and when to share with others, listening to the Spirit's guidance. And for our own questions, we know to study and learn from the Word and to pray and ask for wisdom and understanding, knowing God will richly give it [James 1:5].

Prayer:
Lord, we don't want to stay simple and lazy like the doodlebug, down in our holes, hoping what we need might just drop on us. Help us to seek to know and learn and to be wise and discerning in how we share with others.

Scripture of the Day:
"O ye simple, understand wisdom." -[Proverbs 8:5]

The Word for the Day is "Corrupt."

Quote for the Day:
"Various are the pleas and arguments which men of corrupt minds frequently urge against yielding obedience to the just and holy commands of God." - George Whitfield

We know there are several usages of the word 'corrupt.' It can mean something that has been defiled, changed from good to bad. It can define a crooked, dishonest person or behavior. The Bible warns us about the influence of things that can corrupt. Words can corrupt. A quote of Seneca's says: "Whenever the speech is corrupted so is the mind." Listening to corrupt speech, or speaking corrupt words can corrupt the conscience: "Be not deceived: evil communications corrupt good manners" [1 Cor 15:33]. Whitfield's quote above warns of men who oppose God's Word because they speak from the natural view as brute beasts, speaking evil of spiritual things they know not [Jude 10]. Corrupt minds can speak words of vanity following the lusts of the flesh [2 Peter 2:18]; they can preach another Jesus, resisting the Truth and faith of Jesus [2 Tim 3:8; 2 Cor 11:4]. These corrupt trees bring forth evil fruit [Matt 7:17].

Paul talked of those who corrupted the word of God in his teachings. Corrupt in this sense means to alter from the original or correct version, to change, falsify, manipulate, or distort. Jesus and Paul both had to deal with religious sects and individuals who tried to oppose the truth they were preaching [Luke 20:27; 2 Tim 2:18]. I see the same disturbing opposition today in some new Bible versions. Some new versions delete scripture, or change (in my opinion) the context to diminish the miracles and divinity of Jesus. Some new versions are nothing more than a man's paraphrase! I wonder sometimes if we are heading toward a future, final revision, maybe called 'The Ultimate Bible.' This version will end all doctrinal differences and schisms, it will be understood and received by all men, even secular men. It will be brief, concise, and all men can carry it on their person and boast that they 'know the Bible'. It will be printed in gold lettering on a business card. Its single verse will read: "Let every man do as it seems right in his own eyes, for God (whatever you understand that concept to mean), will surely understand."

Prayer:
Lord, we thank You we are born again, not of corruptible seed, but of incorruptible, by the word of God, which liveth and abideth forever. [1 Peter 1:23]

Scripture of the Day:
"For we are not as many, which corrupt the word of God: but as of sincerity, but as of God, in the sight of God speak we in Christ." - [2 Corinthians 2:17]

The Word for the Day is "Devil."

Quote for the Day:
"The devil's success is contingent upon people's ignorance." – Benny Hinn

For a good lesson on how the devil works and thinks I recommend the classic book by C. S. Lewis titled *The Screwtape Letters.* In the book the worldly wise devil Screwtape writes letters to his apprentice nephew Wormwood about the artful task of luring humans away from God. The book reveals the clever, gentle, gradual and unsuspecting approaches that work best so the human is lured away softly to the dark side without even realizing it. This is exactly the way the devil works—like the most artful enemy you've ever seen in a James Bond movie, like a stalking depraved predator. The Word warns: "Be sober, be vigilant; because your adversary the devil, as a roaring lion, walketh about, seeking whom he may devour" [1 Peter 5:8].

Whether you are aware of it or not there is a spiritual war going on daily and if you are one of God's children, you are right in the middle of it. And you're a daily target. Satan can't shoot at God now that he's cast out of heaven, so he'll shoot at those God created in His Image, keeping the lost from God, luring the saved away from God, sending hurts, sorrows, and problems to the world and to God's people and getting everyone to blame it on God and not him. The devil works diligently twenty-four seven to keep people from God and to blind their eyes to truth [2 Cor 4:4]. He doesn't savor the things of God and he tempts with evil [Matt 16:23; James 1:13-15]; he is a liar and there is no truth in him [2 Cor 4:4; John 8:44]. He steals, kills, and destroys [John 10:10]. He's no silly little caricature in a red suit with horns; he's a heinous enemy God warns you should always 'put on the whole armour of God against, to stand against his wiles.' [Eph 6:11-12]. The good news is you have the victory over the devil through Christ Jesus and if you're submitted to God, resist the devil, use the Word of God and the power of God in you against him, he will 'flee from you' [James 4:7], but if you don't know that, or don't believe that, it won't do you much good. So wise up. Go to boot camp in God's Word to learn your rights against the devil and who you are in Christ Jesus. Gird up your loins; learn how to fight as God intended you to, rather than laying down like a doormat and letting satan walk all over you.

Prayer:
Lord, teach me to become a good soldier of faith, to learn my rights against the devil and how to fight the good fight of faith against him and win—every day.

Scripture of the Day:
"Put on the new man…neither give place to the devil." – [Ephesians 4:24, 27]

The Word for the Day is "Work."

Quote for the Day:
"Keep doing some kind of work, that the devil may always find you employed." -
St. Jerome

People have always had differing attitudes about work. Some hate it, some tolerate it, some accept it, and some enjoy it. I knew a man who had a good job at an Oak Ridge Y-12 facility, but he always bragged that when he retired he was going to "sit back in my lounge chair and rest all day," as if he would be envied. He didn't understand this was an unhealthy lifestyle. The man retired, sat in his recliner every day, soon suffered a fatal stroke, and was buried by his family. This event reminds me of the words of Pascal: "Nothing is so insufferable to man as to be completely at rest, without passions, without business, without diversion, without study. There will immediately rise from the depth of this heart weariness, gloom, sadness, fretfulness, vexation, despair." Many in our society today try to avoid work, looking for an easy way to get by. Others embrace work as the vehicle to achieve their goals. Coach Lou Holtz expressed the differences this way: "Winners embrace hard work. They love the discipline of it, the trade-off they're making to win. Losers, on the other hand, see it as punishment. And that's the difference." Work is good, and the Word of God is clear: "But let every man prove his own work, and then shall he have rejoicing in himself alone, and not in another. For every man shall bear his own burden" [Gal 6:4-5]. "For even when we were with you, this we commanded you, that if any would not work, neither should he eat" [2 Thess 3:10].

Work is a key to happiness: "Blessed is every one that feareth the Lord; that walketh in his ways. For thou shalt eat the labour of thine hands: happy shalt thou be, and it shall be well with thee" [Psalm 128:1-2]. The Word also teaches that 'the hand of the diligent maketh rich,' that 'in all labor there is profit,' and that 'the labor of the righteous is to be enjoyed and tendeth to life' [Prov 10:4,16; 14:23; Is 65:22]. Want to be happy? Work.

Prayer:
Lord, thank You that when we commit and perform our work as unto You, we are rewarded with increase and favor to be blessed as Abraham, that we might be a blessing unto others.

Scripture of the Day:
"And let the beauty of the Lord our God be upon us: and establish thou the work of our hands upon us; yea, the work of our hands establish thou it." -
[Psalm 90:17]

The Word for the Day is "Church."

Quote for the Day:
"There was a time when people went to church, heard the truth, and wept over their sins. Today people go to church, hear a motivational message, and ignore their sins."
– Pastor Ron Smith Jr,

Church can be defined in several ways. Most dictionaries define it is a building used for public worship or a body of religious believers. The New Testament word for church means "the called out ones," called out of darkness and into light. Yet with definitions aside, the church is weaker today than in times past and has less influence on its members. Charles Spurgeon wrote: "I believe that one reason why the church at this present moment has so little influence over the world is because the world has so much influence over the church." Many studies found this one of the primary reasons why people stopped going to church—they weren't changed by going. Eric Clarke said: 'The problem with the church today is an identity crisis, not fully knowing who they are in Christ.'

The church may be confused about its identity but the Word is still clear about what the church is meant to be. It is to be a place filled with saved people, adding to its numbers "daily such as should be saved" [Acts 2:47]. Many sit in the pews unredeemed and the primary message of salvation is seldom taught or presented only in a weak way. Yet those in the church are expected to be 'sanctified in Christ Jesus and saints of God,' holy and virtuous with a deep personal closeness to God' [1 Cor 1:2; Eph 5:27; 1 Peter 2:5]. The possibility of this closeness and of the rights of the believer cannot be known without teaching, without those in leadership walking in a strong place in God and feeding the church of God true, strong Biblical wisdom [Acts 11:26, 20:28; 1 Tim 3:15]. Also, when the church comes together they should 'share what God has done and is doing in their lives,' edifying others and building up their faith [Acts 14:27, 15:4; Heb 10:25]. None of this works well without zeal and fervent prayer, without the church and its leaders operating in power and might and 'subject first to Jesus Christ and his leadership' [1 Cor 14:12, 12:28; Eph 3:10, 5:24; Rom 10:14; Matt 21:13.] 'People don't want a church that will move with the world; they want a church that will move the world' [G.K. Chesterson].

Prayer:
Lord, bring revival into our churches, into its leaders and its people, so they can be the light they are intended to be in this world.

Scripture of the Day:
"That he might present it to himself a glorious church....that it should be holy and without blemish." -[Ephesians 5:27]

The Word for the Day is "Answer."

Quote for the Day:
"People are hurting and looking for answers. The Gospel gives us hope." -
Benjamin Watson

Everyone knows early in life the importance and consequences of an answer. From an early age we learn the concept that there are right and wrong answers. When a youngster goes to school he will inevitably be tested and required to give answers to the test questions. The student immediately faces the truth and reality of his ability to answer correctly. Did the student pay attention in class? Did he study? His answers reveal the condition of his mind and preparation.

We also learn early in life there are other types of answers required of us that have more to do with the heart than the intellect, like when a teacher or parent requires an answer for some behavior or ill conduct. The youngster can truthfully admit their guilt of misconduct, or the mind can race to render an excuse, denial, or justification of the misdeed. So we learn early on that both the mind and heart have a part to play in giving answers.

The Lord wants His people equipped to always answer aright, both to believers and non-believers. Both mind and spirit must be exercised in righteousness to do so. The secular world has so many views and opinions that are opposite or contrary to God's Truth. How does the believer respond when challenged for answers? Like a good student, he must first have the knowledge of the subject queried. The believer must know the truth of God's Word, the knowledge, counsel, wisdom, and absolutes of the Bible. Skeptics can make a mockery of those ignorant of God's Word and make their answers sound foolish.

The believer must also have his heart prepared aright to answer spiritual questions. "But sanctify (honor) the Lord God in your hearts: and be ready always to give an answer to every man that asketh you a reason of the hope that is in you with meekness and fear" [1 Pet 3:15-16]. Know too that the 'Holy Ghost will also teach you and help you know what you ought to say' [Luke 12:12].

Prayer:
Lord, we answer all men by knowing your Word and your Spirit, knowing we will then always have the words we need.

Scripture of the Day:
"A man hath joy by the answer of his mouth: and a word spoken in due season, how good is it!" - [Proverbs 15:23]

The Word for the Day is "Fears."

Quote for the Day:
"Fears are no match for the spirit of God who lives inside us." - Christine Caine

Fear is a feeling induced by perceived danger or threat. Most people think of fears as natural or normal. However most fears are learned except for an infant's in-born fear of falling and the early fear of loud noises. We each learn to fear, or are taught to fear, in our lives, beginning with common early childhood fears like a fear of the dark or a fear of spiders, snakes, and monsters. Later we develop more complex social fears, like fears of loneliness, death, change, fears of intimacy and commitment, of failure and rejection, and social phobias like a fear of public speaking. The four usual action responses to fear are either: freeze, flight, fright, or fight. Fear is often crippling in its intensity. Florence Nightingale said: "How little can be done under the spirit of fear."

The Bible teaches that fear is indeed a spirit and not a spirit from God. "For God hath not given us the spirit of fear; but of power, and of love, and of a sound mind" [2 Tim 1:7]. God calls the spirit of fear a bondage, reminding us "for ye have not received the spirit of bondage again to fear" [Romans 8:15]. We no longer need to yield to fears and should fight them with new knowledge and the Word. Our new thought should be: "Fear thou not; for I am with thee: be not dismayed; for I am thy God: I will strengthen thee: yea, I will help thee: yea, I will uphold thee with the right hand of my righteousness" [Isaiah 41:10]. Dale Carnegie wrote that "Fear doesn't exist anywhere except in the mind" and in the Lord we are now new creations with a renewed mind after the Spirit of God and with the mind of Christ [1 Cor 2:16]. Old things are passed away and all things are new [2 Cor 5:17].

The only healthy fear to hold is a righteous and holy fear of God and a wise fear of the enemy of God and the need to be saved and to be God's [Ps 31:19; Matt 10:28]. Beyond that the Word advises again and again not to fear and the phrase "Fear Not" is used eighty times in the Bible. God wisely knows that fear decreases our hope and effectiveness as Christians and limits our victories in Him.

Prayer:
Lord, help us to walk free of fear and to remember the words of Aristotle, as true today as when he wrote them—"He who has overcome his fears will truly be free."

Scripture of the Day:
"I sought the Lord, and He heard me, and delivered me from all my fears." –
 [Psalm 34:4]

The Word for the Day is "Feed."

Quote for the Day:
"Some people wonder why they can't have faith for healing. They feed their body three hot meals a day, and their spirit one cold snack a week." - F.F. Bosworth

We usually think of feeding in the context of giving food to the body. We know that there are consequences of the type of food we feed the body, and this even applies to commercial and business activity. Lin and I enjoyed dining at a local restaurant for several years. Then one day we discovered the restaurant had changed its menu, and our favorite items were no longer offered. The new menu just didn't taste as good or satisfy like the original, so we discontinued eating there. I believe the main reason for restaurant closings is declining service and food quality. Our natural body is also affected by what we feed it. We all know that poor diet choices can lead to health issues, and that healthy, balanced nutrition is fundamental for good physical health.

There is another definition of feed according to the dictionary which means to 'furnish something essential to the development, sustenance, maintenance, or operation of.' I think this is a perfect definition of our need for spiritual food to be all we can be in the Lord. We must essentially be fed the Word of God to grow, develop, and operate in the Spirit in the Lord. In my opinion, this is the reason for declining church attendance in our society today. Pastors and leaders are quick to beat up the flock and condemn the flock for non-attendance. These same pastors never consider that the church may no longer be serving good, satisfying food. Maybe they should consider what they are feeding the flock of God. The flock does not need to be entertained by stories or sharp humor. The flock does not need to hear intellectual, lofty, self-aggrandizing rhetoric which impresses the speaker but adds no edification to the flock. All this worldly conversation can be found at home on the TV or internet. The Word tells pastors to take heed to themselves first before feeding the flock [Acts 20:28]. You can't give out what you don't have yourself. The flock needs, and wants, the Truth of the Word, the guidance of the Holy Spirit, and a pure heart.

Prayer:
Lord, we pray that the flock of God would be fed the spiritual nourishment of the Word and the Spirit of God by loving shepherds, having the heart of the Good Shepherd, that the flock might be established in the development of a holy people to Your glory.

Scripture of the Day:
"Feed the flock of God which is among you, taking the oversight thereof, not by constraint, but willingly; not for filthy lucre, but of a ready mind." - [1 Peter 5:2]

The Word for the Day is "Lost."

Quote for the Day:
"Suppose you could gain everything in the world and lost your soul. Would it be worth it?" – Billy Graham

I read a news article today about a woman among a group of tourists in Iceland who went missing. Her tour bus stopped at the Eldgha canyon to let the tourists get out and enjoy the views. As everyone reboarded, word soon circulated that a passenger was missing, and all began to seek and search for the lost woman. The woman they looked for was actually in the search group. She'd changed clothes and didn't recognize herself from the announced description. The search was called off, of course, when it became clear the lady was safe and accounted for. The story is humorous, but often we, too, are lost in our lives in some way without knowing it.

Many have not found the Lord and don't realize they are spiritually lost. Often they are not seeking after God, either, because the god of this world, satan, blinds the mind of those who don't believe lest they find the light and the truth [2 Cor 4:4]. Even though satan gained a dominion in the earth, God created and fully accomplished a plan to gain our rights back in Him. A. W. Tozer wrote: "The greatest encouragement throughout the Bible is God's love for His lost race and the willingness of Christ, the eternal son, to show forth that love in God's plan for redemption." God is seeking us even before we seek Him. He knows we're lost, misinformed, and confused—often believing some sort of atheistic view or agnostic faith—even before we realize it is not satisfying our heart and soul. Created by God and in His image, we are meant to be His [Genesis 1:27].

Jesus told of God's love for us and His Desire for us to "find Him" in three parables in Luke 15—the parables of the lost coin, the lost sheep, and the lost son. God rejoices when we seek for Him and find Him, sweetly reminding us He comes looking for us with love when we are lost. He then welcomes us home with joy when we come to the truth and into the Kingdom of God at last, no matter how we've lived and what we've done. We might have been blind and lost but God rejoices to welcome us home. God wants all who are lost to be saved and to come to the knowledge of the truth [1 Timothy 2:4].

Prayer:
Lord, if we are lost and have not found You, or if we have wandered away from You, help us find our way back.

Scripture of the Day:
"For the Son of man is come to save that which was lost." – [Luke 19:10]

The Word for the Day is "Upper."

Quote for the Day:
"God pity us that we have swung from the Upper Room with its fire to the church with the supper room and its smoke." - Leonard Ravenhill

We generally regard an upper estate as superior to a lower one. For instance, at the end of each collegiate basketball season, a tournament committee decides and assigns the brackets for the championship. The superior teams are placed in an upper bracket, the inferior teams are placed in a lower bracket with a tougher challenge of winning. In most all rankings for anything, the upper rank is considered more advantageous than the lower rank. It is natural to aspire for an upper ranking or rating in any endeavor.

Mark 14:13-15 tells of Jesus preparing his disciples to meet Him for a last supper in a large upper room. This implies a special place where He and His disciples could have private and holy communion above the noise and clatter of the ground-level world. But notice the scripture also says it was an upper room 'furnished and prepared,' not some sloppy, cheap room, but an ordered, well-appointed room. Jesus wants this environment of beauty and peace for fellowship with all his followers.

But to attain this special upper room of peace and blessed fellowship with the Lord, the Word tells us we must enter it through a lower approach. We must be humble and submitted to the Lord before going up to the upper room. "Though the Lord be high, yet hath he respect unto the lowly: but the proud he knoweth afar off" [Psalm 138:6]. 'He giveth grace unto the lowly' [Prov 3:34], 'with the lowly is wisdom' [Prov 11:2]. We are to walk with all 'lowliness and meekness, with longsuffering, forbearing one another in love.' We are to endeavor to 'keep the unity of the Spirit in the bond of peace' [Ephesians 4:1-3]. The Lord will commune with the humble in an upper, prepared place. But the prideful, and those that exalt themselves in various ways to be seen of men, will not gain access to this special upper place [Matt 23:1-7]. Stay humble and let the Lord bring you up to His special upper room for sweet fellowship.

Prayer:
Lord, we desire to stay humble and submitted to You, walking in love toward the brethren, that we might have special personal fellowship with You in an upper place above the noise and distractions of the world.

Scripture of the Day:
"And he will show you a large upper room furnished and prepared: there make ready for us." - [Mark 14:15]

The Word for the Day is "Lilies."

Quote for the Day:
"Look to the lilies how they grow! 'Twas thus the Saviour said, that we—even in the simplest flowers that blow—God's ever watchful care might see." - D. M. Moir

In June the lilies become especially prolific in Tennessee. A big farm, the Oakes Daylilies Farm near us in Corryton, holds a Daylily Bloom Festival every year in late June. We often took J.L.'s mother to this festival as she loved to buy new daylilies there for her yard. The Oakes farm has over 1000 varieties of lilies in bloom around the grounds for those who visit to enjoy along with dozens of daylilies for sale in yellow, gold, pink, red, lavender, and more colors.

Lilies are mentioned often in the Bible and pure white lilies, especially, have become associated with Easter, based in part on the symbolic and prophetic words like in the Song of Solomon 2:1-2: "I am the rose of Sharon and the lily of the valleys." Lilies also hold symbolism for their variety and beauty and for the fact that they can grow in so many arenas—wild in the fields along the roadways or fastidiously cultivated in wealthy gardens, reminding us that Jesus as the bridegroom is no respecter of persons or places [Acts 10:34].

The lily is hardy, growing in beauty as designed, not worrying or fretting about its life and multiplying profusely. Jesus taught, 'Take no thought and don't worry so over your life; for what does it profit? Do I not take care of the birds, the grass, and the lilies of the field?' [Luke 12:22, 27; Matt 6:34]. "To appoint unto them that mourn in Zion, to give unto them beauty for ashes, the oil of joy for mourning, the garment of praise for the spirit of heaviness; that they might be called trees of righteousness, the planting of the Lord, that he might be glorified" [Is 61:3]. He advised instead to think more toward 'seeking the things of the Kingdom of God' rather than worrying so much over needless things of the day, knowing all would be well if we did [Matt 6:25-34]. Nature so often shows us a strong example of perseverance, endurance, peace, and continuing growth we could well learn from. We are meant to thrive and "grow as the lily" in our daily lives in all aspects and in our spiritual walk [Hosea 14:5].

Prayer:
Father, help us to learn from the lilies, symbolizing purity, peace, and the soul at rest, and to seek daily to live a righteous life at rest in You.

Scripture of the Day:
"Consider the lilies of the field, how they grow; they toil not neither do they spin: and yet I say unto you, that even Solomon in all his glory was not arrayed like one of these."– [Luke 12:27]

The Word for the Day is "Death."

Quote for the Day:
"Death wasn't part of God's original plan for humanity, and the Bible calls death an enemy - the last enemy to be destroyed." - Billy Graham

I recently lost my younger brother and it was a time of sorrow and loss, but also a time of relief knowing he was free from the intense pain and torment of stage 4 cancer. Another Billy Graham quote expresses the loss: "No matter how prepared you think you are for the death of a loved one, it still comes as a shock, and it still hurts deeply." Most of the comments from those at the graveside service were not about my brother's material possessions, his accomplishments, or awards, but about the character of his heart. The simple, kind, and loving things he did were valued most and retained as good memories. I have noticed this at other funerals too, it is the character and heart that is remembered and cherished most.

Death can also be a dreadful thought to the living. Why do some fear death so? I think it is because of their uncertainty of what lies beyond death. Apart from Jesus, men sit in darkness and have not the revelation that there is a natural body and there is a spiritual body [1 Cor 15:44]. Men look at the body lying in the casket, but that is just the house where the person used to live. They're not there anymore. Jesus came "to give light to them that sit in darkness and in the shadow of death, to guide our feet into the way of peace" [Luke 1:79]. The peace Jesus gives is everlasting life in His salvation. The Apostle Paul said to depart this earthly life and to be in glory with Christ was 'far better' [Phil 1:23].

We have everlasting life from the moment of salvation, but Jesus also came to give abundant life in this world [John 10:10]. Jesus wants us to live to our fullest potential in all things. Life in Jesus is a win-win reality. We live on this side of heaven in abundance and blessing, and if we pass, we then live an even greater, glorious destiny with a glorified body [Phil 3:21]. In Jesus we are passed from death to life evermore whether in the earthly body or the heavenly body!

Prayer:
Lord, we shed our tears for departed loved ones here, but we know there are celebrations of loved ones reunited in heaven. In Jesus, we know the 'circle will be unbroken' as the old hymn says.

Scripture of the Day:
"Verily, verily, I say unto you, He that heareth my word, and believeth on him that sent me, hath everlasting life, and shall not come into condemnation; but is passed from death unto life." - [John 5:24]

The Word for the Day is "Tread."

Quote for the Day:
"Fools rush in where angels fear to tread." - Alexander Pope (1712)

In 1775 during the American Revolution general Christopher Gadsden designed a flag depicting a rattlesnake poised to bite with the words below it: "Don't Tread On Me." The concept, of course, was that the snake would bite if stepped on—as the Colonists felt the British were stepping on them and their rights. Liberty often requires a fight. Teddy Roosevelt once advised to "speak softly and carry a big stick"—a good reminder for how to live life as a strong Christian. Too many walk foolishly and tread unsafely.

My husband and I often hike and we know to watch our way in the woods and on the mountain paths. We often marvel at the careless, unprepared hikers we see on the trails—taking off into the wilderness with no map, no knowledge of the area, no understanding of the turnings in the path or the dangers they might encounter. They often hike not dressed for the way, not well prepared, and are often the ones who fall into problems.

In our lives we need to walk prepared. We have an enemy we need to be knowledgeable of and prepared to meet fearlessly. An unexpected enemy always has the advantage. That's why we are told to 'gird up our loins' (Jer 1:17; 1 Peter 1:13), to 'put on the armor of God' daily (Eph 6:11-18), and to walk with the sure knowledge that God is on our side when we stand rightly in faith against His enemy (Ps 118:6-9). We are meant to purposely and aggressively tread over our enemies, to 'be more than conquerors in this world' (Rom 8:37-39). But in our daily walk we are also meant to tread lightly in love and encouragement with our fellowmen, our family, and our brethren in the Lord. Often these spread their dreams and visions before us, and we should watch carefully not to tread on those harshly or unwisely but to walk in love. W. B. Yeats wrote: "Tread softly with your brethren and fellowmen…walking in love, encouraging, exhorting." We are meant to 'edify' and 'exhort one another daily,' to give 'good words that make the heart of others glad' (1 Thess 5:11; Heb 3:13; Prov 12:25).

Prayer:
Lord, teach us to live our lives prepared, to 'fight the good fight of faith' (1 Tim 6:12) daily, walking in power and victory as a good soldier of the Lord.

Scripture of the Day:
"Behold, I give unto you power to tread on serpents and scorpions, and over all the power of the enemy: and nothing shall by any means hurt you." –
[Luke 10:19]

The Word for the Day is "Anything."

Quote for the Day:
"Faith is not believing just anything. It is believing God, resting in Him, and trusting His Word." - E.M. Bounds

In today's world, with so much access to information via the media and the internet, there can be so many conflicting views and opinions swirling around that it can be a challenge for some to know what to believe.

But the Lord does not want His people to be doubtful, wishy-washy, subject to believe just anything they hear. When we are tempted to believe the 'enticing words of man's wisdom' [1 Cor 2:4], we can be confused and unsettled in our faith. God wants us steady and sure in our belief: "That we henceforth be no more children, tossed to and fro, and carried about with every wind of doctrine, by the sleight of men, and cunning craftiness, whereby they lie in wait to deceive" [Ephesians 4:14]. We need a solid faith we can be confident in, hold fast to, and believe in. We are given the measure of true faith when we accept salvation in Jesus our Lord [Rom 12:3]. The new life [2 Cor 5:17] in Jesus comes with the measure of faith given to us.

We then grow, increase, solidify our faith by knowledge of God's Word: "So then faith cometh by hearing, and hearing by the word of God" [Rom 10:17]. We become steadfast and established in God's Truth so that we are not tempted to believe just anything the voice of mammon speaks. We hold fast our faith when things look hard in the natural just as Abraham did, choosing instead to believe God [Gen 15:6]. E.M. Bounds wrote: "Faith rests its whole weight on His Word. Faith believes, is persistent, can hold fast, stand fast, and wait knowing God's Word is truer than anything seen or said."

Our faith must rest in God, trusting His Word, not being fearful or anxious for anything [Phil 4:6]. We must lift our believing to a higher level than earthly thinking, knowing that we stand in the knowledge of eternal truth and that with God all things are possible [Matt 19:26].

Prayer:
Lord, we establish our faith, believing in thy eternal Word, and we will not be moved by anything contrary to Your Truth.

Scripture of the Day:
"And this is the confidence that we have in him, that, if we ask any thing according to his will, he heareth us: And if we know that he hear us, whatsoever we ask, we know we have the petitions that we desired of him." - [1 John 5:14-15]

The Word for the Day is "Rekindle."

Quote for the Day:
"Come, Lord, stir us up and call us back. Kindle and seize us. Be our fire and our sweetness." – Augustine of Hippo

A scripture in Revelation reminds us God isn't pleased when we drift away from Him in our faith. "I have somewhat against thee because thou has left thy first love" [Rev 2:4-5]. An awareness of your need for God will lead you to seek a strong "on fire," fervent relationship again. And when you draw nigh to God, he will draw nigh to you and begin to 'rekindle His fire in you' [James 4:8]. Seeking more of the Lord, repenting for neglecting time with Him, studying His Word more diligently, giving time to prayer, and thinking and meditating on Him will rekindle fading love if your heart and desire is right.

Love is always worth rekindling and you can fall in love all over again with God, with Jesus, and with His Spirit if you hunger for that love, want it, seek for it. It is your choice to keep walking further away, letting your light and relationship with God grow dimmer, or to turn and draw back closer, reconciling with Him, and becoming fervent in your passion again. Scriptures warn about letting the fire of faith dim. In the parable of the ten virgins half let their lamps go out but half kept theirs kindled, properly valuing their relationship with the Lord [Matt 25:1-13]. The story says the foolish 'slumbered and slept.' It is easy to grow lax in faith or to grow lax in most anything. 'A little sleep, a little slumber, a little folding the hands and poverty will come on you like a thief' [Prov 24:33-34]. This wisdom is true in a natural and a spiritual sense.

In the Olympic Games a torch is carried in at the start of the games as a part of the opening ceremonies. The concept comes from the "torch race" relay the Greeks used to hold. The competitors passed the flame from one to another in the relay, running as fast as possible without extinguishing the fire and being eliminated. We, too, are to run our race but to keep our light burning [Heb 12:1-2]. And, like in the torch race, keeping our fire burning is more important than simply winning the race.

Prayer:
Father, we want to always keep our light and our flame burning. If we have slumbered and slept and let our light dim, stir us up and help us rekindle our faith.

Scripture of the Day:
'Wherefore I put thee in remembrance to stir up (rekindle) the gift of God, which is in thee ...' –[2 Timothy 1:6]

July

The Word for the Day is "Infirmities."

Quote for the Day:
"What an absurd thing it is to pass over all the valuable parts of a man and fix our attention on his infirmities." - Joseph Addison

We usually associate the word infirmity with sickness, but it can also be defined as 'any physical or mental weakness' or 'any personal failing'. Any failing or weakness in our human nature or physical body is an infirmity. We too often focus our attention more on our failings than our strengths. As Christians, we frequently condemn and beat ourselves up over failings and problems in our lives, personality or nature, which we haven't overcome yet.

We sometimes seek out people for help—friends, family, counselors, pastors, or others whose advice we respect. We can often get good Godly help from others, too, as when Moses grew weary on the mount: "But Moses hands were heavy; and they took a stone, and put it under him, and he sat thereon; and Aaron and Hur stayed up his hands, the one on the one side, and the other on the other side; and his hands were steady until the going down of the sun" [Exodus 17:12].

However, we have an advocate to help our infirmities that is beyond the abilities of man. Jesus is ever making intercession for us to the Father according to the will of God [Rom 8:26-27]. A.B. Simpson wrote: "Our first great helper is the Lord Jesus Christ, our advocate with the Father. He it is who takes away our imperfect petitions from our hands, cleanses them from their defects, corrects their faults, and then claims their answer."

God wants us to ever trust in His grace to heal and overcome our infirmities and to focus on our salvation in Jesus who was stricken, smitten, and afflicted that we might be healed [Is 53:4-5]. God is always desiring to fulfill our potential and purpose. "The Lord will perfect that which concerneth me: thy mercy, O Lord, endureth for ever" [Ps 138:8]. Thank God for abundant life in Jesus!

Prayer:
Father, we look not at our infirmities, but turn our eyes opon Jesus, the author and finisher of our faith [Hebrews 12:2].

Scripture of the Day:
"Seeing then that we have a great high priest, that is passed into the heavens, Jesus the Son of God....not an high priest which cannot be touched with the feeling of our infirmities....let us therefore come boldly unto the throne of grace, that we may obtain mercy, and find grace to help in time of need." - [Hebrews 4:14-16]

The Word for the Day is "Patience."

Quote for the Day:
"Patience and perseverance have a magical effect before which difficulties disappear and obstacles vanish." – John Quincy Adams

Patience is the capacity to calmly accept or tolerate difficulties or delays without getting irritated, annoyed or provoked. Recent research shows that the rapid pace of technology today is rewiring humans to be less and less patient. This change is to our harm as other studies show patient people experience less depression and negative emotions, less irritability and better health. Those with more patience tend to have more satisfying lives, get more done and achieve their goals, are more forgiving and more self-regulating.

In Christianity patience is meant to increase as one grows deeper in faith. It is one of the seven virtues, a fruit of the Spirit, and an attribute of God we are to emulate [Gal 5:22-23; Ps 103:8]. In today's world though, we often don't exercise patience. We don't want to wait. We want things now—and by acting impatiently, on our own, ahead of God, we often foil God's best plan for our lives and miss out on a blessing. The Bible has many stories that show us the problems created by impatience. Abraham and Sarah got impatient waiting for the heir God promised them and Sarah sent her maid in to Abraham to help things along [Gen 16:2]. Naaman, angry and irritated that Elisha didn't come out personally to speak with him and annoyed the prophet asked him to wash seven times in the Jordan River, almost missed out on being healed of leprosy [2 Kings 5:1-14].

In all things God teaches patience, showing us in nature the process of growth takes time and can't be rushed. It would be foolish to demand a caterpillar to hurry up and get that chrysalis stage over with. Growth works 'precept upon precept, line upon line, here a little, there a little' [Is 28:10]. Arnold Glasow wrote: "The key to everything is patience. You get the chicken by hatching the egg not by smashing it." We are not meant to act with a 'hasty spirit,' to be 'easily provoked,' but instead we are to 'put on patience daily', being 'slow to anger and annoyance,' remembering that 'he who rules his spirit is mighty in God's eyes' [Prov 14:29; 1 Cor 13:5; Prov 16:32; Col 3:12].

Prayer:
Father, help us to be quiet, steady, and even-tempered in this world today which often tries to push us to act impatiently out of Your best will to our hurt.

Scripture of the Day:
"Let patience have her perfect work, that ye may be perfect and entire, wanting nothing." – [James 1:4]

The Word for the Day is "Freedom."

Quote for the Day:
"I believe our flag is more than just cloth and ink. It is a universally recognized symbol that stands for liberty, and freedom. It is the history of our nation, and it's marked by the blood of those who died defending it." - John Thune

Freedom does not come cheap. As we celebrate the 4th of July tomorrow, Independence Day, we should pause to give thanks to God for our nation and its founding. Good men desired a nation, a way of life, founded upon freedom, where men could determine their own destiny by their own free will, no more in bondage to rulers, despots, and government control. To obtain this dream of freedom, of the people, by the people, for the people, they paid a great price. They fought, suffered, and many paid the price of their lives to establish a nation of freedom.

God paid a great price for our spiritual freedom. He gave His Son to be tortured, beaten, and crucified to set us free from the curse of sin. This freedom of life was bought and paid for by Jesus' sacrifice, but God does not violate our free-will decision to accept or reject the Life. Let us who have accepted the gift of salvation in Jesus, give thanks and celebrate our independence in Him. We have been given a new nature whereby we are no longer in bondage to serve the law of sin and death [Rom 8:2]. We are called out of the darkness of this world into His marvelous Light, whereby we are in the world, but not of the world, free from the ungodly mold of the world's ways to serve the living God in truth and righteousness [1Peter 2:9].

The Bible in Acts 22:28 tells us the Roman chief captain paid a great sum for his freedom, but Paul was free born. So it is in Jesus, we are free born through Him. We are born into freedom from the law of sin and death to serve God in righteousness and truth and to be partakers of the divine nature [2 Peter 1:4]. What a great Independence Day in the Lord to celebrate!

Prayer:
Lord, thank You for America and our way of life, and thank You for salvation in Jesus, both gifts of freedom and grace from You.

Scripture of the Day:
"And the chief captain answered, With a great sum obtained I this freedom. And Paul said, But I was free born." - [Acts 22:28]

The Word for the Day is "Self."

Quote for the Day:
"The self you were really intended to be is something that lives not from nature but from God." – C. S. Lewis

In teaching Educational Psychology in college, my students studied about a variety of terms related to the "self," each important to a child's healthy development—self-concept, self-efficacy, self-esteem, self-confidence and more. A child's self-concept refers to all the ideas, feelings, and attitudes a child holds about him or herself. As children grow and begin to compare themselves with others, and hear feedback from others about themselves, they begin to create judgments about their worth, termed self-esteem. All these factors and more began to influence the confidence children have about themselves—impacting how they learn, socialize and get along with others, set and attain goals, communicate and solve problems, and view life. As social beings we are highly impacted by others and we yearn, whether we will admit it or not, for approval.

Yet it is God's approval we should deeply yearn for above all, and the true confidence we most need is not in ourselves—or in what others think—but in Him. 'Blessed is the man who believes in, trusts in, and relies on the Lord, and whose hope and confidence the Lord is' [Jer 17:7]. The wisdom and counsel in psychology, helping to shape a good self-concept in children, is not wrong. It is needed in a world where so many are damaged emotionally by hurtful environments and negativity. All people need love and encouragement but all people also need God. He loves us and we were made in His likeness to fellowship Him.

We are not intended to be sufficient unto ourselves and self-willed [Titus 1:7] but submitted to God [James 4:7]. When we give our lives to Christ, we become new and begin to die out to our old selves. That process of growth in faith gradually brings us into more unity with the Lord, rooted and built up in Him, established in Him with the heart and mind of Christ [Col 2:7; 1 Cor 2:16]. There is no better place in which our "self" can safely rest. Our natural self is never sufficient alone to do all it can do, or be all it's meant to be, in this life as when rightly submitted under the leadership of God.

Prayer:
Father, build within us the true self-confidence we need in You and help us to seek for Your approval and to become more like You in our walk in life.

Scripture of the Day:
"I can of mine own self do nothing...because I seek not mine own will, but the will of the Father which hath sent me." –[John 5:30]

The Word for the Day is "Committed."

Quote for the Day:
"If you do not plan to live the Christian life totally commited to knowing your God and to walking in obedience to Him, then don't begin, for this is what Christianity is all about." - Kay Arthur

As Christians, we should be committed, dedicated, devoted, loyal, and faithful to following the Lord. A.W. Tozer stated: "A true disciple does not consider Christianity a part-time commitment. He has become a Christian in all parts of his life. He has reached the point where there is no turning back." Our Christian commitment should be full, not part-time. I think this desire is true for all sincere relationships. We want something more, we don't want a part-time relationship or a part-time love. In relationships we want someone's heart and soul to be fully engaged; we want commitment. Who can imagine repeating the vow: "I do take this person to be my part-time spouse." An anonymous quote says: "Love is always full time, never part time, never sometimes and certainly not just in your time."

In the natural, in relationships, we expect this. Why would we think God wants anything less? He doesn't want a part-time relationship. He is a jealous God; He doesn't want other priorities or other gods before Him [Ex 34:14, 20:3]. Yet too often we're a part-time Christian who wants a full-time God. We are too uncommitted or lazy to build a rich, full-time relationship with God, but we want Him to give His all to us all the time.

God wants us to trust Him with all our heart and in every way and area of our life to acknowledge Him [Prov 3:5-6]. God wants His words to be the guiding priority of our lives; then we receive His love and our abode with Him [John 14:23]. We must not let the past or things behind us hinder, but be fully committed to God and as the Apostle Paul expressed: "reaching forth unto those things which are before, I press toward the mark for the prize of the high calling of God in Christ Jesus" [Phil 3:13-14]. We can then shake off the past and current hindrances and follow our Lord with a full-time, full-commitment relationship.

Prayer:
Lord, we will not turn back to the old ways, but walk in newness of life with Jesus our Lord with a devoted and committed heart.

Scripture of the Day:
"I know whom I have believed, and am persuaded that he is able to keep that which I have committed unto him." - [2 Timothy 1:12]

The Word for the Day is "Perfect."

Quote for the Day:
"God didn't instruct us to talk about being perfect. He said be ye perfect as your Father who is in heaven is also perfect." – Kenneth Copeland

In our day-to-day life we're often in a hurry, and impatient in the process, but God most often works slowly and methodically—more concerned with the final product than speed. Like a builder working on a house, God wants a solid foundation so the structure won't just look good on the outside but also stand strong, and stand the test of time. Smith Wigglesworth wrote: "The Holy Spirit is coming to take out of the world a church that is a perfect bride"…and despite our beliefs about the impossibility of growing into perfection that is what God wants. "Our heavenly Father has given us the perfect image of Christ to be our example, His perfect law to be our rule, and it is for us to aim at this perfection" [Charles Spurgeon]. Spurgeon confirmed that God doesn't want us to simply strive to be okay or 'as good as we can be' but 'to be perfect as our Father in heaven is perfect' [Matt 5:48]. We all remember giggling at Mary Poppins measuring herself and announcing she was "practically perfect in every way" but that's what God wants us to strive for.

When an angler drops a hook with a worm on it into the water, a passing fish may take a nibble, but if the worm isn't tasty or good, he'll swim away and not bite. When others are drawn to us we want to be sure that what they 'taste and see is good' [Psalm 34:8]. We are God's product, and we need to represent Him well. We can't make excuses and say 'oh, well, no one's perfect, you know' and act lackadaisical about our failings and shortcomings. As fishers of men, we need to ever work to remove our weak areas and to let Christ increase in us more and more [John 3:30].

We represent God in everything we do, say, and write, and we should strive to represent Him well. "Strive for perfection in everything you do. Take the best that exists and make it better…accept nothing as nearly right or good enough." [Sir Henry Royce]. When others encounter us, we want to leave a good taste in their mouths of what a Christian is.

Prayer:
Lord, although we may not be perfect in every way now, we purpose to keep striving, with diligence and patience, for that high goal because of You.

Scripture of the Day:
"Let patience have her perfect work, that ye may be perfect and entire, wanting nothing." – [James 1:4]

The Word for the Day is "Forsaketh."

Quote for the Day:
"He is truly great that is great in charity. He is truly great that is little in himself, and maketh no account of any height or honor. And he is truly learned that doeth the will of God, and forsaketh his own will." - Thomas Kempis

Luke 14:33 tells us the Lord says we must forsake (abandon, give-up) all that we have or we cannot be His disciples. This means more than just walking away from something, it means letting nothing in our lives have a greater priority or importance than our walk with the Lord Jesus. We must value nothing in life more important than Jesus, and let nothing in life have more influence and control than the Spirit of God. It is simply dying out to the old man, that Jesus might perfect the new man, created in Him [2 Cor 5:17].

Jesus said in Matthew 19:29: "And every one that hath forsaken houses, or brethren or sisters, or father, or mother, or wife, or children, or lands, for my name's sake, shall receive an hundredfold, and shall inherit everlasting life." Jesus knew natural man is self-serving and can be reluctant to change his thinking, and that it is difficult to sometimes break away from things and people. When Jesus talks of forsaking brethren, sisters, father, mother, wife, or children, He is talking about giving loyalty and allegiance to Him above all others. We are still to love and care for family and friends [1 Tim 5:8], but we must place Jesus first above their influence and opinions. Houses and lands refer to material pursuits or possessions that we place in importance above the Lord.

The Lord's will may be to keep you where your are to serve Him, or He may change your current circumstance as He did with Simon and Andrew: "And straightway they forsook their nets, and followed him" [Mark 1:18]. But when we keep Jesus on the throne of our lives, forsaking all others, we walk in the blessed assurance that He is directing our path to reward and blessings [Matt 19:29]. And we have the blessed assurance that the Lord will never forsake us: "And they that know thy name will put their trust in thee: for thou, Lord, hast not forsaken them that seek thee" [Psalm 9:10].

Prayer:
Lord, we will forsake all and place You on the throne of our heart always, that You might lead us unto paths of righteousness for thy name's sake. [Psalm 23:3]

Scripture of the Day:
"So likewise, whosoever he be of you that forsaketh not all that he hath, he cannot be my disciple." - [Luke 14:33]

The Word for the Day is "Flow."

Quote for the Day:
"There is a place to reach where all that God has for us can flow through us to a needy world all the time." – Smith Wigglesworth

Whenever we think of anything 'flowing freely' it is usually positive—water flowing freely in a stream or waterfall, water flowing from a fountain when we are thirsty. From early Old Testament times God talked of leading His People to a land "flowing with milk and honey" [Exodus 3:8], a beautiful, positive picture to them, and to us, of how God wants to provide our needs. Sometimes flow is used in terms of protection, that God will protect us so troubles or waters don't overflow us [Is 43:2], and in promise of provision, as when God caused the waters to flow out of the rock for a thirsty people [Is 48:21]. In another way God wants us to be a conduit of His love and grace in the world, to bring love and 'peace like a flowing stream' to others [Is 66:12].

We know that flow is 'the action of moving along in a steady continuous uninterrupted stream,' its opposite when flow is stalled or stopped, as with a clogged fountain. In all works we do for God, we want His goodness, righteousness, and truth to flow through us. For this to happen we need to continually fill ourselves with Him through reading and studying the Word, communing and staying close to Him. If we put nothing in, there will be nothing to flow out.

In psychology, the term flow refers to a state in which individuals are so immersed and focused in an activity that they forget time and self. They become completely absorbed in what they're doing, lost in the enjoyment and fulfillment of it simply for the joy of experience versus what they can get out of it. How blessed it is when we are used of God in this way—lost in our work for Him, whatever it is, without thinking of reward or motivated by self-serving interests. Rick Warren wrote: "your ministry is not about you." It's about Him and finishing the work Jesus left us to do. Our heart should yearn to come into that richer, deeper place in God where He can flow through us freely as He wills, and that out of our spirit flow the acts, the words, and the example that all need to see in order to have their needs met and to be drawn to Jesus Christ.

Prayer:
Lord, fill us and move in us so we can be an overflowing stream to a world thirsty and needy for You.

Scripture of the Day:
"He that believeth on Me, as the scripture hath said, out of his belly shall flow rivers of living water." – [John 7:38]

The Word for the Day is "Happy."

Quote for the Day:
"The first great and primary business to which I ought to attend every day was to have my soul happy in the Lord." - George Mueller

We all cherish our founding principles of life, liberty, and the pursuit of happiness. Men seek to be happy by various mechanisms and attainments: money, fame, security, pleasure, leisure, charity, ambitions, recreations, thrills, and many others. These all can satisfy to a degree, but the key to true happiness is within us: the state of our soul as Mueller's quote above. The Word tells us that happy are the people *saved* by the Lord [Deut 33:29]; 'happy is that people whose God is the Lord' [Ps 144:15]. Salvation makes our heart a new creation, and we then have the mind of Christ, so that our thinking within ourselves makes the happy life as we live for God [2 Cor 5:17; 1 Cor 2:16].

Giving your heart and life to the Lord is the first step to happiness through God's salvation. It is a free-will choice and decision we make. Jesus stands at the door of our soul and knocks, but He doesn't force Himself in, you must open the door and let Him in to be Savior and Lord of your life [Rev 3:20]. Now you are part of a people whose God is the Lord, saved by the Lord. The next step is to grow in the Lord by seeking God's wisdom and understanding according to Proverbs 3:13, and by increasing in the knowledge of His Word [Ps 119:130].

The Lord in His Word gives us wisdom and keys to walking in this happy life with Him. "Blessed is every one that feareth the Lord; that walketh in his ways. For thou shalt eat the labour of thine hands: happy shalt thou be, and it shall be well with thee" [Psalm 128:1-2]. Happy is he who looks to God for help, whose hope is in the Lord [Ps 146:5]. Happy is the man who has mercy (compassion) on the poor [Prov 14:21]. Happy are we if we endure suffering, persecution and reproach for righteousness' sake: 'for the spirit of glory and of God are upon you' [James 5:11; 1 Pet 3:14, 4:14]. Jesus summarized: "For I have given you an example, that ye should do as I have done to you. If ye know these things, happy are ye if ye do them" [John 13:15, 17].

Prayer:
Lord, thank You that we are happy in following and serving You in all our ways, that we might do Your works of love and power in all our ways.

Scripture of the Day:
"Happy is the man that findeth wisdom, and the man that getteth understanding." - [Proverbs 3:13]

The Word for the Day is "All."

Quote for the Day:
"As God is exalted to the right place in our lives, a thousand problems are solved all at once." - A. W. Tozer

An anonymous quote says 'there is no greater act of worship than giving God all of you' but so often we put so many other things in our lives above God, and we suffer needlessly for it. Even business and educational advice books stress that the one who gives his all to anything is the more likely to succeed. We set goals in the world in all sorts of areas, and diligently pursue them, but often set few goals spiritually to give our all more and more to God every day.

Despite the fact that we should yearn to live in this place with God, striving to give Him our all, it is also to our benefit to put God first, to have Jesus living in us [Gal 2:20]. Jesus taught: "I am the vine, ye are the branches: he that abideth in Me, and I in him, the same bringeth forth much fruit: for without me ye can do nothing" [John 15:5]. Our dependence is supposed to be on Him for us to be blessed, successful, and happy. 'For of Him, and through Him, and to Him, are all things: to whom be glory for ever. Amen.' [Rom 11:36]. 'All things have been created by Him and for Him, things on heaven and on earth' [Col 1:16]. He is the center of the Universe and should be the center of our lives. Everything has a center, an essential core. The planets all revolve around the sun. The nucleus is the center of the atom. The center of anything is the focus point from which all activity is directed. God is intended to be our focus point and center. Our lives are intended to revolve around Him, to be centered in Him, and we are meant to draw our life and being from Him. Whatever we do, even what we eat or drink, is to be to the glory of God [1 Cor 10:31].

In a relationship when you deeply love another, you tend to be sacrificial of self. You're willing to sacrifice time to be with them and to sacrifice your own selfish needs and desires to please them. This is what God wants, for us to love Him in that way and to gradually yield ourselves more and more to Him, giving Him our all and our best [Rom 6:13-19].

Prayer:
Father, we know we don't deny ourselves enough to yield and follow after You as we should. Help us to yearn to give more of our heart, mind, and soul to You every day.

Scripture of the Day:
"Jesus said unto him, Thou shalt love the Lord thy God with all thy heart, and with all thy soul, and with all thy mind." – [Matthew 22:37]

The Word for the Day is "Safe."

Quote for the Day:
"The devil says I'm out, but the Lord says I'm safe." - Billy Sunday

Billy Sunday, quoted above, was a professional baseball player before becoming a mighty evangelist in the early 1920s. I can relate to his quote because I lived, played, and breathed baseball in all my youth. I can remember experiences of running the bases at full speed, sliding into home plate in a close call, the crowd perceiving that I was tagged out, then the umpire waving his hands and yelling "safe!" What a thrill. That's how it often is in our walk with the Lord in this life. Life events and problems occur, knocking us into a slide, making it look to all as if we're out—beaten by failures or events, by attacks of sickness, betrayal, or financial setbacks. But then, as we keep holding fast and leaning to God, the outcome changes to good, we're called "safe!"

We can be sure that in this world we are going to have tribulations, trials, problems, temptations, and obstacles of all kinds. But Jesus tells us to be of good cheer, for He has overcome the world [John 16:33]. It is what we do when tribulations come that matters. We are to remain sober and vigilant, because our adversary the devil, as a roaring lion walks about, seeking whom he may devour[1 Peter 5:8]. When trouble comes, we don't yield, we fight.

When trials come, hold on to your faith and the promises of God, knowing 'this is the victory that overcometh the world, even our faith' [1 John 5:4]. Remember 'God is a shield for you, the glory and lifter up of your head' [Psalm 3:3]. Run the bases of life boldly, knowing the Lord is your helper, and you do not fear man or trials that come [Hebrews 13:6].

Hold fast to belief for a 'safe' call. "Therefore, brethren, stand fast, and hold the traditions which ye have been taught, whether by word, or our epistle" [2 Thess 2:15]. 'Hold fast the confidence and the rejoicing of hope firm unto the end' [Heb 3:6]. 'Hold fast the profession of our faith without wavering; for He is faithful that promised' [Heb 10:23]. Run the race; in the Lord, you're "safe!"

Prayer:
Lord, thank You for the power and authority of Your holy name which is our strong tower of safety.

Scripture of the Day:
"The name of the Lord is a strong tower: the righteous runneth into it, and is safe." - [Proverbs 18:10]

The Word for the Day is "Need."

Quote for the Day:
"Wherever there is a human need, there is an opportunity for kindness and to make a difference." – Kevin Heath

The Bible warns and cautions about the dangers of loving the world and lusting after things of the world to excess rather than walking in the love of God toward others [I John 3]. It also warns of shutting up our heart and compassion toward our brethren in need. We tend to readily reach out to others when they've been ill or hospitalized or when they have lost a loved one. That compassion costs us little financially—a card, flowers, a trip to the hospital, a casserole dropped off at the house. But the numbers who reach out when someone is hit with a financial hardship thin out considerably. Research reveals that individuals respond the least freely and compassionately in this area.

People react with less compassion to people who experience financial hardship than they do to people experiencing other sufferings. Surprisingly, social class was found to greatly influence compassion, with those with more social status and wealth pulling back the most. There is a sad tendency for people to quietly distance themselves from those experiencing financial hardship rather than reaching out with love and compassion to help. Social psychology defines this reaction as the "just-world phenomenon," the tendency for people to believe the world is just and that people get what they deserve and deserve what they get. It's a worldly way for people to harden their hearts and justify their culture's familiar social system and their own selfishness. We need to be prayerful and watchful not to be drawn into this worldly system of thinking.

Deep within, we know that hardships and loss can happen to all and we shouldn't harden our hearts and 'shut up our bowels of compassion' when hardship and sorrow strike among those we know. God is a giving God, a helping God, an encouraging God. The Word cautions to never let the love of money harden us [1 Tim 6:6-12].Our admonishment is to freely give as we have received [Matt 10:8] and to remember that as we give, it will be given to us [Luke 6:38].

Prayer:
Father, help us to never close up our hearts of love and compassion but to always look for opportunities to show Your love and kindness and to make a difference.

Scripture of the Day:
"But whoso hath this world's good, and seeth his brother have need, and shutteth up his bowels of compassion from him, how dwelleth the love of God in him?" – [I John 3:17]

The Word for the Day is "Brought."

Quote for the Day:
"Through many dangers, toils and snares, I have already come; 'Tis grace has brought me safe thus far, And grace will lead me home." - John Newton

So often in life it is through a series of small events, a series of small learnings, that we are brought into greater understandings. Even as children our knowledge to read is built on a series of learning steps from recognizing letters, then words, then sentences and more. In any areas of faith we grow by a series of steps, too; "For precept must be upon precept, precept upon precept; line upon line, line upon line; here a little, and there a little" [Isaiah 28:10]. Yet sometimes, because the process is gradual, we fail to see the Lord's hand in our growth. And we fail to see how often God has brought us out of dark and hard places, developed and changed us, protected and blessed us.

We need to always hold the knowledge in our minds that God has a purpose and plan for our lives, that He leads us and guides us, that He brings us into His Will and Best if we are yielded and willing [Jer 29:11; Rom 8:28]. "For we are his workmanship, created in Christ Jesus unto good works, which God hath before ordained that we should walk in them" [Eph 2:10]. He will lead us and bring us in the right way all our days if we yield and follow Him [John 16:13; Ps 48:14].

God will bring us out of dark places, too, out of hard times—out of pits we fall into in error and ignorance, out of trouble the enemy creates and brings, even out of the problems of the earth we all face. David wrote: "He brought me up also out of an horrible pit, out of the miry clay, and set my feet upon a rock, and established my goings. And he hath put a new song in my mouth" [Ps 40:2-3]. He delivers us from troubles and fears and sorrows because He delights in us [Psalm 18:17-19, 34:4, 18:48].

The Israelites carried a carved rod with them, the carvings representing all the ways God had brought them out of trouble into blessing. We should remember all the ways He has led us out of trouble, grown us in faith, and blessed us. "Bless the Lord, O my soul, and forget not all his benefits"[Psalm 103:2].

Prayer:
Lord, thank You that You have brought us forth in knowledge, wisdom, and faith to establish us and set our feet upon The Rock.

Scripture of the Day:
"And they shall know that I am the Lord their God, that brought them forth out of the land of Egypt, that I may dwell among them." - [Exodus 29:46]

The Word for the Day is "Thinketh."

Quote for the Day:
"As a man thinketh, so is he and as a man chooseth, so is he."– Ralph Waldo Emerson

Thoughts are innocent and do no harm, many say. Yet an abundance of research shows that thoughts are not innocent and meaningless. Thoughts are energy and every thought carries an energy level that impacts the brain, mind, body, and emotions. A thought is thus a powerful thing but generally we go through life not taking much notice of our thoughts, not realizing how they impact our life and actions—and the enemy loves this. We may not know how powerful thoughts are, but satan does. If he can get inroads into our minds through our thoughts, he can get us to begin to believe his lies and to begin speaking them to our greater harm [James 3:5-12].

Marcus Aurelius wrote that "the soul becomes dyed with the colour of its thoughts." Studies reveal that too many of our thoughts are fear-based, negative 'what-if' thoughts and more unfortunately, these negative thoughts have been found to affect a like reaction in our lives. Thoughts have a tendency to create your life, and over 60,000 thoughts run through the mind every day. Where do all those random thoughts come from? From sense perceptions, the conscious and unconscious mind, from everything that has a connection to you, but mostly from the outside world. The words of music you listen to, the television programs you watch, the books you read, the people you talk to and listen to are constantly planting thoughts in your mind. Others roll up directly from the enemy of your soul, 'the father of lies,' who knows the power of thoughts and whose sole desire is to 'kill, steal, and destroy' and to harm you [John 8:44, 10:10].

The key to change is to become conscious of your thoughts and not to entertain or accept the negative thoughts you're bombarded with [2 Cor 10:5]. Swat those pesky blood-sucking mosquitoes away. If you've settled into habits and patterns of negative thinking and the habitual voicing of those thoughts, you will have to consciously work to alter those patterns and renew your mind [Romans 12:2].

Prayer:
Lord, help me to become more aware of the power of my thoughts and to take every negative, unrighteous thought captive before it destructively influences my life.

Scripture of the Day:
"For as he thinketh in his heart, so is he." – [Proverbs 23:7]

The Word for the Day is "Prosper."

Quote for the Day:
"How important it is to ascertain the will of God, before we undertake anything, because then are we not only blessed in our souls, but also the work of our hands will prosper." - George Muller

Some believe that it is godly to be poor and needy. They think this is 'their cross to bear' to keep them humble, or that God has afflicted them with want in order to 'teach them something.' Of course when you ask these indiduals what scripture they are basing that on, they have no answer. Because there is no scriptural basis for this foolish notion. They would never inflict this condition on anyone they loved, but they believe God, who is Love, would be so cruel to do so. The scripture 3 John 2 makes it very clear: 'God wishes above *all* things (italics added) that you prosper, and be in health.' Of course a loving God would want this. The scripture verifies that God *takes pleasure* in our prosperity! "Let the Lord be magnified, which hath pleasure in the prosperity of his servant" [Psalm 35:27]. God doesn't take pleasure in your afflictions and want, but in your prosperity as His servant.

Jesus purchased this great benefit, promise, and blessing for us at the cross. "For ye know the grace of our Lord Jesus Christ, that, though he was rich, yet for your sakes he became poor, that ye through his poverty might be rich" [2 Cor 8:9]. Jesus, the Son of God, Creator, Name above all names in the universe, emptied himself on Calvary not only for our sins, but he was stripped bare of all possessions that He might redeem us from the curse: "Christ hath redeemed us from the curse of the law, being made a curse for us: for it is written, Cursed is every one that hangeth on a tree"[Gal 3:13]. This great benefit was included in the salvation we received in Jesus. He shed His blood for our sins, gave us salvation unto eternal life, and redeemed us from the curse at Calvary. This promise of prosperity is included in our salvation as much as forgiveness of sins. God wants us to enjoy and be blessed in our new life in Jesus. And he delights in our prosperity: "The blessing of the Lord, it maketh rich, and he addeth no sorrow with it" [Proverbs 10:22].

Prayer:
Lord, we thank You for our salvation in Jesus so great and full, and we thank You that You delight in giving us the blessing of prosperity.

Scripture of the Day:
"Beloved, I wish above all things that thou mayest prosper and be in health, even as thy soul prospereth." - [3 John 2]

The Word for the Day is "Blood."

Quote for the Day:
"Pardon of sin and love of sin are like oil and water…they will never go together. All who are washed in the blood of Christ are also sanctified by the Spirit of Christ."
– JC Ryle

In a blood transfusion blood is transferred from the blood of one person into the veins of another. It is often done as a life-saving maneuver but it is important that an individual is given blood that is the right blood type and compatible. Blood is often called the life of the body. It carries oxygen and nutrients to all parts of the body and carries out waste. The blood cells help heal injury and fight against infection.

There are such parallels in the understanding of the blood in a natural sense and in the spiritual sense. We know Jesus 'shed his blood so we could be saved and cleansed from all sin' [1John 1:7]. It is a blood transfusion, sought by us, and accepted willingly, that washes the sin out of us, 'cleansing us of all unrighteousness,' 'making us new creations' and beginning the 'ongoing work of redemption and change in us'[1 John 1:9; 2 Cor 5:17; Heb 9:12-14]. How wonderful that God made this way for us to come back into His Kingdom with all fullness and might and that Jesus was willing to come to earth and pay the price of death for this to happen.

We always view a person a hero who willingly lays down his life for another. It is a sacrifice few are willing to make in this world. Jesus made that sacrifice for us—coming to earth, living a sinless life, 'laying down His life to save us from sin and death, making peace with God for all by His blood' [Rom 5:9; Col 1:20]. Should we not be grateful for that transfusion of His Blood every day and work to 'cleanse our lives and conscience from dead works to serve Him,' being ever thankful for the 'blood-bought change' going on within us? [Heb 9:14] Sometimes it is good to sing out loud the old hymn written in 1876 by Robert Lowry: "What can wash away my sin? Nothing but the blood of Jesus. What can make me whole again? Nothing but the blood of Jesus." To Him be all glory.

Prayer:
Lord Jesus, may we ever be mindful and grateful for Your willingness to come down to earth so we could have a blood transfusion of New Life through You.

Scripture of the Day:
"In whom we have redemption through his blood, even the forgiveness of sins."
 - [Colossians 1:14]

The Word for the Day is "Hate."

Quote for the Day:
"You cannot pray for someone and hate them at the same time. Even if you are asking God to restrain their evil actions, you should also be praying that He will change their hearts. Only eternity will reveal the impact of our prayers for others." - Billy Graham

It seems in our society today that it is a taboo to hate, feel intense or passionate dislike, for anything. You would probably be accused of being 'hateful' or 'judgmental' if you did so. But a true Christian if asked if he has any hate, should respond: "Of course I do, I fear the Lord and I love the Lord, therefore I hate evil." What?! People would say "That can't be true!" The Word of God is clear: 'The fear of the Lord is to hate evil', as Proverbs 8:13 says. Also, 'Ye that love the Lord, hate evil' [Psalm 97:10]. The Spirit within us loves and compels us to righteousness, and gives a godly hatred of sin and evil. God hates evil too [Psalm 5:5, 11:5], but He so loved the world that He gave His Son that whosoever believeth in Him should not perish, but have eternal life [John 3:16].

God hates the corrupted nature that the devil has brought upon man through the fall. He knows where the source of evil comes from: "He that commiteth sin is of the devil; for the devil sinneth from the beginning. For this purpose the Son of God was manifested, that he might destroy the works of the devil" [1 John 3:8]. The devil is a deceiver of mankind, and there is no truth in him, for he is a liar [John 8:44]. Jesus said it is the Truth that you know that will set you free; the truth of His salvation can set you free from the sin nature [John 8:32].

If we truly love, we will share the truth of God's Word that all have sinned and need a Saviour [Romans 3:23]. He that fears God and loves God will share the gospel of truth: he will call sin and wickedness evil and he will declare the wages of sin is death. He will share the good news, too, that Jesus offers salvation from the law of sin and death and wants to translate the sinner out of darkness into His marvelous Light so each can live in newness of life [Rom 6:23; Col 1:13]. Hate evil enough to boldly share the truth of God's love and deliverance.

Prayer:
Lord, may all men be set free from the law of sin and death through salvation in Christ Jesus that they might love His right way and hate every false way.

Scripture of the Day:
"The fear of the Lord is to hate evil: pride, and arrogancy, and the evil way, and the froward mouth, do I hate." - [Proverbs 8:13]

The Word for the Day is "Joy."

Quote for the Day:
"If you have no joy, there's a leak in your Christianity somewhere." – Billy Sunday

Joy has many faces and definitions. Basically it is an emotion evoked by well-being or a state of happiness. The word's origin is from the Greek, meaning 'to rejoice.' In the world, we experience moments of joy when momentous things occur—at births, weddings, graduations, promotions. We also experience joy in small moments—holding hands with someone we love, seeing a beautiful sunset, receiving flowers or a special gift. However, inner, ongoing joy is a sign of the presence of God. I remember feeling the joy of God rush in when I came to know the Lord, and I have felt a rising, overwhelming flow of that joy many times since in the presence of God and in quiet moments of study with Him. C.S. Lewis in his book *Surprised With Joy* wrote that: "Joy…has one characteristic…the fact that anyone who has experienced it will want it again." This is so true. And there is nothing else in this world, no other earthly joy, to compare with the joy found in God daily—and in the surprising moments when He moves dramatically in our hearts and being.

I am always troubled by Christians who express little joy in their actions, speech, or countenance. Many look like they were weaned on a dill pickle. Something is deeply wrong when joy is absent. Joy is a 'fruit of the Spirit' and as Christians 'we're known by our fruit' [Gal 5:22-23; Matt 7:16-20]. We should always be as Frederick Faber wrote—'the kind of souls who have the gift of finding joy everywhere and leaving it behind wherever we go.'

Canaries were taken into the coal mines in the past. If they quit singing, it meant dangerous gas levels were rising. Losing your joy is a sign of spiritual danger, too. If your spiritual life is rich you will have joy, a deep, abiding inner joy that can't be put out by outer circumstances [John 15:10-11]. Jesus said 'nobody could take that joy from you' but you can let your relationship with God slip until your joy dims and diminishes [John 16:22]. If your joy is not strong and healthy, smell the gas today, and seek to get your joy back. "The Christian should be an alleluia from head to foot" [Augustine].

Prayer:
God, we know that when You are richly in us that we will have joy. Help us back into a deeper place in You if we have slipped from living in the fullness of joy.

Scripture of the Day:
"Thou wilt shew me the path of life: in thy presence is fullness of joy; at thy right hand there are pleasures forevermore." - [Psalm 16:11]

The Word for the Day is "Shield."

Quote for the Day:
"A safe stronghold our God is still. A trusty shield and weapon." - Martin Luther

The Word in Ephesians 6:16 talks about taking the shield of faith. We know a shield is a type of armor, and in Paul's day, it was expertly employed by the Roman army. They used a small shield for close fighting, but the main shield used of the Romans was a larger, slightly curved instrument about four feet tall and three feet wide. A soldier could protect his whole body behind this shield, and soldiers could stand side by side together with these shields to form a wall of protecton, very hard for the enemy to penetrate. The shield protected the soldiers from attacks by sword and spear, attacks of rocks and arrows from above, and from flaming darts coming too fast to see.

We are to take the shield of faith. Faith is the absolute conviction and confidence in God's Word. It is total trust in all of God's promises. When we put total trust in God and His Word, another amazing thing happens: God Himself becomes our shield. 'The Lord is my strength and my shield; my heart trusted in him, and I am helped' [Psalm 28:7]. "Every word of God is pure: he is a shield unto them that put their trust in him" [Prov 30:5]. "He shall cover thee with his feathers, and under his wings shalt thou trust: his truth shall be thy shield and buckler" [Psalm 91:4]. We can have confidence in trusting in the Lord by faith. God Himself becomes our shield, and we have nothing to fear, nothing can get past God!

Ephesians 6:16 says 'above all' take up the shield of faith. This has to be the high covering of all the armour of God described in Ephesians 6. We have to 'take' the shield of faith; we have to exercise our faith and trust in God to get the shield's benefits and protection. Just as the Roman soldier who failed to lift up his shield could get injured, we can get hurt by the wicked if we're lazy and fail to trust and exercise our faith. If we succumb to the lust of the flesh, lust of the eyes, or the pride of life, we should quickly repent and receive the forgiveness of Jesus. Then we should take up our shield of faith, regaining the protection God provides, and return to the battle!

Prayer:
Lord, we place our trust in You, believing Your Word and Your promises, and we thank You that You are our shield to protect us and give victory over all the attacks of the enemy.

Scripture of the Day:
"Above all, taking the shield of faith, wherewith ye shall be able to quench all the fiery darts of the wicked." - [Ephesians 6:16]

The Word for the Day is "Respect"

Quote for the Day:
"Respect begins with this attitude: I acknowledge that you are a creature of extreme worth." - Gary Chapman

All people yearn for respect, to be admired for their good qualities, abilities or achievements, but we also know that in the world we have to earn that regard in some way. People receive respect and admiration for many different reasons. We may respect others for their character and fine moral attributes. People often respect others, too, for more materialistic reasons—for how much money they have, for how affluently they live, for their homes, property, clothes, social positions, or rank.

The world's standards for respect are not God's standards. God doesn't look on the outward man but on the inward. When Samuel was seeking a king, he overlooked David as a candidate. "But the Lord said to Samuel, Look not on his countenance or on the height of his stature … for the Lord seeth not as man seeth; for man looketh on the outward appearance, but the Lord looketh on the heart" [1 Sam 16:7]. We are fortunate that God looks past the outer appearance of our life, which may not be all it should be, to look with compassion to the inner heart and the potential of every man or woman. When the scribes and Pharisees were preparing to stone a woman taken in adultery, they reminded Jesus of the law and asked what he thought they should do. He said 'let he that is without sin cast the first stone' and when they'd all left he encouraged the woman to go and live a righteous life and 'sin no more' [John 8:3-11]. Jesus didn't condone the woman's current state but He saw the potential for who she could be and reached out to encourage it. Respect doesn't overlook what is but it always encourages better.

God looks on us with love and sees us as a creature of worth and potential. What God did for any one person, he can do for us because He is no respecter of persons [Rom 2:11]. He sees our potential, our possibilities, and He wants us to rise to our best. If He did miracles for one, He can do them for all. The love and favor He showed to any, He can show to us. Like the old hymn "What He has done for others, He will do for you." Walk in that knowledge.

Prayer:
Father, may we realize our worth in You and rise to our highest potential through Your power and strength and love.

Scripture of the Day:
"For there is no respect of persons with God." - [Romans 2:11].

The Word for the Day is "Secret."

Quote for the Day:
"May we have communion with God in the secret of our hearts, and find Him to be to us a little sanctuary." - Charles Spurgeon

When I was a kid I watched a TV game show "I've Got a Secret." On each show a guest whispered his secret to the show host. The "secret," usually something unusual, amazing, or humorous, was flashed upon the TV screen for viewers to see. Then the show panel of three celebrities were given clues to the secret and allowed to ask the guest yes-or-no questions to try to guess the secret. The guest won money if the secret was not guessed. I enjoyed the show, but was surprised at how seldom the guest's secret was discovered.

In a similar manner, men have always searched for clues to uncover the 'secrets' of God. Who is He? What is He like? What does He want of mankind? What will He do for mankind? Is there an afterlife? Like in the old TV show, people search for clues to the secrets of God by asking questions and probing. Unfortunately, like in the old country song that says people look for love in all the wrong places, they usually look for answers about God in the wrong places, looking to the opinions of men, the philosophy of scholars, or the views of so-called mystics and gurus. But the secret of the Lord is not revealed through any of these channels.

The secret of the Lord is openly revealed through Jesus and His Word. Jesus fulfilled prophecy by His works and by His words, saying in Matthew 13:35: "I will utter things which have been kept secret from the foundation of the world." The revelation of the mystery of God was made manifest by Jesus and by the scriptures [Rom 16:25-26]. Want to know what God the Father is like? Learn of Jesus, hear His words. Jesus said: 'he that hath seen me hath seen the Father' [John 14:9]. The secret of the Lord is with them that fear Him [Psalm 25:14], that seek to know Him and His Word more and more, and who let the Holy Spirit guide them into all truth.

Prayer:
Lord, we thank You that You sent Your Son into the world as a man to show the secrets of the Lord by His works and by His words. Thank you for the gift of the Holy Spirit who is the Spirit of Truth leading and guiding us in Your way.

Scripture of the Day:
"The secret of the Lord is with them that fear him; and he will shew them his covenant." - [Psalm 25:14]

The Word for the Day is "Perform."

Quote for the Day:
"You have to perform at a consistently higher level than others; that's the mark of a true professional." – Joe Paterno

A Zig Ziglar quote says: "if you don't see yourself as a winner, then you cannot perform as a winner." A renewing aspect of faith is learning that God sees you as strong and able—and usually more able than you see yourself. We dwell on our doubts that many things are too hard or impossible for us, but Jesus said instead: "If thou canst believe, all things are possible to him that believeth [Mark 9:23]. 'With men it is impossible, but not with God: for with God all things are possible' [Matthew 19:26].

We often love the revelation of those words, the idea of them, but we are not always fully persuaded they apply to us. Yet God's promises are eternally and always true. 'He is not a man that He can lie' and He is not changeable [Num 23:19; Mal 3:6; 2 Cor 1:20; Heb 13:8]. However, two things are needed. Each of us has to make a decision, as a child of God, that God is reliable and that His Word and promises are true, and always true, for others and for us. Second, we must seek to learn what those promises are so we can stand in them. This means reading the Word, studying, and looking for those promises of God. When you find them, write them down, claim them, and know they are for you. Deuteronomy 11:20 says 'write them on your doorposts and gates' and Proverbs 7:3 says 'bind them on your fingers, write them on the table of your heart.'

The idea is to get them before your eyes and mind, to commit them into your heart and spirit, to be persuaded of their truth. Then as a convinced Christian you will consistently perform at a higher level than you once thought possible in yourself, with confidence that He is working in you.

Prayer:
Father, may we collect your promises and hold them fast in our hearts and thoughts like treasures, knowing they are meant for us.

Scripture of the Day:
"And being fully persuaded that, what He had promised, He was able also to perform." - [Romans 4:21]

The Word for the Day is "Darkness."

Quote for the Day:
"Darkness cannot drive out darkness; only light can do that." - Martin Luther King

In nature there is a natural darkness, we call night, and a natural light, we call day. I think most reasonable people agree that light is superior to darkness. In winter, we become weary of the short days of sunshine and eagerly await the longer days of sun in the spring and summer. In climes with longer winter seasons there can even be a mental disorder called seasonal affective disorder (SAD). It can cause depression, anxiety, low energy, and other symptoms that cause the inhabitants of such climes to yearn for the long days of summer sunshine.

There is also the reality of spiritual darkness and light. Without Jesus, all are separated from God and in the spiritual darkness of sin [Rom 3:23]. God gave man a freewill and he can choose to stay in spiritual darkness, and many do. "And this is the condemnation, that light is come into the world, and men loved darkness rather than light, because their deeds were evil. For every one that doeth evil hateth the light, neither cometh to the light, lest his deeds be reproved" [John 3:19-20]. All who stay in darkness are taken by the powers of spiritual wickedness in high places [Eph 6:12]. "The way of the wicked is as darkness: they know not at what they stumble" [Prov 4:19]. Those who walk in the ways of darkness rejoice to do evil, and delight in the froward, perverse, unyielding, disobedience of the wicked [Prov 2:13-15].

Jesus is the light of the world: "Then spake Jesus again unto them, saying, I am the light of the world; he that followeth me shall not walk in darkness, but shall have the light of life" [John 8:12]. Jesus came to deliver man from the power of darkness and to translate us into His kingdom of light [Col 1:13]. He came to open our eyes to turn from darkness to light, to receive forgiveness of sins, and to receive an inheritance of divine promises [Acts 26:18]. Jesus gives His Light to 'guide our feet into the way of peace' [Luke 1:79]. Jesus calls us out of darkness into His marvelous light that we might show forth the praises of Him, walking in His light, His promises, and His divine life now [1 Peter 2:9].

Prayer:
Lord, we once stumbled in darkness, blinded by spiritual wickedness, slaves to the law of sin and death. But the Light of Life came by Christ Jesus, and now we see, now we live, now we show forth His praises forever more. Hallelujah!

Scripture of the Day:
"Ye are all the children of light, and the children of the day: we are not of the night, nor of darkness." - [1 Thessalonians 5:5]

The Word for the Day is "God."

Quote for the Day:
"We need to find God, and He cannot be found in noise and restlessness. God is the friend of silence. See how nature—trees, flowers, grass—grow in silence; see the stars, the moon, and the sun, how they move in silence…We need silence to be able to touch souls." – Mother Teresa

A wise proverb says, "Those that seek me early shall find me" [Prov 8:17]. To seek early means 'to seek first before other things' rather than just to seek early in the morning. But the concept of early morning is a speaking one, because then—before the business and noise and hustle of the day—it is quiet. The main point is that God wants us to seek after Him, to make time for Him above other things, to get quiet with Him so we can hear from Him, so He can fill us in times of prayer and study to be useful for Him in the world.

The heart of most Christians is to know God better, to be closer to God, to be able to hear from Him. The Word promises that 'his ear isn't heavy that it can't hear' [Is 59:1]; it is mostly that we are just not listening. As we spend time with a friend, sharing and listening, we come to know that friend. It is no different with God. If we 'draw near to Him, He will draw nigh to us' [James 4:8]. Also as we come to know a friend more, we grow to love them more. God says "I love them that love me" [Prov 8:17]. Should that surprise us to read this? God made us in His image, to fellowship with Him, to talk with Him, 'to hear His voice' [Deut 4:36]. Why do we think of Him as so distant and disinterested instead?

Amazing though it seems, God Almighty, the creator and ruler of the universe, seeks our fellowship. Isn't that a wonder? God yearns to be present with His people, to be more present in His world. He created it all for His pleasure and called it 'good' [Gen 1:1-31]. I think this is sometimes why we can feel God's presence so much more keenly in nature, amid His creation. Or standing quietly looking up at the stars and moon in the dark sky at night. When we get quiet, away from the noise and restlessness of the world—away from all the spirits of unbelief—it is easier to find Him, to connect to Him, to feel His presence. Find time to be with God, friend. He desires it and you need it.

Prayer:
Father, we know You said "Call unto me and I will answer thee" [Jer 33:3] but we do not seek out time to call on You often enough. Help us to seek You more.

Scripture of the Day:
"But if from thence thou shalt seek the Lord thy God, thou shalt find Him, if thou seek Him with all thy heart and with all thy soul." - [Deuteronomy 4:29]

The Word for the Day is "Truly."

Quote for the Day:
"It is a grand mistake to think of being great without goodness and I pronounce it as certain that there was never a truly great man that was not at the same time truly virtuous." - Benjamin Franklin

God delights in those that deal truly [Proverbs 12:22]. It refers to those who walk and live honestly. We see many in our culture today that walk in a dishonest way. Politicians who lie, distort facts, and contrive false arguments to advance themselves or to hurt their political opponents. We see the abomination of lying lips in the media, in academia, in business and commerce, and sadly, even among individuals we know. We all want leaders in every walk of life to be fair, honest, and upright. Everyone wants to be treated fairly. We do not want to be deceived, misled, or exploited by someone unjust in order to get a personal gain at the expense of another.

Men can appear truly upright and virtuous in public, but in private, in secret, they can be corrupt and dishonest. The game of golf can illustrate this behavior. I love golf; of all the sports it has no referees or umpires walking and observing the player. The game is founded upon the noble principle that each player is responsible for fairness and for calling a penalty upon himself for breaking a rule. Most of my golf experiences have been with golfers who play by the rules. But a player can be tempted to ignore the rules if no one sees him use a "foot wedge" to improve his lie in the rough. And it happens at times, regrettably. True character is revealed in golf, and life, when nobody is looking.

God is good to the man that deals truly, 'even to such as are of a clean heart' [Psalm 73:1]. If we have received Jesus as Savior He has given us a clean heart through His redemption. He also gives us the promise of the Holy Spirit to fill us with power, and judgment, and might to empower us to walk in uprightness [Micah 3:8]. Jesus was true in all His teachings, not conformed to the world, but walking in 'the way of God truly' [Luke 20:21]. Let us be true to God's righteous ways in open or secret, that we might shine as lights of truth in a dark world.

Prayer:
Lord, we will watch and pray that we enter not into temptation [Mark 14:38], but that we live and deal truly to be Your delight.

Scripture of the Day:
"Lying lips are abomination to the Lord: but they that deal truly are his delight."
- [Proverbs 12:22]

The Word for the Day is "Limited."

Quote for the Day:
"Faith in God is the gift that takes us beyond our limited self." – Vincent Nichols

Often people put limits on their lives by their beliefs and actions. For things to happen in your life, you need to believe that they can happen and you need to act on those beliefs. This is true for life in general but even more true for life in faith. A minister once said: "You need to give God something to work with."

When we know the Bible promises us that "with God nothing shall be impossible" [Luke 1:37], why do we limit Him so? Why do we falter so in our faith that God can and will do the impossible in our lives? I believe there are four main reasons for this. First, I think we hold misconceptions about God and about what He can do and wants to do in this world today. We forget the Bible is as true and reliable today as it was when written, that God 'is the same yesterday, and to day, and for ever' [Heb 13:8]. God's words and promises never go out of date and out of style, even though people, even learned people, try to tell us God has changed with the times. Second, because of a lack of knowledge of God's Word, we are easily swayed into limited beliefs because we don't know for ourselves the Bible's truths and promises. Third, we all find it easier to walk in faith until things get tough or don't go our way like we thought they would. Then, like the house built on the sand, our faith washes away because the foundations weren't sure [Matt 7:24-27]. Finally, I suspect we hold an often secret belief that God is a faithful and true God in general but we lack the confident trust that He will be faithful to us individually. We read the Bible stories; we hear others' strong faith stories. But inwardly, we don't really believe God will be true for us in the same way, so we too often 'lean to our own strength and understanding' [Prov 3:5]. We don't 'stand firm' as we should [Gal 5:1]. Often our limited beliefs are the real enemies we need to fight and conquer.

What is the answer? We have to 'fight the good fight of faith' and determine in our hearts we are going to trust and believe God [1 Tim 6:12]. We need to 'build ourselves up on our most holy faith,' moving past our limited selves to confidently believe in God [Jude 1:20].

Prayer:
Lord, help us to take the limits off our faith, to believe in You more fully and to not weaken in faith when a few storms and trials come our way.

Scripture of the Day:
"Yea, they turned back and tempted God, and limited the Holy One of Israel." - [Psalm 78:41]

The Word for the Day is "World."

Quote for the Day:
"If I walk with the world, I can't walk with God." - D.L. Moody

We are programmed from an early age to start conforming to the rules, standards, or ways of our society. As children, we learn there are rules for students in school. For example, students are expected to be on time, to sit at the right desk, and to not disturb class or interfere with the teacher. Later in life as employees we learn to conform to the company's rules and requirements for the job. All military personnel must conform to the rules and standards of the military. I learned this lesson one day when I made a misstep during marching drills. The Drill Sergeant got right up into my face and yelled: "Stepp, do they have any schools in Tennessee?!"..."Yes, Drill Sergeant!"..."How come you didn't go to any of 'em?!" I made sure I conformed to the platoon's marching cadence after that.

The Bible says "be not conformed to this world' [Rom 12:2]. God is not talking about our individual responsibilities to society. We are to obey the laws, respect our fellow man, perform our jobs and civic duties, pay our required taxes, and be a good, responsible citizen. God is talking about our heart and mind values. We are in the world, but not of the world [John 17:16]. The scripture is telling us not to conform to the prevailing standards, attitudes, customs, and practices of the world that are contrary to His Word. God's absolutes of truth must be our guide in thinking and behavior. We are not to love the world, for the world passes away, but they that obey the will of God abide forever [1 John 2:15-17].

'But be ye transformed by the renewing of your mind' [Rom 12:2]. God wants a major change in the believer in character and nature. To transform something into something else means to convert it into that thing. We are to be transformed to the image of Jesus [Rom 8:29], by being born-again, and by renewing our minds, or thinking, by the Word of God. We learn God's absolutes of truth to control our thinking and behavior that His Spirit might lead us into His good, and acceptable, and perfect will.

Prayer:
Lord, we will not love the things of this world, but will be conformed to the image of our Lord Jesus by renewing our minds in the truth of God's Word.

Scripture of the Day:
"Love not the world, neither the things that are in the world. If any man love the world, the love of the Father is not in him." - [1 John 2:15]

The Word for the Day is "Meet."

Quote for the Day:
"If we meet and you forget me, you have lost nothing, but if you meet Jesus Christ and forget Him, you have lost everything." –Anonymous

Although Jesus walked and ministered on the earth over 2000 years ago, we can still meet Him by faith. Jesus came to earth and died for our sins to make it possible for us to meet Him, the Lord, and the Holy Spirit personally again. He broke the veil, between the physical and spiritual realms, separating us from fellowship with God to restore our relationship with Him [2 Cor 3:15-18].

We can now know Jesus through faith. In our day-to-day walk on earth, we often think of people we'd like to meet some day—usually famous people, individuals we admire. We'd like to spend time in their company to learn from them. In many ways we often wish we could be more like them. A relationship with Jesus gives you all this and more—a personal relationship, a lifelong friend like no other, and eternal life [John 15:15]. In addition, knowing Jesus gives you power for daily living. 'But as many as received Jesus, He also gave power to those that believed in His name to become the sons and daughters of God' [John 1:12].

What else happens when you meet Jesus? You gain a new security and confidence as you grow in faith and begin to find your purpose. You become 'a new creation,' a better person, more at peace, with more wisdom, and knowledge [2 Cor 5:17]. You show more love than you did before, because Jesus' perfect nature begins to merge into yours [Gal 3:27; Rom 8:29]. He gives you counsel, help, and leadings you need every day and will be your help in trouble. The benefits of meeting Him continue to grow, too. The longer you know Him, the deeper your fellowship with Him. And when your life here is finished, you move on into heaven to live forever with Him and with those who have gone on before. 'Old things are passed away and all things become new' [2 Cor 5:17].

Prayer:
Lord Jesus, we are so grateful for the sacrifices You made so we could come to know You here on earth and know of a surety our home eternally will be with You.

Scripture of the Day:
"Then we which are alive and remain shall be caught up together with them in the clouds, to meet the Lord in the air: and so shall we ever be with the Lord." -
[1 Thessalonians 4:17]

The Word for the Day is "Avoid."

Quote for the Day:
"Our society strives to avoid any possibility of offending anyone—except God."
- Billy Graham

So many warnings in the Bible caution us to stay away from trouble, to pass by it, but we don't always do that. While on vacation one summer at Edisto Island, South Carolina, Lin and I were riding our bikes around the island. As we passed by a water hazard close to the golf course, I noticed a motionless alligator in the grass beside the water. The beast was so still as I approached on my bike, I thought it must be dead. Lin cautioned me not to get close, but I wanted to see what had killed the gator—injured by an auto? gunshot? I was curious. Just then the gator snapped its head up with jaws agape and I exited stage left like a lightning bolt. Our own personal decisions are responsible for most of our troubles.

Trouble and evil can have a tempting quality that can lure us. If sinners entice us to join them in their plots to prey on others to 'find all precious substance, to fill our houses with spoil,' do not walk with them in their way [Prov 1:10-19]. Many do not fall into sin in a huge way at first, but little by little. They don't avoid the little acts, little temptations, little wrongs, which lead to more. Someone steals a little money from the company at first and no one knows. Then that person is tempted to embezzle more and more as the sin grows, usually leading to a very bad ending. It's the little foxes that spoil the vines [Song of Solomon 2:15].

The Bible gives us helpful insight to many temptations and errors to avoid. We are to avoid those that cause divisions and offences against the faith of God and those that want to argue a different view contrary to God's truth [Rom 16:17]. We are to avoid fornication and avoid profane and vain babblings and oppositions of science falsely so called [1 Cor 7:2; 1 Tim 6:20]. We are to avoid those that cause dissensions, strife, quarreling, and arguing for the sake of arguing [Titus 3:9]. "But foolish and unlearned questions avoid, knowing that they do gender strifes" [2 Tim 2:23]. Our best advice is simply to abstain from, to avoid, all appearance of evil [1 Thess 5:22].

Prayer:
Lord, thank You for Your help in avoiding all evil by Your promise: "This I say then, Walk in the Spirit, and ye shall not fulfil the lust of the flesh" [Gal 5:16].

Scripture of the Day:
"Enter not into the path of the wicked, and go not in the way of evil men. Avoid it, pass not by it, turn from it, and pass away." - [Proverbs 4:14-15]

The Word for the Day is "Things."

Quote for the Day:
"Expect great things from God. Attempt great things for God." – William Carey

John Rushkin maintained "the best things in life aren't things." However, we worry a lot about things—material possessions, day-to-day happenings, looks, clothes, money, accomplishments and position, and so much more. But the best things in life aren't objects or inanimate entities—or even people and their opinions we often get overly focused on. We're called to a higher life, in which our focus should be on higher things—things more eternal and everlasting.

Things are simply things. God made all things in heaven and earth for our pleasure and called them good but we aren't meant to set our mind on those things. And we are never to set our minds and affection on the base things of the world and things which God despises [1 Cor 1:28]. Instead we're to set our minds on the things of God. We're to water and plant the seeds God shows us and to trust God to bring the growth. Worrying over them doesn't help anything. Whenever we get overly anxious, impatient, frustrated and fretful over things or people in our lives, we move over into sin. We're meant to keep our peace and trust in God, to 'be anxious for nothing,' to 'set our minds on things above' [Col 3:2].

The things of earth, that so often trouble us, shouldn't. Jesus died so we could have the victory over things of the earth, 'putting all things under his feet' [1 Cor 15:27]. Yet people often feel if they're not worrying over things, it means they aren't caring enough. They equate worrying as caring. Martha, busy about so many things, was annoyed at Mary sitting at Jesus feet learning. 'Lord, don't you care that I have all this load on my own shoulders, that Mary isn't helping?' she asked. But Jesus tried to help her see that her focus wasn't on the right things [Luke 10:38-42]. Over-loving or over-caring about people or things can be damaging and hindering to the important things in life and get in the way of the things God does want you to do. We need to learn to set our thoughts on heavenly things more than on earthly things.

Prayer:
Lord, help us to rise above the problems, worrisome patterns of living, and the love of things of this earth to walk in a higher place in You.

Scripture of the Day:
"Finally, brethren, whatsoever things are true, whatsoever things are honest, whatsoever things are just, whatsoever things are pure, whatsoever things are lovely, whatsoever things are of good report: if there be any virtue, and if there be any praise, think on these things." – [Philippians 4:8]

The Word for the Day is "Wash."

Quote for the Day:
"There may be some sins of which a man cannot speak, but there is no sin which the blood of Christ cannot wash away." - Charles Spurgeon

It is obvious that things when washed clean have more appeal, satisfaction, and beauty. After washing both my vehicles in the hot July sun, I sat down with a cool glass of water and felt better about both clean cars. One time years ago I had purposed to trade in my vehicle with high mileage for a new one. I cleaned the car thoroughly and headed for the dealership. When I returned shortly, Lin asked "What happened?" I replied that I had changed my mind: I was so much more pleased with the nice, clean vehicle that I knew I would never get the value I had for it in trade-in; so I decided to keep it.

Mankind needs to be washed and cleansed from the filthiness and defilement of sin [Rom 3:23]. Some think they can create their own righteousness and cleanse themselves with good works or good thoughts. "Not by works of righteousness which we have done, but according to his mercy he saved us, by the washing of regeneration, and renewing of the Holy Ghost" [Titus 3:5]. But without the shedding of blood there is no remission [Heb 9:22]. Jesus shed His pure blood to pay the price of sins for all: 'Unto Him that loved us, and washed us from our sins in His own blood' [Rev 1:5]. And it is through accepting His salvation that we are redeemed and washed from sin. Yet some men will not acknowledge their need to be washed: "There is a generation that are pure in their own eyes, and yet not washed from their filthiness" [Prov 30:12].

But once born again in our spirit through Jesus we are washed from sin, made the righteousness of God in Him [2 Cor 5:21]. We can then draw near to God with a clean heart: 'we are sanctified, and justified in the name of the Lord Jesus, and by the Spirit of God' [1 Cor 6:11]. We can then come to Him 'with a true heart in full assurance of faith, having our hearts sprinkled from an evil conscience' [Heb 10:22]. We are born into newness of life that we might glorify Him and draw men unto His salvation. What a blessed way to live, to be washed clean, to love and be loved of God, and to love one another as He loved us .

Prayer:
Lord, thank You for washing us clean by Your blood, and we 'will publish with the voice of thanksgiving, and tell of all thy wondrous works' [Psalm 26:7].

Scripture of the Day:
"Wash me thoroughly from mine iniquity, and cleanse me from my sin." - [Psalm 51:2]

August

The Word for the Day is "Temptation."

Quote for the Day:
"Temptation is the devil looking through the keyhole. Yielding is opening the door and inviting him in." -Billy Sunday

It's always easier to act and talk spiritual when we're not facing any difficulties, trials, or temptations. But a wise thought to keep in mind is that the devil is always watching, stalking, following your life—peeping into your keyholes and looking for a chance to cause trouble. Satan is a predator ever on the prowl and we, unfortunately, are the prey.

Too often when satan comes knocking at the door, we foolishly open it, invite him in and politely entertain him. The little temptations he offers under guise, like the wolf in sheep's clothing, seem innocent—look tasty and appealing—and like Adam and Eve with the apple, before we know it we're taking a bite into big trouble. David Wilkerson wrote: "Temptation is an invitation or enticement to commit an immoral act and no one is immune." It's not a sin to be tempted but it is a sin to give in to temptation and fall away [Luke 8:13].

The devil will see to it that everyone is tempted, so we need to ponder the path of our feet, walk wisely every day, and guard our hearts and lives with all diligence [James 1:13; Prov 4:23,26]. We're not to conform to the pattern of the world and what everyone else is doing, but to continually grow in faith and stay strong in our mind to pass any tests sent our way, staying safe in God's will [Mark 7:20-23; Romans 12:2; 1 Peter 1:13].

What did Jesus do when tempted? He stood firm, quoted the Word of God, and resisted the devil [Matthew 4:1-11]. We should do the same, fighting any temptation that comes our way. We should also 'put on the shield of faith and the armor of God every day so we'll be able to quench all the fiery darts of the enemy' [Ephesians 6:10-18]. Then we can triumph against any sneaky or outright attack satan sends our way. Remember: "He that is begotten of God keepeth himself, and that wicked one toucheth him not" [1 John 5:18].

Prayer:
Lord, help us to not be foolish and careless, ignorant of satan's devices, so we are easily swayed into temptations he sends our way. Teach us to fight well.

Scripture of the Day:
"Blessed is the man that endureth temptation: for when he is tried, he shall receive the crown of life, which the Lord hath promised to them that love Him."
- [James 1:12]

The Word for the Day is "Plow."

Quote for the Day:
"We should be a holy people eager to greet our Lord...busy in evangelism, hands on the plow, eyes on the prize." - David Jeremiah

An old Irish proverb says: "You will never plow a field by turning it over in your mind." Plowing is hard work and takes a committed disciplined effort. A farmer knows he plows and plants, trusting for growth and a harvest. So should we, as Christians.

We must first plow up the 'fallow ground' in our lives [Jer 4:3]. The hard, worldly, uncultivated heart must be broken up, cleansed of thorns, made soft, to receive the seed of God's truths, to grow and harvest righteous blessings. How do we plow up fallow ground? There must be a commitment to effort first; the lazy person will not plow, and cannot expect a harvest [Prov 20:4]. A farmer may encounter hard, rocky soil to plow and he needs a plow of strong metal to break up the ground. He then needs a strong source of power, such as a tractor or mules, to pull the plow. Our strong metal is the sheer decision, resolve, and determination to break up the fallow ground of our heart. Our source of power to pull us through to victory is the Holy Spirit [Acts 1:8]. He is our Helper, our Comforter, and leads and guides us into all truth.

When you start plowing, you must continue plowing even if the going gets rough and you hit rocks or hindrances. Jesus has told us already that we will face obstacles, but if we stay the course He overcomes all things [John 16:33]. The plower must stay focused on preparing his field (heart) for a harvest. My granddad used to put blinders on the eyes of his mules so they would stay focused and not be distracted. We must fight to finish the course, too [2 Tim 4:7].

We plow up the fallow ground, we make our heart ready, we plant seed, we reap the harvest sown [Mark 4:26-29]. This is how God's kingdom operates.

Prayer:
Lord, we will plow up our fallow ground that we might sow seeds of righteousness into our heart and reap a harvest of blessings. We pray that we might also sow the seeds of the Light of the Gospel into this dark world that the Father might reap a harvest of souls.

Scripture of the Day:
"For our sakes, no doubt, this is written: that he that ploweth should plow in hope; and that he that thresheth in hope should be partaker of his hope." -
[1 Corinthians 9:10]

The Word for the Day is "Heart."

Quote for the Day:
"Upon green grass, beneath green leaves, by gentle streams my heart receives." – Jane Merchant

God wants us to 'trust in Him with all our heart' but sometimes in a noisy, and busy world our hearts—that central and innermost part of our being—gets worn and tired [Prov 3:5-6]. The heart, or soul, is the seat of the will, feelings, and mind and it is intricately linked to our physical body and to our spirit, the center of our spiritual being. When our bodies or heart get worn and weary it can impact our spiritual life and awareness. In those times we need restoring.

Leslie Schmucker once wrote: "God's voice is steady and unwavering. But we must quiet ourselves to hear it." When feeling worn and frazzled, we need to pull away to God, to get quiet so He can strengthen and refresh our hearts [Psalm 119:28; Is 30:15]. When we pull away into His presence to seek Him, pray, study, meditate and quietly wait for Him, we will richly find Him again [Matt 7:7; Acts 3:19]. "In returning and rest shall ye be saved; in quietness and in confidence shall be your strength" [Isaiah 30:15].

Often in nature, the restoration our hearts need can be found more easily. "He maketh me to lie down in green pastures; he leadeth me beside the still waters; he restoreth my soul" [Psalm 23:2-3]. God's nearness is felt in the quiet beauty of growing things, in the natural world. It is hard to stay care-worn in the beauty of nature. All of nature seems to speak of the Word of God.

We should be quick to realize when we need to pull away. In stressful, busy times we need to find time to clean our hands and hearts of all our cares, concerns, and problems, giving them to God and repenting for carrying them around and worrying over them, for leaning too much to our own thoughts and understandings in how to handle them [Phil 4:6-7; 1 Peter 5:7; James 4:8]. When we turn to the Lord, seek Him in quietness and faith, he'll refresh our hearts and cover us with a blanket of peace. By gentle streams and in purposeful quiet times, our heart receives.

Prayer:
Lord, help us to remember that we don't hear Your Voice best in the clamor and cacophony of the world but in quiet times with You, seeking your company.

Scripture of the Day:
"Create in me a clean heart, O God; and renew a right spirit within me." -
[Psalm 51:10]

The Word for the Day is "Perilous."

Quote for the Day:
"A strength to harm is perilous in the hand of an ambitious head." - Elizabeth I

As I write this today, America has once again suffered horrible acts of violence. In the last two days two cities in the US have been victims of random shootings, leaving dozens dead. These random, evil acts of murder have left many grieving the cruel loss of loved ones. One of the signs of the last days according to scripture is that perilous (dangerous) times shall come [2 Tim 3:1]. Every generation has had cause to consider the evils of its day and reasonably suppose that they were seeing the last days. The dangers and evils of our day could support this assumption also.

The apostle Paul was no stranger to perils in his day either. Many dangers that Paul faced are listed in 2 Corinthians 11:26. Two of the perils are unexpected though. Paul faced perils of 'his own countrymen.' And secondly, he faced perils 'among false brethren.' You don't reasonably expect danger from your fellow citizens or from those claiming to be believers. How could this be? The scriptures tell us perilous times come because men are lovers of their own selves, covetous, fierce, false accusers, among other things [2 Tim 3:2-7]. The murdered today haven't even been buried yet, and politicians and pundits try to exploit the tragedy by blaming and falsely accusing rivals, not out of sorrow for the deceased, but for personal attention.

Paul also suffered perils of false brethren—unholy men, blasphemers, having a form of godliness, but denying the power thereof. The compromised church today also blames everything except the real cause of evil: "The thief (satan) comes not but to steal, and to kill, and to destroy" [John 10:10]. The evil work of satan in men's hearts will not be remedied by political or societal opinion, but only by the heart becoming a new creation in Christ Jesus [2 Cor 5:17]. Let us intercede and pray for spiritual revival in our churches, in our homes, and in our land.

Prayer:
Lord, open the eyes of Your people to know that we wrestle not against flesh and blood, but against spiritual wickedness. We thank You that peril shall not separate us from the love of Christ, that in all things we are more than conquerers through Him that loved us [Rom 8:35-37].

Scripture of the Day:
"This know also, that in the last days perilous times shall come." [2 Timothy 3:1]

The Word for the Day is "Two."

Quote for the Day:
"Two becoming one is less about aligning preferences and more about uniting in purpose." – Krista Ortiz

The concept of the Trinity is often difficult for people to grasp—how God the Father, Son, and Holy Spirit are three distinct beings yet also one. They are always in perfect unity, hard for us as human beings to understand as we often find being in unity with others difficult. The concept of "two becoming one" is presented to us with marriage. Genesis 2:24 says: "Therefore shall a man leave his father and mother, and shall cleave unto his wife: and they shall be one flesh." The words are beautiful but the process of becoming one involves a journey of love, submission, and selflessness.

From the first God paired creatures, male and female, to bond for their good and to facilitate procreation. Many animal and bird species are bonded through life, just as God formed Adam and Eve to be bonded as lifelong helpmeets. "And the Lord said, it is not good that the man should be alone; I will make him an help meet for him" [Gen 2:18]. Man and woman were meant to cleave to one another, one with Him, staying rightly unified [Gen 2:22-24; 1 Pet 3:7].

On the hiking trail I have often observed two vines so entwined and embedded into each other that they have become one. This "growing into one" process took time just as the relationship in a marriage—and even a good friendship—takes time, persistence, and loving effort. The old natural self wants to assert its rights first, to have its own way. But as two gradually bind and twine into one, they are strengthened and become better as one [Eccl 4:9-12]. Learning to be submissive, loving, and caring in a marriage relationship teaches a deeper righteousness because we begin to emulate the Trinity relationship. We begin to model the unified heavenly relationship we'll know for eternity after death [1 John 3:1-3; Rom 8:29; 2 Cor 3:18]. Earth is a bit of a training ground, for eternity and marriages teach us how to be "one with another." As a couple lives to please God, becoming more "one with Him" daily, becoming more unified as a couple becomes easier, too.

Prayer:
Father, help us in our marriages and our relationships to better model the loving oneness shown in the Trinity.

Scripture of the Day:
"And they twain shall be one flesh: so then they are no more twain, but one flesh."
- [Mark 10:8]

The Word for the Day is "Neighbor."

Quote for the Day:
"Definition of a good neighbor: someone to be trusted; a courteous, friendly source of help when help is needed; someone you can count on; someone who cares." - Edward B. Rust, Jr.

Lin and I recently returned from a vacation and it felt good to be back home. I was also thanking God for good neighbors. While we were away my neighbors saved my mail, watched over our house, and my neighbor Ken even mowed my lawn without being asked. We have been blessed many years with good neighbors on our street that embody the qualities of a good neighbor as defined in our quote above: 'trustworthy, courteous, friendly, helpful, dependable, and caring.' We try to be good neighbors in return, recalling the words of Harry Truman: "All will concede that in order to have good neighbors, we must also be good neighbors. That applies in every field of human endeavor."

Another definition of neighbor is 'one that does us good, and pities and relieves us in distress.' The story of the good Samaritan found in Luke chapter 10 illustrates this. The story tells of a certain man traveling the road from Jerusalem to Jericho who fell among thieves who stripped him, wounded him, and left him half dead. Both a priest and a Levite, two religious types, passed by on the other side of the road, refusing to help the man. But a Samaritan, an outsider, stopped, bound up the man's wounds, carried him to town to an inn to be cared for, and paid all the expenses for his care! Jesus pointed out that the Samaritan was the true neighbor because he showed mercy. The 'religious' types may have talked the talk, but they didn't walk the walk. The Bible tells us we are to love God with all our 'heart, soul, strength, and mind, and thy neighbor as thyself' [Mark 12:30; Lev 19:18]. Jesus said 'this do and thou shalt live' [Luke 10:28].

"Lord, who shall abide in thy tabernacle? who shall dwell in thy holy hill? He that walketh uprightly, and worketh righteousness, and speaketh the truth in his heart. He that backbiteth not with his tongue, nor doeth evil to his neighbor, nor taketh up a reproach against his neighbor" [Psalm 15:1-3].

Prayer:
Lord, we thank You for good neighbors. We will love God with all our heart, and our neighbor as ourself.

Scripture of the Day:
"Thine own friend, and thy father's friend, forsake not; neither go into thy brother's house in the day of thy calamity: for better is a neighbor that is near than a brother far off." - [Proverbs 27:10]

The Word for the Day is "Draw."

Quote for the Day:
"Only when He dwells within our hearts will our lives truly honor Him and truly draw others to Him." – William Barclay

The Law of Attraction suggests that people attract into their lives what they most focus on. Like always attracts like, positive attracts positive, and negative attracts negative. This law, as wise as it is, tends to overlook the role that God plays in human affairs and it tends to forget that when we live close to God, we draw others to God through the light of God living and shining in us.

A point missed by many is that mankind was made in God's image. That innate heredity and potential divinity, that spiritual heritage, draws His own to Him. He is our Father and Creator and the inward being of ourselves is drawn to unify our lives and heart with His. He's our daddy. We might have been separated from Him by sin, but His love ever draws us. 'I have loved you with an everlasting Love; therefore have I drawn you with loving devotion' [Jer 31:3].

Through Jesus, God showed how His Spirit could draw others to us, too. Jesus said: "And I, if I be lifted up from the earth, will draw all men unto me" [John 12:32], teaching that through us He would continue to draw others to God. He taught, "The spirit of the Lord is upon me because He has anointed me" and "I am the light of the world" [Luke 4:18; John 8:12]. When we belong to God, when we know Jesus and are born again, when God's Spirit lives strong within us, we are anointed, too, and our light and the power of God within us, will draw others.

Prayer:
Lord, lead me closer to You so I can draw others to You by my life and ways, letting my light shine.

Scripture of the Day:
"And I, if I be lifted up from the earth, will draw all men unto me." - [John 12:32]

The Word for the Day is "Sound."

Quote for the Day:
"No matter what the circumstances, we Christians should keep our heads. God has not given us the spirit of fear, but of power, of love and of a sound mind. It is a dismal thing to see a son of heaven cringe in terror before the sons of earth."
- A.W. Tozer

One of the most troubling and sad conditions of our society today is the ever increasing cases of mental disorders, particularly Alzheimer's disease and dementia. These disorders of the brain cause millions to suffer mental and social problems which interfere, diminish, and can destroy ordinary daily functions, and can be fatal. In 2015 these disorders affected almost six million Americans, and the number grows yearly both in the U.S. and worldwide. We are bombarded with drug ads in the media for these disorders, and the ads often not so subtly imply that senior citizens can more or less expect these afflictions.

It is even more disturbing that many Christians accept and expect these disorders to afflict them. This is not the case at all according to God's eternal truth. God's Word in 2 Timothy 1:7 says we have been given a sound mind: free from injury or disease, free from flaw, defect, or decay, solid, firm, and stable. If we let our minds think and dwell on worldly media instead of God's Word, we can open a door for the enemy to afflict us this way. We should boldly praise God every day that we are not given a spirit of fear, but of a sound mind, regardless of age! If we think we're inevitably going to be afflicted, and our mouths start speaking this lie, we can indeed open the door to receive it. "Death and life are in the power of the tongue" [Prov 18:21]; "For as he thinketh in his heart, so is he" [Prov 23:7]; "For by thy words thou shalt be justified, and by thy words thou shalt be condemned" [Matt 12:37].

The sound doctrine of God's Word is given that the aged men be sober, clear headed, grave, temperate, self controlled, sound in faith, sound in charity, and sound in patience [Titus 2:1-2]. God has given us a sound, solid, firm, mind. Claim it, accept it, praise God for it, and enjoy it!

Prayer:
Lord, we will believe and receive the truth of Your eternal Word, and we will walk with a sound mind to glorify You.

Scripture of the Day:
"For God hath not given us the spirit of fear; but of power, and of love, and of a sound mind." - [2 Timothy 1:7]

The Word for the Day is "Sea."

Quote for the Day:
" *The sea, once it casts its spell, holds one in its net of wonder forever.*" - Jacques Cousteau

I always see the wonder of my God in His creation—and time by the sea especially inspires me, as the sea and its beauty seem to speak to the soul. Rossetti wrote: "The sea hath no king but God alone"—and few people spend time at the ocean without feeling God's presence.

The sea is a place of relaxation, rest, and tranquility. The rhythm of the water and the waves, the sun and sound of the gulls, begin to relax the inward being and set the soul free. Here it is easy to visualize 'the Spirit of God moving upon the face of the waters, creating the sea and all that is within it and calling it all good [Gen 1:2, 9, 10]. Robert Henri wrote that the sea "has some potent power to make us think things we like to think." "The ocean stirs the heart, inspires the imagination and brings eternal joy to the soul" [Wyland].

There are so many lessons at the sea. The waves come and go, ordained in their patterns. The mystery of the waves and tides remind us of the mystery of God. Simply the sheer wonder of the sea and all its creatures, great and small, and its infinite riches speak to us of the greatness of God [Psalm 104:24-25]. The sea reminds us to simplify and relax, to just see beauty and enjoy it, to get back to ourselves—and back into that deeper place with God.

Despite the passing of time, despite the storms, the sea goes on. That understanding of continuity comforts us and gives us peace, knowing that God will see us through our storms and trials, too, bringing us back out of trial and trouble into a better place [Deut 31:6; Psalm 34:17-20; Nahum 1:7]. The Word promises: "He maketh the storm a calm, so that the waves thereof are still" [Psalm 107:29].

Prayer:
Father, thank You for the glory of Your creation and for the wonder and beauty of the sea. Help us to stop and see the wonder and beauty of creation around us every day and not only when we journey to the ocean.

Scripture of the Day:
"The sea is his, and he made it: and his hands formed the dry land." - [Psalm 95:5]

The Word for the Day is "Vision."

Quote for the Day:
"Now lift your vision above all these, look at Me alone and see in Me the God who is enough and stand upright in uncompromising faith." - A.B. Simpson

Among the definitions for the word vision are: 'the faculty or state of being able to see, a mental image of what the future will or could be like, or a sight of unusual beauty.' It seems that all men who have accomplished the most have had vision, seeing a bigger picture of a future destiny or goal, and then being willing to hold fast to that vision and act upon it. Explorers, like Columbus, had a vision of a new place and pressed toward it. Moses had a vision of leading his people to a promised land. In both instances God had given both men a vision and a task to follow. Both men persisted against all obstacles to their visions because they knew they had received the vision from God.

We seek direction for our lives and desire to achieve something more. But it is in God that we find the right direction. We have God's promise: "I will instruct thee and teach thee in the way which thou shalt go: I will guide thee with mine eye" [Psalm 32:8]. We need only to believe the all-sufficiency of the great I AM to give and to obtain the vision He has for us.

But to obtain the big vision God gives we must first be faithful in the smaller matters. "He that is faithful in that which is least is faithful also in much: and he that is unjust in the least is unjust also in much" [Luke 16:10]. When we do all things as unto the Lord, we are showing ourselves to God as faithful and able to be entrusted with greater visions.

We find then that true happiness only comes from following God faithfully in the path and individual vision He has for each of us. We are assured that happy is the man who seeks God's wisdom and understanding for all things, who trusts in God's help and whose hope is in the Lord [Psalm 146:5, Prov 3:13]. God wants us to hold on and to pursue our vision despite all obstacles, for He has willed good toward us and promises an expected end [Jeremiah 29:11].

Prayer:
Lord, we will be faithful in the small things and press toward greater visions in faith and obedience, knowing that You alone are sufficient to bring it to pass.

Scripture of the Day:
"Where there is no vision, the people perish: but he that keepeth the law, happy is he." - [Proverbs 29:18]

The Word for the Day is "Door."

Quote for the Day:
"The door of the human heart can only be opened from the inside."- Wm Hunt

Above the altar at the front of a church we visit, there is a large wooden cross hanging in the middle of an arched doorway. But there is no doorknob on the door. In thinking about that later I saw several lessons in that altar door. The first is that the door, with the cross hanging on it, represents that at the forefront of our beliefs as Christians is Jesus. He is the door into the sheepfold and into the Kingdom of God.

The second lesson is that the only way into the richness of the Kingdom Of God is through Jesus. He holds the key and the only way in is through and by Him. Jesus said: "I am the door: by me if any man enter in, he shall be saved, and shall go in and out, and find pasture" [John 10:9]. There is no doorknob, no man's way in, because only through Jesus is there a way in. Isaiah prophesied: "And the key of the house of David will I lay upon his shoulder; so he shall open, and none shall shut; and he shall shut, and none shall open" [Isaiah 22:22].

The third lesson relates more to what we'll find inside the door. Some people enter in but never fully explore and adventure into the fullness of all that God is, like getting into a secret garden but never walking further into the garden to travel all its paths and to see all its beauty. That personal journey is one that only you, individually, can take. 'Seek, and you will find; knock and it shall be opened' [Matt 7:7]. You get out of anything, including faith, about as much as you're willing to put into it. You have to consciously spend time praying, studying the Word, seeking for more of God, and asking Him to reveal more of Himself to you. Ultimately, only you can decide how much of God you want to let into your life.

Prayer:
Lord Jesus, You said, "Behold, I stand at the door and knock: if any man hear my voice, and open the door, I will come in to him, and will sup with him, and he with me" [Rev 3:20]. That's intimate. That's communion and fellowship, and the sweet thing is that You offer us this invitation every day…calling out to us in the busyness and clamor of our world, amid its opinions and ideas that are often confusing and loud and not scripturally based. May we seek for You, and come to know You in all fullness, letting You into every aspect of our lives.

Scripture of the Day:
"I am the door: by me if any man enter in, he shall be saved, and shall go in and out, and find pasture." - [John 10:9]

AUGUST 12
The Word for the Day is "Scripture."

Quote for the Day:
"Even those with a good grasp of scripture, and who spread the gospel accurately and honestly, can enrich their testimony and comprehension through continued Biblical study and instruction." - Brad Archer

"Pilate saith unto him, What is truth?" [John 18:38]. This question has been asked, pondered, and debated since the beginning. Jesus said the Word of God is truth [John 17:17]. The Bible tells us that all scripture is inspired of God: infallible, inerrant, and eternal [2 Tim 3:16]. The true believer has to stand on the side that all scripture in the Bible is inspired and written as God ordained and directed. Of course most outside the church place little or no value in the scriptures at all. As evangelist Milton Green once said: "They've got something else figured out." Sadly, many in the church today cast doubt and unbelief on the scriptures. To doubt one part is to cast doubt over all. "To stay away from Christianity because part of the Bible's teaching is offensive to you assumes that if there is a God, He wouldn't have any views that upset you. Does that belief make sense?" (Rev Timothy Keller). Even many church leaders harbor unbelief about the Bible's truth. A prominent seminary professor once tried to insult my belief in the Bible's truth by calling me a 'naive literalist'.

The Word also tells us there are profits and benefits to believing the inspired scripture: it is profitable for doctrine, for reproof, for correction, for instruction in righteousness. But to acquire these advantages we must know and study the scriptures, we must read the Bible. Jesus asked: 'Have you never read the scriptures?' [Matt 21:42]. The same holds true today, many form their opinions without ever reading the scriptures. Jesus also said: "Ye do err, not knowing the scriptures, nor the power of God" [Matt 22:29]. If we do not live and base our faith on God's absolutes of truth, then 'we have not His word abiding in us'[John 5:38]. Let the unbelievers, both in and out of the church, those that are unlearned and unstable, distort the scriptures with their own interpretaton to their own destruction [2 Pet 3:16]. But let the disciples of the Lord stand on the firm and eternal inspired holy scriptures which are able to make us wise unto salvation and to give us a rich, abundant life through Jesus Christ [2 Tim 3:15].

Prayer:
Lord, we will study, stand on, and believe Your inspired scripture "That the man of God may be perfect, thoroughly furnished unto all good works." [2 Tim 3:17]

Scripture of the Day:
"All scripture is given by inspiration of God, and is profitable for doctrine, for reproof, for correction, for instruction in righteousness." - [2 Timothy 3:16]

The Word for the Day is "Renewed."

Quote for the Day:
"Unlike getting born again, which happens instantly, being renewed in the spirit of your mind involves a process. It takes place as you spend time in God's Word and let it change your soul." – Gloria Copeland

To be renewed means to be restored to a former or better estate after being in decay or disrepair. It also means to revive, make new again or transform. When we are born again, an inward renewal begins and we become a new creation [2 Cor 5:17]. However, this is only the beginning of change for us. Our soulish being, our will, thinking, feelings, and emotions, have lived in the world and been dominated by the world's thinking and programming for a long time. But as we yield to the Lord to allow Him to remake and renew us, the Potter's hands will renew and make of us something new and beautiful if we allow it [Colossians 3:9-10; Jeremiah 18:1-4].

As we become renewed in the Lord, we are not simply inanimate, passive lumps of clay on the potter's wheel. We are alive and actively involved in the process of change. We participate by desiring change and by working with God to bring it into being through studying and reading the Word, through having an open seeking heart, and through prayer and yielding to God's hands to remake us [Psalm 119:9; Romans 12:1-2]. Daily our heart prayer should be: "Create in me a clean heart, O God; and renew a right spirit within me" [Psalm 51:10].

Sadly, we have an enemy in this earth who does not want us to be changed and renewed into God's image, who wants us dominated by the thinking and destructive ways of this world. To see ongoing renewal occur we will have to fight to continue to move forward [1 Tim 6:12; James 4:7; 1 Peter 5:8]. To be renewed involves a warfare to grow and become all God wants us to be, 'to be renewed after his image' and 'to walk in newness of life' [Col 3:10-12; Rom 6:4].

Prayer:
Lord, we are grateful to be a new creation in Christ Jesus but we also want to be renewed in the inner man by the Spirit. Help us to continue to pass from our old state into a wholly new one—ever being reconditioned and remade into Your image.

Scripture of the Day:
"Be renewed in the spirit of your mind; and…put on the new man, which after God is created in righteousness and true holiness." - [Ephesians 4:23-24].

The Word for the Day is "Refresh."

Quote for the Day:
"In short, I can settle for things that are less than God's best, if I do not learn to live life in refresh." - Randy Rice, Pastor

After mowing my lawn on a hot August day, it was good to take a little time to relax and refresh myself. I have a bench next to the house in my driveway, and I like to sit there and enjoy a tall glass of iced cola. I gradually cool down and the cold drink is exceptionally satisfying to my thirsty throat. It is easy to get run down physically not only from lawn chores, but from the business of everyday life as well. Sometimes to renew our strength and reinvigorate our bodies, we just need to take some time off, to relax, to slow down, and have a little "me time." God established this principle in the Word when He taught that a day of rest (sabbath) after six days of labor was for refreshing and renewal [Ex 23:12, 31:17]. A day of rest to renew the body is also good for the mind and spirit.

The Bible tells us ways to find refreshment for the spirit-man also. The Bible tells us that Paul in his ministry was refreshed amongst his friends. The company of good friends in the Lord can refresh and uplift our heart [Philemon 7]. We can renew our spiritual strength by the comfort and spirit of others in the Lord [2 Cor 7:13]. We can be refreshed by speaking inspired words that God gives us. Elihu, speaking to Job, had been given instruction by the Almighty and said: "I will speak, that I may be refreshed" [Job 32:20]. Simply speaking the Word of God can revive and restore our spirit. Following and being obedient to the will of God will refresh. Paul said: "That I might come unto you with joy by the will of God, and may with you be refreshed" [Rom 15:32]. And when we supply the needs of others, we refresh them and ourselves [1 Cor 16:17-18]. But the surest way to secure the times of refreshing is in the Lord. To glory in Jesus' salvation, love and grace, and in God's comforting Holy Spirit and precious promises, will give new strength and refreshing to spirit, soul, and body [Acts 3:19-20].

Prayer:
Thank you Lord, that although we may get weary in body and soul, we are always promised the time of refreshing in You.

Scripture of the Day:
"And the next day we touched at Sidon. And Julius courteously entreated Paul, and gave him liberty to go unto his friends to refresh himself." - [Acts 27:3]

The Word for the Day is "Consider."

Quote for the Day:
"A true Christian does not consider Christianity a part-time commitment. He has become a Christian in all parts of his life. He has reached the point where there is no turning back." – A. W. Tozer

Every now and then it is good to sit down and consider your life. Look at the past and learn from it. Look to the future and set goals and plans. Consider the present to see if you are walking in your best every day, using your life and time for good. Consider, also, in this time how faithfully you are following the Lord. As Tozer said, "a true Christian does not consider Christianity a part-time commitment." It is his all with no turning back.

In the Word, we see that God often rehearsed the past to remind His people of how they'd grown in Him and of all He'd brought them through. It's good sometimes to consider your growth in God, to remember and be thankful for all the ways God has protected, sheltered, and grown you, opened doors for you, given you wisdom and understanding [Num 15:40; Ps 77:11; Is 46:9]. A remembrance of the past like this often spurs a desire to continue growing more positively toward God in the future. The sins of our past are forgiven but the past, present, and future are linked and people who don't remember their past are prone to repeat the same problems again.

Thomas Monson wrote: "The past is behind, learn from it. The future is ahead, prepare for it. The present is here, live it." We can learn from the past and plan for the future, but life is made up of the hours of each current day in the present, and God always wants us to consider well our ways and walk with Him aright in every day [Ps 119:15]. For each of us our daily goal is to walk in righteousness, to become more and more like Jesus, and to finish His Work [John 4:34; Phil 1:6]. So we always need to consider how our goals and actions lead us ever on to that legacy. That should be the race we run and think toward—that higher calling above any earthly one [Heb 12:1-3; Phil 3:13-14; 1 Cor 9:24-27].

Prayer:
Lord, let us ever be mindful of all we've gained through You and to yearn to keep moving forward every day, in every way, with a dedicated, sold-out heart.

Scripture of the Day:
"Now therefore thus saith the Lord of hosts; Consider your ways." - [Haggai 1:5]

The Word for the Day is "Side."

Quote for the Day:
"I say, be not discouraged, for God is on our side if we really trust in Him, as is indicated by every coin in your pocket and every bill in your wallet." - Dr. Ben Carson

As children, we often played team games with two opposing sides or teams. The players for both sides were usually picked by the team captains or leaders. Kids instinctively wanted to be picked on the side with the most talented players, knowing the chances of winning were better on that team.

What a blessing it is to know that if we walk with the Lord in truth, trust, love, obedience and devotion, He is on our side in life as Dr. Carson pointed out, and not just a slogan on a dollar bill or coin. With God on our side, we are protected from terror and destruction, and we are protected when men rise up against us to bring harm and hurt [Psalm 91:7, 124:1-2]. With God on our side, we are comforted on all sides when troubles come [Psalm 71:21; 2 Cor 4:8]. As Psalm 118:6 confirms: with God on our side, what can man do to us?

But we must be on God's side first. The question each man must answer today is the same that Moses asked: "Who is on the Lord's side?" [Ex 32:26]. In Moses' absence from the people, to be with the Lord on the mount, the people turned away from God to serve the lusts of the flesh and the lust of the eyes. They created a substitute for God, and worshipped a golden calf made by hands. Moses then made distinction between those truly on the Lord's side, and those not. Today, there is a great war and conflict going on in our world as to which side we will choose. Satan has used lies and deception to try to get man to choose the side of worldly thinking over God's truth. The enemy has even deceived many in the church to compromise and accept the current cultural and social norms over God. He deceives man into thinking he can embrace the world and God at the same time; but "Ye cannot serve God and mammon" [Matt 6:24]. As John Hagee states: "You will either offend the world and please God, or please the world and offend God." Multitudes, multitudes stand in the valley of decision today [Joel 3:14], as the Spirit asks: "Who is on the Lord's side?"

Prayer:
Lord, we will commit ourselves wholly to be on Your side, and will then walk in peace knowing You are on our side.

Scripture of the Day:
"The Lord is on my side; I will not fear: what can man do unto me?" -
[Psalm 118:6]

The Word for the Day is "Voice."

Quote for the Day:
"God's voice is still and quiet and easily buried under an avalanche of clamor."-
Charles Stanley

A sweet quote, author unknown, says "Your voice is my favorite sound." We all understand that quote and smile—thinking of someone's voice we love, that we always delight to hear. God is like that with us, like a loving Father. And He loves to hear our voice. Deuteronomy reminds us God made us to hear His voice—"Out of heaven he made thee to hear his voice that he might instruct thee" [Deut 4:36]. God made us in His image and gave us voice that we might speak and commune with Him. "While they are yet speaking, I will hear" [Isaiah 65:24]. 'Then shalt thou cry and the Lord shall answer and guide thee continually' [Isaiah 58: 9,11].

Many people think that God just knows your thoughts and that this is all that is needful. Although God does know your heart and thoughts, He also wants you to commune and talk with Him; He wants you to ask for the things you need [Matthew 7:7-8; Luke 11:13]. And He wants you to bring your requests to Him orally. We are even advised we often do not receive because we ask not [James 4:2-3; John 16:23-24]. 'Ask Me and I shall give thee' he advises [Psalm 2:8]. "If ye abide in me and my words in you, ye shall ask what ye will and it shall be done unto you" [John 15:7].

In a loving relationship we talk and share our hearts. In a close fellowship and relationship with God, when you are right with Him, He will begin to speak with you, too—through the Word, through your Spirit. You will even hear His voice in your inner being—counseling, advising, comforting, strengthening. What a lovely privilege to hear from God in those secret times just with Him, knowing He hears our voice and inclines His ear to us and speaks to us in return [Psalm 116:1-2; Jeremiah 33:3].

Prayer:
Father, what a privilege to know You made us to commune with You and that, like a loving Father, you not only want to hear our voice but You love hearing it.

Scripture of the Day:
"My voice shalt thou hear in the morning, O Lord…make thy way straight before my face." - [Psalm 5:3,8]

The Word for the Day is "Rain."

Quote for the Day:
"Rain is grace; rain is the sky descending to earth; without rain there would be no life." - John Updike

What a beautiful thing rain is, watering the earth, making things grow, created by God as He created all things. Especially in the heat of summer the rain seems most welcome to not only plants, but to the animals and mankind as well. I can remember how grateful my grandfather was when rain came down on his crops after a dry spell at his farm in Tellico Plains. But aside from the natural benefits of rain, the Word of God gives us some spiritual meanings as well. Psalm 72:6 paints a picture of the Lord coming down (to us) like 'rain upon the grass, as showers that water the earth.' God's refreshing and replenishing sustenance is always there for His people.

Our walk of faith with God follows a pattern like the scriptures about rain in the Bible. At first in the world there was no rain, God's creation was in perfect balance. 'For the Lord had not caused it to rain upon the earth...But there went up a mist from the earth and watered the whole face of the ground' [Gen 2:5-6]. So when the Lord told Noah that he would 'bring a flood of waters upon the earth' [Gen 6:17], Noah had to make a leap of faith to build the ark. Noah's natural eyes had never seen rain, but he had to believe in the spiritual truth of God. We have to do that to enter into the Kingdom of God, to trust and believe on God's promise in the spirit, even though we can't see it with the natural senses. In this sense, rain is symbolic of rebirth and renewal by the washing away of the old and the growth of something new from God.

God gives us more rain, more faith as we move forward in our faith walk. 'If ye shall hearken diligently unto My commandments to love the Lord and to serve Him with all your heart and soul, I will give you the rain of your land in his due season, the first rain and the latter rain' [Deut 11:13-14]. In each season as we move on with God we receive more rain—more knowledge, more wisdom, more growth in Him. We also hold to a future hope that God will bring a latter rain, filled with more of His power and might than we have ever seen before!

Prayer:
Lord, we will walk and serve You in every season, looking forward to Your blessings of the first and latter rains of promise.

Scripture of the Day:
"He shall come down like rain upon mown grass: as showers that water the earth."
- [Psalm 72:6]

The Word for the Day is "Find."

Quote for the Day:
Though we travel the world over to find the beautiful, we must carry it with us or we find it not." – Ralph Waldo Emerson

Studies in child development show that we can teach children from a young age to see and notice beauty. As we age and become more distracted, we often lose our easy ability to see beauty and to take joy in it; neither do we seek it out. Yet appreciation of beauty and excellence is a virtue. Holding that characteristic boosts happiness and lowers depression. It helps us connect to something greater, and it makes us want to be better and more loving.

It shouldn't surprise us to learn that beauty is an aspect and part of God's nature. There is a beauty, not just within God himself, but in holiness [Psalm 90:17; Zechariah 9:17; Psalm 29:2]. After creating nature and all the world, God saw all that He made and called it good [Genesis 1:31]. Many times the Bible shows God as a creator of beauty and excellence and as an appreciator of both. 'For by Him were all things created in heaven and in earth' and all 'declare the glory of God' [Colossians 1:16; Psalm 19:1].

If you want to become more sensitive to beauty and excellence and to appreciate both more you may need to consciously 'think more on those things—things that are lovely and good' [Philippians 4:8]. Remember the old line advising you to stop and smell the roses? You may need to stop some of the busyness in your life to do just that, 'to seek that you will find,' to cultivate the art of seeing beauty again more readily, to carry with you the desire to find the beautiful [Matthew 7:7]. While you are at it, seek to see God in that beauty and draw closer to Him. Many who have sought to see more beauty in the world have found more of God along the way. 'Blessed are they that seek Him with the whole heart' [Psalm 119:2].

Prayer:
Father, in our busy lives, we often fail to see the beauty of your glorious world and we also miss seeing the beauty of Your nature. Help us seek to see both more.

Scripture of the Day:
"And ye shall seek me, and find me, when ye shall search for me with all your heart." – Jeremiah 29:13

The Word for the Day is "Filled."

Quote for the Day:
"What you're filled with eventually comes out." - Pastor Shane Idleman

We can present an image to others, but eventually, as others come to know us, they see clearly if the image is real and genuine or mostly pretense. Our actions, behavior, and words reveal us and show what is truly in us. Sooner or later, people show their true colors. "A person playing a role will eventually forget the act. Be patient and watch closely" [Tony Gaskins]. Being a Christian isn't a label, like being an American, it's a lifestyle, a reality, a relationship. True Christians show by their lives, their actions and words, who they really are. "The way you view God will eventually show up in the way you live your life" [Charles Spurgeon].

Words, as well as actions, reveal what a man is. If you listen to someone long enough, you will hear who they are. "A good man out of the good treasure of his heart bringeth forth that which is good; and an evil man out of the evil treasure of his heart bringeth forth that which is evil; for of the abundance of the heart his mouth speaketh" [Luke 6:45]. The Lord wants our heart filled with Him and with His Spirit [Eph 5:18]. Then our hearts and words can bring forth blessing to others. We can be filled with God's wisdom [Ex 28:3], His praise and honor and His goodness [Ps 71:8, 104:28]. We can be filled with His knowledge [Rom 15:14], His rich comfort, deep joy [2 Cor 7:4; 2 Tim 1:4] and His fullness in every area [Eph 3:19].

Sadly, some change the truth of God into a lie, though, and allow themselves to be filled with unrighteousness, becoming foolish [Rom 1:22-32]. They grow full of mischief [Prov 12:21], wrong ways [Prov 14:14], anger, envy, and even madness [Luke 4:28; Acts 13:45; Luke 6:11], losing right knowledge and becoming reprobate [Rom 1:28]. The Lord wants us to wholly give ourselves to Him and to be filled with His Spirit, and to enjoy the treasures of a good heart. "Being filled with the fruits of righteousness, which are by Jesus Christ, unto the glory and praise of God" [Phil 1:11].

Prayer:
Lord, fill us with your Holy Spirit that out of a good heart we will manifest the fruits of righteousness unto Your praise and glory.

Scripture of the Day:
"Blessed are they which do hunger and thirst after righteousness: for they shall be filled." - [Matthew 5:6]

The Word for the Day is "Little."

Quote for the Day:
"You can't jump from little things to big things. It takes time and patience." –
Nadia Comaneci

We often underestimate the influence and importance of little things. But all learning comes little by little in a building progression. Our faith and growth in spiritual things is progressive, too. Often when people become Christians late in life they expect to jump from 'little child' to ' young man' to 'strong adult father' in one mighty leap but the Bible advises growth in faith is a gradual overcoming process [1 John 2:13]. In anything we must start at the beginning, learn the basics, work, study, practice, and grow. We have to let patience have its perfect work [James 1:4].

The little things also begin to show clearly who we are in our walk in faith as in life. Lawrence Bell wrote: "Show me a man who can't bother to do little things, and I'll show you a man who cannot be trusted to do big things." God will not give us big things to do, either, until we show we can be trusted with the small things that He gives first. 'He that is faithful in that which is least is faithful also in that which is much' [Luke 16:10]. Likewise, the little things carelessly done or left undone reveal a problem with maturity and often with the heart. 'The little foxes spoil the vines' [Song of Solomon 2:15] and need to be dealt with.

Too often in our fast paced world we want to skip past the little stuff, but each part of our growth in faith is important, just as seed time, watering, and harvest are important in the process of producing a rich crop [John 4:35-38]. Our coming to be all we're meant to be in all areas in our faith walk is a slow incremental process, like a tree growing down deep roots, planted by the water [Col 2:6-7; Jer 17:7-8]. God is always the gardener, too. He prunes, cuts, and trains, if we will allow it, so we will grow strong spiritually, little by little, precept upon precept, to bear more fruit and be all we're meant to be [Isaiah 28:10; Col 1:10-11].

Prayer:
Lord, help us to faithfully allow You to grow us to maturity in You so we can become all you want and need us to be in the earth.

Scripture of the Day:
"Though thou be little among the thousands…yet out of thee shall he come forth unto me that is to be ruler." – [Micah 5:2]

The Word for the Day is "Ready."

Quote for the Day:
"The fool, with all his other faults, has this also, he is always getting ready to live."
- Epicurus

Although still in the heat of late summer, August is a month when football teams get ready for the upcoming Fall season. It's amusing to listen to the sports media excitedly analyze and try to predict results of the coming schedule for the local teams. In our area, it's mostly about the Tennessee Vols and the SEC schedule. As the Vols practice and get ready for the scheduled competition, the fan base prepares with hope of good results for the coming season.

Just as a football team has to prepare for it's schedule, Christians have to get ready and stay ready for opposition. But whereas the football competition lasts only one season in the year, the believer's challenge requires readiness year-round. We have to prepare for the challenges of life itself and all the day to day demands, trials, and tribulations of living. A football team gets ready for all the skills and strategies of its scheduled opponents. Our constant opponents in life are the pull of the flesh nature [1 John 2:16] and the wiles of our adversary, the devil, always trying to defeat us [1 Pet 5:8].

How do we get ready for our "life" schedule? A football team tries to remedy its faults and increase its strengths by coached practices. But we have the advantage of having One that is perfect and all-powerful within us: 'because greater is he that is in you, than he that is in the world' [1John 4:4]. And we have a victory over the faults and lusts of the flesh by that same One: "This I say then, Walk in the Spirit, and ye shall not fulfil the lust of the flesh" [Gal 5:16]. Our faults are replaced by the overcoming perfection of Jesus, the Captain of our salvation, bringing us to glory and sanctification in Him [Heb 2:10-11]. We simply die out to ourselves and let the Captain have total control. "Now thanks be unto God, which always causeth us to triumph in Christ, and maketh manifest the savour of his knowledge by us in every place" [2 Cor 2:14]. What a blessed feeling knowing we are season-long victors in our Lord!

Prayer:
Lord, thank You, that submitted and led by your Spirit, we are ready to overcome all challenges and walk as victors in You.

Scripture of the Day:
"But sanctify the Lord God in your hearts: and be ready always to give an answer to every man that asketh you a reason of the hope that is in you with meekness and fear." - [1 Peter 3:15]

The Word for the Day is "People."

Quote for the Day:
"God's people are a people of excellence…Do your work well, take care of the re-sources that God has given you, and live in such a manner that when people see you, they will be attracted to your God." - Joel Osteen

What do people think of you? What kind of image do you project? Countless studies have examined the impact of first impressions. Companies work hard at creating images favorable to buyers. You also project an image wherever you go whether you like it or not. Right or wrong, the image you present shapes how someone perceives you. When you tell them the business you work for or the church you attend, your image also impacts how people perceive that business or church. As a representative and ambassador for Jesus Christ, do you look and act like an ambassador?

The other day I was watching footage of the queen of England in a public set-ting—poised, immaculately dressed, congenial, stopping to shake hands and greet different people, acting with grace, courtesy and wisdom—in every way a beautiful ambassador for her country. What if she had been rude, drunk, sloppily dressed, humped into a seat ignoring people, texting, only talking with the few people she knew well, gossiping, telling dirty jokes, popping a few curse words into her speech? You'd have been shocked and disappointed. Why? Because you expected better of someone in a high position, representing a kingdom. Yet you are a child of Almighty God, a royal priesthood, a part of the Kingdom of God, a representative of God Almighty wherever you go [2 Cor 5:20; 1 Pet 2:9; Matt 19:14; 1 Cor 1:30]. Jesus said "I have chosen you and ordained you" [John 15:16]. You have been called 'to the obtaining of the glory of the Lord Jesus Christ,' 'chil-dren of the most High,' 'His anointing abiding in you' [2 Thess 2:14; Psalm 82:6; 1 John 2:27]. Oh, that you could see who you are in Him and so respect that high place that in every moment you would reflect His glory and act as a King's child, showing forth His office, His Kingdom, and His Honor in everything you do and say, in every way you look and act.

Prayer:
Lord, remind us today that we are not only your children but sons and daughters of royalty and ambassadors for Christ. Help us 'to walk in a manner worthy of that calling' [Ephesians 4:1-3].

Scripture of the Day:
"But ye are a chosen generation, a royal priesthood, an holy nation, a peculiar people; that ye should shew forth the praises of him who hath called you out of darkness into his marvelous light." - [1 Peter 2:9]

The Word for the Day is "Guide."

Quote for the Day:
"I've learned that no matter what, my faith will guide me. However I play on the field, I know my faith will guide me. After sports, my faith will guide me. As I've grown in my faith, that's something that's given me comfort. God has taught me that I can trust in Him." - Marcus Mariota

We can learn things on our own, but it is often helpful to have an experienced guide to lead us. Two friends of mine are both professional fishing guides. They help people who don't have time to fish often to enjoy the sport. These guides have special talents and knowledge they utilize to achieve successful results. First, they know the natural habits, patterns, and preferences of the fish species whether it be bass, stripers, trout, crappie, catfish or other species. They know the waters they fish, how to adjust to the best locaton and depth depending on the season. They know the best baits, lures, and equipment for each type fish and how to properly present them. And, they know how to communicate all these factors to their clients to ensure a happy outcome.

If we are yielded and trust totally in the Lord, we have a special guide for our lives. The Lord gives us the Holy Spirit to guide us into all truth [John 16:13]. The Spirit has the knowledge of all the realities of our lives that we cannot know with our natural eyes. He not only knows us, but He knows all the people in our life. Like the fishing guide, He sees the conditions that exist below the surface of the water. He knows and discerns all the hidden things that we cannot know with the carnal senses. And He knows the best knowledge, wisdom, and skills He needs to impart to us to achieve our goals in God's will. We are assured He will instruct and teach us in the way, guiding us with His counsel [Psalm 32:8, 73:24].

My fishing guide friends have emailed me many photos of their excited, happy clients holding their catches with wide smiles on their faces. I know my guide friends were delighted too. God wants to put a smile on our face by guiding our way continually and guiding us into the way of peace [Isaiah 58:11; Luke 1:79].

Prayer:
Lord, "thou art my rock and my fortress; therefore for thy name's sake lead me, and guide me" [Psalm 31:3].

Scripture of the Day:
"I will instruct thee and teach thee in the way which thou shalt go. I will guide thee with mine eye." - [Psalm 32:8]

The Word for the Day is "Charge."

Quote for the Day:
"The Lord cares enough about His people that He charges the army of heaven with their care." – Pastor Gilbert Moore

Media, movies, and books bombard us with entertaining and fascinating depictions of the supernatural—from werewolves, vampires, and witches, to good and evil superheroes. Yet it is rare we read or see stories about angels. Generally when they are depicted, they are not biblically portrayed. It is rare to hear any sermons or teachings about angels either, so it is little wonder we are so ignorant of them. Yet God's angels are a mighty reality and their love bears us up. "Bless the Lord, ye his angels, that excel in strength, that do his commandments, hearkening unto the voice of his word" [Psalm 103:20].

The number of angels is far beyond counting and the Word tells us there are "ten thousand times ten thousand, and thousands and thousands" of them [Gen 2:1; Matt 26:53; Rev 5:11]. Besides the knowledge that the angels serve God and carry out the work of the Kingdom as God ordains, there are 'ministering angels' concerned with our personal lives and rejoicing when anyone on earth repents, is saved, and comes into the Kingdom of God [Heb 1:14; Luke 15:10]. In the Bible we learn angels bring protection, supply needs, give strength, direction, wisdom, and vision from God. They excel in strength, patrol the earth as God's representatives, watch over us, and fight for us against God's enemies [Psalm 103:20; Ex 23:20; Psalm 34:7]. "For He shall give His angels charge over thee, to keep thee in all thy ways" [Psalm 91:11].

We should be grateful for the ministry of angels on our behalf, expectant of their help, and eager for God to teach us to know more of them. Everything they do at all times is for our good. Billy Graham wrote: "We know they are watching but in the heat of the battle, I have thought how wonderful it would be if we could hear them cheering." Vance Havner similarly said "We shall play a better game if...we remember who is in the grandstand."

Prayer:
Father, thank You for the angelic host and for the angels assigned to watch over and guard our lives. Help us to keep a right focus on the true supernatural, to avoid erroneous beliefs and false spiritual knowledge and to not seek out dangerous darkside activity [2 Cor 10:4-5; Deut 18:10-13; Lev 19:31].

Scripture of the Day:
"For he shall give his angels charge over thee, to keep thee in all thy ways." - [Psalm 91:11]

The Word for the Day is "Presence."

Quote for the Day:
"The more time you spend in God's Presence, the more you will act and think like Him." - Kenneth Copeland

Children watch and emulate their parents when small. My son used to follow me around the yard when I mowed with my push mower, pushing his little plastic toy mower behind me. We are naturally inclined to want to learn from, or emulate, our parents and those we admire and spend time with. And the more time we spend with God, the more we will act and think like Him.

As Christians, we should desire to conform more and more to the image of Jesus. We should be desiring and seeking more time in God's presence. But we must come into His presence with a right heart and attitude. "Let us come before his presence with thanksgiving" [Psalm 95:2]; "Serve the Lord with gladness" [Psalm 100:2]. We should come to His presence as a privilege, not as an obligation. How do we come into God's presence? We come through His Word. Reading, studying, and meditating the Bible. We can hear His Word through faithful ministers of His Truth. And we come into His presence with prayer. We have the faithful promise that He will honor our seeking with His presence: "Draw nigh to God, and he will draw nigh to you" [James 4:8].

When we draw near to God we can enjoy the benefits of His presence. We grow in our faith as we possess more of God's Word in our heart [Romans 10:17]. It grows our understanding and trust in God. It causes our desires to line up more with God's as we turn from the carnal, flesh nature [Galatians 4:9].

Our motive and purpose should be to dwell, to ever be living in, God's presence. "Surely the righteous shall give thanks unto thy name: the upright shall dwell in thy presence" [Psalm 140:13]. We should acknowledge His continual presence with us by His Spirit. Even as we perform our daily work and duties we possess the 'knowing' that God is always with us. We glory then that His 'times of refreshing shall come from the presence of the Lord' [Acts 3:19].

Prayer:
Lord, we vow to spend more time in Your presence that we might conform more and more unto the image of Jesus.

Scripture of the Day:
"Thou wilt shew me the path of life: in thy presence is fulness of joy; at thy right hand there are pleasures for evermore." - [Psalm 16:11]

The Word for the Day is "Grasshoppers."

Quote for the Day:
"When a man makes alliance with the Almighty, giants look like grasshoppers." –
Vance Havner

As a child, my friends and I used to play out in the field on warm summer days, enjoying the beauty of daisies, Queen Anne's lace and blue bachelors buttons, listening to the humming of the bees, and watching the green grasshoppers leap into the air again and again. The grasshoppers might have felt powerful leaping so high into the air above other insects, but in our young minds we were the true giants of the field, the grasshoppers only small and insignificant.

To the Almighty, we are like the small green grasshoppers, but in our earthly self-focus and self-importance we often forget that. Being made in God's image, a little higher than most of God's creation with a powerful intellectual capacity, we are prone to sometimes act a little smug and to become too sufficient in ourselves. However, Jesus' example taught us to be humble before God, to stay out of vainglory. 'For Jesus made himself of no reputation, and took upon him the form of a servant, and was made in the likeness of men…humbled himself and became obedient unto death' [Phil 2:6-8]. For this He was exalted, not for being pompous, cocky or self-sure, but for being obedient and sub-servient to God. Jesus was ever aware of his earthly limitations as a man and of the necessity to lean fully to the Father for his wisdom, strength, guidance, and power.

We serve a mighty God and when we walk with Him, are led and guided by Him, His Might is given to us, too [2 Peter 1:3-4; Col 1:11-13]. We are lifted up through Him and can "run through a troop and leap over a wall" with strength beyond ourselves [Ps 18:29]. Through Jesus we 'become the children of Almighty God, invested with His power and might' [John 1:12; Acts 1:8]. As God's own, when we make a committed alliance with Him, and lean to His understanding and strength, the giants we encounter in our lives begin to look like grasshoppers, too.

Prayer:
Lord, thank You that through Your strength we can do valiantly and that You will tread down our enemies [Psalm 60:12]. Help us daily to ever trust in Your strength and Your might and never in ours alone.

Scripture of the Day:
"It is he that sitteth upon the circle of the earth, and the inhabitants thereof are as grasshoppers." - [Isaiah 40:22]

The Word for the Day is "Vow."

Quote for the Day:
"What is a vow...but the mouth repeating what the heart has already spoken." - Jane Yolen

Most have heard the old saying: "Don't make a promise you can't keep." This concept has Biblical origins for God takes very seriously making vows to Him or vows to people that are not performed or kept. What is a vow? One simple spiritual definition for vow is 'a dedicated or covenant promise to God to do or perform something.' A vow is serious business with God and should never be taken lightly or with indifference. Any vow we make should be made thoughtfully and deliberately and not in a casual way. When God makes a promise or a vow He keeps it according to His perfect holiness. "People with good intentions make promises, but people with good character keep them" [anon].

As God's people we should be true to our words, true to our vows. The Bible gives us instruction and wisdom concerning vows. "When thou vowest a vow unto God, defer not to pay it; for he hath no pleasure in fools: pay that which thou hast vowed" [Eccl 5:4]. As stated before, we should be very deliberate about our vows: not rash with our mouth or hasty to utter any thing before God [Eccl 5:2]. "Better it is that thou shouldest not vow, than that thou shouldest vow and not pay" [Eccl 5:5]. God wants us to give serious prayer and devotion to any vow we make to Him, not hasty or impulsive without commitment.

We observe many today that do not keep their word or promises, beguiling for personal gain or uncaring that they don't stand firm in their vows. God's people should be holy unto Him and keep their word, making a difference in the world. Speaking of vows, fifty years ago on this date, August 28th, this East Tennessee boy gave his marriage vows to his beloved. I am so blessed to have Lin in my life I can only say with all my heart Thank You, Lord, Thank You.

Prayer:
Lord, we have put off the old man and put on the new, therefore we will only speak truth and reverently fulfill the vows of our mouth.

Scripture of the Day:
"If a man vow a vow unto the Lord, or swear an oath to bind his soul with a bond; he shall not break his word, he shall do according to all that proceedeth out of his mouth." -[Numbers 30:2]

The Word for the Day is "Him."

Quote for the Day:
"What's closest to your heart is what you talk about, and if God is close to your heart, you will talk about Him." – A. W. Tozer

Our conversation tells a great deal about who we are, where we come from, and how we think. What people feel and believe tends to slip out in their words. Actions may speak louder that words, but words are telling, too. What you love and are avidly interested in is usually what you tend to talk about, whether it's your kids, your work, your favorite football team, or the Lord.

Jesus told his disciples 'You are the salt of the earth,' an obvious metaphor for how they would positively "season" the world around them with their words and actions [Matt 5:13]. He also said 'Let your light shine before men, that they may see your good works and glorify your Father in Heaven' [Matt 5:16]. We should both talk and act differently if God is alive and well within us. People should hear and see God through us and be drawn by Him in us [John 12:32; Phil 2:13].

Our talk should be real and sincere, though—never phony, contrived, or legalistic—and always shared as led by the Spirit of God exactly if, when, and how He shows us to share [2 Cor 3:6]. Surely all the many Bible stories about the Pharisees way of doing things showed us the wrong way to share faith. We're to be known by our love, by the fruits of the Spirit in us, and we're to follow God's perfect timing and Spirit in all things, being "wise as serpents and harmless as doves" [Matt 10:16]. The concept of being prudent and Spirit-led in our sharing, however, doesn't imply leaning to the opposite pole and never sharing at all—too timid or embarrassed to share even when opportunities come and doors open [Mark 8:38, 16:15]. If we love God and live close to Him we want to talk about Him as much as we talk easily about other things we love and we yearn to lead others closer to Him.

Prayer:
Lord, let us be as quick to share about You, with love and excitement, like anything else we share with others, not denying You or worrying about what others might think and missing the chance to share how wonderful You are.

Scripture of the Day:
"For of him, and through him, and to him, are all things: to whom be glory for ever. Amen." - [Romans 11:36]

The Word for the Day is "Mark."

Quote for the Day:
"The greater danger for most of us lies not in setting our aim too high and falling short; but in setting our aim too low, and achieving our mark." - Michelangelo

With deer archery season coming up next month in this area, a lot of bow hunters start going to the archery range to sharpen up their skills. Typically, this involves shooting at a target attached to a hay bale or using an indoor target facility. The target bullseye is the mark or target the archer tries to achieve. When I was a youngster learning the basics of becoming a baseball pitcher, my coach gave me the best advice. He said: "Son, don't worry about the mechanics of the throw, just keep your eye focused on the catcher's mitt." I found this is true in most things in life we aim for: keep your focus on the mark, or target, you're trying to obtain or achieve.

In writing to the Philippians, the apostle Paul stated "forgetting those things which are behind, and reaching for those things which are before, I press toward the mark for the prize of the high calling of God in Christ Jesus" [Philippians 3:13-14]. What is the mark? The mark for us is to be conformed to the image of Jesus. Our target or goal is to always be more and more like Jesus in our heart, our mind, our ways, and in our impact and ministry to others. To achieve this mark we must always have Jesus as our focus: "Looking unto Jesus the author and finisher of our faith" [Hebrews 12:2].

Paul says this is a "high calling." We are never to be complacent or satisfied where we are now, for there is always a higher calling, a more excellent mark in Jesus to aim for. Jesus is always the higher calling, wanting to lift us up above the ordinary to greater things in Him. All shooters know that to hit a mark or target that is far, they must aim high or above the mark to hit it. The Lord wants us to aim high, to be increased more and more [Psalm 115:14]. And the Lord equips us to achieve this high calling in and through Him. "I will instruct thee and teach thee in the way which thou shalt go: I will guide thee with mine eye" [Ps 32:8]. "For that which is urged onward by the Almighty's hand cannot miss its mark" [Charles Spurgeon]. Let us press on, aiming for the high mark in Christ Jesus!

Prayer:
Lord, in all our ways we will keep our eyes and our focus on Jesus that we might achieve the mark of being conformed more and more unto His image.

Scripture of the Day:
"I press toward the mark for the prize of the high calling of God in Christ Jesus."
-[Philippians 3:14]

The Word for the Day is "Quit"

Quote for the Day:
"When you start living by faith, you don't quit work. You change employers. You go to work full time for God." – Kenneth Copeland

In the world today most people look forward to quitting their jobs and retiring at some point. The idea of quitting from all labor, sitting back and taking it easy, and filling each day indulgently with pleasures is very appealing to most people. But you will never find the words "quit" or "retire" spoken of in this way in the Bible. God's heart is for you to be "Refired" as you grow older not "Retired."

The enemy has planted a concept in our minds that the ideal life is one in which we never have to labor or work. Society has helped this idea along with retirement entitlements and the initiation of the Social Security Act in 1935, originally designed to lessen economic hardship brought on by the Great Depression. In 1935 the average life expectancy was age 61, so the concept was to benefit the infirm and elderly who could no longer usefully work. Now with our average life expectancy at about eighty years of age, most people can expect many long, useful, healthy, and strong years beyond what was once considered old age.

In truth, our lives and years, including our retirement years, don't belong to us if we are in the Lord, they are His. It is God who should be ordering our steps and lives at every age and stage [Ps 37:23; 1 Cor 6:19-20]. Think what a workforce for God there would be if all those in their "second adulthood" retirement years went to work utilizing their skills and gifts for God as He directed and began doing those "good works" they always told God they wished they'd had time for earlier? Henry Emerson Fosdick wrote: "Don't simply retire from something, have something to retire to." Give those years willingly to the Lord. Be assured the bugle doesn't sound for God's Calvary to retire from action until it's time to go home.

Prayer:
Lord, help us to open our hearts to begin to see our retirement years as a time to be dedicated and sold out to You, not to cease from work and duty, but to be willing and eager to spend our latter years working for You in the Kingdom of God.

Scripture of the Day:
"Watch ye, stand fast in the faith, quit ye like men, be strong." -
[1 Corinthians 16:13]

September

The Word for the Day is "Words."

Quote for the Day:
"Words are containers. They carry faith, or fear, and they produce after their kind."
- Charles Capps

One of the greatest impacts to my faith and my walk with the Lord was when I discovered what the Bible said about the importance and impact of the words we speak. Charles Capps' book *The Tongue-A Creative Force,* was a helpful aid in understanding the importance of words according to the scriptures. Jesus said that a man would speak out of the abundance of the heart, either good or evil, depending upon the heart's condition [Matthew 12:34-35]. Matthew 12:37 states 'that by our words we are justified or condemned.'

How should we speak to be justified? Jesus said that the words He spoke were spirit and life [John 6:63]. So when we speak the words of Jesus we create a force for spirit and life, which is why we need to have an abundance of the Word of God in our heart. God's words contain wisdom and understanding. They 'are life to those that find them, and health to all their flesh' [Prov 4:20-22]. We need to seed our minds with good words and truth and guard our hearts with diligence, knowing that the words we put into our minds and hearts and the words we speak matter [Prov 4:23]. The Bible gives many cautions about being watchful over the words we say—to put away a froward, willful, proud mouth and to not use offensive, perverse, and critical speech[Prov 4:24]. Instead our mouths should speak good, right, edifying and fruitful words of faith [Prov 12:14]. Instead of complaining to God about our problems, we should remember, too, that we have the authority to speak to the problems and mountains in our lives and command them to be removed [Mark 11:23]! Speaking God's Word will always bring God on the scene for He is watching over His Word to perform it [Jeremiah 1:12].

The enemy knows the power of your words. That is why he tries to bring you into condemnation by filling the heart with worldly error, doubt, unbelief, and fear. He knows you will then speak what is in your heart, and it is what a man speaks that defiles him [Matt 15:11]. Get your heart filled with God's truth, and quit praying the problem, and start praying and speaking the answer.

Prayer:
Lord, we will fill our heart with more abundance of Your Presence, Your Word, Your Spirit, that our words may speak spirit and life for ourselves and others.

Scripture of the Day:
"For by thy words thou shalt be justified, and by thy words thou shalt be condemned." -[Matthew 12:37]

The Word for the Day is "Virtue."

Quote for the Day:
"Love is the sum of all virtue, and love disposes us to good." - Jonathan Edwards

We use the term "virtue" less in our society today than in times past but it refers to moral excellence. A virtuous person is one who conforms his or her life and conduct to high moral and ethical standards. In Latin the term *virtus* refers to moral perfection. Surprising to many, God has called us to virtue and wants our lives to be of moral excellence.

Many great philosophers have debated what virtues are most important for people to hold and created lists, charts, and hierarchies of them. One listing from Isaiah of the virtues of the Holy Spirit includes wisdom, understanding, counsel, might or fortitude, knowledge, piety, and the fear of the Lord [Isaiah 11:2-3]. The three better known Christian virtues, faith, hope, and charity, are given in 1 Corinthians 13:13. In all the listings of virtues most agree they are attained by practice and habit which involve submission of the will.

The Bible counsels that we are to think virtuously and act virtuously, giving all diligence to that practice, 'adding to our faith virtue and to virtue knowledge' [2 Peter 1:5; Phil 4:8]. When virtue becomes strong within us, it can come out of us to touch others in a positive way. As Jesus walked through the multitudes, people sought to touch him "for there went virtue out of him and healed them all" [Luke 6:19]. Jesus was also aware when virtue went out of him [Mark 5:30; Luke 8:46]. Perhaps from this example we should yearn for good, power, and virtue to so reside in us that they would touch and impact others, too. Dr. Greg Herrick wrote: "The theological virtues—faith, hope, and love—are so named because they relate primarily to the inner disposition of the heart toward God and are intimately connected to and find their expression in our relationships with others." We develop virtue as we grow in the Lord; then it shows in our lives and reaches out to touch others.

Prayer:
Lord, may we strive to be virtuous people of moral excellence so that those Godly traits shine out of our lives and bring You honor and glory.

Scripture of the Day:
"According as His divine power hath given unto us all things that pertain unto life and godliness, through the knowledge of him that hath called us to glory and virtue." - [2 Peter 1:3]

SEPTEMBER 3   **J.L. Stepp**
The Word for the Day is "Miracles."

Quote for the Day:
"How can we call ouselves a church and not believe in healing and in miracles? I cannot read four pages anywhere in the Bible without encountering miracles! And the God of the Bible is the same today!" - T.L. Osborn

You've probably heard someone say "Miracles have passed away." Some denominations even hold this dogma. But one scripture entirely refutes this erroneous belief—Hebrews 13:8: 'Jesus Christ the same yesterday, today, and forever.' Has Jesus done miracles yesterday, or anytime in the past? Of course. Then the same Jesus is doing miracles today, and will do miracles tomorrow. If Jesus did miracles then, but denied men miracles today, He would violate the scripture. This cannot happen. "For I am the Lord, I change not" [Mal 3:6].

God wants His people to receive miracles. Why do "believers" have such a hard time believing for and receiving a miracle? The primary reasons for the failure to receive God's blessings are a lack of faith and unbelief through ignorance of His Word. If you were raised to believe miracles had passed, you had no faith to believe for miracles, because you had never heard the scriptures about miracles presented. God's people are destroyed for a lack of knowledge [Hosea 4:6], and renewing the mind and heart to faith only comes by hearing the Word of God [Rom 10:17]. Unbelief robs us of receiving of God. God is love, as is Jesus [1 John 4:8; Heb 13:8], and nothing is impossible with God [Luke 1:37]. The most impossible looking situation is 'just a piece of cake' to Jesus. So it pleases Him for us to receive by faith the miracles we need to have the "life more abundantly" He promised. The childlike faith simply believes that He said it, that settles it!

God not only wants us to receive, but also to perform miracles. We are to be His ministers to the world. Miracles draw men to Jesus. They want a God of miracles! Miracles manifest forth the glory of the Lord [John 2:11], and 'many believed in His name when they saw the miracles He did' [John 2:23]. Let us strive to be like the followers of Jesus, full of faith and power, to show the world a God of love, salvation, and great wonders!

Prayer:
Lord, turning the water to wine was just the beginning of Your miracles, and we thank You that You are the same today: still performing miracles and wonders!

Scripture of the Day:
"And Stephen, full of faith and power, did great wonders and miracles among the people." -[Acts 6:8]

The Word for the Day is "Wisdom."

Quote for the Day:
"True wisdom begins and ends with God." - Anonymous

Wisdom is simply the quality or state of being wise, of being able to think and act using good understanding, knowledge, experience, common sense, and insight. Wisdom is often also defined as accumulated learning. The more we learn and study in an area, the more expertise we gain in that area. All these understandings may be good, but as Christians we cannot afford to overlook the spiritual aspect of wisdom. In the Lord, we should place all wisdom under New Management. As long as we seek wisdom first from the world, we will only have problems.

Throughout the Bible we are encouraged to seek God's wisdom and 'to not lean to our own understanding' [Prov 3:5]. All wisdom that is good comes from and originates in God [Prov 2:6]. His understanding is infinite. It has no limits and it has no end [Psalm 147:5]. 'Wisdom and might are His…and the Light dwells with Him' [Dan 2:20, 22]. True humility recognizes the need to always lean to God's wisdom first, for it is 'better than rubies; and all the things that can be desired are not to be compared to it' [Prov 8:11-12].

Fortunately, God gives His Wisdom liberally to all who seek it. "If any of you lack wisdom, let him ask of God that giveth to all men liberally and upbraideth not" [James 1:5; 3:17]. We seek and find God's wisdom through study in the Word, prayer, asking and seeking for it. And thereby are we enriched.

Corrie Ten Boom wrote: "Faith is like radar that sees through the fog—the reality of things at a distance the human eye cannot see." God's Wisdom coming in to us, rising up in us—as from out of a fog—gives us wise ideas we could not know of ourselves to create witty inventions, to write songs, paint, and create artistry to the glory of God, to run businesses in wise and successful ways. God's wisdom is always higher and deeper than ours and gives us, through Him, abilities, knowledge and skills beyond our own—a beautiful benefit of God's wisdom working in and through us to better our own lives and to better the world.

Prayer:
Lord, may we strive to be virtuous people of moral excellence so that those Godly traits shine out of our lives and bring You honor and glory.

Scripture of the Day:
"In the hearts of all that are wise hearted I have put wisdom, that they may make all that I commanded thee." - [Exodus 31:6]

The Word for the Day is "Harvest."

Quote for the Day:
"I grew up on a farm. We learned that there was a season to plant, a season to water, and a season to harvest. The planting and watering could be laborious, but without those stages, there would never be a harvest." - John Wooden

This season in East Tennessee is a time of harvest for many fruits and vegetables for the farmers. God established from the beginning that there would always be seedtime and harvest [Gen 8:22], and God desires an abundant and joyful harvest for His people [Gen 9:7]. The eternal principle is that you will reap and harvest what you have sown [Gal 6:7]. This Kingdom law also works in the natural concerning the works of our hands. Any good thing that God plants in our heart to desire, we must first plant the seeds to produce the harvest we want. If it be a skill or vocational talent we want to perfect, we must learn, practice and work that talent to produce the fruit and the harvest desired. Simply, we set our hands to sow the seeds, work and tend the sown ground, then exercise patience for the fruit to be produced for harvest.

God also wants us to use the seed/harvest principle in a spiritual application to harvest men's souls for the Kingdom. The whole world is the potential harvest, and the harvest is always ready, but Jesus said that the labourers are few [Luke 10:2]. The harvest of souls is not solely dependent upon pastors and ministers, but each individual believer is a potential laborer too. Never minimize the importance of sowing any good seed you can for God's harvest. We can share the gospel, we can sow love and kindness, compassion and mercy, help and assistance, encouragement and counsel. These godly seeds planted into a person's heart may grow the fruit of a soul ready to receive salvation in Jesus. And the sower of the seed is just as vital to the harvest as the reaper or laborer. Both he that soweth and he that reapeth rejoice together for the harvested soul [John 4:36]. Bring forth a harvest of the best for your own life, and always be a labourer in the harvest of souls for the Lord.

Prayer:
Lord, we will plant seeds of faith in our hearts for a blessed harvest, and we will always be ready to sow the Gospel Truth into hearts that we might harvest souls for the Kingdom of God.

Scripture of the Day:
"Then saith he unto his disciples, The harvest truly is plenteous, but the labourers are few; Pray ye therefore the Lord of the harvest, that he will send forth labourers into his harvest." -[Matthew 9:37-38]

The Word for the Day is "Gospel."

Quote for the Day:
"Let us remember this: one cannot proclaim the Gospel of Jesus without the tangible witness of one's life." - Pope Francis

The term Gospel, in a broad sense, refers to words or teachings that are infallible, unfailing, and without error. To us, as Christians, it is the message of the full revelation of Christ, his birth, death, and resurrection. Christians are united and defined through their belief in Jesus, the repentance of sin, and acceptance of Him through salvation. One of the church's missions, and the mission of individual Christians as well, is to preach and share this gospel to others.

An important point in being able to share the Gospel is to be assured you have personally experienced it. In all areas you can't share well what you haven't experienced, you can't teach what you don't personally know, and you can't lead where you haven't walked. Each of us is empowered by experience. Our personal testimony becomes powerful when shared because it's real [Rev 12:11].

Don't assume, like many, that people will hear the Gospel at church. Bill Armstrong, a US Senator and strong Christian, wrote that "most of those who need to hear the gospel will never come to church…nor will they ask for spiritual help unless someone else begins the conversation or, in some way, gives them an opening to do so." In addition a recent study revealed that over half of Protestant churches do not engage in evangelism and over half of church-goers have never shared their testimony or how to become a Christian with even one other person. However, sharing your faith and sharing the Gospel should be one of every Christian's priorities. "How shall they believe in Him of whom they have not heard?" [Rom 10:14]. Jesus said "go ye into all the world and preach the gospel to every creature" [Mark 16:15], 'be lights to bring salvation' [Acts 13:47]. We should always be willing to share sincerely with others what God has done, and is doing, for us. Never underestimate how many people hunger for a relationship with God but have no idea how to find it.

Prayer:
Lord, help us to be open and willing to share with others about our faith and to talk about all You have done for us and about the wonderful difference You have made in our lives.

Scripture of the Day:
"For I am not ashamed of the gospel of Christ: for it is the power of God unto salvation to every one that believeth." - [Romans 1:16]

The Word for the Day is "Refuse."

Quote for the Day:
"You must every day make higher ground. You must deny yourself to make progress with God. You must refuse every thing that is not pure and holy." - Smith Wigglesworth

The Dictionary tells us that 'refuse' means 'not willing to do something; not willing to accept or grant something.' We see that the decision to refuse something is a function of our free-will; it is an act by our own conscious choosing. Of course the Lord wants His followers to do as He did: 'to refuse the evil, and choose the good' [Is 7:15]. Before salvation in the Lord, the carnal nature is toward the evil, to choose the ways of the law of sin and death. The Bible gives us insight to the specific 'bad' choices that the carnal man makes. The carnal man refuses to humble himself before God [Ex 10:3]. He walks in arrogancy in his own way in the pride of life. And because of pride he refuses to hear God's Word; he refuses instruction and God's wisdom [Prov 8:33, 1:24]. The prophet Jeremiah spoke of those who refuse God's words and way as walking in the imagination of their heart and walking after other gods, to serve and worship them [Jer 13:10]. When man rejects God, he walks and serves the god of this world by default whether he acknowledges it or not. His carnal mind rejects the correction and ways of the Lord: "Because the carnal mind is enmity against God: for it is not subject to the law of God, neither indeed can be. So then they that are in the flesh cannot please God" [Rom 8:7-8].

We praise God because in Christ Jesus we are given a new heart or nature, made a new creation in His salvation [2 Cor 5:17]. We are also given the advantage of His Spirit of truth living within us, to help guide us in the way of righteousness [John 14:16-17]. We strive to keep our heart with all diligence then, for out of it are the issues of life, and the governance of the will whereby we choose good, and refuse evil [Prov 4:23]. The believer refuses the carnal ways of the flesh as stated above, renewing his mind to God's word, instruction, wisdom, and knowledge. Blessed is the man that chooses God's ways, finding life and obtaining the favour of the Lord [Prov 8:34-35].

Prayer:
Lord, thank you for the new creation we are in You, living in Your love and Spirit, that we find it easy to choose good and refuse the evil of the old man.

Scripture of the Day:
"See that ye refuse not him that speaketh. For if they escaped not who refused him that spake on earth, much more shall not we escape, if we turn away from him that speaketh from heaven." -[Hebrews 12:25]

The Word for the Day is "Rock."

Quote for the Day:
"In matters of principle, stand like a rock." - Thomas Jefferson

T. S. Eliot once wrote: "The True Church can never fail for it is based upon a rock" but unfortunately the church as a whole today has slid from that solid foundation into weakened compromise. In many areas, important to strong faith, the church has grown silent. "The silent church allows false teaching because they don't want to rock the boat. They are liberal in twisting or reinterpreting the truth or they avoid it all together. "Can't we all just get along? Is their rallying cry…Pastors encourage but rarely convict" [Pastor Shane Idleman]. This is sad because the strength of the church has always been its rock-like adherence to the principles and truth of God.

Recent surveys reveal there is growing confusion in Christian churches. Less than half of those surveyed believe the Bible as the Word of God, believe God the author of scripture, or believe Jesus the only route to salvation and eternal life. Even Christian colleges are teaching beliefs that attack the authority of the Bible and challenge foundational tenets. An old hymn claims 'on Christ the solid rock we stand' but the church has something else figured out now.

The Bible tells many accounts of people compromising their faith and falling away and their end is never good. Stories like Lot settling in Sodom and Gomorrah [Gen 19] or Aaron allowing the people to fashion a golden calf [Ex 32] show that condoning wrong can only bring sorrow. "No man can serve two masters… Ye cannot serve God and mammon" [Matt 6:24]. The true church is built on the rock of Jesus Christ and it is upon the rock, the Son of God, and upon the foundation of God our Creator and His Word that our faith must be built [1 Cor 3:11, 10:4; Ps 18:2; 2 Sam 22:32]. Jesus is the rock upon which we can stand safely and without fear in all the life storms we face. To begin to compromise is to allow the foundation of the structure of our faith to be weakened—like building a house upon the sand [Matt 7:26-27; Ps 40:2, 27:5]. We need to build and keep our feet on the rock so we will have a firm and safe place to unwaveringly stand.

Prayer:
Father, may we purpose to stand firm in our faith, keeping our beliefs strong and uncompromising and built on the rock.

Scripture of the Day:
"Whosoever heareth these sayings of mine, and doeth them, I will liken him unto a wise man, which built his house upon a rock." [Matthew 7:24]

The Word for the Day is "If."

Quote for the Day:
"If you believe what you like in the gospels, and reject what you don't like, it is not the gospel you believe, but yourself." - Saint Augustine

"If it doesn't rain tomorrow, I will mow the grass." It is so common that many times we set conditions for doing certain things, for fulfilling certain things, or for expecting certain things. When we start the sentence with 'if,' then what follows is the introduction of a condition or event that must happen before we act or think a certain thing. The truth is, we often impose these conditions to excuse ourselves from works, duties, obligations, or tasks we might not want to do. 'I will look for a job tomorrow if I can get my resume finished.' 'I will help my sick neighbor if I don't have to go to Kroger's for groceries.' 'I will catch up on my housework if I can get over this sniffle.' The "if" word can be played like an exemption card to keep from doing what you don't want to do.

We can even play the "if" card in spiritual matters with God. 'If I can ever catch up on my work, I'm gonna pray and read the Word more.' 'If God will just give me a special sign, I will believe for my healing, for my finances, for my loved one's salvation,' or some other thing. We try to add these extra conditions or events sometimes to excuse our unbelief for not standing in faith on God's Word and promises.

The Bible gives us some good remedies from having to apply the 'if" condition to God's Truth. The Bible tells us we must be willing and obedient to receive: "If ye be willing and obedient, ye shall eat the good of the land" [Isaiah 1:19]. We must make a conscious decision and commitment that we are going to humble ourselves in following God. Then we must be obedient to God, turning away from the ways of the world and the carnal nature. We must place no if's, and's, or but's about the decision to submit to the Lord's righteous ways. We must then build our faith and simply believe God's Word without any additional conditions. Jesus said that all things are possible if we believe. Then our only "if" condition will be: "If God said it, that settles it!"

Prayer:
Lord, we set our will to follow You only and to obey Your Word. And we commit to grow in the Word that our faith might open to us all possibilites.

Scripture of the Day:
"Jesus said unto him, If thou canst believe, all things are possible to him that believeth." -[Mark 9:23]

The Word for the Day is "Envy."

Quote for the Day:
"People are often vain of their most criminal passions; but envy is one passion so mean and low that nobody will admit to it."- Francois de La Rochefoucauld

Envy is a begrudging or resentful feeling of discontent aroused by someone else's accomplishments, money, attributes, or possessions. It is "a response to another person who has success, skills, or qualities that we desire and it involves feeling a lack in comparison to that person" [Dr. Seth Meyers]. At its root envy is linked to competition and low self-esteem, and studies have found the more fulfilled and confident a person is, the less they envy others. None of us want to admit when the temptation to envy comes, but occasionally it will come knocking on every door.

When envy comes knocking don't let it in! Satan will send envy as a thought but we're not to entertain envious thoughts and should not let them grow and fester in our minds. Envy causes division and bitterness. Our hearts should rejoice for others when blessings come to them and we should be quick to pluck up envious thoughts as soon as we see them. This is our old nature trying to rise up, the enemy's nature, and our job as new creations—eager to please God and to be more like Him—is to resist any instance of envy that comes our way [Gal 5:19-21; 1 Pet 2:1]. When we steadfastly resist the devil and his ugly thoughts he will flee from us [James 4:7].

People have often jokingly called envy the green-eyed monster and think it's normal to feel and acknowledge envy. But envy is a hateful, destructive, and hurtful monster. From the story of Cain killing his brother over envy, to Saul envying David's favor with God and trying to kill him, we see again and again the destructive end of envy unchecked [Gen 4; 1 Sam 19]. What's the answer? Honestly recognizing envy for what it is and taking those hostile, jealous feelings and that envious sin straight to God [1 John 1:9]. We should then re-focus our thinking, concentrating on all our blessings, not letting envious talk come out of our mouths, and training ourselves in godliness to rejoice in others successes as we'd want them to rejoice in ours.

Prayer:
Father, may we fight envy for the foul spirit it is and seek to stamp it out of our lives anytime it rears its snakelike head.

Scripture of the Day:
"A sound heart is the life of the flesh: but envy the rottenness of the bones." - [Proverbs 14:30]

The Word for the Day is "Wait."

Quote for the Day:
"Our willingness to wait reveals the value we place on the object we're waiting for."
- Charles Stanley

We all have times in life when we have to wait—like it or not. We're in a hurry, but we get caught in a traffic jam. We need to speak to someone via the phone, and we hear the message: "Please wait for the next available service rep." These annoying waits are just part of daily life. But the believer sometimes faces a greater challenge when he is waiting on the Lord. Maybe he has prayed and is waiting for an answer concerning health, finances, relationships, or any life issue. The enemy will always try to dissuade our faith to get us to give up believing, and to give up waiting. But the Bible gives us wisdom and helps us to know how to behave and handle waiting on the Lord.

First, we must hope in full assurance on the solid foundation of God's Word [Ps 130:5]. It is good to hope and quietly wait on the Lord knowing that He is good to those who wait on and seek Him [Lam 3:25-26]. But it is essential to establish an upright condition of the heart while waiting. We must maintain integrity and uprightness which will preserve us and keep us steady and sure in our waiting time [Ps 25:21]. The Lord promises to strengthen our heart when we are of good courage [Ps 27:14]. The enemy will tempt us with impatience and fretfulness, but we must rest in the Lord, wait patiently for Him, and keep His way and our expectation solid [Ps 37:7, 34]. The world and the enemy will tempt us to doubt and turn away and give up, but we must keep our trust in Jesus [1 Thess 1:9-10].

We must also have the revelation that with God there is a due season, an ordained time [Psalm 104:27]. "For the vision is yet for an appointed time, but at the end it shall speak, and not lie: though it tarry, wait for it; because it will surely come, it will not tarry" [Hab 2:3]. God loves us and knows when we are best prepared in faith, wisdom, maturity, and ability to fulfill the vision to God's glory. So stay prepared, wait patiently, for the vision will surely come!

Prayer:
Lord, our heart is fixed, trusting in You, believing Your Word, and waiting patiently to receive in due time that we might glorify You in all things.

Scripture of the Day:
"But they that wait upon the Lord shall renew their strength; they shall mount up with wings as eagles; they shall run, and not be weary; and they shall walk, and not faint." -[Isaiah 40:31]

The Word for the Day is "Plans."

Quote for the Day:
"Your plans for your life don't compare to what God has planned for you." – T.J.
Tison

We often make plans for our days and lives without giving thought to whether
God approves of them or not. But God does have a plan for each of our lives and
we can seek and find it. First, though, we cannot ever hope to find God's plans for
our lives without knowing Him well. "If you want the perfect plan that God has
for your life, you will have to go by the way of Calvary to get it." [Billy Graham].
Each of us has to come to a submitted place where we believe God has a plan
and then seek to grow closer to God so He can reveal Himself and that plan to us
[James 4:7-10].

In one of Sarah Young's devotionals, she wrote: "True dependence is not simply
asking [God] to bless what you have decided to do. It is coming to [Him] with
an open mind and heart, inviting [Him] to plant [His] desires within you." This
is hard. We like to control our own lives. We'd prefer to make our plans and then
ask God to bless them. We like being the ruler of our lives, in the driver's seat. To
change and yield to God we need to crucify self-will, get past the restricting expectations of others, and stand against the assaults of the enemy continually trying to derail God's plan along its route [Gal 2:20]. Often a long journey of work,
study, experience and changes are needed before we can arrive at the place where
we can really begin to walk in God's purpose [John 15:5; Psalm 127:1].

An old quote by Minnie Pearl says: "God has a plan for all of us but He expects
us to do our share of the work." We dream instead that God will drop His plan
and purpose on us like a miner striking gold—but we forget the long, hard days
in which the miner believed in his vision and worked in inclement conditions
before finding even the first nuggets. Walking in God's plan and purpose involves
work and this reluctance to work holds many back from the fullness of God's
best plans and purposes [Col 3:23-24; 1 Cor 15:58]. God is only "ready to assume
responsibility for the life wholly yielded to Him" [Andrew Murray].

Prayer:
Father, we yearn to be in Your best plan but humbly admit we often get in our
own way of it coming to pass. Help us yield to Your leadership and trust in Your
process to ready us for all You have for us to do and accomplish for You.

Scripture of the Day:
"For I know the thoughts (plans) that I think toward you, saith the Lord, thoughts
of peace, and not evil, to give you an expected end." - [Jeremiah 29:11]

The Word for the Day is "Ask."

Quote for the Day:
"It is not begging, it is not worrying, it is not fighting; but it is asking that gets results from God." - Bob Rodgers

A child may ask: "Daddy, can I have some candy?" The child expects to receive something. Our heavenly Father is pleased to answer prayer as much as the natural dad loves to give to his child. But God's children are sometimes reluctant to ask, feeling unsure or unworthy. Or they grow discouraged because they have not yet received what they asked for. There are many promises in the Word of God that relate to asking, but I think living close to God and knowing the Word are the key foundations to rightly asking of God. We must abide in Jesus, staying fixed and constant with our life in Him. And we must have His Word abiding in us, rooted and grounded in our heart, to govern our life direction and decisions.

Here are some Bible insights as to how abiding in Jesus confirms our prayer of asking. Abiding in Jesus gives us the confidence to ask, for we are promised that everyone that asketh receiveth [Matt 7:7-8]. We delight ourselves in the Lord, and know 'he shall give us the desires of our hearts' [Ps 37:4]. Some think we should not ask for our desires, but godly desires are planted by the Lord, they are not whims. I like evangelist Bob Rodgers' quote: "But a desire is embedded and rooted in the heart or spirit of man. God plants desires within people." We abide in Jesus keeping His commandments and doing those things pleasing in His sight: we are promised that 'whatsoever we ask, we receive of Him' [1 John 3:22]. If we do not abide in Jesus we can ask and not receive because we ask amiss, 'that we may consume it upon our lusts and our carnal, sinful ways' [James 4:3].

His Word must abide in us because the Word grows and establishes our faith [Rom 10:17]. The Word teaches us His will, so that we know what to ask [1 John 5:14-15]. Our faith establishes our asking in believing, not wishing: "And all things, whatsoever ye shall ask in prayer, believing, ye shall receive" [Matt 21:22]. The abiding Word enables us to walk by faith, not by sight, so we believe we receive when we pray [Mark 11:24]. If the Word abide not in us, the enemy can steal our patience and faith through lack of knowledge [Hosea 4:6].

Prayer:
Lord, as we abide in You, and Your Word abides in us, we have confidence in asking in faith: therefore, we will believe big, we will ask big, and receive big!

Scripture of the Day:
"If ye abide in me, and my words abide in you, ye shall ask what ye will, and it shall be done unto you." -[John 15:7]

The Word for the Day is "Lying."

Quote for the Day:
"The Bible is straightforward in saying that lying is a sin and offensive to God." –
Pastor John Ong

Lying is one of the character traits universally condemned around the world in
every culture and faith. Yet recent studies found people lie at least one time a
day on average, men more than women, adolescents the most, and 91% reported
their lies were about matters they considered trivial. Over 70% admitted to lying
to friends, siblings and parents, and 69% to spouses. Why do people lie so much?
The main reasons found were to shift blame, avoid confrontation, save face, get
their way, make themselves feel and look better, and be seen as nice.

Although the majority of people seem to think it all right to lie, God disagrees.
First, God does not lie and he detests and hates lying [Num 23:19; Prov 6:16-
19]. Proverbs 6:17 lists lying as one of the six things the Lord hates and calls an
abomination to Him. The Bible warns liars can expect a prophetically scary fate
[Prov 19:9; Rev 21:8] and stories like Ananias and Sapphira, lying to the apostles
and then dropping dead after, show the seriousness to which God views lying
[Acts 5:1-11]. The Lord is a God of truth and He wants only truth in our lives
[Psalm 51:6, 31:5].

Lying is a sinful habit that begins with a little lie that soon gives birth to more.
Any sinful act we engage in, justify and continue, versus repenting of and striving
not to repeat again, can sear our conscience and cause us to repeat until it seems
normal and right. Lies were brought into the world by satan. He lied to Eve [Gen
3:4] and he is the father of all lies, still perpetuating his lies and still behind every
lie we tell [John 8:44]. People can lie to themselves, to others, and to God, but it is
always wrong. Even the concept of "little white lies that do no harm" needs to be
adjusted. Austin O'Malley said "those who believe it is all right to tell little white
lies soon grow color blind." No matter what we've decided about lying, we need to
stop it in all ways in our lives because no matter what we call it, God calls it sin.

Prayer:
Father, we're grieved to learn of the prevalence of lying in the world and grieved
to realize we have probably bought into the concept that small lies don't matter
much. Help us to change and to walk and speak only truth.

Scripture of the Day:
"Lying lips are abomination to the Lord: but they that deal truly are his delight."
- [Proverbs 12:22]

The Word for the Day is "Kingdom."

Quote for the Day:
"I pldedge allegiance to the Christian flag, and to the Savior, for whose Kingdom it stands, one Savior, crucified, risen, and coming again, with life and liberty for all who believe." - Dan Quayle

The Apostle Paul, praying for the saints and faithful brethren in Christ in the city of Colosse, gave thanks to God the Father "Who hath delivered us from the power of darkness, and hath translated us into the kingdom of his dear Son" [Col 1:13]. Before coming to Jesus Christ, the men of Colosse lived in darkness, living worldly, carnal lives, subject to the law of sin and death. But in Jesus, they changed kingdoms, translated out of the worldly darkness into the kingdom of God: righteousness, peace, and joy in the Holy Ghost [Rom 14:17]. God's will is that all be saved, coming into the marvelous light of the Lord Jesus [1 Pet 2:9].

The Word of God reveals the truth of this divine kingdom promised to them that love Him [James 2:5]. "Jesus answered and said unto him, Verily, verily, I say unto thee, Except a man be born again, he cannot see the kingdom of God" [John 3:3]. Jesus explained to Nicodemus this was not a flesh birth, but an entrance to the kingdom of God by being born of the Spirit [John 3:5-8]. This receiving of salvation in Jesus gives us immediate benefit of the kingdom of God for Jesus said "behold, the kingdom of God is within you" [Luke 17:21].

What a glorious salvation we have in Jesus, being made a new creature in Him [2 Cor 5:17], and having the kingdom of God within us. We are promised that if we 'seek first the kingdom of God, and His righteousness, all these things shall be added unto you' [Matt 6:33]. All our needs are supplied [Phil 4:19], and we are given exceeding great and precious promises that we might be partakers of the divine nature [2 Pet 1:4]. And as the sun and blue of the firmament is always there above the storm clouds, the kingdom of God is always there even when tribulations come, for we have received a kingdom 'which cannot be moved' [Heb 12:28]. And we have peace, for in Jesus we overcome the world [John 16:33]. Therefore, 'let us have grace to serve God with reverence and godly fear' [Heb 12:28].

Prayer:
Lord, thank You that by Your salvation and the kingdom of God within us, we are in the world, but not of the world [John 17:16].

Scripture of the Day:
"Neither shall they say, Lo here! or, lo there! for, behold, the kingdom of God is within you." - [Luke 17:21]

The Word for the Day is "Something."

Quote for the Day:
Any definition of a successful life must include service to others…Caring and sharing is everything and everyone has something to give." - Barbara Bush

What is a successful life? Many people have given answers to that question. Coach John Wooden defined success as "self-satisfaction in knowing you made the effort to do your best, to become the best you are capable of becoming" while CEO Kara Goldwin defined it as "knowing that what you are doing is helping you and others live a better, happier, healthier life." The concept of giving, caring, and serving underlies both definitions. Jesus taught: 'The Son of Man did not come to be served but to serve, and to give his life a ransom for many' [Matt 20:28].

We all have something that we can give and share with others. It might be money, time, service, encouragement, gifts, talents, and more. The smallest act of caring has the potential to turn lives around and make a difference, but we must be open for God to pour His love and sharing through us. Most philanthropic organizations started with small efforts and grew, like Dolly Parton's Imagination Library and Larsen Jay's Random Acts of Flowers. God loves to multiply our giving in big ways beyond what we can imagine and we should never view anything as too small to matter [Luke 6:38].

Made in God's image, and with His Purpose, there are ways in which each of us are designed and ordained to work, serve, and give—often in different ways at different times and stages of our lives. Albert Einstein wrote: "It is every man's obligation to put back into the world at least the equivalent of what he takes out of it." Everyone has something to give. Each of us can live his or her life after God's plan, giving and sharing as He leads, or we can live our lives totally as we wish, putting self and self-interests ever first [Luke 9:23; Gal 5:24].

Prayer:
Father, help us remember, as You have given so much to us in love, blessings, gifts and talents, to also give back into the world to help and bless others.

Scripture of the Day:
"For if a man think himself to be something, when he is nothing, he deceiveth himself…as we have therefore opportunity, let us do good unto all men, especially unto them who are of the household of faith." - [Galatians 6:3,10]

The Word for the Day is "Kindness"

Quote for the Day:
"No act of kindness, no matter how small, is ever wasted." - Aesop

Have you noticed that it is difficult to have a bad attitude around someone showing kindness? Kindness seems to have a power of reciprocity. "Kindness gives birth to kindness" [Sophocles]. When someone is kind to us, we tend to be friendly, generous, and considerate in return. This kindness for kindness principle is verified in the Bible with stories including that of Abimelech and Abraham, and of Rebekah and the servant of Abraham [Gen 21:22-24, 24:1-22]. Give kindness and you will receive kindness.

God's kindness is marvelous and has a special eternal quality [Psalm 31:21; Jer 31:3]. The special expression 'lovingkindness' is derived from the Hebrew word *checed*, literally meaning "covenant loyalty." Lovingkindness is God's eternal love and kindness to those who are His own. "Yea, I have loved thee with an everlasting love: therefore with lovingkindness have I drawn thee" [Jer 31:3]. This tells us that God has had a faithful, unfailing, merciful, and gracious kindness and love for us since the beginning. God's lovingkindness is excellent and continues to those that know and trust Him [Psalm 36:7,10].

Kindness is a characteristic of those upright in heart before the Lord. It is an essential trait in approving ourselves as the ministers of God [2 Cor 6:4-10]. We show ourselves as the elect of God when we embrace kindness, mercy, and forgiveness [Col 3:12-13]. And we acknowledge that we were also once sinners, but after the kindness and love of God appeared toward us we were saved by Jesus Christ our Savior [Titus 3:4-6]. Kindness is an essential addition to our faith that we might have revelation knowledge of the Lord. We are instructed to add to our faith virtue, knowledge, temperance, patience, godliness, brotherly kindness, and charity [2 Pet 1:5-7]. Verse 8 continues: "For if these things be in you, and abound, they make you that ye shall neither be barren nor unfruitful in the knowledge of our Lord Jesus Christ."

Prayer:
Lord, as You have shown Your merciful and comforting kindnesses toward us, we will sow seeds of kindness to others to show Your love in our heart.

Scripture of the Day:
"For his merciful kindness is great toward us: and the truth of the Lord endureth for ever. Praise ye the Lord." -[Psalm 117:2]

The Word for the Day is "Judgment."

Quote for the Day:
"People don't like to think of God in terms of wrath, anger, and judgment. They prefer to fashion God after their own preferences and give God characteristics they want Him to have. People try to remake God to conform to their own wishful thinking to make them comfortable in their sins." – Billy Graham

It is popular today to quote one line of scripture to fashion a life philosophy without exploring the whole Bible in its entirety. That scripture is "judge not that you be not judged" [Matthew 7:1]. The story in John 8 is often used in example where Jesus spoke to a group of unrighteous scribes and Pharisees ready to stone a woman caught in adultery. He admonished them: 'Let he that hath no sin cast the first stone' [John 8:7]. Convicted, they walked away. Jesus didn't say it was all right for the woman to live as she did and when the group left he said to her, 'Go and sin no more.' The sin was not condoned. Jesus later said he didn't judge 'after the flesh' like the world, but 'after the Spirit.' In this way 'if he judged his judgment was true' and right [John 8:15-18].

God is a loving God but also a righteous judge and "the Lord loveth judgment" [Ps 37:28]. He hates evil and admonishes us that "the fear of the Lord is to hate evil…and the evil way" [Prov 8:13]. God expects His People to hold fast to the good, abstain from any appearance of evil, and "execute true judgment" ordered after God's Word [1 Thess 5:21-22; Zech 7:9; Ps 119:133; Is 1:16]. We are not to refashion God as we'd like to excuse sinful ways or to avoid conviction or judgment. Joubert wisely wrote: "Man pictures God like himself—the indulgent man worships an indulgent God, the stern man a stern God." Many today have created an indulgent nonjudgmental God who always understands and lets them do as they like. With the twisting of scripture about judgment many would invite the devil himself in for a cup of tea and put a cushion under his feet. For he has so cleverly convinced the world no one should dare judge another or name evil, even when it sits right before them.

Prayer:
Lord, help us not to go along with erroneous teachings justifying wrong, fearful of ever speaking truth and standing up for righteousness.

Scripture of the Day:
"For the time is come that judgment must begin at the house of God: and if it first begin at us, what shall the end be of them that obey not the gospel of God?"
- [1 Peter 4:17]

The Word for the Day is "Treasure."

Quote for the Day:
"Unless we place our religion and our treasure in the same thing, religion will always be sacrificed." - Epictetus

We all have things in our lives of special treasure. As we look back over our lives, some things we treasure are material, but our greatest treasures are usually life experiences and people. I still recall the thrill of my first bicycle, and later my first vehicle, and I remember pitching a no-hitter as a little leaguer and the treasure of seeing my name in bold on the sports page of the local newspaper. But my greatest treasures were the heart experiences of love, kindness, and goodness of family and friends. These far outweighed all others.

Jesus' teaching in Matthew reminds us that where our treasure is, our heart will be also, and that we need to lay up treasures in heaven more than on the earth [Matt 6:19-21]. The worldly seek the treasures of fame, fortune, wealth, the esteem of men to satisfy the pride of life. When these treasures are for self glory with no relation to God, they profit nothing [Prov 10:2]. The Christians' treasure should be the Lord Jesus Christ in their hearts. God has commanded the light to shine out of darkness, and this light in the Lord shines in our hearts giving us wisdom, knowledge of the glory of God, stability and strength in salvation [2 Cor 4:6; Is 33:6]. Seeking to live righteous and upright in obedience to His will and truth is our treasure. We access other divine treasures in His salvation, such as wisdom, which gives us understanding of the fear of the Lord, and finding the knowledge of God [Prov 2:4-5]. In Jesus are all the treasures of wisdom and knowledge [Col 2:3]. "A good man out of the good treasure of the heart bringeth forth good things" [Matt 12:35]. God will also give us material things and prosperity to bless and fulfill His will. How could anyone not treasure the kingdom of God with it's divine nature and blessings [2 Peter 1:4]?

Placing our treasure in living for the Lord has an additional marvelous consequence. It causes *us to* become a treasure to God! "Now therefore, if ye will obey my voice indeed, and keep my covenant, then ye shall be a peculiar treasure unto me above all people" [Ex 19:5]. Treasure the Lord and be a treasure to Him!

Prayer:
Lord, we will treasure our salvation and newness in Jesus Christ above all else, walking in love, truth, and righteousness that we might be a treasure to You.

Scripture of the Day:
"For where your treasure is, there will your heart be also." - [Matthew 6:21]

The Word for the Day is "Peace"

Quote for the Day:
"Don't let people pull you into their storm. Pull them into your peace." –Kimberly Jones-Pothier

We just spent two weeks in the South Carolina Lowcountry at Edisto Island. In our second week at the coast, reports of Hurricane Dorian began to come in. The storm was still far away at sea but I noted with interest three types of reactions: (1) those panicked, fearful, and talking the worst; (2) those concerned, anxious, focused on the negative; and (3) those more at peace, seeing realistically the storm was far away, that storms come and go, and that they would have plenty of time to prepare and leave the coast if needed later.

This situation reminded me of the story of Jesus asleep in the boat when a great tempest was at sea, washing waves overboard. The disciples were panicked but Jesus lay asleep in the boat. Probably annoyed at this, they woke him up and said, 'Lord, don't you care we might die here? Save us!' Jesus woke and said 'Why are you afraid? Where's your faith?' And he rebuked the winds and sea, bringing a great calm and peace [Matt 8:23-27]. The disciples marveled that the sea obeyed Him and wondered at His peace and calm in the midst of the storm.

It's a lesson for us to walk in a place more spiritually than carnally minded [Rom 8:6]. Jesus counseled, 'I want you to walk in a place of peace. Yes, you'll have tribulations in this fallen world. Storms will come, but keep in mind I have overcome the world and am greater than your enemy in the world who brings tribulations, troubles, destructions, and problems' [Rom 8:6; John 16:33]. We should work, pray and study to find a way to stay in peace as we walk through our days, to focus on knowing God is with us, and that Jesus came and died, not only to redeem us, but to leave us with the peace of God [Rom 5:1]. That peace can rise up as needed to counter carnal fears and threatening situations. Jesus said 'I am with you always' but how little we draw on that—leaning to Him and keeping the spiritual aspect versus carnal aspect of ourselves uppermost and in the lead [Matt 28:20]. We often sadly live at such a low level of faith, forgetting what we've been given and what we have in Christ Jesus.

Prayer:
Lord, help us remember the power left us through Jesus and abiding in us, and to always speak to the storms in our lives and expect them to calm and be still.

Scripture of the Day:
"Thou wilt keep him in perfect peace, whose mind is stayed on thee: because he trusteth in thee." – [Isaiah 26:3]

The Word for the Day is "Hinder."

Quote for the Day:
"At that instant he knew that all his doubts, even the impossibility of believing with his reason, of which he was aware in himself, did not the least hinder his turning to God. All of that now floated out of his soul like dust. To whom was he to turn if not to Him in whose hands he felt himself, his soul, and his love?" - Leo Tolstoy

We all sometimes experience difficulties and obstructions that hinder our lives in the natural. We come to an unexpected road closure due to construction and we have to delay and detour our route. A widespread pandemic closes schools and businesses causing disruption of our normal work and life routines. These hindrances are common to all men in all places from time to time.

The most important hindrances we must address are those that impede our Spiritual life in the Lord. The Word in Galatians 5:7 asks 'who did hinder you that ye should not obey the truth?' The hindrance can come from forces outside ourselves. Satan can hinder, and the enemy will use other men to attack, persecute, or tempt us away from a right walk with the Lord [1 Thess 2:18]. He will also use our old worldly nature to tempt us to backslide through the lusts of the flesh and eyes, and the pride of life [1 John 2:16]. 'The carnal mind is enmity against God ...So then they that are in the flesh cannot please God' [Rom 8:7-8].

We hinder ourselves most through our own personal habits and ignorance. We can fall into habits of consuming our time with TV, sports, family or work leaving no time for spiritual fellowship and growth in the Lord. "Bad habits are our enemies because they hinder us from being the person we want to be" [Joyce Meyer]. Ignorance of God's Word can hinder even worse: "My people are destroyed for lack of knowledge" [Hosea 4:6]. We learn the truth of God's absolutes through His Word. We gain the spiritual wisdom through the Word to guide us in our decisions and actions. The Word is the Light unto our path to guide us in our behavior and thinking [Psalm 119:105]. Each must make his own free-will decision to give the Truth and will of God priority over hindrances of man, the flesh, or the devil. Having put your hand to the plow, it's your own decision to look back, or go ever forward in the Lord [Luke 9:62].

Prayer:
Lord, we will seek first the kingdom of God and His righteouness, letting nothing hinder our walk in love, truth, and obedience to the Gospel of Jesus Christ.

Scripture of the Day:
"Ye did run well; who did hinder you that ye should not obey the truth?" - [Galatians 5:7]

The Word for the Day is "Sickness."

Quote for the Day:
"God has been taking the blame for sickness and disease for centuries…this idea has contributed to the lack of faith prevalent in the church today for healing and deliverance." – Pastor Troy Edwards

The concept that we have a good and loving God and an equally crafty and evil devil was established in Genesis and continues to Revelation. Most people of faith know they are engaged in spiritual warfare while on this earth between Good and Evil. One of the biggest lies the enemy has perpetuated, even in many churches, is to assign the blame for sickness, disease, pain, and calamities to God—suggesting God sends such sorrows and hurts as an aid to spiritual growth and piety. What a clever lie—because if a person believes this is true, how can they have faith for healing or deliverance? Or how can they totally trust a God who would willingly abuse them? In the natural world abusive parents tell their children evil lies like these when they afflict harm on them. We are morally shocked over such behavior. So should we be in the spiritual. Our God is not an abusive Father. Be watchful for lies about His good character, remembering 'satan is a liar, the father of lies and there is no truth in him.' [John 8:44]

Believe steadfastly instead what God says: 'The thief comes only to kill and destroy: I have come that you may have life and have it more abundantly' [John 10:10]. "I will put none of these diseases upon thee…for I am the Lord that healeth thee" [Ex 15:26]. 'Forget not all My benefits…who forgiveth all thine iniquities, who healeth all thy diseases, who redeemeth thy life from destruction, who crowneth thee with loving kindness and tender mercies' [Ps 103:2-4]. Remember, too, that 'the Son of God came and was manifested that He might destroy the works of the devil' [1 John 3:8]. There is no instance in the Bible where Jesus put sickness, disease, or sorrow on anyone. He came to 'free us' and give us 'power and authority over all devils and to cure diseases' [Luke 9:1].

It is your right as a child of God, and born again of Jesus, to walk in health. Any opposing attack is not from God but from the devil. Yet many 'are destroyed for a lack of knowledge' on this subject [Hosea 4:6]. Trust in God's Word above all and stand in it.

Prayer:
Father, thank You for ordaining health for us and for sending Jesus to free us from satan's dominion. Teach us to stand in truth and on Your Word.

Scripture of the Day:
"… and I will take sickness away from the midst of thee." – [Exodus 23:25]

The Word for the Day is "Strength."

Quote for the Day:
"Make sure you are doing what God wants you to do—then do it with all your strength." - George Washington

Age is the measure of time something has existed. Old describes something no longer young. Yet, we always hear asked "How old are you?" and seldom "What is your age?" We are programmed early on with the concept of 'old' as a perpetual condition that naturally escalates as the age increases. This leads to the assumption that as people accumulate more age, they automatically increase more conditions of oldness, like sickness and weakness. But this is a clever deceit of the enemy, for age (the measure of time) is not the same as a condition, like strength or weakness, wellness or sickness.

Too many people expect, and accept, deteriorating strength and health as they age because they have equated age to condition. But in the kingdom of God, believers should not accept this if we live in the Spirit of God and not of this world. Both Old and New Testament truth verifies this. Moses was 120 years old when he died, but his eye was not dim, nor his natural force abated or diminished [Deut 34:7]. When Caleb was 85, his strength was the same as it was at 40: 'as my strength was then, even so is my strength now' [Joshua 14:7-11].

We, as the redeemed in Jesus, have an even greater right to strength by promise and by covenant. The Lord is the 'strength of our life', and the Lord will 'give strength unto His people' [Psalm 27:1, 29:11]. Jesus came to give us life more abundantly [John 10:10], and the Lord wants us to serve Him with joyfulness, and with gladness of heart, for the abundance of all things (which includes strength) [Deut 28:47]. Jesus has redeemed us from the curse of the law [Gal 3:13], and His Spirit within us quickens (makes alive, vigorous) our mortal body [Rom 8:11]. The Lord satisfies our mouth with good things (His Word and promises), so that our youth is renewed like the eagle's [Ps 103:5]. This is not a vanity thing, but a purpose: God wants you to have perpetual strength to fulfill the works and visions He wills for you, that you might glorify Him!

Prayer:
Lord, we will serve You with joyfulness and gladness of heart for the abundance of strength and all things that we might fulfill Your will and glorify You.

Scripture of the Day:
"But they that wait upon the Lord shall renew their strength; they shall mount up with wings as eagles; they shall run and not be weary; and they shall walk, and not faint." -[Isaiah 40:31]

The Word for the Day is "Signet."

Quote for the Day:
"Each of us has our own unique stamp that reveals how we're created in God's image...it's our call and privilege to act as this signet ring in God's world." – Amy Boucher Pye

Signet rings are a part of heraldry dating back to 2500 BC. The signet ring, made of ivory, stone, or fine metals and later of pure gold, was a symbol of authority, adorned with a family crest or office. The signet ring was an inseparable, valuable possession, always worn—usually on the little finger of the left hand—to show office or rank. Jewish and religious leaders had signet rings as did Pharoahs and kings; so did early Christians—both men and women. In Biblical times the signet ring was used not only as an outward sign of the authority of its owner but to press into hot wax as a signature. Signet rings were passed down in families, transferring authority, and utilized by rulers to pass on authority. Pharoah took off his ring and put it on Joseph's hand setting him over all of Egypt [Gen 41:42]. In the book of Esther, King Ahasuerus took off his ring that he had given Hamen and gave it to Mordecai, giving him authority [Esther 8:2]. The father in the prodigal son put his family ring back on his son's hand [Luke 15:22], symbolic of God's forgiveness to us when we turn from error and wrong, humble ourselves and repent.

In a symbolic way the Word teaches that we are chosen to represent the Lord, as if we wore His signet ring of authority, that we are sealed by the Holy Spirit of promise, and that the name of God and Christ are stamped in our foreheads—a seal of the believer, a protection over us [Hag 2:23; Eph 1:13; 2 Tim 2:19]. What a great gift that the Father has bestowed his family crest, his power and authority, his ownership on us. We are His and He knows those who are His. 'Nevertheless, the foundation of God standeth sure, having this seal; The Lord knoweth them that are His" and 'if we walk in His ways, we will be a vessel of honour unto His use, prepared unto every good work' [2 Tim 2:19, 21]. Jesus paid a great price for you to be welcomed back into the Lord's family, into royalty, into The Kingdom of God. Keep it in your heart that you are sealed with His own signet ring, a stronger seal than any king's [Dan 6:17; Eph 1:13].

Prayer:
Lord, help us to be always conscious that we are your children, royalty in the Kingdom of God, wearing Your signet and seal, loved and protected by You.

Scripture of the Day:
"In that day saith the Lord of hosts I will...make thee as a signet: for I have chosen thee." – [Haggai 2:23]

The Word for the Day is "Crooked."

Quote for the Day:
"One cannot think crooked and walk straight." - Anonymous

Did you ever notice how annoying and vexing it is for things to be crooked that are supposed to be straight? Have you ever taken a road that looked straight on a map, only to have so many curves you would have been better off taking the longer route? Other crooked things that annoy are twisted electric cords, gnarled fishing line on the reel, golf shots that hook or slice, and many other things we all could mention.

The Bible also talks about how our life pathways can be crooked. Moses prophesied to the children of Israel how they had corrupted themselves and become a perverse and crooked generation. How? They had become fat (prosperous) and had forsaken God and lightly esteemed Him (didn't take Him seriously anymore). They had provoked Him with strange (false) gods and abominations (perverse behavior). They had forgotten God, had no faith, were void of counsel and understanding in their vanities [Deut 32:5-28]. The Word tells us that all who turn to crooked ways will go with the workers of iniquity [Psalm 125:5], and they shall not know peace [Isaiah 59:8].

But we have a Deliverer to turn our crooked paths straight. John the Baptist came prophesying of Jesus: "Every valley shall be filled, and every mountain and hill shall be brought low; and the crooked shall be made straight, and the rough ways shall be made smooth" [Luke 3:5]. If we are in a valley or rut, Jesus can lift us out; if we face mountains of problems or cirmumstances that seem too great to be moved, Jesus will remove them; if our life seems rough and crooked, Jesus will make the way straight and give us peace. What a blessing for us to have the eternal promises of God, His love and faithfulness and His Holy Spirit to comfort and guide us, so that we may make our way straight and smooth and 'shine as lights in the midst of a crooked and perverse nation' [Phil 2:15].

Prayer:
Lord, we will make every crooked way within us straight, so thay we may shine the glorious light of Your gospel to the world.

Scripture of the Day:
"That ye may be blameless and harmless, the sons of God, without rebuke, in the midst of a crooked and perverse nation, among whom ye shine as lights in the world." - [Philippians 2:15]

The Word for the Day is "Forever."

Quote for the Day:
"Forever is for a purpose…God intended for us to live forever in His presence." –
Robert Smith, Jr.

We live in a world that always seems to be shifting and changing. History and
even old movies show us the incredible changes that have occurred in our world
since its inception and even in the last fifty years. We often wonder: Is anything
permanent? Even social mores and norms shift and change, along with the ideas
as to how people should live.

In all the changeableness of the world, God is permanent. God always was and
always will be, and He is unchanging [Heb 13:8]. "For I am the Lord, I change
not" [Mal 3:6]. There is no variation in God, in Jesus, in the Holy Spirit, and they
will not pass away or be destroyed [Dan 7:14]. God's Word, also, is living and enduring and will not change [1 Pet 1:23]. How comforting it is, sometimes, when
people all around us are casting doubt on faith, wishing to change it to be more
relevant, deciding it is now obsolete and unneeded, to know God always was, is,
and always will be God. His truth will reign forever. 'He is the same yesterday,
and today, and forever' [Heb 13:8]. People may change but God and His truths
do not change.

So many things are settled forever and established of God: God's love, God's mercy and favor, God's truth, God's blessings and promises, God's care and concern,
God's strength and might. Our list could go on and on. "For Thou blessest, O
Lord, and it shall be…forever" [1 Chron 17:27]. What joy it is to know that we
go on forever with Him, too. The 'gift of God through Christ Jesus is eternal life'
[Rom 6:23]. Because we are His we have life forever, too, life eternal, and we will
'be with the Lord forever' [1 Thess 4:17].

In a world where little is lasting or permanent, God is permanent, established,
immortal, from generation to generation forever [Ps 9:7; 1 Tim 6:16]. 'The world
is firmly established; it will not be moved'…'the Lord shall reign forever and ever'
[Ex 15:18; Ps 93:1]. He will reign forever and we with Him.

Prayer:
Father, we thank You that in this world where so many are trying to reinvent You
and change Your Word, that we can stay at peace, knowing you are not changeable.

Scripture of the Day:
"I know that, whatsoever God doeth, it shall be for ever." – [Ecclesiastes 3:14]

J.L. Stepp

SEPTEMBER 27
The Word for the Day is "Delay."

Quote for the Day:
"Trust His wisdom knowing that He will honor you and bless you, and He will do it in His timing, which is always the right timing. If you experience delay, know this: a delay is not a denial." - Jesse Duplantis

Delays are common in life for various reasons and causes, some short term, and some longer term. Some are by natural means: road construction narrows the road to one lane and we have to wait on a three minute red light. Others are by men: decisions that affect us are delayed by legalities or other obstacles. We deal with natural delays and go on our ways with alternative plans.

But what about delays in the Lord when we have not yet received an answer to prayer? Delays in the spirit realm are as real as those in the natural. If our prayer is founded on the truth of God's Word, we must know that delay is not a denial as the quote of the day states. So how do we handle delays to our prayers?

We must stand. The enemy will try to deceive and dissuade you from believing God. But we must put on the whole armour of God including truth, righteousness, the gospel of peace, faith, the helmet of our salvation, and the word of God; and having done all, to stand [Eph 6:13-17]. We must stand in God's faithfulness and not let unbelief rob us of our promises [Mark 6:5-6].

We must have patience. When we fall into various trials of our faith, we must know that 'the trying of our faith worketh patience. But let patience have her perfect work, that ye may be perfect and entire, wanting nothing' [James 1:2-4]. Besides the enemy, man can cause delays to our prayers. Man has a free will, and sometimes God has to find a willing man to fulfill His purpose. Just because we don't see the desired result yet, doesn't mean God isn't working.

When we face delays, we need to 'hold resolutely to our hope and faith, knowing we can trust God to keep His promises' [Heb 10:23]. We must stand firm and patient in our trust in the truth of God's Word and His faithfulness. We must walk by faith, not by sight, ever trusting God. Delayed? Stand fast. The enemy lies and says the answer is no, but God's answer in Jesus is always YES.

Prayer:
Lord, we will stand fast and patient in Your Word knowing that delay does not void the Truth that all the promises of God in Christ Jesus are yea and Amen.

Scripture of the Day:
"I made haste, and delayed not to keep thy commandments." - [Psalm 119:60]

SEPTEMBER 28
The Word for the Day is "Heirs."

Quote for the Day:
"Our Father is very wealthy. And the news is out; the richest One in the universe has designated us among His heirs. How eagerly we should be searching His will and testament to find out exactly what it is He has bequeathed us." – Catherine Marshall

Most of us would be thrilled if we learned tomorrow we were heirs of a wealthy man's fortune. Few have not indulged an idle dream now and then of walking into an unexpected and undeserved legacy. Yet as Christians, born again through Christ Jesus, that is exactly what has happened. However, few of us are aware of all we have inherited. I often think the church has not always taught us well, that through Jesus, we are more than heirs to eternal life [Gal 3:29; Eph 3:6; Rom 8:17]. Although it is glorious to think about eternal life with the Lord, we are also heirs of the promises of Abraham, the same promises of the people of Israel, grafted into that bloodline through Jesus [Heb 6:17; 11:9; Rom 11:17-19].

In a will, specific inheritances are written down and recorded. Your gifts of inheritance are written in the Word of God and recorded, but until you read them and realize they are for you, and receive them, they are of little profit. To be saved you need to believe, repent of your sins, and ask Jesus into your heart and life. You read or heard this message first somewhere, believed and responded to it. Here is a beautiful thought for you today: you are heirs of sweet and precious promises and rich blessings beyond salvation alone. Yet you must search them out in God's Word for yourself, receive and accept them by faith, and then begin to walk in the fullness of all you've received.

'You are all heirs of God and joint heirs with Christ' [Rom 8:17], 'heirs of the kingdom' [James 2:5], and 'fellow heirs of the same body' [Eph 3:6]. 'All the promises in the Word of God are yours,' [2 Pet 1:4], and all are 'yea and in Him amen, unto the glory of God' [2 Cor 1:20]. You can let someone talk you into thinking you haven't been given much or you can go seeking in the legal document of God's Word to see exactly what you've been given.

Prayer:
Lord, thank You that You have made us heirs of Yourself and joint heirs with Christ, partakers of all your wonderful promises. Help us to seek and find all You've so freely given to us.

Scripture of the Day:
"That being justified by his grace, we should be made heirs according to the hope of eternal life." – [Titus 3:7]

The Word for the Day is "Magnify."

Quote for the Day:
"If we magnified blessings as much as we magnify disappointments, we would all be much happier." - John Wooden

The two primary definitions of magnify are: to make something appear larger than it is, and to extol, glorify, esteem, or praise greatly. Both meanings have application to the believer's life. God wants us to magnify Him above all, and not magnify our cares, trials, and tribulations. The Wooden quote above is often true in our daily lives. We too often make 'mountains out of mole hills.' We worry, fret, and dwell on every little problem until it consumes our thinking and despairs our heart. But Jesus commands us to cast all our cares upon Him, trusting that He supplies all our needs [1 Pet 5:7; Phil 4:19].

The true believer wants to magnify God in all things, and the Word gives us wisdom to please the Lord. "Let all those that seek thee rejoice and be glad in thee: let such as love thy salvation say continually, The Lord be magnified" [Ps 40:16]. We magnify the Lord when we offer up our thanksgiving and praise [Ps 69:30]. Our soul magnifies the Lord when we acknowledge His strength, His mercy, His great works, His help and provision for us [Luke 1:46-55]. We magnify the Lord when we appropriate His blessings by faith: "Let the Lord be magnified, which hath pleasure in the prosperity of his servant" [Ps 35:27].

The Lord also magnifies. The Lord has magnified His Word. "Thou hast magnified thy word above all thy name" [Ps 138:2]. God's Word reveals the lovingkindness of His salvation to mankind, and His established, eternal Truth. God also graciously magnifies the righteous to show that He is with us [Josh 3:7], and to show the reality of Jesus in us [Phil 1:20]. God will also magnify our ministry efforts to add believers to the Lord [Acts 5:13-14] and to exalt His name [Acts 19:17]. The Lord rewards those that purpose to magnify God in their righteous and true ministry. The key is to humble ourselves and always magnify the Lord in all things: "Humble yourselves in the sight of the Lord, and he shall lift you up" [James 4:10].

Prayer:
Lord, we purpose to walk humbly and upright before You, giving thanksgiving and praises to Your Name that we might magnify and exalt our God.

Scripture of the Day:
"O magnify the Lord with me, and let us exalt his name together." -[Psalm 34:3]

The Word for the Day is "Add."

Quote for the Day:
"We are admonished not to add to or take away from scripture…it is God-breathed and it is life's final and ultimate authority." – Charles Stanley

God designed a plan for our lives to give us an abundant, blessed life, and a happy one. He laid down commandments and Kingdom guidelines after His best will, for us to follow in obedience. These were created to ensure our steps would follow the best life path, bringing us joy, keeping us protected in God's love. God also left His Word, which has survived all these centuries as our guide. Within it, along with His loving guidance, He offered cautions He knew we would face—to not wrongly follow after other gods, to not drift from our faith, to not pick up the habits and ways of the ungodly around us. He also cautioned 'not to ever add to His Word and not to diminish or take away from it' [Deut 4:2].

God's Word 'was established forever,' 'true and right' [Ps 119:89; Heb 4:12]. The Bible is not a regular or normal book but a divinely inspired one [2 Tim 3:16]. Naturally for this reason satan and his minions work hard to devalue and diminish it. Satan started this type of argument in the garden, "Hath God said?" —knowing that doubting God's Word would only lead to sorrows [Gen 3:1]. Warnings are given in many scriptures to be watchful for these tactics, to not get 'itching ears seeking out teachings to suit our own passions, turning away from the truth' [2 Tim 4:3-4], to be watchful for those 'with smooth talk who teach contrary to God's Word knowing satan is behind such tactics' [Rom 16:17-20; 2 Pet 3:16; 2 Cor 11:14-15].

God's Word doesn't shift with time. To begin to add to or to take away from it is dangerous. If you've begun to take lightly the idea of picking and choosing what you want to believe in the Bible, adding a little here, diminishing a little there, give prayerful thought today to God's view on this in Revelation 22:18-19: 'If any man shall add unto these things, God shall add unto him the plagues written in this book; if any man shall take away from the Word…God shall take away his part out of the book of life, and from the blessings in this book.' God does not take this matter lightly.

Prayer:
Father, we sometimes forget to reverence Your Word as we should. Help us not to be led into error adding to or diminishing it unwisely.

Scripture of the Day:
"Ye shall not add unto the word which I command you, neither shall ye diminish aught from it." – [Deuteronomy 4:2]

October

The Word for the Day is "Forgive."

Quote for the Day:
"Forgiving is not about forgetting, it's about letting go of the hurt." - Mary McLeod
Bethune

What a glorious and joyous blessing it is to know that in Jesus we are forgiven. We were dead in sins once, separated from God, but by the blood of Jesus and His salvation, we were quickened and made alive to God, having forgiveness of all our trespasses [Col 2:13]. As believers and made the righteousness of God in Him, having our sins forgiven, how could we not extend the same grace to those who have trespassed against us? Yet, for some it is difficult to forgive.

God does not want us carrying the sorrows, anger, and resentment of past hurts. This can impede our heart of receiving the abundant life of peace and joy in Jesus. The Word teaches that there are consequences if we do not forgive. The Lord's prayer tells us: "And forgive us our debts, as (taking place at the same time) we forgive our debtors" [Matt 6:12]. Receiving and giving forgiveness are to be integral to our prayer, necessary and essential. Jesus said: "But if ye forgive not men their trespasses, neither will your Father forgive your trespasses" [Matt 6:15]. We must cast this care of a past hurt upon Jesus and forgive so that we can move on with Him [1 Pet 5:7]. You suffered enough when you were wronged; the Lord does not want your heart afflicted longer by continuing to carry that hurt. Forgive and let it go.

Holding on to unforgiveness can act like a toxin within to steal the joy of our hearts and can also damage our natural body. A lady with a long illness once asked me to pray for her. As she described her ailments, the Lord showed me by the Spirit that her problem was a long-harbored unforgiveness against someone that had hurt her. When I told her this, she burst into weeping acknowledging this truth. She prayed, asking forgiveness of God, and forgave that person. She regained her peace in the Lord, and received her healing! Forgive and walk in the joy of the Lord through the redemption and forgiveness of sins in Jesus [Eph 1:7].

Prayer:
Lord, we will shake off the past, forgive our trespassers, and receive forgiveness as we walk on in newness of life and joy in Jesus.

Scripture of the Day:
"And when ye stand praying, forgive, if ye have ought against any: that your Father also which is in heaven may forgive you your trespasses." - [Mark 11:25]

The Word for the Day is "Seasons."

Quote for the Day:
"I'm so glad I live in a world where there are Octobers." - L.M. Montgomery

We are blessed in Tennessee to enjoy four distinct seasons, each with its own beauty and character. There is something beautiful in every season of the year in Tennessee. J.L. and I hike often in the Smokies and we've noticed how uniquely different the same trail is in different seasons. In fall, it's a joy to crunch leaves underfoot and look up into the canopy of trees dressed in their fall colors of russet red, vibrant orange, and rich gold. In winter, the beauty of the bare trunks is visible and with the leaves gone, vistas out over the mountains delight us on the high points. As spring begins, lovely fresh yellow-green leaves pop out and wildflowers dot the trailside. By summer, the forest has created a rich, lush wonderland of shady green overhead with mountain laurel in early summer and in mid summer rhododendron, flame azalea, fire pinks and black-eyed Susans.

The Bible teaches us in Ecclesiastes that: "to every thing there is a season, and a time to every purpose under the heaven" [Ecclesiastes 3:1]. I wonder if we relish and appreciate each season in our world, and each season of our lives, as we should. I have friends who have complained through every season of their lives—complained when they weren't married, complained about their mate when they were, complained when raising their children, complained when their nest was empty, the children gone, complained when they worked, complained when they didn't, yearned to be older and wiser, and then complained when they were.

Look around. 'Taste and see that the Lord is good" (Psalm 34:8). Savor the world and life you have. No matter how bad some of your days may seem, someone in the world wishes they could live your life for even a day.

Prayer:
Lord, help us to be more grateful in every day, in each time and season in the earth, and in our lives. Show us Your Purpose for every day and season and help us find a way to be a blessing and a light.

Scripture of the Day:
"A man hath joy by the answer of his mouth: and a word spoken in due season, how good is it!" - [Proverbs 15:23].

The Word for the Day is "Snare."

Quote for the Day:
"There is one thing that all Satan's cunning and all the snares of temptation cannot take by surprise - an undivided will." - Soren Kierkegaard

Simply defined, a snare is a trap for catching prey, much like we put a worm on a hook to deceptively catch a fish. Other definitions include: 'something by which one is entangled, an instance in which one is involved in difficulties or impeded, or a situation or a trick through which one is deceived.' Many snares we face are of the devil since his objective is to steal, kill, and to destroy [John 10:10].

Satan can deceive us into snaring ourselves. He gets us to divide our will from wholly following God to turn to the carnal ways. When we mingle with, learn the works and ways of, and serve the idols of the world, we can be snared into serving the ways of the world instead of God [Deut 7:16; Ps 106:35-36]. When we live in agreement and accord with the world, we are snared: "Ye cannot serve God and mammon" [Matt 6:24]. When we talk unbelief like the world instead of the truth of God's Word, we are snared: "Thou art snared by the words of thy mouth, thou art taken with the words of thy mouth" [Prov 6:2]. We are snared when our heart falls into foolish and hurtful lusts for things rather than the will of God [1 Tim 6:9]. All these snares trap us when we mind the carnal flesh more than the Spirit.

The devil also uses men to lay wicked snares to catch us [Ps 119:110]. The wicked and proud take delight in tricking with their deceits. They imagine mischief in their heart for the purpose of 'overthrowing our goings' [Ps 140:1-5]. They speak deceit with 'sharpened tongues and poisoned lips' [Ps 140:3]. With 'much fair speech' and flattery they entice to yield to the lusts of the flesh [Prov 7:21].

But in the Lord we are promised His deliverance from the snares of the wicked and all pestilence [Psalm 91:3]. The law of the wise and the fear of the Lord is a fountain of life to depart from the snare of death [Prov 13:14, 14:27]. Keeping the will undivided in serving the Lord and walking in the Spirit keeps us free from the snares of the devil.

Prayer:
Lord, thank You that You keep us safe from the snares of the enemy. As the hymn says: 'Tis grace has brought me safe thus far, and grace will lead me home.'

Scripture of the Day:
"Surely He shall deliver thee from the snare of the fowler, and from the noisome pestilence." - [Psalm 91:3]

The Word for the Day is "Holy Spirit."

Quote for the Day:
"The Holy Spirit is the most influential mentor in your life. He is always willing to teach and guide you in all truth." – Alisa Hope Wagner

We have all met people who seem to know God better than others, who know Jesus well, His nature shining through their lives and witness. We've also met those who know the Holy Spirit better than others. To many, the Holy Spirit seems elusive, a wispy mystery. What do we know of the Holy Spirit? He has mind, will, personality, and knowledge just as God and Jesus do. He can command, speak, teach and love. He can help woo and lead us to God, to Jesus, and then into deeper faith. Blessedly, once we have given our hearts to God, He lives within us, and will ever stay and be with us and help us [1 Cor 3:16; Acts 2:38].

In Old Testament times the Spirit was given only to certain people of God's choosing, to prophets, priests, or kings, 'by measure', in a limited way [2 Pet 1:21]. But when Jesus came, He left us—among all the blessings of salvation and inheritance—the gift of the Holy Spirit. 'And I will ask the Father and He will give you another Comforter, another helper, that he may abide with you forever' [John 14:16-18]. Those who walk in a rich relationship with the Holy Spirit manifest a lot of wisdom, allowing them to speak truth, not of themselves but of the Lord, enabling them to witness, testify, and share more effectively [John 14:26, 16:13, 15:26]. The Holy Spirit is the secret of power in ministry. Remember Jesus told His disciples to wait until they received the Holy Spirit before they went out to preach and teach [Acts 1:8, 4:31; Luke 24:49].

Regardless of our various religious teachings, we know and have seen that the Holy Spirit manifests Himself more fully in many lives, but only because He is allowed to. Just as more of God, more of Jesus, come into your life as you seek and grow in faith, more of the Holy Spirit will come, too, as you are open and begin to seek for more of Him. God will not give you what you do not want and do not seek. "It is your part to believe. It is your part to receive. Nobody else can do it for you." [Billy Graham].

Prayer:
Lord, thank you for the Holy Spirit in my life. Help me to seek more of Him and to welcome more of Him.

Scripture of the Day:
"If ye then, being evil, know how to give good gifts unto your children: how much more shall your heavenly Father give the Holy Spirit to them that ask him?" – [Luke 11:13]

The Word for the Day is "Lamp."

Quote for the Day:
"Genius without religion is only a lamp on the outer gate of a palace; it may serve to cast a gleam of light on those that are without, while the inhabitant sits in darkness." - Hannah More

I remember as a Boy Scout spending a week at a camp on Norris Lake. The camp had crude wooden cabins and an outdoor latrine set back in the woods. At night, we were required to be in our bunks at 10:00 pm and *no* lights were allowed on after that. One scout asked the Scoutmaster what to do if he needed to use the latrine in the night. The Scoutmaster simply replied, "Well, be careful." Sometimes a lamp or light comes in handy in the dark.

There are times in life we may feel we are in darkness and need a light. Maybe we need guidance for the path, direction, or life decision we face. We need a lamp to light our way. The Bible teaches us that the Lord is our lamp to lighten the darkness we face [2 Sam 22:29]. The scripture also gives us insight to receiving and utilizing the divine lamp. Our first step to receive the light of life is to receive Jesus as Lord. We are then translated (moved) out of darkness (not knowing the right way) into His marvelous Light (divine direction, counsel, wisdom) [Col 1:13]. The Lord will always give us the best light, or direction, when we seek Him. The enemy deceives, but God's Holy Spirit guides to all truth [John 16:13].

The Bible is also a lamp unto our feet, and a light unto our path [Ps 119:105]. You can see a path or direction in life with your natural or carnal eyes, and it can look good, like the right or best way. Yet carnal darkness can deceive. The path ahead may look good, and smooth, and right, but further on the path, out of sight, the way may become rocky, steep, difficult and dangerous. Perhaps you thought you knew the reality of the path, but you were in spiritual darkness and were fooled and misguided. Only the light of God's Truth can reveal the reality of each path choice in life, and which is God's best for your good. There is always light in Jesus, for 'he leadeth in paths of righteousness for his name's sake' [Psalm 23:3].

Prayer:
Lord, thank You that You are the lamp of our life, and You will always show us the path for our life when we seek You, for we are in the kingdom of Light.

Scripture of the Day:
"For thou art my lamp, O Lord: and the Lord will lighten my darkness."
 -[2 Samuel 22:29]

The Word for the Day is "Honey."

Quote for the Day:
"If you want to gather honey, don't kick over the beehive." – Dale Carnegie

I think we all remember our first times of tasting or eating honey—in a spoon from a jar, spread on warm toast or a biscuit, or dripping off a honeycomb taken from a beehive. A definition and synonym for honey is sweetness, and it is easy to see why. In the Bible again and again, God said He would take the people of Israel to a 'land flowing with milk and honey' [Exodus 3:8] and we easily understand that to mean a good, fertile place of rich nourishment and sweetness.

I like the concept God so often gives that He wants us to have the basics we need in life but also the "sweetness of life." The old proverb 'You catch more flies with honey than vinegar' reminds us, too, that the Lord wants our lives to show sweetness, goodness, and kindness in the world [Psalm 34:8; Prov 16:24]. We will not draw others to us, or to God, with a sour, vinegarish, and bitter disposition. The scripture "taste and see that the Lord is good" [Ps 34:8] reminds us that when people get around us they should come away with a smile and a good taste in their mouths. We are to show the Love of God to others through our lives, actions, and words.

A read through the Psalms should remind us quickly that God's Word and law should be our delight [Psalm 1:2] and His knowledge sweet to our ear and taste [Psalm 19:10]. We should treasure His Word and teaching above gold, happy to think on it, knowing it enriches us and makes us wiser [Ps 119:97-99, 127]. Just as the bee heads daily to the flower rich with sweet nectar, we should head daily to God and His Word to be fed, enriched, and nourished, too.

Prayer:
God, help us not to let the sorrows in this life steal our sweetness and help us to be like your "honey" in the world, drawing others to You.

Scripture of the Day:
"The statutes of the Lord are right, rejoicing the heart…more to be desired are they than gold…sweeter also than honey and the honeycomb…and of keeping them there is great reward." – [Psalm 19:8-11]

The Word for the Day is "Slow."

Quote for the Day:
"Be slow to speak, and only after having first listened quietly, so that you may understand the meaning, leanings, and wishes of those who do speak. Thus you will better know when to speak and when to be silent." - Saint Ignatius

The word 'slow' is neither positive or negative by itself, but depends upon the circumstances and conditions of its use. Example, most Southerners love the delicious savor of slow-roasted barbeque. But if we're eating that sandwich while driving and are slow to hit the brakes when a dog darts in front of the car, that's not so good.

The righteous are admonished to be slow to anger. An angry or wrathful man stirs up strife but he that is slow to anger appeases, soothes, and defuses strife instead [Prov 15:18]. The Proverbs paint many pictures of the Godliness of a man slow to anger—that he is wise, shows discretion, defers anger, pauses when provoked to study how to answer in order not to cause offense or stir up more strife [Prov 16:32, 15:28]. 'He that is slow to wrath is of great understanding' and knows it is a 'glory to pass over a transgression' [Prov 14:29, 19:11]. Not responding or acting in the heat of anger, 'the heart of the righteous studieth how to act and answer' and by the Spirit he discerns and considers the heart of the other person [Prov 15:28]. Is that person's heart slightly ajar to receive truth? We must then proceed slowly and deliberately so as not to cause the door to be slammed shut. If the door is open to receive, we can then proceed to share God's Word by the Spirit. All these are examples of sharing truth in a positive, slower way.

Jesus gives us a warning as to when the slow way can be negative. He admonishes to not be 'slow of heart' to believe the scriptures [Luke 24:25]. A heart conditioned more by carnal, worldly thought, will be slow or even reluctant to receive and believe the truth of God's Word. If the world's voice and opinion dominates the thinking, then we become sensitive to the world, but hardened to the Word of God. Our heart should not be slow, but quick and alive to believe the Word. Jesus said: "If ye continue in my word, then are ye my disciples indeed; And ye shall know the truth, and the truth shall make you free" [John 8:31-32].

Prayer:
Lord, we purpose to be slow to wrath and deliberate to answer by Your Spirit. But we purpose to not be slow of heart, but ready to believe Your Word.

Scripture of the Day:
"He that is slow to wrath is of great understanding: but he that is hasty of spirit exalteth folly." -[Proverbs 14:29]

The Word for the Day is "Direct."

Quote for the Day:
"We cannot direct the wind, but we can adjust the sails." – Dolly Parton

An old Lewis Carroll quote says: "If you don't know where you are going, any road will get you there." Too often the roads we choose, after our own understanding or in following along after others, take us into sorrows and troubles. Although we try to be wise in life about our choices, many times we look back in hindsight and realize we missed it. Leaning to our own limited understanding alone just doesn't always work out well.

Proverbs 3:6 counsels that if 'we will seek God's will in all that we do that He will direct our paths.' It doesn't say He might; it says He will. So often we rush ahead, feel pressured to act, to make a decision, without stopping to pray, to get still and quiet before the Lord, to get His counsel and direction. We get presumptuous and think we can figure it out without Him. We can, of course, but the results are not always what we hope for and then we often wrongly blame God.

We can 'devise our own way but it is a lot better when we allow the Lord to direct our steps' [Psalm 32:8, 37:23]. Haste makes waste and too often we act and order our days, our decisions, in too much of a hurry. The push we feel to hurry and decide, to hurry and do, is a push from the dark side. Satan doesn't want us to wisely 'wait on the Lord.' When we do, God will help to direct us in the right path for our best joy, happiness, prosperity, and health [Lam 3:25; Prov 3:5-8]. Adjust your sails, today, away from any direction you're following that is not of God's design. 'God will instruct you and teach you in the way which you should go; He will guide you with his own wisdom and eye' [Psalm 32:8].

Prayer:
Father, thank You that it is Your heart's desire to guide us and lead us in all the paths in our life. Help us not to get hasty and follow our own way.

Scripture of the Day:
"In all thy ways acknowledge him, and he shall direct thy paths." – [Proverbs 3:6]

The Word for the Day is "Grow."

Quote for the Day:
"Consider the tree for a moment. As beautiful as trees are to look at, we don't see what goes on underground—as they grow roots. Trees must develop roots in order to grow strong and produce their beauty. But we don't see the roots. We just see and enjoy the beauty. In much the same way, what goes on inside of us is like the roots of a tree." - Joyce Meyer

We know things, plants or animals, grow from small to larger as a normal course of nature. The Christian, besides natural bodily growth, has another dimension of growth to consider: spiritual growth. The Bible tells us that God promises to flourish and grow the righteous [Psalm 92:12]. Of course our main aim is to grow into the image of the Lord [2 Cor 3:18]. But spiritual growth is not automatic like natural growth. It takes a different effort to grow spiritually in the Lord.

The Bible uses the analogy of natural growth to help our understanding. We start out, as do natural babies, as newborn spiritual babes. And as natural babes need milk, we need 'the sincere milk of the Word, that we may grow thereby' [1 Peter 2:2]. The truth of God's Word grows our faith, wisdom, and understanding of God [Rom 10:17]. And we mature spiritually as we grow in grace and knowledge of the Lord Jesus Christ [2 Peter 3:18].

But whereas natural growth is easily observed, we can go through seasons when spiritual growth doesn't seem so obvious. We may be going through a time when nothing seems to confirm our spiritual growth, when nothing outstanding in our natural or spiritual walk seems to be happening. But this is also a time to stay committed to grow in the Lord. It can also be a time of growing deeper roots in the Lord. The bare tree in winter may look barren or dead, but it is putting down deeper roots in this season to sustain future increased growth and beauty. We can also put down deeper roots in the Lord in this season by getting closer to God through prayer, fellowship, and His Word. God can use this quiet time of growth in Him to prepare each of us for His greater works, blessings, and beauty that He has planned for us in His due time.

Prayer:
Lord, we purpose, in all seasons, to continue to grow in grace and knowledge of the Lord Jesus Christ that we can show His Light to those that sit in darkness.

Scripture of the Day:
"The righteous shall flourish like the palm tree: he shall grow like a cedar in Lebanon." -[Psalm 92:12]

The Word for the Day is "Affection."

Quote for the Day:
"Whatever a man depends upon, whatever rules his mind, whatever governs his affection, whatever is the chief object of his delight, is his god." – Charles Spurgeon

The world of itself is not evil unless it draws you away from God. Saint Ignatius wrote that "everything has the potential of calling forth in us a deeper response to our life in God," but everything can also pull us to lavish more love, affection, and more obsession in the wrong direction. God made the world and all that was in it and called it good. He meant for us to joy in it, to love it, but He still wants to be first in our thoughts and affection. "And thou shalt love the Lord thy God with all thine heart, and with all thy soul, and with all thy might" and 'thou shalt have no other gods before Him' [Deut 6:5; Ex 20:3].

In general a god is any thing, person, or object we idolize or deify. It is easy to let things and people in the earth, at work, home, and in general, begin to consume our thoughts and time, soon taking on too much importance. A look at statistics on what people spend the majority of their time and affections on doesn't include God in the listings, which is sad and to our hurt. Jesus taught, 'Do not love the world or the things in the world. If anyone loves the world, the love of the Father is not in him' [1 John 2:15]. Have you allowed "other gods" to creep in and take over your life, crowding God out? You can change that and change what you reverence and put first. You 'can set your mind on things above more than things on earth' [Col 3:2]. You can do a reset. You can purpose 'to be more spiritually minded, to be less conformed to the world, to be transformed and renewed in your mind' [Rom 12:2].

What profit is it for you if you gain the whole world but lose closeness to God, become reprobate, and forfeit your relationship to Your Father [Matt 16:26]? If you have lost a righteous respect and fear for God such that you think it of no consequence, if you neglect Him, dishonor Him, give Him little to none of your time, and if you have other gods of the world before Him, you are on dangerous ground [Matt 6:24]. The enemy stalks those weakened, not under the care and covering and abiding friendship of God.

Prayer:
Lord, the world around us has its own way of labeling sin and wrong. Help us to order our ways and thoughts after Your Word and Will rather than the current views around us.

Scripture of the Day:
"Set your affection on things above, not on things on the earth."-[Colossians 3:2]

The Word for the Day is "Walked."

Quote for the Day:
"If you've walked with me, you pretty well know me." - Anonymous

I believe there is a lot of truth in the quote above. When you walk with some-one you do get to know them better. How does this happen? I think this occurs through harmony and communion. When Lin and I take walks together around the neighborhood we usually walk in stride, or harmony, together. If one walks faster or slower than the other, then we're apart and not in unison. We often share thoughts, especially spiritual thoughts, and feelings with each other as we walk. I've noticed this happens even when friends or neighbors join the walk, they always seem to want to share what's going on in their lives and they ask of ours.

The Word tells us that Noah walked with God. But in Noah's day the men of the earth had turned wicked, corrupted their way, and the earth was filled with vio-lence [Gen 6:1-12]. Noah had no church or fellowship around to encourage him, so what made him walk with God? Noah made a decision to walk with God by his own free will. I can imagine him simply praying: "O God, Maker of heaven and earth, I want to know you." This pleased the Lord and Noah found favor with God as he walked in His ways. And as we know, the wicked were destroyed off the earth; only Noah and his family were saved.

There are only two ways to walk in this life—in the ways of the Lord or in our own ways. D.L. Moody once said: "If I walk with the world, I can't walk with God." To walk in God's ways is to try to do that which is right in His eyes and to keep His commandments, to walk uprightly according to the truth of the gospel, to walk in integrity, and to trust in the Lord's ways [1 Kings 11:33; Gal 2:14; Psalm 26:1]. Abiding in Jesus is the surest way to walk as we should, and anyone who abides in Him should try to walk as Jesus walked and by His example [1 John 2:6]. When we choose to walk in the Lord's ways instead of our own ways or the ways of the world, God reserves special promises for us. We're promised that every man who fears the Lord and walks in His ways will be abundantly blessed and that all who walk uprightly and honorably will dwell close to God's heart [Psalm 15:1-2, 128:1]. Walk in step with God, talk with God, and be blessed of Him.

Prayer:
Lord, we will commit all our ways to the Lord Jesus to walk righteously and speak uprightly that we might 'dwell on high' [Is 33:15-16].

Scripture of the Day:
"These are the generations of Noah: Noah was a just man and perfect in his gen-erations, and Noah walked with God." -[Genesis 6:9]

The Word for the Day is "Leaves."

Quote for the Day:
"Trees lose their leaves every year and they still stand tall and wait for better days to come." – Anon

Nature is such a lovely teacher. Here in October as fall moves into East Tennessee and over The Great Smoky Mountains, the leaves are turning glorious colors. Across the hills, valleys, and mountains are splashes of vivid red, rich orange, and golden yellow. It's a beautiful time and a beautiful season, reminding any who drive through the mountains of the glory of God's handiwork and creativity. As J.L. and I hike in the mountains, we pick up leaves to study them, marveling at how distinctively each is made—as are we. God says each of us is individually and wonderfully made, special and unique in His eyes [Psalm 139:14].

Like the leaves, we have our seasons and times, our purposes under the heaven [Eccl 3:1]. As the trees move through their seasons, we move and change through our seasons, growing and changing each year. We don't know or understand clearly the times and seasons of life as God does [Acts 1:7; Psalm 104:19]. We occasionally walk through hard, heavy times, but looking at the trees and the leaves reminds us that after any bleak time of winter, any barren time, spring will always come again. At the end of our seasons we know, too, that our leaf never withers and dies because we have eternal life to look forward to [1 Peter 1:6; Psalm 1:3].

The beauty of the fall leaves give us joy and we should take joy in our lives and days [Hab 3:17-18; Ps 16:11]. God also wants us to be useful for Him as we pass through our seasons of life, putting down deep roots unto Him, sheltering and giving joy to others, our roots reaching down to His living Water and our lives bringing forth fruit [Ps 1:3; Jer 17:8]. Trusting in God we should not be anxious when things in our days or seasons are not perfect, when things grow hard, staying confident that we are in the palm of His Hand and are the apple of His eye, protected in His loving arms [Is 49:16; Ps 17:8; Deut 33:27].

Prayer:
Father, as we look around us at the beauty of the trees and leaves, when it looks like You took your watercolors out to paint a glorious landscape, may we learn lessons from all we see and rejoice in the beauty You've created.

Scripture of the Day:
"The leaves thereof were fair, and the fruit thereof much, and in it was meat for all...and all flesh was fed of it." – [Daniel 4:12]

The Word for the Day is "Gladness."

Quote for the Day:
"A kind heart is a fountain of gladness, making everything in its vicinity freshen into smiles." - Washington Irving

We find in Deuteronomy 28 the glad promises of joy that God gave to the children of Israel if they followed the voice of the Lord. God promised them awesome blessings of prosperity, increase, abundance, health, protection, promotion and more. But God then listed the awful curses that would come if they turned away from the Lord. How could they possibly turn from God having such promises? Verse 47 reveals a surprising cause: "Because thou servest not the Lord thy God with joyfulness, and gladness of heart, for the abundance of all things." How could the heart lack joy and pleasure in serving the Lord for such awesome blessings? The Word gives us insights to this answer.

Gladness is sown for the upright in *heart* [Psalm 97:11]. So there is some fault with the heart condition to not have this promised gladness. It should be our hope and desire to walk every day with gladness. 'The hope of the righteous shall be gladness" [Prov 10:28]. Hope is the positive image in our mind of the thing desired. And since faith is the 'substance of things hoped for' [Heb 11:1], absence of this divine hope is a form of unbelief. Unbelief negates faith and robs us of the joy and gladness of *expecting* to receive from God.

Another fault of the heart is when one has no root in themselves. In Mark 4 Jesus tells the parable of the sower, who sows the Word. Some immediately receive the Word with gladness, but when affliction or persecution comes for the Word's sake, immediately they are offended because they "have no root in themselves"'[Mark 4:16-17]. Instead of a solid, committed vow to hold God's truth above all else, these are influenced more by carnal circumstances and by the world's opinion rather than faith in the truth of God's promises. It is easier to serve the Lord with joyfulness, and gladness of heart for the abundance of all things, when we walk upright in heart and receive the light of God's Word sown in our hearts [Deut 28:47; Psalm 97:11].

Prayer:
Lord, we will serve You with gladness and come before Your Presence with singing, giving praise and thanksgiving for the abundance of all things.

Scripture of the Day:
"Serve the Lord with gladness: come before His presence with singing."
-[Psalm 100:2]

The Word for the Day is "Abomination."

Quote for the Day:
"If sin becomes an abomination to you, you will have a hundred percent victory over it." – Sunday Adelaja

God provides commandments and guidelines for living a righteous, clean, and blessed life. He also lays out ways that are sinful and wrong in His eyes that we are not to walk in, believe in, or participate in. He clearly labels behaviors that are wrong, sinful, and abominable to Him, like in Proverbs 6 and Exodus 20. An abomination can be defined as something that causes disgust, often more extreme than sin, so we might want to become particularly mindful of those ways God labels an abomination.

Often in knowing and hearing of the mercy and grace of God, we forget that He is also a God of judgment and that many things thought okay in the world today are wrong in His eyes and an abomination to Him. A quote by Michael Horton says: "God's Word does not merely impart information; It's…God speaking." We can pick and choose which parts to believe in God's Word or accept it as truth [John 17:17; 2 Tim 3:16-17]. Through Jesus, we can receive forgiveness when we repent of wrong ways, but we are not to knowingly seek out ways that are sinful and an abomination to God. As with all sinful ways, if we seek them out and walk in them habitually, eventually we will become blinded to the truth about them and begin to condone them [Prov 17:15; Jer 8:12; Luke 16:15].

God laid out listings of behaviors that are abominable in order to protect us from the destructive results that can occur in our lives from freely walking those paths [Deut 18:10-11; Prov 26:25; Ezek 5:11]. It would be wise for you to utilize a concordance or to Google "abomination-kjv" to read about all those behaviors God hates. My opinion in these areas matters little, but God's view matters greatly.

Prayer:
Lord, help us to order our ways and thoughts after Your Word and Will.

Scripture:
"Ye shall therefore keep my statutes and my judgments, and shall not commit any of these abominations." – [Leviticus 18:26]

The Word for the Day is "Beg."

Quote for the Day:
"We have been deceived into believing prayer is all about persuading God to release His power. We no longer need to beg or plead; we need to exercise the authority He has given us and receive His blessings." - Andrew Wommack

As a boy I cannot remember many people, if any, praying to God with confidence in faith expecting an answer from God. It seemed that most either begged and pleaded with God to please notice their need, or they just accepted whatever happened must be God's will. *Que sera sera,* whatever will be will be.

The quote for the day sadly confirms that many today still think they have to beg and plead to get anything from God. Why is that? I think the two main reasons are ignorance of the Word and a beggarly attitude in appropriating and executing their rightful authority in the Lord. God's people can be destroyed for a lack of knowledge of His truths [Hosea 4:6]. Without renewing the mind by the Word, you can be ignorant of the blessings God has promised [Rom 12:2]. You can feel unworthy if you don't have the revelation that in Christ Jesus you are righteous [2 Cor 5:21], that you are a joint heir with Christ [Rom 8:17], and that He wants you to have an abundant life [John 10:10]. It's impossible to pray in faith confidently if you don't know your position in God and His will and promises.

You can have the knowledge of the scriptures, but still turn to the beggarly (weak and pleading) elements if you do not utilize and execute your rightful authority in Christ [Luke 10:19]. The name of Jesus is above all names, and He has given us authority in that Name [Phil 2:9; Acts 3:6]. We can forfeit our blessings if we don't exercise the authority we have in Jesus. God does not want us to be timid or beggarly but to 'be strong in the Lord, and in the power of His might' [Eph 6:10]. In Jesus we are no longer a beggar but are raised and lifted up to glory in Him! Praise be to God!

Prayer:
Lord, we come boldly before Thy throne in confidence knowing all the promises of God in Jesus are yes, and Amen, unto the glory of God by us! - [2 Cor 1:20]

Scripture of the Day:
"He raiseth up the poor out of the dust, and lifteth up the beggar from the dunghill, to set them among princes, and to make them inherit the throne of glory."
-[1 Samuel 2:8]

The Word for the Day is "Destruction."

Quote for the Day:
"The friends you choose are the catalyst to your own happiness or destruction." –
Greg Trimble

The old proverb "Choose Your Friends Wisely" is good counsel at every age and stage of life. Most of the temptations, problems, and pitfalls we face have links to the friends and associates we spend the most time with. Friendships are generally made among those who cross our paths most often, those we spend the most time with and share similar life activities and interests with. Friendships are also made because 'like is drawn to like.' We're drawn to people similar to ourselves, with similar looks and social skills we feel comfortable with. A Joan Walsh Anglund quote says: "A friend is someone who likes you and you like them." A warm connection and drawing often initiates friendship.

Good, rich friendships are a treasure. They enrich and sweeten our lives. With good friends we can be ourselves and know we are treasured for who we are. But, sometimes friendships can become problematic. Friends, like elevator buttons, can take you up or take you down. People change, as we do, but not always to the good. Negative, toxic friends run off positive friends that might prove better companions for us. Dark and light don't mix well. Unwise, froward, negative friends can also negatively affect our behavior. It's hard to stay strong enough to withstand the daily influences of people you hang around with the most. When that influence is bad, it takes you down.

It's hard, but important, to separate from destructive friendships and companions. The Word of God warns us not to keep company with those who walk in sinful lifestyles [1Cor 5:1, 6:9-11; Psalm 1:1,2]. As God changes us, sometimes we have to break away from problem friendships, even if those friends grow angry and scornful toward us for doing so [2 Cor 6:17; 1 Pet 4:3-5]. If we continue to stubbornly keep company with wrong friends they can bring ruin to our lives. If we wisely follow God's leading instead, He will be a loving friend to us, and in time bring sweeter, healthier friendships into our lives [Prov 18:24].

Prayer:
Father, help us to examine our friendships and to makes changes as we should.

Scripture of the Day:
"Enter ye in at the strait gate: for wide is the gate, and broad is the way, that leadeth to destruction, and many there be which go in thereat: Because strait is the gate, and narrow is the way, which leadeth unto life, and few there be that find it." – [Matthew 7:13-14]

The Word for the Day is "Laughter."

Quote for the Day:
"Take one cup of love, two cups of loyalty, three cups of forgiveness, four quarts of faith and one barrel of laughter. Take love and loyalty and mix them thorougly with faith; blend with tenderness, kindness and understanding. Add friendship and hope. Sprinkle abundantly with laughter. Bake it with sunshine. Wrap it regularly with lots of hugs. Serve generous helpings daily." - Zig Ziglar

You've probably heard the expression "Laughter is good for your soul." Laughter from a good soul is especially good. Ziglar's quote above describes this beautifully. His recipe for joy combines love, loyalty, forgiveness, faith, tenderness, kindness, understanding, friendship, hope, hugs, and lots of laughter. One of my fondest rememberances of the pure joy of laughter was a scene in the movie *Mary Poppins.* It was when Uncle Albert and Bert laughed so heartily while singing "I Love to Laugh" and got so filled with glee they floated up to the ceiling. I laugh just remembering that scene. Soon the two kids joined in laughing and they floated up too. Of course when Mary Poppins called the children down, they all came back to the floor. "Oh, that's sad" said Uncle Albert. Nothing deflates joy and laughter like sadness.

There is also a perverted laughter that is not so edifying. The loud laughter over silly folly, vulgar things, and vanity amuse but cannot fill the heart with glee or true joy. The laughter of mockery and derision spews from a darkened heart. These kinds of laughter produce noise, but cannot elevate the heart like Uncle Albert's kind.

God gives the oil of joy for our happiness [Isaiah 61:3], and a merry heart also "doeth good like a medicine" [Prov 17:22]. Clinical studies have shown that patients induced to laughter improved their recovery time. God wants us to serve Him with joy and gladness for the abundance of all things [Deut 28:47]. So if you're going through a hard time, keep your faith and trust in the Lord. He will turn your captivity and fill your mouth with laughter and so much joy in your heart you might float up to the ceiling!

Prayer:
Lord, thank You for the precious fruit of joy that the Holy Spirit gives us. We will share that joy to show the world the love and goodness of God.

Scripture of the Day:
"When the Lord turned again the captivity of Zion, we were like them that dream. Then was our mouth filled with laughter, and our tongue with singing." -
[Psalm 126:1-2]

The Word for the Day is "Clamour."

Quote for the Day:
"Solitude with God repairs the damage done by the fret and noise and clamour of the world." – Oswald Chambers

Clamour, or clamor, refers to loud and continuous noise, complaints, outcries, or demands, and it speaks of the noisy clamour all around us. There is a lot of noise and distraction in our world—mixed with unkindness, angry words, bitterness, slander, gossip, and open hostility. It's wearying and tiring, making us yearn for peace and quiet [Prov 17:1; Psalm 63:1]. In a normal day, with so much clamour coming at each of us—even on the best of days—it's difficult to stay centered and in peace.

Getting away from the clamour of life on a trip, vacation, hike, walk in the park or just taking some time away to linger in the quiet of a library, garden, museum, gallery, or scenic spot is healthy and provides a needed break. Time away mitigates stress and anxiety, getting us off the treadmill of a busy world [Is 32:17; 1 Pet 3:4; Gen 3:8]. Surprisingly many people are uncomfortable with solitude, often anxious with time alone by themselves. They've become so used to noise, media, television, commercial or city noise, people ever talking, or machines clacking that being alone seems an abrupt shock. But quiet times help you to renew, rediscover what's important, relax, and get in touch with your inner self.

As Christians the sweetest aspect of a break from the clamour of the world is spending it quietly with the Lord [Psalm 46:10; Matt 6:6]. Here true renewal and rest occur, with the peace of God coming into your heart and life as you take time away with Him. Quiet time with God helps you connect with God to hear His Wisdom, renew your mind, regain your peace, and become refreshed [Psalm 51:12; John 14:26; Rom 12:2]. As God's children we're meant to have personal time with Him. That time should include time in God's Word, time in thought and prayer, time for gratitude and praise, and time to listen. Spending time alone from the clamour of life is refreshing and beneficial in and of itself but time alone with God brings blessing and renews your soul.

Prayer:
Lord, help us always to find time to be still with You, to be refreshed and renewed.

Scripture of the Day:
"Let all bitterness, and wrath, and anger, and clamour, and evil speaking, be put away from you, with all malice." – [Ephesians 4:31]

The Word for the Day is "Comfort."

Quote for the Day:
"The vigour, and power, and comfort of our spiritual life depends on the mortification of the deeds of the flesh." - John Owen

What a pleasure it is to be in comfort. Sometimes we need physical comfort like a pair of shoes or clothing that fits just right. Or maybe we have an easy chair that gives our body sweet rest when weary. I always found that a purring kitty on my lap helped to alleviate my stresses. Sometimes we need mental, emotional, or spiritual comfort for hurts, distresses, sorrows and griefs. A kind and loving word from a friend can help comfort us in these times.

There are many things we can hope for in the natural and among people to comfort us, but there is one sure way to obtain comfort. The Bible tells us God is the God of *all* comfort [2 Corinthians 1:3]. No matter whether it be a natural comfort as ease from pain, or an emotional comfort from sorrows, God will supply the comfort we seek by our faith and by His Word.

A woman had a disease of an issue of blood for twelve years, had spent all she had on doctors, but could not be cured. She heard of Jesus, and believed that if she could just touch His garment she would be healed. When she touched His garment, Jesus turned and told her to be of good comfort, her faith had made her whole [Matthew 9:22]. Blind Bartimaeus was comforted when he called out to Jesus and received his sight through faith [Mark 10:46-52].

The Word of God will comfort us in any affliction. The merciful kindness of the Lord to comfort us is revealed through His Word [Psalm 119:76]. *All* the promises of God are yea and Amen in Jesus [2 Corinthians 1:20]. And we are assured comfort and rest when we walk in the fear of God and comfort of the Holy Ghost [Acts 9:31]. Trust in God's Word and reach out in faith today to receive from God the comfort you need.

Prayer:
Lord, thank You that no matter the need or affliction, You comfort us by faith in Your Word, and by the Comforter, the Holy Ghost.

Scripture of the Day:
"This is my comfort in my affliction; for thy word hath quickened me." -
[Psalm 119:50]

The Word for the Day is "Expected"

Quote for the Day:
"I've always tried to go a step past wherever people expected me to end up."
- Beverly Sills

Many have said it is the unexpected moments of beauty that move us the most but I think the "expected" moments move us, too. To Expect means we are 'looking for and hoping for something any minute'—like awaiting the birth of a child or expecting a special phone call. In a sense to "expect" is to Hope. When we expect something is likely to happen, we look forward to it, think about it, and envision it. I think we can live in "an expectancy of faith"…if we would. God says 'I will walk with you and talk with you' [Jer 29:12] and we can hope and expect for that. He promises 'I will give you rest and peace"[Matt 11:28; John 14:27] and don't we all need that? He assures us 'I will supply all your needs' [Phil 4:19] and that is comforting, too, in so many ways. The Bible is full of promises of hope and faith we can Expect, count on, and look forward to. Like waiting for the leaves to turn in October, our expectancy may be tested a little bit sometimes. But if we hold fast in faith and confidence, it will come [Heb 10:23].

Some people like to live with low expectancy, feeling it is safer and will lead to less disappointment. But in the Lord we have hope and the Lord's encouragement that He has high expectations for us. 'For I know the thoughts I have toward you, thoughts of peace and not evil, to give you a future and a hope' [Jer 29:11]. God has dreams and plans for us beyond the expectations others see and often beyond our own expectations. God's plans are always good plans, and "Faith expects from God what is beyond all expectation" [Andrew Murray]. So we should always live our days expectantly.

I often think God is watching us expectantly, too—in every season—to see if we will learn and grow and strengthen. How will we grow in Him? Will we accomplish all He hopes, letting Jesus increase in us more and more? 1John 3:2 promises: 'It doth not yet appear what we shall be: but we know that, when He shall appear, we shall be like Him.' Isn't that a glorious hope and expectation?

Prayer:
Lord, may we live daily with an "Expectant Heart"—expectant to see and appreciate beauty, seeking and expectant to grow in You.

Scripture of the Day:
"For I know the thoughts that I think toward you, saith the Lord, thoughts of peace, and not of evil, to give you an expected end." - [Jeremiah 29:11]

The Word for the Day is "Return."

Quote for the Day:
"This is the truth: as from a fire aflame thousands of sparks come forth, even so from the Creator an infinity of beings have life and to him return again."
- Marcus Tullius Cicero

The act of returning can be either good or bad, depending upon what we are returning to. It is always pleasant to return home after being away, whether on a trip for pleasure or business. We might have enjoyed recreations away, but returning to the peace and comfort of home gladens the heart. It is always easier to relax and recover from fatigue when we return home.

However, we can return to ways that do not bring true joy. If we have walked with the Lord, and return to the old ways of the flesh and of the old man, we cannot have peace. Anyone who has seen a loved one go astray from the Lord knows the grief and sorrow we feel for the backslider. We pray and intercede for the loved one astray, and know the joy and gladness when that one comes back to the Lord. The Lord is always ready to restore and heal the one that wants to return to fellowship with Him. Jesus has promised that He will never refuse any that come to Him: "and him that cometh to me I will in no wise cast out" [John 6:37]. The Lord's mercy endureth forever to those who call on Him [Ps 136:1].

As believers, we should also expect a good return on the words we speak in faith. We should believe and expect for the answers and requests we pray to return to us in manifestation. The Word that goes forth out of God's mouth does not return void; that is, it does not come back with no results, but it accomplishes the will and purpose that God desired. When we speak the scripture, the Word of God, it is God's living Word coming out of our mouths. And we should expect it to prosper, or accomplish, our requests and not return void. So believe the promises of God for yourself and for those you pray for to prosper and accomplish the requests you ask in faith.

Prayer:
Lord, thank You for Your grace and mercy that if we have fallen away from You, we can repent and return in forgiveness to grace and fellowship with You again. Thank you that we can speak Your Word and expect that it will not return void, but will prosper and accomplish our request in the Name of Jesus.

Scripture of the Day:
"So shall my word be that goeth forth out of my mouth: it shall not return unto me void, but it shall accomplish that which I please, and it shall prosper in the thing whereto I sent it." -[Isaiah 55:11]

The Word for the Day is "Time."

Quote for the Day:
"The more time you spend with someone, the more like them you will become. The same is true of God." – Amber Fox

Few people, at the end of their lives, think: "O, I wish I'd gone shopping more, gone on more cruises, had finer cars and a grander house." When people are at the end of life, ready to meet God, their thoughts shift toward eternity. Sometimes even Christians are uncomfortable and fearful about going on to meet God because they know Him so little. God, Jesus, the Holy Spirit were only words in creeds they read, recited, or heard about in church. They have no real personal relationship with any member of the Trinity, and this is sad. Just as most people, in the natural, would hate to think of moving in and spending the rest of their life with someone they hardly know, many are anxious at life's end about moving on to spend eternity with God in heaven.

How do we come to know God better? In the same way we make time to come to know anyone better. We reach out, we make an effort to form ties with another, to build a relationship with them. To know God better we have to be willing to seek out His company, to spend time with Him, talk and listen to Him [Deut 4:29]. We have to study and read God's Word where He reveals Himself to us and speaks to us, and we must make space for time in prayer, to share with God from our hearts [1 Chron 16:11]. We can also learn of God by seeking out knowledge and wisdom about Him as we would about any subject or individual we wanted to know more of. Frankly, we all make time to learn about and grow in whatever is most important to us. We all have the same 24 hours in every day and we all have been given the same measure of faith. Those close to God, to Jesus, to the Holy Spirit, have given time to attain that place [1 Cor 1:5].

Prayer:
Lord, help me in this busy life to make time to form a strong true relationship with You so I'll be eager to move on to spend eternity with You.

Scripture of the Day:
"Knowing the time, that now it is high time to awake out of sleep: for now is our salvation nearer than when we believed." - [Romans 13:11]

The Word for the Day is "Change."

Quote for the Day:
"There is nothing wrong with change, if it is in the right direction." - Winston Churchill

I love the weather in the month of October. The hot, humid days of summer are behind, and the days of October are mostly sunny, clear days with low humidity. It just feels good to be outside this month, to go hiking and enjoy the mountains, to play golf or sports, or even to work in the yard seems pleasant. Every season is special in God's creation. Each season has its unique delights and comforts. We know a brief weather front can bring a temporary discomfort, but it passes and the climate resumes its change to the next season.

Our growth in the Lord can be like the seasons. God wants us to stay constant and without change in some ways. He wants our heart to stay constant in always putting Him first in all things. Our commitment, devotion, fellowship, trust, and obedience must stay constant. Malachi 3:6 tells us the Lord does not change in His love to us, and we should not change in our love to Him.

But the Lord wants change in our lives in other ways. God also wants changes in the right directions. He wants us always changing more and more into the image of Christ Jesus by renewing our minds to His truth and wisdom and walking uprightly before Him [Rom 8:29]. He wants us to grow in each season of life that we might be blessed, and be a blessing [Gen 12:2].

Maybe you're in a season of growth that seems slow to change. You want to receive from the Lord and achieve the next level of growth, but you're not there yet. Seasons change gradually to the next, and you will move into your next season if you stay constant in the Lord. Stay committed and trusting God's faithfulness: "But let patience have her perfect work, that ye may be perfect and entire, wanting nothing" [James 1:4]. Remember the Lord's desire is to always change you from glory to glory!

Prayer:
Lord, thank You for the unique beauty of each season in nature. And thank You for each season in our growth in You, knowing we are being changed from glory to glory as we conform more and more to the image of our Lord Jesus.

Scripture of the Day:
"For I am the Lord, I change not." -[Malachi 3:6]

The Word for the Day is "Yield."

Quote for the Day:
"God must do everything for us. Our part is to yield and trust." – A. W. Tozer

A definition for "yield" is to give way or surrender control to another. Most of us think of total surrender in terms of defeat, in being forced to give up because all hope is lost. That idea makes it harder to understand the concept of surrendering all voluntarily to the Lord, trusting our lives fully into His hands. Jesus said "follow me" but in honesty, we like to lead, not follow; we don't like giving up control [Matthew 4:19].

Why is yielding to God so hard? It's because we're wired naturally to put self first, to protect the self. The world teaches us mistrust early in life, training us that to trust too much in another is risky, even dangerous. Satan uses this knowledge to build mistrust, slithering about in the world seeking to harm us and to use others to hurt us, causing us to build protective walls around our hearts. Because our life experiences have shown us people are often not to be trusted, it is easy for our minds to cast that shadow of mistrust over onto God, to wonder if He can be trusted.

It takes humility to surrender and to yield to God, to do things His way, letting Him lead and guide. But the more we come to know and trust God, the more we begin to let Him take the driver's seat in our lives. The benefits of yielding to God are not always ones we readily see at first, but they come as we grow in faith and trust [Jer 17:7-8]. A peace and release begins to come that all is well when we rest in Him. We find life is easier, yoked with God, as He carries more of the load [Matt 11:29]. Surrendering self and yielding to God reaps only good. 'No good thing does God withhold from those who are fully His' [Psalm 84:11].

Prayer:
Father, teach us to trust You more every day and to yield every aspect of ourselves to Your care.

Scripture of the Day:
"Yield yourselves unto God…and your members as instruments of righteousness unto God." - [Romans 6:13]

The Word for the Day is "Purpose."

Quote for the Day:
"We need to give our total focus to the business of reaching this world with the Gospel of Jesus Christ and stop running down meaningless rabbit trails that get our focus off of our heavenly purpose." - Jerry Falwell

Some men seek for and try to discover their purpose in life, the reason for which they exist, or their individual calling, work, or mission in life. Some find this purpose or calling at an early age, usually by recognizing a special talent or gift they have, or by being drawn to a particular activity or work that appeals to their personality. Probably the majority accept work that is suitable or adequate, but not of what you would consider profound purpose. But where would society be without all the people that do the ordinary, but needed and essential jobs? God is no respecter of persons [Acts 10:34], and every man has a special purpose in Christ Jesus, and often several purposes over a lifetime.

If you asked someone the purpose of Jesus, they would probably say 'He came to save the world,' which is true. The Bible states, however, that Jesus came for a specific purpose: He was manifested "that he might destroy the works of the devil" [1 John 3:8]. He came to destroy the works of the devil (in each individual) through the new creation we become through His salvation. He wants us to then walk and be led in His Spirit to overcome the lusts of the flesh [Gal 5:16-17]. Jesus renews our mind by the Word of God and gives us the help of the Holy Spirit to overcome the flesh and works of the devil if we are committed to follow Him. "But thanks be to God, which giveth us the victory through our Lord Jesus Christ" [1 Cor 15:57].

Every man in Christ Jesus then has an eternal holy calling and purpose given by God [2 Tim 1:9]. We are called to show the love of God through Christ Jesus our Lord, to share the good news of the gospel, and to make disciples of all men that Jesus might fulfill His purpose of destroying the works of the devil in their lives. We also share this purpose through our prayers, intercessions, and ministry by the Spirit to men needing deliverance and salvation in the Lord.

Prayer:
Lord, thank You for Your salvation in Jesus. Help us with our purpose in Him to show, share, and deliver that Gospel to others that they might be free also.

Scripture of the Day:
"He that commiteth sin is of the devil; for the devil sinneth from the beginning. For this purpose the Son of God was manifested, that he might destroy the works of the devil." - [1 John 3:8]

The Word for the Day is "Trouble."

Quote for the Day:
"Just 'cause trouble comes visiting doesn't mean you have to offer it a place to sit down." - Appalachian saying

Trouble comes knocking at everyone's door now and then—but like the old saying above, that doesn't mean you need to make trouble welcome. When troubles do come your way, stop and pray, and also look inward at your own life. Sadly, many of our troubles are caused by our own behavior. For example, we've been late to work far too often, lose our job, and then complain to our friends and the Lord about the unfairness of it all. We act immorally or unkindly, break up a loving relationship in our lives and then whine to God, feeling the victim. I'm sure you see the point. Many times our own erroneous, careless actions and ways are the roots of our troubles. Change and repentance are needed and prayer for God's loving help and guidance [1 Peter 5:7; 1 John 1:9; Acts 3:19].

Sometimes, the enemy of God has his nasty hand in helping to bring trouble to our door through calamitous events or through people he utilizes. He hates us because we belong to God and he never ceases finding ways to instigate ways to breach our spiritual defenses to bring hurt. In these instances of trouble pray for God's help, intervention, and restoration [Deut 20:1-4; Psalm 34:6]. Don't ever accept that trouble is "just the way it is in life.' An old quote says: 'Trouble is the devil's first name' and it is a thought worth holding in mind. When satan made trouble for God in heaven, God fought and cast him out and you should do the same every time he comes knocking at your door. Whenever trouble comes, fight the good fight of faith. Stay on the right side of God and know, with confidence, that He will always help you in any time of trouble when you reach out to Him [Isaiah 65:24; Psalm 46:1].

Prayer:
Lord, thank You that even when we are troubled on every side, You are always with us, our refuge and strength, a very present help in trouble.

Scripture of the Day:
"The Lord is good, a strong hold in the day of trouble; and he knoweth them that trust in him." - [Nahum 1:7]

The Word for the Day is "Sacrifice."

Quote for the Day:
"If Jesus Christ be God and died for me, then no sacrifice can be too great for me to make for Him." - Charles Studd

We are familiar with natural sacrifices we make in life, when we give up things for somebody else's sake. A husband gives up a round of golf to help the wife clean house; parents deny themselves so their kids can have their needs supplied. Whatever the sacrifice is, we are denying ourselves and giving priority to another's wants or needs.

We learn of sacrifices for spiritual purposes in the Bible. The Old Testament describes sacrifices of thanksgiving and praise to God by offering the first fruits of crops. Blood sacrifices of animals were offered to receive mercy and pardon for sins. Blood was required for the remission of sins [Heb 9:22]. In the New Covenant, the reconciliation of God and humankind was fulfilled in the sacrifice of Jesus Christ for the sins of the world. Jesus shed His blood and gave His life for salvation forever [Heb 10:12]. "For there is one God, and one mediator between God and men, the man Christ Jesus" [1 Tim 2:5].

Romans 12:1 tells us we are now to present ourselves a 'living sacrifice' to God. Our human body stays alive, but we are to sacrifice and die-out to the old self-centered nature of the flesh. We are self-centered from birth, and it is natural for our flesh to be self-serving. The Lord wants us to die to self, and live totally in His will. This takes a strong-willed decision and commitment to be a living sacrifice. It is not an automatic, instantaneous reality. The flesh resists the spirit [Gal 5:17], and we must determine to always give God's way priority over self. If we yield to the flesh and make mistakes, we repent, receive forgiveness, correct our course, and continue our goal that Jesus be ever increasing in our heart. This mind of Christ in us over self-will is always our priority. "Be not conformed to this world"[Rom 12:2]; sacrifice the old ways of self, and live in ever-newness of life, peace, joy, and blessing in the Lord.

Prayer:
Lord, we will sacrifice the old self-serving ways, and be a living witness of the new creation we are in our Lord Jesus.

Scripture of the Day:
"I beseech you therefore, brethren, by the mercies of God, that ye present your bodies a living sacrifice, holy, acceptable unto God, which is your reasonable service." - [Romans 12:1]

The Word for the Day is "Reins."

Quote for the Day:
"As the traveler who has lost his way, throws his reins on his horse's neck, and trusts to the instinct of the animal to find his road, so must we do with the divine animal who carries us through this world." – Ralph Waldo Emerson

Reins are used to give subtle cues and commands. The reins in a horse's mouth teach him to follow the will of his master and, in time, with a good and wise master, the reins are hardly needed as horse and master become so in tune. Likewise, a team of horses hitched to a carriage or yoked together at the plow, learn to move in oneness and harmony when yielded to their master's leading. The lesson for us is that life is best, and blessed, when God holds the reins and control of our lives. Too often we let our own heart and ideas plan our way but God wants to establish our steps [Prov 16:9]. We may deceive ourselves and others about how yielded to God's leadership we are, but God isn't deceived about whether He really holds control and reign in our lives or not. He searches and tries the hearts and reins and He knows all that are fully His, yielded to Him [Psalm 7:9; Rev 2:2-3; Psalm 139:1-13].

In all ways possible God wants us to be in company with others yielded and following after God, too. Dark and light have no fellowship and push against each other in uncomfortable disharmony like the wrong ends of a magnet pressed together. Our lives are happier hooked into strong relationships in family, work, organizations, and church with like-minded believers. God is grieved and our hearts should be grieved, and we should be pricked in our reins, our conscience, when we fall into spending too much time with people not in the Lord and not following after His ways [Psalm 73:21; Rom 6:13].

Our hunger and desire should be for God to hold our reins more and more. "Examine me, O Lord, and prove me; try my reins and my heart" [Psalm 26:2]. We should hunger for more of God, for Him to reign more and more in our lives and hearts, to be directed more by Him every day. We should pray that He would show us stubborn areas of our lives where He is still not in full control.

Prayer:
Lord, help us to see the areas of our lives where You are not Lord and Master, in loving control, and help us lay down stubborn, willful ways unpleasing to You.

Scripture of the Day:
"I the Lord searcheth the heart, I try the reins, even to give every man according to his ways, and according to the fruit of his doings." – [Jeremiah 17:10]

The Word for the Day is "Marvelled."

Quote for the Day:
"There's only two times recorded in scripture that Jesus marvelled." - Andrew Wommack

What could possibly cause Jesus to marvel? The instances recorded in scripture describe two events, one positive where Jesus was amazed thinking highly and with respect and appreciation for the circumstance, the other where He was negatively bewildered and perplexed at the situation. These two events help us to see the real difference between belief and unbelief.

The first event, where Jesus marvelled in a positive way, is found in Matthew 8:5-10 where in Capernaum, He encountered a centurion seeking His help. The centurion, a Roman military officer, told Jesus that his servant 'lieth at home sick of the palsy, greviously tormented.' "And Jesus saith unto him, I will come and heal him." But the centurion told Jesus to just speak His word only, "and my servant shall be healed." How did the centurion have such faith? He understood authority saying "For I am a man under authority, having soldiers under me: and I say to this man, Go, and he goeth; and to another, Come, and he cometh; and to my servant, Do this, and he doeth it." The centurion did not ask Jesus to come to his house or for any physical touch because he believed the spiritual authority of Jesus and knew Jesus only needed to 'speak the word' in that authority. Jesus then marvelled at this centurion's great faith in His Authority and Word.

The second event, a negative example, is recorded in Mark 6:1-6 where Jesus went to His own country, among His own kin, to minister. But they looked on the physical man and said 'Is not this the carpenter...is not his own family here among us?' And they were offended. And Jesus "could there do no mighty work." And "he marvelled because of their unbelief." These walked in the flesh, limited by natural, physical, carnal realism, which opens the door for unbelief. The centurion related to Jesus in the Spirit realm and was therefore blessed by believing Jesus to 'speak the word only.' So we see that it is best to walk in the Spirit believing God's Word by faith, not needing physical or tangible evidence first. "If we live in the Spirit, let us also walk in the Spirit" [Galatians 5:25].

Prayer:
Lord, we purpose to walk by faith, not by sight, believing Your Word regardless of circumstances, because all things are possible if we believe [Mark 9:23].

Scripture of the Day:
"When Jesus heard it, he marvelled, and said to them that followed, Verily I say unto you, I have not found so great faith, no, not in Israel." - [Matthew 8:10]

The Word for the Day is "Pharisee."

Quote for the Day:
"Sometimes we emulate the Pharisees more than we imitate Christ." - R.C. Sproul

We tend to quickly vilify the Pharisees today for their opposition to Jesus and for being instrumental in putting him to death. We should remember, however, that Jesus was born among the Jews, taken to the temple to be circumcised, taught the Torah and faith of the Pharisees. He frequently talked with and socialized with those who were Pharisees and taught in the synagogue [Luke 7:36-50]. The Pharisees weren't an alien people to Jesus but the message he brought was in many ways alien to them. Pharisee leaders were educated and some of the few who read and knew God's Word. In a harsh time of Roman rule and disrespect for God, the Pharisees were striving to preserve their faith. But they had become misguided because they had become obsessive about their structured religious rules and laws and had moved away from a true relationship with God.

As R. C. Sproul taught 'they looked good on the outside but inside they hid impurity; they pretended a righteousness they did not live.' They'd settled into a form of religion that wasn't sweet and genuine anymore, but based on rote and ritual. Corruption had also crept into the midst of the priesthood; they had a cushy thing going. They went through the rituals, but their heart wasn't close to God anymore. Jesus, on the other hand, walked in true righteousness and holiness [1 Peter 1:15-16]. People were drawn to that and to the true anointing on his life. Nothing shows up a counterfeit like the genuine, and nothing makes the counterfeit more uncomfortable than being around the genuine. The constant ongoing contrast was between the surface, literal mind and walk of the Pharisees and the spiritual mind and walk of Jesus. Jesus often pointed that out, too: "Do not ye after their works: for they say and do not" [Matt 23:3]. The Pharisees had come to a place where their system was killing the effectiveness of the church. Holding their religious system above Truth, they missed seeing who Jesus was. And even hated Him for the Truth he brought.

Prayer:
Father, help us not to get lost to venerating a religious system and its beliefs more than having a true relationship with You—and in the process missing You and even persecuting and condemning those walking in a right way with You.

Scripture of the Day:
"Woe unto you scribes and Pharisees, hypocrites! For ye shut up the kingdom of heaven against men." - [Matthew 23:13]

The Word for the Day is "Offend."

Quote for the Day:
"I just feel truth is truth, and sometimes I probably offend some people."
 - Franklin Graham

It is impossible not to offend someone with your own views. For this not to be true the world would all have to be the same in every viewpoint for no possibility of offense to occur. There are many viewpoints about religion, too, but the Christian holds and knows the absolute truth of the gospel of Jesus. We are to live and share that gospel with others [Mark 16:15]. And if we do not share the truth of God for fear of offending, then our fear has voided that truth. We claim to hold a truth, but by never proclaiming that truth, we show that it is not truth to us in reality. Thus we become dishonest and hypocritical by our silence of the truth.

Faith by its nature is built on absolutes. Our world today, however, is leaning more and more toward relativism versus faith, holding the doctrine that there are no absolutes and that all knowledge, truth, and morality exist only in relation to culture, historical time, or society. But we must not back away from our faith and the integrity of Biblical truths even if it offends someone. Pastor David Jeremiah wrote: "When culture changes around us, God's standard of living does not." God's absolutes cannot be altered just to make men feel comfortable in their sins.

Our calling as believers is to speak the truth in love [Eph 4:15]. The Holy Spirit, who is the Spirit of Truth [John 16:13], will always guide us in the best and appropriate way to share the truth. If we love others as Jesus does, we will speak the truth in love to them because their destiny and relationship with the Lord is priority over all. God's truth is a spiritual power that may offend some because it discerns the thoughts and intents of the heart and convicts [Heb 4:12]. We cannot share the truth of God's Word effectively unless we live it; otherwise, we are truly offensive because the hypocrisy is obvious. It we truly love as Jesus, we will be true witnesses undismayed by whatever hate and rejection we incur for speaking His truth; for only God's truth sets man free [John 8:32].

Prayer:
Lord, we will share the good news of the gospel of Jesus, ever being led by His Holy Spirit, speaking the truth out of an upright and obedient heart.

Scripture of the Day:
"Many therefore of his disciples, when they had heard this, said, This is an hard saying; who can hear it? When Jesus knew in himself that his disciples murmured at it, he said unto them, Doth this offend you?" - [John 6:60-61]

November

Quote for the Day:
"Grace: You need it. You can't live without it, but you can't purchase it and you can't earn it. It only ever comes by means of a gift and when you receive it, you immediately realize how much you needed it all along, and you wonder how you could've lived so long without it." – Paul Tripp

As a young girl grace only meant one of two things—a blessing my dad said at dinner and an effortless, elegant way of moving that some lovely women seemed to possess. I didn't understand Spiritual Grace until I was born again as a young adult. Then, like the quote above, I suddenly realized the beauty of what grace is and wondered how I could have lived so long without it. What is grace in the spiritual sense? It is the unmerited, free favor of God that comes to us through salvation. Jesus purchased a grace for us on the cross that we couldn't attain ourselves [Eph 2:8-10; 2 Cor 5:21]. In a sense no one can be here on earth without grace, we cannot attain salvation without grace, or return to God at death without grace.

Although grace is an essential part of God's character, it doesn't come until we reach for it. Grace is like a gift there waiting until we finally unwrap it [Eph 4:7]. Then when the Spirit of God, the Spirit of Truth, comes into us, our spiritual blindness begins to lift. We walk in wonder and gratitude into God's favor and love. We grow in grace and truth; we become new creations [John 1:16; 2 Cor 5:17]. Grace transforms us, makes us new, teaches and trains us as we grow in faith to renounce ungodliness and worldly passions, to live self-controlled, upright, and godly lives [Titus 2:11-12]. We keep receiving grace on and on.

New doctrines of grace are emerging that teach election, divine sovereignty, and a grace without a cross, stressing God is tolerant of all beliefs, not requiring repentance or salvation or urging a holy life. Carefully avoid beliefs contrary to God's Word and stay in the wonder and truth of His love and favor [2 Pet 3:17-18]. "A true understanding of grace—of God's unmerited favor—always provokes a life of gratitude and obedience." [R. C. Sproul]

Prayer:
Lord, help us to continue to grow in You, to be ever grateful for Your love and your unmerited grace and favor.

Scripture of the Day:
"For by grace are ye saved through faith; and that not of yourselves: it is the gift of God: Not of works, lest any man should boast." [Ephesians 2:8-9]

The Word for the Day is "Persuaded."

Quote for the Day:
"People are generally better persuaded by the reasons which they have themselves discovered than by those which have come in to the mind of others." - Blaise Pascal

In our society today we are being assaulted by persuasive tactics at almost every turn. Marketing and advertising strategists try to convince us of the need and advantage of buying their products. Politicians and media disregard truth and use "the illusory truth effect" that if you repeat a lie enough people will think it's true. Unfortunately, many will not take the effort to discover truth and reasons for themselves, and they become convinced by the deceptions of others. But Pascal's quote is true, we are better persuaded by the reasons we acquire by our own effort, rather than just lazily accepting the opinion and argument of others.

Our mission as Christians is to persuade the world of the love and salvation in Christ Jesus. However, we must be fully persuaded of our own faith before we can convince others. We can try to persuade someone to a certain way of thinking or belief, but our words have little power or effect unless they are confirmed by our own lives. No one will value your argument if you can't convince others that you believe it yourself.

We cannot be fully persuaded in faith unless we first *know* the Lord ourselves [2 Tim 1:12]. We must have a real experience where He has come into our hearts, being born-again, made a new creature in the Spirit [2 Cor 5:17]. We must be convinced fully of the absolute truth of His Word. A double minded man is unstable, ineffective, and unable to persuade others to Christ [James 1:8]. We must be bold, solid, unwavering in our convictions of God's truth to persuade others [Acts 19:8]. If Jesus is truly Lord and first priority in all things in our lives, then we are fully persuaded in faith to enlighten and convince the world with powerful witness of the eternal glory and life in Jesus Christ.

Prayer:
Lord, help us not to be 'almost' [Acts 26:28], but fully persuaded of all the truth and reality in Christ Jesus that we might be witnesses to the world to draw men to salvation in Him.

Scripture of the Day:
"For I am persuaded, that neither death, nor life, nor angels, nor principalities, nor powers, nor things present, nor things to come, nor height, nor depth, nor any other creature, shall be able to separate us from the love of God, which is in Christ Jesus our Lord." - [Romans 8:38-39]

The Word for the Day is "Shepherd."

Quote for the Day:
"A true shepherd leads the way. He does not merely point the way." – Leonard
Ravenhill

Individuals in most any walk in life need teaching and guidance. Sheep are often used to exemplify this piece of wisdom because all sheep are in need of a shepherd. Sheep, by their nature, are apt to go astray without a good shepherd to lead them and care for them. Although sheep are gentle, and surprisingly intelligent, in their desire to flock together, they will often follow one another to hurt and peril. Biblically, sheep have always represented human beings, needing God's care, protection, and guidance.

One of the most beautiful passages about the Lord as a good shepherd is in Psalm 23: "The Lord is my shepherd: I shall not want. He maketh me to lie down in green pastures; he leadeth me beside the still waters. He restoreth my soul." This is the type of shepherd our souls yearn for. Jesus, too, is spoken of as the Great Shepherd (Hebrews 13:20), the chief Shepherd (I Peter 5:4), and 'the good shepherd who giveth His life for the sheep' (John 10:11). A good leader is one we can safely follow and trust in but Jesus explained that not everyone who calls himself a shepherd of the sheep and a leader of others, is a good shepherd or leader. He sorrowfully acknowledges that many shepherds or leaders don't really love the sheep in their care and that they would run, leaving the sheep and not fighting to protect them, if a wolf or trouble came.

David was a young shepherd before he fought Goliath. He kept his father's sheep and singularly fought and protected them from a lion and a bear with God's help. He felt confident that God would deliver him out of the hand of Goliath, too [1 Samuel 17:33-37]. This is a good lesson for us to remember about the delivering and saving power of God when we are faced with the lions, bears, and Goliaths in our lives. We need to keep in mind the words: 'The Lord thy God will not fail thee, nor forsake thee' [Deuteronomy 31:6]. We are safe in God, knowing that the Lord Jesus, the Holy Spirit, and the angels of heaven are always with us, watching over and keeping us.

Prayer:
Lord, may we take comfort, knowing that You are our good shepherd, a loving Father we can count on to always guide, lead, and protect us.

Scripture for the Day:
"I am the good shepherd, and know my sheep, and am known of mine." -
[John 10:14]

The Word for the Day is "Idols."

Quote for the Day:
"Just because you don't bow down and worship a golden statue does not mean you don't have idols in your life." - West McAdam

What is an idol? It is anything that takes the place of God in our heart. Idols can be objects, desires, or people. Anything that consumes our attention and priority of thought and desire above God becomes an idol to us. Idols can be people we admire so much that they become objects of devotion or worship. Sports stars, movie stars, TV celebrities, or anyone the culture elevates to elitist status can become an idol. Money, power, position, and possessions can become idols when they become our total focus. Activities like work, family, sports, recreations, or other interests can consume our time and attention away from God. "An idol of the mind is as offensive to God as an idol of the hand" [A.W. Tozer]. If we allow anything to usurp the place of God in our heart, it becomes an idol, and we practice idolatry. All idolatry is a work of the flesh and carnal desire [Gal 5:19].

Giving one's heart over to idols can have adverse consequences. Idols are a snare that can capture your desires and attention so as to hinder and eliminate focus on the Lord. "And they served their idols: which were a snare unto them" [Psalm 106:36]. When we get so devoted to an idol, like money or position, that we boast of it, we become confused and confounded: "Confounded be all they...that boast themselves of idols" [Psalm 97:7].

"Know ye not that ye are the temple of God, and the Spirit of God dwelleth in you? And what agreement hath the temple of God with idols" [1 Cor 3:16; 2 Cor 6:16]. God is a jealous God [Ex 34:14], and is intolerant of idols. To the Lord, an idol in the temple of God is a defilement. He asks: "what fellowship hath righteousness with unrighteousness? and what communion hath light with darkness?" [2 Cor 6:14]. The excessive attention and devotion to an idol can become as a god to us. God alone wants our heart: "Thou shalt have no other gods before me" [Ex 20:3]. God's directive and commandment is clear and simple as the scripture states: 'keep yourselves from idols' [1 John 5:21].

Prayer:
Lord, help us reject idols, as Jesus declared: "for it is written, Thou shalt worship the Lord thy God, and him only shalt thou serve" [Matt 4:10].

Scripture of the Day:
"Little children, keep yourselves from idols. Amen." - [1 John 5:21]

The Word for the Day is "Read."

Quote for the Day:
"When you read God's Word, you must constantly be saying to yourself, 'It is talking to me, and about me.'" – Soren Kierkegaard

When we are small, our parents read to us so we can learn. As we grow older, we read to ourselves to learn. Through reading we tap into the great world of wisdom and knowledge. Frederick Douglass wrote "Once you learn to read, you will be forever free." Even Dr. Seuss taught that the more you read, the more things you will know.

Even in Old Testament times when paper was scarce and few knew how to read, God still recorded his Word on stone and parchments, to be read to His People. Again and again we see where God's leaders read "all the words of the law, the blessings and the cursings, according to all that is written in the book of the law" [Joshua 8:34]. The Word was revered and precious then, and the people would sit for hours to hear it read. We should be of the same mind today, but Bibles are so easily found and so readily available, that many have forgotten the wise admonishments of God to faithfully read the Word.

The Bible, unlike other books, is God-inspired, so when we read it, we gain much more than from other reading because the Spirit helps to give deeper understanding. We profit and grow every time we read in the Word and gain more of God's knowledge. "Whereby, when ye read, ye may understand my knowledge in the mystery of Christ as it is now revealed…by the Spirit" [Eph 3:4-5]

Sometimes a sweet way to read and study the Bible is to realize that the words, promises, and directives given are not distant and directed to someone else, but written to you. I like to sometimes change the words a little to direct them toward myself and to read them out loud that way. Instead of just reading "Blessed is the man that trusteth in the Lord" [Jer 17:7], I'll read it "Blessed am I when I trust in the Lord." As Kierkegaard wrote, it helps to remind me God is talking to me and talking about me, that His Word is specifically for me and to me. Perhaps you might try personalizing God's Words the next time you read.

Prayer:
Lord, quicken us to find time to read more in Your Word, to learn it, know it, and keep it, and to realize it is written to us and for us personally.

Scripture of the Day:
"Seek ye out of the book of the law and read." - [Isaiah 34:16].

The Word for the Day is "Difference."

Quote for the Day:
"Regardless of whatever I do, I know what my purpose is: to make a differnce in people's lives." - Tim Tebow

Recently I was thinking on what a difference Jesus has made in my life. I listened to the old Ronnie Milsap song "What A Difference You've Made In My Life" and was moved to tears remembering the Lord is 'my sunshine day and night.' Before Jesus I walked in the mold of this world and was so arrogant, thinking I walked with the in-crowd, so with-it and cool. But when Jesus came into my heart, I was different, and I knew it. I looked the same in the mirror, but my heart was different: I felt the presence and love of God and the peace of God that I had never known. I had a lot of garbage in my mind to clean up, but I knew I only wanted to follow and please Jesus from then on and saw daily what a difference He'd made in my life and ways.

God makes a difference in our lives, and we are then His instruments to make a difference in others' lives. We must have the revelation that we are still in the world, but not of this world [John 15:19]. A Christian is not the same as the world in his thinking or values. God has always put a difference between holy and un-holy, between clean and unclean, righteous and unrighteous, good and evil [Lev 10:10]. God's absolutes of truth are established forever. We are not the same as the world in behavior, turning away from the world's ways in seeking only to please the Lord by living uprightly before Him. Our motive, and goal, is to follow and please God above all by seeking His will and direction for our lives. "And be not transformed to this world: but be ye transformed by the renewing of your mind, that ye may prove what is that good, and acceptable, and perfect, will of God" [Rom 12:2].

We can make a difference in others' lives, too. Charles Stanley wrote: "When you become an instrument in God's hands, as He transfers someone from the realm of darkness into the Kingdom of His Son, you make a difference in the person's eternal destiny. Not only that, but satan also receives a devastating blow." How do you make a difference to someone in darkness? By turning on the Light of the gospel truth and helping them find their way to the Lord.

Prayer:
Lord, thank You for the difference You've made in our lives. Help us to share the Good News in Jesus that others might receive this blessed difference too.

Scripture of the Day:
"And of some have compassion, making a difference." - [Jude 22]

The Word for the Day is "Talent."

Quote for the Day:
"There is no such thing as a great talent without great will-power." – Honore de Balzac

A talent is a natural mental or physical aptitude or ability. All people have talents of different types. Psychologist Howard Gardner claims people possess multiple types of intelligence, abilities and creativity. Our gifts, unfortunately, are not all recognized and nourished in our homes, schools, or world. A beautiful realization to grasp is that God knows our gifts and sees them when no one else does. He formed them in us, formed us in our mother's womb endowed with potential, talents, and purpose. "Before I formed thee in the belly I knew thee: and before thou camest forth out of the womb I sanctified thee, and I ordained thee" [Jeremiah 1:5]. God is your designer, and the Word says "God saw every thing that He made and, behold, it was very good" [Genesis 1:31]. That includes you.

Because of satan in the world, it is guaranteed that stumbling blocks will be put in your path to keep you from meeting the potentials and purpose God laid in you. Also God works on a different timetable and via different methods than ours. "So are my ways higher than your ways, and my thoughts than your thoughts" [Isaiah 55:9]. There may be seasons in which we are developing character, knowledge, or life skills to ready us for a higher purpose.

The parable of the talents in the Bible, which could refer to money or personal abilities, shows us how God feels when we will not use and grow our talents. The master in the parable was angry with the servant who hid his talent away and didn't use it [Matt 25:14-30]. God wants us to use the talents and abilities He has given us wisely and well so He can multiply and increase them. It grieves God's heart when we do not value the gifts and abilities He has planted in us. He wants us to learn to use our talents, to prosper and succeed. Remember, you are God's unique handiwork, His creation, and 'His workmanship, created in Christ Jesus unto good works, which God hath ordained you should walk in' [Ephesians 2:10].

Prayer:
Father, help us to know the gifts and talents You have given to us and to use and develop them to Your glory.

Scripture of the Day:
"Unto one He gave five talents, to another two, and to another one; to every man according to his several ability." - [Matthew 25:15].

The Word for the Day is "Jealous."

Quote for the Day:
"God is jealous for your heart." - Pastor Kyle Idlem

Jealousy can be possessive and protective; it can be good or bad. Some of the more negative dictionary definitions of jealous are: 'feeling or showing suspicion of someone's unfaithfulness in a relationship, being unhappy and angry because someone has something that you want, or envying someone's achievement or advantages.' Pastor Randy Smith expressed bad jealousy this way: "Unrighteous jealousy is centered on self, rooted in pride and offensive to God. Jealousy is a warning light that you are not rejoicing in the success of others and loving those who have offended you. It's a warning light that you are not trusting in the providence of God for your own life. It's a warning light that there is too much self-worship and not enough Christ worship." I like this idea of a 'warning light' that the focus can be too much on self, instead of reliance, faith, and trust in the Lord's goodness, provision, and grace.

There is also a godly jealousy [2 Cor 11:2], and some of the definitons that fit this type are: 'very watchful or careful in guarding or keeping something; intolerant of rivals; vigilant, heedful, mindful, and protective of one's possessions.' Exodus 34:14 tells us that God is a jealous God. This is an expression of God's love and care for us in the best sense. When we come into salvation in Jesus, we die out to self and God lovingly possesses us as His own. And God is vigilant, and fierce in His desire to protect, guard, and keep us safe, secure, and blessed in Him. It is hard to comprehend our value to God, but C.S. Lewis expressed it this way: "It passes reason to explain why any creatures, not to say creatures such as we, should have a value so prodigious in their Creator's eyes."

If God is so jealous for our good, we also should be jealous for Him. We should exalt and worship Him above everyone and everything else in our lives, and be devoted to following His will and path for our lives. "The primary goal of our lives will be to show the world that our God is the one true and living God - that He alone makes life meaningful and worthwhile" [Richard Strauss].

Prayer:
Lord, thank You that we are so valued to You that You are jealous for us. We in turn, will guard and protect Your place in our lives above all else.

Scripture of the Day:
"For thou shalt worship no other god: for the Lord, whose name is Jealous, is a jealous God." - [Exodus 34:14]

The Word for the Day is "Righteousness."

Quote for the Day:
"Righteousness is a status achieved through divine intervention and human obedience." – Joel Dahlstrom

In a general sense righteousness is the quality of being morally upright, but in a more Biblical sense righteousness is a new estate we move into only by salvation through divine intervention. We cannot attain this estate on our own. We attain righteousness unto eternal life by Christ Jesus [Rom 5:21], and this state is not the "end" but only the "beginning" of a new life and walk. We come into God's righteousness and into His Kingdom as babes. Charles Fowler wrote, "You are born supernaturally through faith by the grace of God into the Kingdom of Righteousness; but…born a babe." He added that then you make progress from that point on with your own efforts combined with God's continuing help and grace.

We must individually pursue and follow after righteousness [Prov 21:21]. It doesn't come seeking after us. We must personally desire to come into more of God and more of His righteousness. That's why Jesus taught "seek, and ye shall find; knock, and it shall be opened unto you…and he that seeketh findeth; and to him that knocketh it shall be opened" [Matt 7:7-8]. As children, our parents saw to it that we were trained up in the way we should go [Prov 22:6] but God won't push us into spiritual growth. He wants us to yearn for it for ourselves, to zealously seek it [Jer 29:13; 2 Chron 15:2].

In our everyday lives, where we are in faith and righteousness is seen not only by God but by others who come to know us. We know from Jesus' counsel to the Pharisees that not all of what many people call righteousness is pleasing to God either [Matt 5:20]. "Little children, let no man deceive you; he that doeth righteousness is righteous…whosoever doeth not righteousness is not of God" [1 John 3:7, 10]. People sometimes talk a good talk but don't walk a good walk. What we should want is a genuine life of righteousness, not something errant or deceptive, like John Wesley wrote 'a soul that hungers and thirsts after righteousness,' yearning to grow more and more in the knowledge of God.

Prayer:
Lord, we are grateful for salvation but help us to yearn to grow more in faith and righteousness every day, always seeking more of You.

Scripture of the Day:
"Blessed are they which hunger and thirst after righteousness: for they shall be filled." - [Matthew 5:6]

The Word for the Day is "Stiffnecked."

Quote for the Day:
"I find the term 'a stiffnecked people' very interesting. I believe that it means this was a group who were narrowly focused, inflexible, and close-minded to the ways of God." - Dr. Keith Wagner

A stiffnecked person is one who is stubborn, intractable, not to be led, and haughty. We read in Exodus, Chapter 32, that the Israelites grew impatient when Moses tarried on the mount with God. They then fashioned a molten calf and worshipped it. God told Moses the people had quickly turned away from the way He had commanded them, and had become a stiffnecked people [Ex 32:1-9]. How could a people so quickly turn from God having seen the glorious works He had done: performing the miracles in Egypt, parting the Red Sea, bringing water from the rock, sending bread from heaven, and more? The Bible gives us some answers for why people are unable to turn from their old ways to serve God.

A stiffnecked person does not have his heart fully set on God. He does not fear the Lord, reverencing and esteeming Him above all. He does not serve the Lord by loving and fellowshipping God above all. He does not cleave unto the Lord by developing a close relationship with Him. And he does not make God his praise and delight above all else. "Thou shalt fear the Lord thy God; him shalt thou serve, and to him shalt thou cleave, and swear by his name. He is thy praise, and he is thy God, that hath done for thee these great and terrible things, which thine eyes have seen" [Deut 10:20-21].

We are not meant to be stubborn and stiff-necked, but to yield ourselves unto the Lord. A stiffnecked person continues to follow his own ways instead of first seeking God's will and direction for all his decisions. "Ye stiffnecked and uncircumcised in heart and ears, ye do always resist the Holy Ghost" [Acts 7:51]. The stiff-necked follow the old carnal ways instead of the Holy Spirit. The Spirit is sent to guide us into all truth [John 16:13], but we must be yielded to follow His leading. The flesh nature will war against and try to dissuade us from the Spirit's leading if we are not fully committed to follow Him [Gal 5:17]. A stiff neck hurts, but 'Happy is that people ...whose God is the Lord' [Psalm 144:15].

Prayer:
Lord, we will stay committed and yielded in all our ways to You, that Your Holy Spirit may always lead us into paths of righteousness for thy Name's sake.

Scripture of the Day:
"Now be ye not stiffnecked, as your fathers were, but yield yourselves unto the Lord." - [2 Chronicles 30:8]

NOVEMBER 11

Lin Stepp

The Word for the Day is "Created."

Quote for the Day:
"Thou hast created us for Thyself and our heart cannot be quieted 'til it may find repose in thee." – Saint Augustine

People spend a lot of time and money today paying for DNA tests and searching genealogical records to learn of their ancestry. There is a drawing and yearning within people to know about the people they have birthright to.

There is also a hunger and desire within each of us to find our spiritual Father and Creator. Jesus said He would 'draw all men unto Him' [John 12:32] and although God will not force us to find Him, He will seek and draw us. A piece and part of us knows He designed and made us, and we yearn for union with Him. We yearn to be united to Him, the One who made us. "For I have created him for my glory, I have formed him; yea I have made him" [Is 43:7]. God is our Father. He yearns for us to know Him and there is a restlessness and drawing in every soul also yearning to know Him.

We were not created randomly. We were created by design, for communion with God and for His pleasure. 'For we are His Workmanship created in Christ Jesus unto Good Works, which God hath before ordained that we should walk in them' [Eph 2:10]. Each of us were made in His Image and for His pleasure—and we come Home when we become His, when we are reborn in Christ Jesus. We are back to our rightful heritage, our rightful estate. And we are at rest and at peace. "Rest in the Lord" Psalm 37:7 tells us. And when we find Him, when we become His, our hearts can be quieted and at rest at last.

Prayer:
Thank you, Lord, that You created us in Your Image, for Your pleasure and to walk after You in goodness and righteousness, love, and joy. We give you praise for this gracious privilege and for this blessed heritage.

Scripture of the Day:
"Thou art worthy, O Lord, to receive glory and honour and power: for thou hast created all things, and for thy pleasure they are and were created." -
[Revelation 4:11]

The Word for the Day is "Able."

Quote for the Day:
"There is no place nor time where He is not able and willing to walk by our side, to work through our hands and brains, and to unite Himself in loving and all-sufficient partnership with all our needs and tasks and trials, and to prove our all-sufficiency for all things." - A.B. Simpson

We often look at ourselves in the natural and are prone to think that we are not able, capable, competent, or skilled enough to accomplish much. We look at others who have achieved and think 'I could never do that.' But as a Christian we should be comforted to know that God is not limited by our natural abilities, for He will enable us to perform the things He wants us to do.

This wonderful fact is illustrated by the story found in Exodus 35:30-35 when the children of Israel came together to build God's tabernacle in the wilderness. They had been slaves in Egypt, not exactly a skilled, competent, educated, or wealthy group. But 'as many as were willing hearted' [Ex 35:22] came together to build God's glorious tabernacle. Because they were willing, not regarding their natural estate as former slaves, 'the Lord put wisdom and understanding' in them to know how to accomplish all manner of work for the sanctuary [Ex 36:1]. The tabernacle was built according to God's specific plans not by super-architects, but by the common people who were willing to follow God and let Him give them the wisdom and ability to accomplish the work.

God doesn't just make this grace possible for the work of ministers in the pulpits on Sunday, but also for all of us for the common, everyday works and tasks of Monday to Saturday. God wants to enable us to be blessed in 'the factory, the workshop, the business office, the school-room, and even for the kitchen' (A.B. Simpson). "And he said unto me, My grace is sufficient for thee: for my strength is made perfect in weakness" [2 Cor 12:9]. God is able to "do exceeding abundantly above all that we ask or think, according to the power that worketh in us" [Ephesians 3:20], so that we might accomplish much and glorify Him in the common tasks of life, and in Jesus be the shining Light of Life to the world.

Prayer:
Lord, we take the limits off our thinking, and the limits off Your grace, knowing that we can do all things through Christ which strengtheneth us [Phil 4:13].

Scripture of the Day:
"And God is able to make all grace abound toward you; that ye, always having all sufficiency in all things, may abound to every good work:" - [2 Corinthians 9:8]

The Word for the Day is "Knock."

Quote for the Day:
"Jesus says: 'Look! I stand at the door and knock. If you hear my voice and open the door, I will come in'." – Tim F. LaHaye

When the children were still at home and life more hectic day to day, a common call of mine was: *Would somebody please get the door?* There was always somebody knocking—someone selling something or soliciting a service, children wanting mine to come out to play, or a delivery. It seemed as if there was always someone knocking on the door wanting something. Life is busy in a different way now. The demands are more emails and texts to answer, work to complete, errands to run, writing to finish. But still ongoing demands and interruptions.

It's little wonder that when God knocks, wanting a little more of our time, we're often too quick to put off that knock. It's almost as if we say to his requests and knocks: *Would somebody else please get the door?* Or *"I'll be there in a minute!"* Then, of course, we immediately feel guilty for putting God off, for not stopping everything to answer and open the door of our time to Him. God's knock is always given at the right time, though, and God's knock will always bring us something precious, wondrous, and unexpected if we will stop and open the door [Luke 14:16-24]. I always smiled over the story in Acts when Peter came to the door where his disciples gathered praying for his release. He knocked to come in but when Rhoda came to tell them he stood outside, they thought her crazy. He had to keep knocking before they would let him in [Acts 12:12-16]. Their answered prayer was at the door but they didn't want to answer the knock.

God wants us to open the door to Him when He knocks, to take time in our busy lives to allow Him in. He wants to fellowship us, be a friend and help to us, guide our life and way [Deut 4:36; Psalm 32:8] but He can only do that if we are willing to take the time to answer His knock, to let Him in to the busyness of our lives.

Prayer:
Lord, too often we don't answer Your knock when we should. Help us to know that whenever we do, we will always be immeasurably blessed.

Scripture of the Day:
"Behold, I stand at the door, and knock; If any man hear my voice, and open the door, I will come in to him, and sup with him, and he with me." -
[Revelation 3:20]

The Word for the Day is "Alive."

Quote for the Day:
"Man is spiritually dead and does not originate in himself a movement toward God and spiritual life. It's supernatural, and it is a work of divine power. Spiritual renewal accordingly is a divine miracle in which that which was dead is now alive."
- John F. Walvoord

Are we being fully alive or just existing? Some people seem to fit the quote by e.e. Cummings: "Unbeing dead isn't being alive." We've all met people that fit this mode of existence, seemingly having no zeal for life, no aspirations, no works, no goals, no deep interests: 'just gettin' by.' Others have purpose, joy, service, and an enthusiastic mission or aspiration for their own life, and desire to benefit others as well. But we are truly only spiritually alive in Christ Jesus: "For as in Adam all die, even so in Christ shall all be made alive" [1 Cor 15:22].

Alive means not only the opposite of dead but fully alive, fully aware, vibrant and expectant, living each day to the fullest with joy. In the Lord, we don't live in boredom and despair anymore. God yearns for us to be fully alive, our being lit up from the inside out. Jesus said 'I have come to bring life and to bring life in all its fullness' [John 10:10]. In the Lord we can walk into this fullness, this new-ness, where energy and power flow into us and out of us. When we are fully in the Lord, we show the world what life is like in Him—and what a difference God makes. As Irenaeus of Lyon, a second century church father, wrote: "The glory of God is a human being fully alive."

Being fully alive in the Lord we can relish all aspects of living. We can enjoy and appreciate the simple and natural things of life—the beauty of a sunset, the sound of birds singing, the delight in a child's laughter. We can also enjoy the challenge and accomplishment of higher callings and achievements of living. We can dare to dream, to plan, and to do any purpose in the Lord, for 'we can do all things through Christ Who strengthens us' [Phil 4:13]. So celebrate living fully in the di-vine nature [2 Pet 1:4] and enjoying all the kingdom benefits in the Lord [Psalm 103:1-5] that sound too good to be true—but in Jesus are always "Yes!"

Prayer:
Lord, we thank You for the divine miracle of making us alive to You through the salvation of our Lord Jesus Christ. We will live this new life devoted to Jesus and devoted to sharing the gospel that others may be made alive in Christ.

Scripture of the Day:
"Likewise reckon ye also yourselves to be dead indeed unto sin, but alive unto God through Jesus Christ our Lord." - [Romans 6:11]

The Word for the Day is "Well."

Quote for the Day:
"All shall be well and all shall be well and all manner of things shall be well." –
Julian of Norwich

The presence of God is the living water we all need to be healthy in our souls, just as we need water in life to live. God and Jesus speak of themselves often as the well of life…that 'with joy we can draw water out of the wells of salvation' [Is 12:3], that 'if we ask, God will give us living water to drink' [John 4:10], that 'if we are thirsty and seek, God will pour His spirit and blessing upon us' [Is 44:3].

Life will go well for us, too, when we walk in the Lord and walk rightly in His ways. God said to Jesus He was well-pleased with Him as His beloved son [Matthew 3:17], and many scriptures affirm God is pleased with us, too, when we follow rightly in His ways. When 'we are faithful over little, God will move us to be faithful over more' [Matt 25:23], if 'we don't weary in well-doing, we will reap in due season' [Galatians 6:9]. If 'we walk in righteousness and do well, we will eat the fruit of our doings' [Is 3:10]. When we do well and walk rightly, God is well-pleased [Heb 13:16].

I love the sweet concept of faith, too, that if we are well in Him, do well in Him, and live well in Him, that it will be well with our souls. We cannot out give God, and all that we do to live well for Him comes back to us in a rich joy and well-being—a peace, a comfort, a sense of rightness. How sweet it is to know that we are His, in the palm of His Hand, safe and secure in His Love and to know He is with us wherever we go [Ps 91:4; Is 49:16]. Never be weary in living for God, in seeking more of Him, for the rich blessing of His Presence within will always be more than enough in return. Fix your eyes on what is eternal. Be at peace and be joyful always when it is well with your soul [2 Cor 4:18].

Prayer:
Father, we all seek peace in our souls but often forget that to attain it, we need to draw closer and closer to You, living the righteous life you designed for our happiness and well-being.

Scripture of the Day:
"Say ye to the righteous, that it shall be well with him: for they shall eat the fruit of their doings." - [Isaiah 3:10]

The Word for the Day is "Poor."

Quote for the Day:
"What does love look like? It has the hands to help others. It has the feet to hasten to the poor and needy. It has eyes to see misery and want. It has ears to hear the sighs and sorrows of men. That is what love looks like." - Augustine

Do you want to be blessed upon the earth? Then consider the poor [Ps 41:1]. We will always have abundant opportunities to minister this grace and kindness because we will always have the poor with us [Matt 26:11]. The term poor is usually associated with the condition of poverty and need: for material things, money, help and assistance, or bodily handicaps. In this fallen world, satan seeks to steal, kill, and destroy any way he can through circumstances both natural and man-made. Some are rendered poor through circumstances and need help. God instructs us to open our hand wide, generously, to the poor and needy [Deut 15:11]. Giving out of a loving, compassionate heart is blessed of God [Luke 6:38]. But men can often cause their own poverty and need kind reproof, wisdom, counsel, and intruction most. "He becometh poor that dealeth with a slack hand" [Prov 10:4], and a person that won't work or help themselves needs repentance more than charity. The poor can be negligent and lack judgment in their affairs causing poverty [Prov 12:23]. The righteous give material goods and godly counsel to help the poor out of both natural and self-inflicted hurts.

A poverty worse than natural want is to be poor and lacking in spirit. A rich man can have abundance yet be poor and foolish in spirit because he knows not the way of the Lord [Jer 5:4]. One can boast of possessions and say they need nothing, but in God's eyes they are poor and wretched [Rev 3:17]. This type of poverty needs the truth of God's Word to remedy a poverty of Spirit. The righteous must give the truth of God's love and salvation in Jesus Christ to deliver out of this worst kind of poor condition void of God's life inside.

In Christ Jesus we are redeemed from the curse of poverty: "For ye know the grace of our Lord Jesus Christ, that, though he was rich, yet for your sakes he became poor, that ye through his poverty might be rich" [2 Cor 8:9]. Share your love and help and share the good news of salvation in Jesus Christ with the poor.

Prayer:
Lord, we will open our hand to the poor, and we will open our heart and mouth to share the redemption and abundance of life that is in Christ Jesus our Lord.

Scripture of the Day:
"Blessed is he that considereth the poor: the Lord will deliver him in time of trouble." - [Psalm 41:1]

The Word for the Day is "Fixed."

Quote for the Day:
"He who is fixed to a star does not change his mind." – Leonardo da Vinci

Often when out driving in the car or when working around the house I'll tune in to a favorite radio station. Even as I travel or do housework, I'm tuned in mentally to that station and when a song comes on I especially love, I listen more closely to the words or I might even sing along. Although the radio is in the background of my primary activity, its song or message can quickly be brought to the foreground. It's as though my mental "antenna" is up, staying tuned in or fixed to the station even when working or traveling.

We should be tuned in to the Lord, to His Spirit, like this, fixed and stayed in Him, always ready to hear and to listen to Him. Staying tuned in to God keeps us on the right track, warns us of danger, directs us with all our tasks, and helps us stay in safety and righteousness in our hour-by-hour walk [Heb 12:2]. When you balance your checkbook, you are enabled to do so quickly because you learned and memorized the needed addition, subtraction, and multiplication facts in school. To hear rightly from God you need to have learned and hidden in your heart God's Word [Ps 119:11] and you need to know God's Voice well enough from dedicated time in Him that you recognize it like sheep would their shepherd's voice [John 10:3-4].

Jerry Bridges wrote: "God's Word must be so strongly fixed in our minds that it becomes the dominant influence in our thoughts, our attitudes, and our actions." When our lives are fixed on God and on Jesus, when we hear the check and guidance of the Holy Spirit, life goes well for us. We are then victors rather than victims in our daily lives. We are not afraid of evil tidings when our heart is fixed [Psalm 112:7]. We walk in calm, in surety, and in peace when our hearts and minds are stayed in God [Is 26:3]. We hear from God and get the direction we need when we remain established and dependent upon Him [Is 30:21; John 10:27, 16:13]. We need to stay ever fixed to the true star and to stay clearly tuned to Channel W-GOD every day.

Prayer:
Lord, help us to keep our antenna tuned in to You every day, purposed to hear Your Voice and Direction to guide us in every aspect of our lives.

Scripture of the Day:
"He shall not be afraid of evil tidings: his heart is fixed, trusting in the Lord." – [Psalm 112:7]

The Word for the Day is "Exercise."

Quote for the Day:
"The spirit, like the body, can be strengthened and developed by frequent exercise. Just as the body, if neglected, grows weaker and finally impotent, so the spirit perishes if untended." - Wassily Kandinsky

After a strenuous two hours of leaf raking today in my yard, I was glad to put up the tools and come inside to sit for awhile. I was very tired, but I felt good to have exercised my body knowing that physical activity benefits the body's muscles, organs, and even the brain (who wouldn't welcome help there!). We know we are to take care of our bodies to glorify God [1 Corinthians 6:20], but God places a greater priority upon exercising ourselves unto godliness, for this is more profitable unto all things, both in this life, and that which is to come [1 Timothy 4:7-8]. We are to exercise care for our natural body, but we are to exercise deliberate effort in developing our spiritual man.

Taking the effort to know God's Word is the essential requirement of our growth of the inner, spiritual man. Our natural man progresses from a baby state to adult state as we grow. The Word tells us that we grow from babes, ignorant and unskillful in the word of righteousness to one of full age as we progress from milk, as a babe, to strong meat as our spiritual man matures. The full aged spirtual man by reason of use has his senses exercised to discern both good and evil [Hebrews 5:11-14]. This discernment of good and evil is essential in growth of godliness and the Bible says: "Thy word have I hid in my heart, that I might not sin against thee" [Psalm 119:11].

We can be sure to exercise aright our spiritual man if we exercise the same as God does. "But let him that glorieth glory in this, that he understandeth and knoweth me, that I am the Lord which exercise lovingkindness, judgment, and righteousness, in the earth: for in these things I delight, saith the Lord" [Jeremiah 9:24]. So if we exercise lovingkindness, judgment, and righteousness, we show God's love to this world and delight the Lord.

Prayer:
Lord, help us to keep our natural body strong to glorify You, and help us to apply ourselves to exercise godliness in greater measure that we may grow into the fullness of our Lord Jesus.

Scripture of the Day:
"And herein do I exercise myself, to have always a conscience void of offence toward God, and toward men." - [Acts 24:16].

The Word for the Day is "We."

Quote for the Day:
"We are the Bibles the world is reading; we are the creeds the world is needing; we are the sermons the world is heeding." – Billy Graham

Like it or not "we" are examples every day to those around us—to our children and our families, to our coworkers, to our neighbors, to our friends, to the people in our churches and organizations. Whether we know it or not, believe it or not, we may be the only Christians some people ever meet, and when we say we are Christians, then all of Christianity is partly judged and evaluated by how we represent and present it. That's why the Bible teaches that 'we are all ambassadors for Christ' [2 Cor 5:20]. It's an important leadership role.

Role models are important in every stage of life. A role model is one who influences others by serving as an example. From the beginning of our lives we learn through observation and imitation. Countless studies show the impact of a parent's example, actions, and teaching on a child's life. Children constantly watch, listen, and model the behavior they see. But all through life we continue learning from example. Others around us and the people whose lives we touch learn from the example of our Christian walk. That's why Paul, as a mentor, stressed to Timothy the importance of being an example in love, faith and purity that others would want to emulate [I Tim 4:12], and he urged Titus to live in a sensible, righteous, and godly way [Titus 2:12-13]. If you think your example doesn't matter much, think again.

The most powerful leadership tool you have is your example. You can't really expect others to rise above the example you set, either. Madeleine Barat, a devout nun, wrote: "Your example, even more than your words, will be an eloquent lesson to the world." We are meant to live godly in this world, to not be conformed to the world but to the ways and mind of God, to show the love of God in our lives, and to be a visible light in an often dark world [Titus 2:11-12; Rom 12:2; John 13:34-35; Matt 5:14-16]. Your life and your example are a story for all to see. Give others something to be inspired by.

Prayer:
Father, help us to realize more fully that we are the role models for Christianity in the world and to keep in mind that people will not listen to our advice and ignore our example.

Scripture of the Day:
"For we are His workmanship, created in Christ Jesus unto good works, which God hath before ordained that we should walk in them." – [Ephesians 2:10]

The Word for the Day is "Steadfast."

Quote for the Day:
"Whatever happens, abide steadfast in a determination to cling simply to God." -
Saint Francis de Sales

The KJV spelling of the word of the day is 'stedfast,' but in modern English is spelled 'steadfast,' which means resolutely or dutifully firm and unwavering, loyal, faithful, committed, devoted, or dedicated. I like the idea of 'steady and strong,' which is how every believer should be in the Lord. But the enemy is always trying to get us to waver in our trust and reliance in God and, unfortunately, many times succeeds. The Word gives us counsel as to his evil devices and traps to ensnare and cause one to waver from following God wholly.

A heart that is not right with God, not loyal to His covenant, will cause us to waver [Psalm 78:37]. This is being double-minded, trying to follow the worldly ways and please God too. You cannot serve mammon and be steadfast in God at the same time [Matt 6:24]. A stubborn and rebellious spirit that refuses to accept God's absolutes of truth will sabotage devoted commitment to the Lord [Psalm 78:8]. A hardened heart is akin to rebellion and resists the way of righteousness [Heb 3:15]. Following the unlearned and unstable who wrest the scriptures to justify their own error and ways is compromise to God's truths [2 Pet 3:16-17]. Each must steadfastly resist the devil remembering that "greater is He that is in you, than he that is in the world" [1John 4:4].

God is steadfast forever [Dan 6:26], and our being steadfast in Him has benefits for us and others. When we are steadfast in the work of the Lord, living and sharing his truth to the world, God rewards us and our 'labor is not in vain' [1 Cor 15:58]. In this world we will have tribulations [John 16:33], but our steadfast hope is that despite sufferings, we also partake of the consolation [2 Cor 1:7]. Steadfast hope in God also acts as an anchor to our souls, keeping us strong and steady amidst the storms of life [Heb 6:19]. Steadfast confidence makes us partakers of Christ: 'because as he is, so are we in this world' [1 John 4:17].

Prayer:
Lord, we purpose to keep a steadfast and upright heart before You, that we might witness Jesus to the world and bring joy to our fellow brethren [Col 2:5].

Scripture of the Day:
"For we are made partakers of Christ, if we hold the beginning of our confidence stedfast unto the end." - [Hebrews 3:14].

The Word for the Day is "Battle."

Quote for the Day:
"Whether or not you are aware of it, a war is raging all around you, and the battle is for your mind." –Joel Osteen

As a child I remember being read the great battle stories in the Bible—how Joshua fought the battle of Jericho—and hearing and reading of many other great battles in which God enabled His People to triumph over their enemies. World and American history is full of accounts, too, of wars and battles, how good victored over evil, and sometimes, sadly, how a despotic regime triumphed over good instead.

We may not have personally experienced wars or battles, but whether we realize it or not we are in a daily warfare and battle. That battle is for our souls and the battleground begins in our minds. In the classic book *The Screwtape Letters*, the senior devil advises his apprentice that the way to gain a man's soul is to "keep knowledge out of his mind." As this book depicts so well, we are constantly wrestling with a spiritual enemy interested only in hurting and destroying us, yet our daily temptation is to overlook this. Too often we get our focus, our mind, on problems with people or happenings, not seeing the real enemy whose intent is behind the problems we face. "We wrestle not against flesh and blood, but against principalities, against powers, against the rulers of the darkness of this world, against spiritual wickedness in high places" [Eph 6:12]. Our daily battle is spiritual.

Jesus wisely stressed the importance of loving the Lord not only with all our heart, soul, and strength but with all our mind [Mark 12:30]. Yet, often we are careless about guarding our mind and thought, not seeing it as important. We let down our hedges, allow gaps to form in our defenses, and let the enemy creep in with delight [Ezek 13:5; Prov 4:23]. Our goal as good soldiers in the Lord is to let God's mind and will reign in us, to have the mind of God and of Jesus dominant is us [1 Cor 2:16; Phil 2:5-11]. We need to daily battle to keep our minds 'stayed on Him' [Is 26:3]. If we battle with a full and wise heart, we can also be assured that God will battle as strongly on our side.

Prayer:
Father, help us to know that our minds shape everything we do, as well as all we perceive, and to train and guard our minds with all diligence.

Scripture of the Day:
"For thou has girded me with strength for the battle: thou has subdued under me those that rose up against me." – [Psalm 18:39]

The Word for the Day is "But."

Quote for the Day:
"Doubt isn't simply unbelief—it's more of an attitude that says, 'I believe but'....or 'I want to believe, but'....! Doubt is active opposition to faith, and it tries to push faith aside." - Joyce Meyers

Have you ever heard someone say: "I know the Bible says that, but ...."? You know when you hear the conjunction "but," you are next going to hear something contrasting with what has already been mentioned. Whenever you hear "but" it is usually a statement of doubt, trying to push faith in the Bible aside. If you are new in the faith or walk with God, you may likely repeat this word "but" also. Why does this happen? You have to realize the carnal mind has been trained to think according to "reasonable, sensible, common sense" logic, and the Word of God may sound too good to be true. The mind has been programmed to reject as fantasy such thoughts as "God shall supply all your need according to his riches in glory by Christ Jesus" [Phil 4:19]. The carnal mind argues 'The Bible says that, but that can't be true, that's just wishful thinking.' The believer must have the revelation that the Bible is the inspired Word of God, that it is established forever, that it will never pass away [2 Tim 3:16; Psalm 119:89; Matt 24:35]. The Word may sound too good to be true, but it is true forever!

Another truth that causes some to stumble and say "The Bible says that, but ...", is the fact that God's Word is very clear in establishing absolutes of truth. The carnal, unrenewed thinking has often been programmed by the philosophy of relativism that there are no absolutes, and that everyone has the right to decide for themselves what is right or wrong. We are supposed to be 'tolerant,' 'non-judgmental,' 'open' to different values. But again, God's absolutes of truth are established forever, and cannot be voided by popular or societal opinion. It is only the truth of God's Word that can set men free from spiritual darkness with it's hurt and destruction [John 8:32]. Commit yourself to God's Word and renewing the mind to Truth. God gives us a great help and advantage in this quest by giving us the Holy Spirit who "will guide you into all truth" [John 16:13].

Prayer:
Lord, we purpose not to live by our own understanding, but by every Word of God. If God said it, there are no ifs, ands or buts. His Word is settled in our hearts.

Scripture of the Day:
"And such were some of you: but ye are washed, but ye are sanctified, but ye are justified in the name of the Lord Jesus, and by the Spirit of our God." -
[1 Corinthians 6:11]

The Word for the Day is "Persons."

Quote for the Day:
"A person's a person no matter how small." – Dr. Seuss

How a person treats others shows the level of their walk and relationship with God. Miguel Ruiz counseled that "respect is one of the greatest expressions of love" and Johann Goethe wrote: "You can easily judge the character of a man by how he treats those who can do nothing for him." In our hearts most of us know that Jesus counseled and taught that 'what we wanted others to do toward us, we should do toward them' [Matt 7:12]. We all want to be treated with dignity, respect, and kindness and we should treat others in the same way.

Christians often decide the way to show love and respect for others, especially those less fortunate, is by writing a check to charity, serving at a soup kitchen, or giving of time or money to mission works at church. These kindnesses are good, but I think our love for others should show daily in all the many small actions and ways we don't examine often enough. How do you act toward others every day at home, work, shopping, or out to dinner? Do you show more respect for those with more position, more wealth, more lavish clothes or possessions? The heart of God, when alive and well in us, doesn't look first on the outer man to judge worth. Do you seek out in friendship those who have more than you or those whose relationship can most benefit you? Or do you look, like God, first at the heart? [I Sam 16:7]

The true nature of God is to look on the potential of a person. We're advised in the Bible to 'esteem each other highly in love, to encourage one another and build one another up' [1 Thess 5:11-13]. In working with the young in age, in knowledge, or in faith, remember always that you once walked there. Encourage all to their best selves. I love this quote by Carl Rogers to close: "The degree to which I can create relationships, which facilitate the growth of others as separate persons, is a measure of the growth I have achieved in myself." Show no respect for any person except to help them to their best self and to help them be the person God yearns for them to be.

Prayer:
Lord, help us to be respectful of all, to encourage growth in others, and to not show erroneous respect unduly based on outward circumstances and worldly attainments.

Scripture of the Day:
"It is not good to have respect of persons in judgment." – [Proverbs 24:23]

The Word for the Day is "Thanksgiving."

Quote for the Day:
"People who intentionally count their blesssings, express their thanks, and cultivate the quality of finding thanksgiving items in every circumstance - those are the people who live on Gratitude Street." - Dr. David Jeremiah

The Thanksgiving Holiday is a time we look forward to each year, spending time with family and loved ones, enjoying the special dinner, good times, and giving thanks to God for His Goodness. Thanking God has special benefits. The Word encourages us to glorify God by telling of His wonderous works [Ps 26:7], to pay our vows to God [Ps 50:14], to magnify the Lord [Ps 69:30], to praise and bless His name [Ps 100:4], to declare His works with rejoicing [Ps 107:22], and to call upon His name [Ps 116:17]. We are exhorted to give thanks always for all things unto God [Eph 5:20].

It is easy to give thanksgiving when things are going good, but we must also offer thanksgiving when times are difficult. The Word tells us to: "Be careful for nothing; but in every thing by prayer and supplication with thanksgiving let your requests be made known unto God" [Phil 4:6]. We see then that prayer and thanksgiving are integral: "Continue in prayer, and watch in the same with thanksgiving" [Col 4:2]. Thanksgiving is an essential element in living 'rooted and built up in Him, and established in the faith' [Col 2:7].

We give thanksgiving to God not because of present circumstances, but because of our relationship to Him, knowing the victory He faithfully gives us through Jesus. "But thanks be to God, which giveth us the victory through our Lord Jesus Christ" [1 Cor 15:57]. "Now thanks be unto God, which always causeth us to triumph in Christ, and maketh manifest the savour of his knowledge by us in every place" [2 Cor 2:14]. By Jesus "let us offer the sacrifice of praise to God continually, that is, the fruit of our lips giving thanks to his name" [Heb 13:15]. God wants us to live on 'Gratitude Street' every day and enjoy His blessings.

Prayer:
Lord, You give us so much to be thankful for, and we come to You with thanksgiving and with praises for all Your wondrous works.

Scripture of the Day:
"Enter into his gates with thanksgiving, and into his courts with praise: be thankful unto him and bless his name." -[Psalm 100:4]

The Word for the Day is "Example."

Quote for the Day:
"A good example is far better than a good precept." – D.L. Moody

My mother often taught us in proverbs and one I remember hearing often was: "Actions speak louder than words." It's true. When our example is wishy-washy and when we constantly change our stance on important beliefs or issues we are shown up to be weak and unstable. "Do as I say but, please, not as I do" doesn't cut it in the Christian walk.

From the time we're small, we are all looking for those we can look up to and follow, people who can serve as patterns we can emulate—and not just in our Christian walk. I remember when wanting to become an author that I visited several writers' groups around town. The words of advice and counsel sounded so good at first but over time I saw that the members did little writing, that few had completed any books or ever been published. My enthusiasm for the group waned. As H. B. Peterson wrote, "If our words are not consistent with our actions, they will never be heard above the thunder of our deeds." Followers need a model or example to benchmark against—a strong and inspirational standard for them to follow.

Your Christian life should be one that others will want to follow and not run from for its hypocrisy and insincerity [Phil 3:17; John 13:15]. We're supposed to be changed and transformed, different, and not like the world anymore [2 Cor 5:17; Rom 12:2]. In our words and conversation, in the way we love and care, in our behavior and actions, in our continuing growth in faith, we are to exemplify what we say we believe [2 Tim 2:21-26; Eph 5:1-5].

Being a good example is a powerful thing and the righteous example you live can turn you into an instrument of God. As John Maxwell wrote: "A leader is one who knows the way, goes the way, and shows the way."

Prayer:
Lord, help us to realize that when we talk, teach, or advise a righteous course of action, while our lives are to the contrary, that our words have little effect.

Scripture of the Day:
"But be thou an example of the believers, in word, in conversation, in charity, in spirit, in faith, in purity." – [1 Timothy 4:12]

The Word for the Day is "Believe."

Quote for the Day:
"Not long ago I heard a man who was asked what he believed. He said he believed what his church believed. 'What does your church believe?' 'The church believes what I believe.' And that was all they could get out of him." - Dwight L. Moody

Lin and I often travel to craft shows, book signings, and events where we have been invited to come as a vendor to market our books. It is always good to have Lin's readers come by to get a new title, and it's always an opportunity to add new readers, too. Often, a new reader will ask Lin what she writes. Lin will reply: "I write contemporary Southern fiction with a little romance, a dash of suspense to keep you guessing, and a touch of inspiration." Lin can give this brief, concise answer because she knows what's in her book. I see a parallel to the quote above with this example. People who can readily share their belief with you do so because they know what's in The Book. Some, like the man in the quote, can only say "Well, you know I'm a ....," naming the denomination or church they attend. They seem to abide under a broad umbrella of tenets, but no specifics.

God wants us to be strong in our believing and faith, both for our benefits and for others sake, too, by knowing what's in The Book, the Bible. We appropriate and receive all the benefits and blessings of Kingdom living through strong and sure belief and faith. We must realize this is a work of the heart in seeking God and His truth above all [Rom 10:10,17]. God is a rewarder of those that diligently seek Him [Heb 11:6], and He will show the exceeding greatness of His power to us who believe [Eph 1:19]. What a blessing to be a partaker of the divine nature by believing all His precious promises and to know *all* things are possible to those who believe [2 Peter 1:4; Mark 9:23]!

When Jesus returned to the Father, he left His believers to continue His work on earth. Believers are now to show His love, mercy, grace, and power to those in darkness that they might come into His kingdom [John 14:12]. Dare to believe—that you might be the vessel the Lord uses to touch someone and translate them out of darkness into His Marvelous Light!

Prayer:
Lord, our heart will be rooted and grounded in belief of Thy truth, and we will bear witness of the Light that other men might believe on the Lord Jesus.

Scripture of the Day:
"But without faith it is impossible to please him: for he that cometh to God must believe that he is, and that he is a rewarder of them that diligently seek him."
-[Hebrews 11:6]

The Word for the Day is "Heed."

Quote for the Day:
"Take heed lest you stumble." – Horace

One of the subtle dangers in the Christian walk is growing careless and apathetic and drifting away from a genuine closeness with God. The pull or "drift" is often not readily felt. Playing in the ocean waves, it is easy to suddenly look around and realize you have drifted too far away from shore and into danger. Many are drowned because of this. In a canoe or boat, drifting down river on a warm, sunny day, it is easy to get caught up in the enjoyment of the moment before realizing your craft is caught in the pull of the current with the sound of a waterfall ahead. "Drifting off course is one of those great evil influences which affects the believer as much as the unbeliever…no warning bell is ever sounded; we drift away softly and silently" [anon].

In Christian circles, teaching often focuses on salvation and growth in God while failing to focus on the subtle ways in which the walk with God can grow dim. No one purposely means to slip away from God, to drift from closeness to Him, but it happens to us all from time to time. We get busy, we fall into bad company and wrong influences, we pray less, study the Word less, forget the fervency in which we once walked. Jesus warned, "Take heed therefore that the light which is in thee be not darkness" [Luke 11:35].

Innumerable times in the Bible scriptures warn to "Take Heed." "Wherefore let him that thinketh he standeth, take heed lest he fall" [1 Cor 10:12]. The influences warned about that can cause one to drift, stumble, and gradually fall away from God are many, including unrighteous influences [Mark 8:15], deception [Matt 24:4], greed and covetousness [Luke 12:15], leaning to one's own understanding and ways [Prov 3:5-6], and growing careless in words [Ps 39:1]. Remember the enemy is watching every minute to see God's people grow careless so he can move in [1 Pet 5:8]. Drifting is a sin…and one "that will take you further than you want to go, keep you longer than you want to stay, and cost you more than you want to pay" [unknown]. So be watchful. "The mark of the true child of God is that he does not drift for long" [John Piper].

Prayer:
Lord, let us check our hearts and lives, and take heed that we don't slip in our faith or drift into danger and harm, but stay always anchored and close to You.

Scripture of the Day:
"Take heed to thyself, and keep thy soul diligently, lest thou forget the things which thine eyes have seen, and lest they depart from thy heart." - [Deut 4:9]

The Word for the Day is "Confession."

Quote for the Day:
"Your success and usefulness in the world is going to be measured by your confess-tion and by the tenacity with which you 'hold fast' that confesssion under all cir-cumstances." - F.F. Bosworth

We know, in a legal definition, that to make confession is to admit, declare, or acknowledge something in words, usually a confession of guilt for a misdeed or crime. To admit or declare something hidden is also an example of confession, like in a novel or story where a person confesses their unfaithfulness to a partner or spouse. A spiritual confession is more a declaration of solid belief and relation-ship with God, or an admittance of sins and faults to be forgiven by the Lord.

The Bible definition of confess is to acknowledge a specific belief as one's own and to publicly own it. To accept and declare Jesus as our own Savior and Lord is a vital element in salvation. "That if thou shalt confess with thy mouth the Lord Jesus, and shalt believe in thine heart that God hath raised Him from the dead, thou shalt be saved. For with the heart man believeth unto righteousness; and with the mouth confession is made unto salvation" [Romans 10:9-10]. What a blessing to know that as we confess Jesus as our own, He confesses us as His own to the Father in heaven [Matt 10:32].

F.F. Bosworth stated that we must "hold fast" our confession at all times. We must hold our confession of faith with tenacity under all circumstances, whether good or evil. The devil will always attempt to steal the Word in our heart. The enemy will try to use contrary worldly opinion and persuasion to deceive and dissuade us. He will use trials and troubles to attempt to discourage us. He will even try to use prosperity to divert our attention away from the Lord. But Jesus ever makes intercession for the elect, and in all these things 'we are more than conquerors through Him that loved us' [Rom 8:31-37]. And if we stumble due to sin, we con-fess our sin and receive forgiveness [1 John 1:9]. "Blessed is he whose transgres-sion is forgiven, whose sin is covered" [Ps 32:1]. So hold fast your confession, for "Whosoever shall confess that Jesus is the Son of God, God dwelleth in him, and he in God" [1 John 4:15].

Prayer:
Lord, we will declare and profess Jesus as our Lord and Savior and hold fast our confession of faith at all times, in all circumstances, to all people. Amen.

Scripture of the Day:
"For with the heart man believeth unto righteousness; and with the mouth con-fession is made unto salvation."   - [Romans 10:10]

The Word for the Day is "Oaks."

Quote for the Day:
"God sees his children like acorns—born small and fragile, and one among many. But when we're planted, fed, given light and allowed to grow, we're capable of transforming into mighty oak trees." – Jennifer Preyss

An old proverb says: "From little acorns mighty oaks grow." An oak tree produces a huge crop of acorns but not all will become an oak tree. God's heart plan, though, is for you to grow into a mighty oak of righteousness. Think of an oak tree for a minute—solid, strong, stable, fixed in place, not vacillating or changed by day to day situations, by weather or storms, drawing much of its strength from an unseen source, through roots reaching deep into the ground. This is what our hearts should yearn for as God's children, to become strong and admirable in the Lord. John Hames wrote that 'a tree is a great instructor, showing us what can be accomplished through time, perseverance and patience.' In a humorous sense an oak tree is simply an acorn that never gave up.

I love the scripture in the Bible that says 'the trees of the field know God' [Ezek 17:24]. Shouldn't we equally yearn to know God and to want to grow up to become all we can be in Him? That's what He wants, too. Like the oak, He wants us to be planted in a good place in fertile soil by abundant waters [Ezek 17:5}, ever increasing in faith and strength 'so our leaf doesn't wither and all we do prospers' [Psalm 1:1-3]. It is never God's design for us to stay an acorn. He wants us ever growing, vibrant in our faith, healthy with ever deepening roots, and bearing much fruit [Matt 7:18; Is 11:1]. Just as an oak is easily identifiable for what it is, God wants us easily identifiable as His, too. His heart yearns to raise us up to be all we can be, to make our low tree grow high, to preserve and lift us up even when the enemy tries to hurt us, attack us, or cut us down [Ezek 17:24; Job 14:7; I Peter 2:24]. God wants to make us oaks of righteousness for His glory, a tree visible for its faith and strength to all and one able to provide strength and safety for others [Dan 4:20-21; Matt 13:32].

Prayer:
Father, may we be determined to continue growing in You, becoming mighty oaks of righteousness.

Scripture of the Day:
"To appoint unto them that mourn in Zion, to give unto them beauty for ashes, the oil of joy for mourning, the garment of praise for the spirit of heaviness; that they might be called trees [oaks] of righteousness, the planting of the Lord, that he might be glorified." - [Isaiah 61:3]

The Word for the Day is "Man."

Quote for the Day:
"When a brave man takes a stand, the spines of others are often stiffened." - Billy Graham

In today's devotion, we are using the word "man" in the singular context, one person, not plural persons as mankind. It seems the popular societal focus today is on the collective concept of man, rather than the individual. People want to emphasize group membership such as political party, social, ethnic, sex, age or any number of group classifications. And there is less emphasis on the importance of the individual man. The collective is viewed as the answer to societal issues. Yet it is individuals within any group that make the decisions for that group's directions. Each man will stand before God in judgment for his own decisions, not the group's. I think God wants us to focus on the importance of our singular, individual life course and our influence on others.

God has had a people from the beginning, but He has always had a special man in each time to direct the people after His will. We could list many individuals like Abraham, Moses, David, the prophets, the apostles and others that God used to lead, direct, deliver, and counsel the people in the way of God. God never called out a group or commitee, but always a single man to stand for His purposes. An example of this is found in Ezekiel 22:30 when the people had profaned God in their ways and deserved judgment. God says: "And I sought for a man (not a group) among them that should make up the hedge and stand in the gap before me for the land, that I should not destroy it (one man could have saved the land): but I found none." One man can make all the difference.

God sent one man, His Son, to be the Savior of all mankind. Jesus showed by His life and by His Word the image that each person should follow if we accept Him as Lord and Savior. God wants the Light and Life to shine from each single believer to enlighten the darkness of the world. Don't forfeit your own witness and impact on others by assuming some group will do the work for you. Each believer following God's will helps His church accomplish the divine mission. You're just one person, but one man in God can make a difference in this world!

Prayer:
Lord, we do not follow "group think" but follow the Holy Spirit in living Your will for our individual lives for our sake and for our witness of Jesus to the world.

Scripture of the Day:
"For there is one God, and one mediator between God and men, the man Christ Jesus." - [1 Timothy 2:5]

December

The Word for the Day is "Water."

Quote for the Day:
"What water is down in your well comes up in your bucket." – Old Proverb

We turn on our faucets to get water, often forgetting that our ancestors—and many around the world still today—dig wells into the ground to reach the water they need. There is a skill and an art to finding the best location to dig for a well. Every person has a need for water. We need it for life and health. We need it to survive. Knowledge is often called "the water of life." As human beings we seek for the knowledge and truths we need to live successfully in this life. We instinctually seek for truth and are frustrated when we pursue knowledge and endeavors that lead to dry and erroneous ends. Within all people, too, is a hunger for the truth of God, a hunger to find and reunite with the source of life, even if people are unaware of that hunger. When Jesus talked to the Samaritan woman at the well, He told her that only the water He could give satisfied and was a "well of water springing up into everlasting life" [John 4:10-14]. So it is for us.

In the natural, wells can go dry. Rains fill and refresh natural wells. The water of the Word replenishes our spiritual well and keeps it full. It fills us, cleanses us, enriches us, keeps us. The words we put in our spiritual well will never dry up or pass away [Heb 4:12; Ps 119:9; Is 40:8; Matt 24:35]. Just as the rain keeps replenishing a natural well we need to also keep replenishing our spiritual well with the Word, continually filling and enriching that well of life within us. When you feel dry, that is the place to go to quench your thirst and be refreshed.

When a natural well is full of rich, pure water, there is water to share with others. When our spiritual wells are full, and not dry and depleted, we have spiritual water to share. You can't pull up spiritual wisdom to give to others in need when there is nothing much in your well. Those who give a cup of cold water to the thirsty are always appreciated in the natural or the spiritual [Mark 9:41]. If your inner spiritual well is full of the Holy Spirit you can pull from that so that the needed knowledge and understanding others need can rise up to come out of your mouth and to refresh others [John 7:38; Prov 2:6].

Prayer:
Father, thank You that You provide all we need for an abundant life now and eternally in the well of salvation if we choose to drink of it and be filled.

Scripture of the Day:
"Therefore with joy shall ye draw water out of the wells of salvation." –
[Isaiah 12:3]

The Word for the Day is "Hearing"

Quote for the Day:
"Hearing the truth is a jolting experience. It presses us and pushes us to get out of our comfort zone and do something different." - Jesse Duplantis

The world is full of noise today and with advances in social media and communications, people are bombarded with information. Many people often feel overwhelmed and experience Sensory Overload today from the overload of words, noise, and stimuli they experience. Church and religious leaders can often make the situation worse, pushing religious dogma and offering little truth. This was true in Jesus time with the Pharisees and Sadducees. Both taught and pushed strict adherence to the religious system of their day. They had developed rules and regulations for almost all human behavior and had corrupted the faith and the church of their time. True righteousness had not been taught so when Jesus began to teach truth, they became angry and threatened. They did not want to hear Jesus' teachings, which threatened their religious structure and rules, and they did not want the people to hear the truths Jesus taught.

People today, as then, need to hear God's truth but, unfortunately, may not often be hearing it. Whenever people hear truth, when they've long been fed distortions of truth, they can find the experience jolting and upsetting. It conflicts with the comfortable religious traditions and cultural views they've been hearing so long. Bertrand Russell wrote: "New truth is often uncomfortable, especially to the holders of power." Any discomfort in hearing absolute truth is worth the pain, because Jesus said it is the truth you know that sets man free [John 8:32].

When people are fed a diet of deceit, compromise, and lies, the heart can become hardened to truth. Their eyes become closed and the ears dull to hear the truth. God's people should always seek His truth with a heart to know Him better, and to follow Him better. "And be not conformed to this world: but be ye transformed by the renewing of your mind, that ye may prove what is that good, and acceptable, and perfect, will of God" [Rom 12:2].

Prayer:
Lord, we will keep our hearts open and our ears open to hear Your Truth that we might grow in deeper faith and understanding to fulfill Your Will in us.

Scripture of the Day:
"For this people's heart is waxed gross, and their ears are dull of hearing, and their eyes they have closed; lest at any time they should see with their eyes, and hear with their ears, and should understand with their heart, and should be converted." -[Matthew 13:15]

The Word for the Day is "Apple"

Quote for the Day:
"Even if I knew that tomorrow the world would go to pieces I would still plant my apple tree." - Martin Luther

I associate apples with Christmas…the smell of apple pies and sweet breads, cinnamon and apple candles, bright red and green apples mixed in with decorations for mantles and tables. God promised that He would 'Keep us as the apple of His eye…and make us ride on the high places of the earth' [Deuteronomy 32:10,13]. Isn't that a lovely picture?

Apples were once more precious than they are today. When my mother was a child in a big family of twelve children, during the Great Depression, getting an apple in the toe of one's Christmas stocking was a coveted gift. Just seeing a shiny red or green apple gives us a lift in our Spirit. On a hike in the mountains one fall day, my husband and I discovered an apple tree loaded with ripe apples behind a deserted cabin up a trail. We enjoyed a sweet moment sitting on the porch of that old cabin munching on two apples, crisp and warm from the sun.

We each hold special memories about apples. And how sweet it is that God sees us as the "apple of His eye." The Lord says, too, that we are "precious in his sight" [Isaiah 43:4], made with purpose and plan. Like a good earthly father loves his children, God loves us, too, but with a deep, unfathomable love. He created us in His image, calls us sons and daughters, and knows even the number of hairs on our heads.

In Jeremiah 31:3 God reminds us: "Yeah, I have loved thee with an everlasting love." Pull that vision tight into your heart whenever the enemy tries to make you feel unworthy, when the world and its ways weary your soul. You are indeed the apple of God's eye.

Prayer:
Lord, make us mindful and grateful for the simple things here at the holiday season and for the message of Your love. We ask that You would keep us through the coming year as the apple of Your eye and hide us ever under the shadow of Your wings [Psalm 17:8]…In Jesus blessed name, Amen.

Scripture of the Day:
"He kept him as the apple of His eye…he made him ride on the high places of the earth." - [Deuteronomy 32:10,13]

DECEMBER 4   J.L. Stepp
The Word for the Day is "Outward."

Quote for the Day:
"It is not your outward appearance that you should beautify, but your soul, adorning it with good works." - Clement of Alexandria

"Do ye look on things after the outward appearance?" [2 Cor 10:7]. If you do, you're not the Lone Ranger. Men generally judge by the outward appearance first, and in some ways this is reasonable. This is the first thing we observe in a person. And sometimes it shows the true condition of the heart. An outward pleasantness can reflect a good heart. A mean person, sour-faced, scowling, and sarcastic in manner and speech, often abides in darkness. Sometimes the appearance looks good, sounds good, behaves good, but first impressions can be false for man can give false outward impressions and yet have a heart full of hypocrisy and wickedness. Even so-called religious people can appear beautiful and righteous on the outside, but inwardly, be full of hypocrisy and iniquity [Matt 23:27-28].

Some men evaluate their own status and worth by the outward appearance, comparing and measuring themselves to others [2 Cor 10:12]. If they judge themselves superior to others, they lift up themselves in pride. If they think themselves inferior to someone else, they can easily envy and covet the other's superior appearance. Such men that compare and value themselves by comparing themselves to others are not wise [2 Cor 10:12].

"But the Lord looketh on the heart," not on the outward appearance [1 Sam 16:7]. For the heart determines a man in the Lord's eyes. "For every tree is known by his own fruit" [Luke 6:44]. A righteous heart will yield righteous words and righteous behavior. It is the hidden man of the heart that the Lord sees [1 Pet 3:4], and this is what we should want others to see in us. The new man of our spirit, the Lord Jesus Christ, should shine the Light both inwardly and outwardly in our life.

Prayer:
Lord, we pray for Your spiritual gift of discernment that we might not be misled or deceived by outward appearances, but that we might rightly know the true heart and spirit of man.

Scripture of the Day:
"But the Lord said unto Samuel, Look not on his countenance, or on the height of his stature; because I have refused him: for the Lord seeth not as man seeth; for man looketh on the outward appearance, but the Lord looketh on the heart."
-[1 Samuel 16:7]

The Word for the Day is "Music."

Quote for the Day:
"Next to the Word of God, the noble art of music is the greatest treasure in the world." – Martin Luther

I've always thought Christmas music one of the most beautiful parts of the holiday season. The old carols fill the radio station selections, are sung in the churches and performed in concerts and recitals around every city of the nation. Christ's name is in the word "Christmas" and He is proclaimed in nearly every carol we sing. His name sings on the wind and in the air everywhere—proclaiming His birth and His glory to those who know Him, to those who know Him not, and even to those who reject Him.

Praising God with voice and instruments dates back to the earliest of times in the stories of God's people. When David brought the ark of God home he appointed 'singers with instruments of music, psaltries, harps, and cymbals all lifting up praise to God with joy' [1 Chron 15:16]. At Jesus birth the angels sang and worshipped God as we know they also do in the heavens [Luke 2:13-14]. Worship, music, and praise bring glory and pleasure to God [Ps 135:1-3] and scriptures say 'God inhabits the praise of His people' [Ps 22:3]. I know many times I have felt the presence of the Lord in singing or even in listening to a beautiful Christmas performance like "The Hallelujah Chorus."

So many scriptures remind us to praise the Lord—'to praise Him in the sanctuary, to praise Him with stringed instruments and organs, to praise Him with our voices, with the timbrel and the dance'….and to "Let everything that hath breath praise the Lord" [Psalm 150:1-6]. As a girl, I loved the old German folk song "Music Alone Shall Live," and I think we can feel confident that good and righteous music will always live and not die—and that we will continue to enjoy it in the heavens as we do here on the earth.

Prayer:
Father, let us not forget to praise You with singing and music here at this Christmas season and at all times like the Psalm says: "Be Thou exalted, Lord,…so will we sing and praise" [Psalm 21:13].

Scripture of the Day:
"It came even to pass, as the trumpeters and singers were as one…they lifted up their voice with the trumpets and cymbals and instruments of music and praised the Lord." - [2 Chronicles 5:13]

The Word for the Day is "Mystery."

Quote for the Day:
"Biblical mystery is something hidden from natural man, yet God has fully revealed it. It is an open secret which sinful humanity cannot see. It is a truth that God must reveal to individuals." - Dr. Lloyd Jones

As you probably know, my wife Lin is an author of romance novels. But she is also a prolific reader of novels. Recently, she has enjoyed a series of mystery novels by one of her favorite authors, Agatha Christie. Lin loves the hidden clues and secrets of the story, trying to guess which of the characters is the culprit. Of course this is fictional mystery, but there is also spiritual mystery when it comes to the kingdom of God. Some men ponder these mysteries, some don't.

The things of the Spirit are foolishness to the natural man [1 Cor 2:14], but a man seeking truth may ask: "What would God be like if He were on this earth in a body like I have?" Ministers of Christ and stewards of the mysteries of God [1 Cor 4:1] have the answer to that question: God *has* come in the flesh and shown himself to man. He was born of woman, living in a flesh body just like us, experienced the sweaty, tough work as a carpenter, a plain looking man aquainted with common grief and sorrows, tempted as we are, yet without sin [Rom 1:3; Mark 6:3; Is 53:2-3; Heb 4:15]. He always followed the Spirit showing love, mercy, and miracles as man had never known. He proclaimed the Truth of God and defended Truth against the false teachers of His day. This man was faithful to His calling in God, even to His death on a cross at Calvary, and He was raised up to be Lord and Savior to all who believe on Him. [Acts 16:31].

The next mystery question might be: "How do we get 'right' with God?" You must become a new creature, born-again in your spirit, receiving 'Christ in you, the hope of glory' [2 Cor 5:17; John 3:3; Col 1:27]. The Spirit in you will then guide you into all truth [John 16:13] as you follow and grow in the image of Jesus, and it will be given unto you to know the riches of the glory of the mysteries of the kingdom of heaven [Matt 13:11; Col 1:27].

Prayer:
Lord, we look unto Jesus, the author and finisher of our faith, and thank Him for the Holy Spirit that leads us into all truth and revelations of the mysteries of the kingdom of heaven as we renew our mind in His Word.

Scripture of the Day:
"And without controversy great is the mystery of godliness: God was manifest in the flesh, justified in the Spirit, seen of angels, preached unto the Gentiles, believed on in the world, received up into glory." -[1 Timothy 3:16]

The Word for the Day is "Life."

Quote for the Day:
"No beauty shines brighter in life than that of a good heart." – Anonymous

Proverbs 4:23 admonishes to 'Above all else, keep or guard your heart with all dil-igence, because out of the heart come the issues of life.' Everything we do in our lives flows from the heart. So, how do you guard your heart above all else? First, it's important to remember the scripture is talking about your Spiritual Heart, the deep inner part of you connected to God. The essence of who you are, the core of your being. That is the lifeblood of your soul and your life, which must be guarded as diligently as any sentry guards his station.

Somehow we must each keep our hearts safe, true, and protected—in a world not very interested in keeping us Spiritually strong, in a world more interested in in-vading our hearts with worldliness, lies, doubt, and unbelief. You and your heart are meant to be in union and meant to be holy. If you and your heart are right and true before God, then you are protecting and guarding your heart wisely and well, and righteousness will flow from your life. From a sincere and true heart will always come the good and noble things of life [Luke 6:45].

King Solomon called the heart the 'wellspring of life.' If your heart is unhealthy it impacts everything in your life. A deeply spiritual and right "understanding is a wellspring of life unto him that hath it... sweet to the soul, and health to the bones" [Prov 16:22-24]. Michael Hyatt wrote: "If your heart is unhealthy, it threatens everything else—family, friends, career—everything." We need to work to keep our heart clean, pure, righteous and holy. Just as a clogged or stopped up spring threatens the life of a well, when our spiritual relationship with God becomes clogged or unhealthy, it will hurt the flow of all we do and all we are. We are to diligently seek to keep a clean and pure heart, knowing this pleases God and will cause our lives to be blessed in very way [Matthew 5:8; Psalm 51:10].

Prayer:
Lord, You said those pure in heart would see and know You. Help us not to let our hearts grow cold, stony, or wayward but to stay sweet and clean before You.

Scripture of the Day:
"Keep thy heart with all diligence; for out of it are the issues of life." -
[Proverbs 4:23]

The Word for the Day is "Suddenly."

Quote for the Day:
"You need to know that in a moment of time God could turn it all around - suddenly." - Joel Osteen

Most men, I believe, like to live their lives in an ordered fashion, having comfortable and reasonable expectations. Events that happen suddenly, quickly, and unexpectedly can either be positive or negative depending upon the effect and consequence of the event. The Bible gives us counsel and revelations about sudden events both good and evil.

The Word of God is very direct in revealing wisdom concerning the sudden negative effects of certain behaviors. "A naughty person, a wicked man, walketh with a froward (false) mouth. He winketh with his eyes, he speaketh with his feet, he teacheth (points) with his fingers; Frowardness (perversity) is in his heart, he deviseth mischief continually; he soweth discord. Therefore shall his calamity come suddenly; suddenly shall he be broken without remedy" [Prov 6:12-15]. This is the law of sowing and reaping: "Be not deceived; God is not mocked: for whatsoever a man soweth, that shall he also reap" [Gal 6:7].

As believers, we are not to be afraid of sudden fear [Prov 3:25-26]. "For God hath not appointed us to wrath, but to obtain salvation by our Lord Jesus Christ" [1 Thess 5:9]. We are redeemed from destruction and made the righteousness of God in Christ Jesus [Psalm 103:4; 2 Cor 5:21]. We know we are to have faith in God and hold on to His Word with steadfast patience [James 1:4]. But God also wants us to be open to believe for His sudden deliverance. An excellent example of this is found in Acts, chapter 16. Paul and Silas were beaten and thrown in the inner prison in stocks. And at midnight they prayed and sang praises to God. Suddenly, there was a great earthquake and all the prison doors were opened and the prisoner's bonds were loosed. Talk about quick and unexpected! Pray and believe God. He can come suddenly as a mighty rushing wind from heaven, or as a light shining down from heaven and suddenly set you free [Acts 2:2; 9:3]. Keep an open expectation—He can send your answer suddenly!

Prayer:
Lord, we know our victory in Jesus is assured, and we hold fast in faith knowing also that our deliverance and answer can come suddenly—thank you, Lord!

Scripture of the Day:
"And at midnight Paul and Silas prayed, ...And suddenly there was a great earthquake, so that the foundations of the prison were shaken: and immediately all the doors were opened, and every one's bands were loosed." - [Acts 16:25-26]

The Word for the Day is "Apart."

Quote for the Day:
"The moment someone chooses to trust in Jesus Christ, his sins are wiped away, and he is adopted into God's family. That individual is set apart as a child of God with a sacred purpose." – Charles Stanley

It is easy, with the hectic pace of the holidays, to forget to have the time we need with the Lord. Suddenly we feel stressed, tense, our peace gone and we wonder why. Our best and sweetest peace is always found in the Lord and we need to make time for Him, and for quiet times away with Him, even amid all the busy events of the season [2 Thess 3:16; Is 26:3]. At Christmas, we celebrate the birth of Jesus, who came to bring peace on earth and to open the way for us to have fellowship with God and to be adopted into the family of God. A precious, precious gift we should not forget.

Often when we first come to know God, and before we grow close to Him, we tend to compartmentalize faith and the rest of our life. We live our everyday life during the week, saving our spiritual time for Sunday. But gradually, and hopefully, as faith grows we start to yearn for more. We begin to realize 'we have to say no to a lot of good things in order to be able to say yes to a lot of great things' [Sean McCabe]. We begin to pull away from the world more often to pull closer to God. We begin to realize that 'God has chosen us to be a peculiar, special people unto Him, holy and set apart,' living first for Him above all, willing to put Him first in our time and thoughts [Deut 14:2]. Joyfully, we find He is eager to spend time with us as well.

Sometimes when my husband J.L. and I pull apart and take off to hike in the Smoky Mountains near our home, we find ourselves restored and replenished in spirit, from getting away from the hectic pace of everyday life. Time apart with God refreshes our lives and spirit, too, and we need to make place for it. "Apart from Jesus Christ, we do not know what is our life, nor our death, nor ourselves" [Blaise Pascal]. We cannot truly find the happiness and peace we need apart from God. We are not really of this world spiritually, just passing through it [John 17:16-26].

Prayer:
Father, help us to remember in the busy days of the holiday season, and in every day, to find time to pull apart, be with You and hear from You.

Scripture of the Day:
"But know that the Lord hath set apart him that is Godly for himself; the Lord will hear when I call unto him." - [Psalm 4:3]

The Word for the Day is "News."

Quote for the Day:
"Evangelism is when the Gospel, which is good news, is preached or presented to all people." - Billy Graham

Years ago I was involved with an evangelistic association that served the local Knoxville area in their outreach. I had come to know the Lord and been filled with the Spirit and I was eager to share the Gospel. I remember the Lord quickened to me that I could not join this outreach until I had first witnessed to my own neighbors. So I knocked on every door and truthfully told my neighbors that I wanted to work with a Knoxville ministry, but the Lord required me to witness to my neighbors first. I was relieved at the friendly reception I received. One thing I observed from this outreach experience was that most people seem to be open and hungry to hear good news. They'd all heard and endured so much negative and bad news in their lives, they were eager to receive some hope.

One of the Proverbs in the Bible reminds us that "as cold waters to a thirsty soul, so is good news from a far country." The Gospel is good news from afar—even from heaven! I learned to engage people by simply first asking: "Could you use some good news?" This almost every time opened up hearts to hear the message of the good news of the Gospel. The Spirit even helped me to write a gospel tract which I entitled *"Could You Use Some Good News?"*

This tract and concept of *good* news helped me to share the essence of the blessed hope of the Gospel. The good news is that: (1) *Jesus Christ is alive* today and *He is the answer* to your need [Rev 1:18; Heb 13:8]; (2) Jesus is alive today for destroying the works of evil and He wants to give *you* abundant *life* [1 John 3:8; John 10:10]; (3) Jesus destroys the works of evil by *living* in *you*, helping you become a *new* creation with *victory* [Rev 3:20; 2 Cor 5:17; Rom 8:37]; (4) You get Jesus' Spirit in you by making Him *Lord* of *your* life [Rom 10:9-10]. That act puts the riches of 'Christ in you, the hope of glory' so you can live life abundantly, trusting Jesus for every detail of your life, and so you can also renew your mind by the Word of God to enable you to follow His will in all things [Rom 10:9-10; Co1:27].

Prayer:
Lord, the news of the Gospel sounds too good to be true to the carnal mind, but it is Your eternal Truth. Therefore we take joy that we are saved and that we can now call upon the name of the Lord with gladness and joy.

Scripture of the Day:
"As cold waters to a thirsty soul, so is good news from a far country." -
[Proverbs 25:25]

The Word for the Day is "Eagle."

Quote for the Day:
"Don't be a pigeon if you were born to be an eagle. Experience God's altitude for your life." – Myles Monroe

Eagles are large, majestic, powerfully built birds admired for their size, beauty, and sharp skills. The American Bald Eagle, unique only to the U.S., is the national bird for our country and a symbol of freedom. Eagles have amazing eyesight and can spot prey two miles away. They mate for life and are loyal to their families. They build their nests high in tall trees or on mountain ledges. Sadly, bald eagles were hunted for sport and nearly wiped out for many decades. Pesticides and chemicals in fish, making up much of an eagle's diet, weakened the birds also. But now U.S. conservation efforts are ongoing to ensure the eagles' protection and the Bald Eagle is no longer on the Endangered Species list.

God often uses the symbol of the eagle in teachings throughout the Bible. In Exodus He talks about how "I bare you on eagles' wings, and brought you unto myself" [Ex 19:4]. A little known fact about eagles is that when the parent eagles are eager to see their eaglets leave the nest, they begin to pluck out the down lining the nest, making the little eaglets uncomfortable on the nettle-like sticks and branches underneath. Little eaglets are not eager to leap from their high nests out into the air. It's a long way down! But if they do not leave the nest the parent eagles push them out, but then fly above them, creating an upsweep of wind to hold the babies up and protect them as they begin to beat their small wings and begin to fly. This is a picture of how God often pushes us on to grow in Him, to move forward and rise higher, but always holding us as we step forth and begin to fly in each new venture.

As a good Father, God says he will 'renew our strength like the eagle's so we can 'mount to high places, run and not be weary, walk and not faint' [Is 40:31] and He promises He will 'renew our youth like the eagle,' too [Ps 103:5]. Eagles lift and fly above the clouds when a storm comes, like God wants to lift us above our cares and troubles. These lovely pictures show God's heart of love toward us…how 'He has set His love upon us, will deliver us in times of trouble, and sets us on high, because He knows our name and we know Him' [Ps 91:14].

Prayer:
Lord, help us remember how much You love Your creation and often compare Your love for us to Your love for the wonders of nature, like the eagle.

Scripture of the Day:
"For thus saith the Lord; Behold, he shall fly as an eagle." – [Jeremiah 48:40]

The Word for the Day is "Nature."

Quote for the Day:
"I love to think of nature as an unlimited broadcasting station, through which God speaks to us every hour, if we will only tune in. " - George Washington Carver

Lin and I have been blessed to enjoy the beauty and wonders of God's creation as we have explored mountain trails for our hiking guidebook and the state parks in Tennessee and South Carolina to produce our state parks guidebooks. Creation declares the glory of God and we feel His presence in nature. Some men worship the creation, but not the Creator. But the things that are made declare His eternal power and Godhead, so that they are without excuse [Rom 1:20].

God's creation and nature can declare to us many spiritual truths, as Carver suggested like a broadcasting station. Nature speaks to us of seasons: "To every thing there is a season, and a time to every purpose under the heaven" [Eccl 3:1]. The bare limbs on the trees at this time do not mean nothing is going on in the tree. The tree is establishing deeper roots and preparing for the future season of lush new growth and fruit. We can use every season in our life for purpose in God, knowing that if we stay committed He will prepare us to fulfill His will and purpose in future seasons ahead, and all things will work together for good [Rom 8:28]. Nature teaches us that all creation works from the seedtime and harvest principle. Every plant produces after the seed of its kind that is sown. The kingdom of God operates on the same principle: we sow seeds of faith, love, good, righteousness, and other godly virtues; we reap a harvest of the same [Mark 4:26]. Nature shows us that all plants and creatures start as newborns and develop to maturity. We start out as newborn babes in Christ and grow in Him as we renew our mind to His Word and continually seek His will in all things [1Pet 2:2].

Prayer:
Lord, what a joy it is to feel Your presence and commune with You in the beauty of nature, or in the quietness of our prayer closet. You are always with us no matter where we are. Thank You, Lord.

Scripture of the Day:
"Wherby are given unto us exceeding great and precious promises: that by these ye might be partakers of the divine nature, having escaped the corruption that is in the world through lust." - [2 Peter 1:4]

The Word for the Day is "Disciples."

Quote of the Day:
"May it please Christ our Lord to grant us true humility and abnegation of will and judgment, so that we may deserve to begin to be His Disciples." – St. Ignatius

Deep in our hearts we balk a little at the concept of being a sold-out disciple or follower of Jesus, giving up our right to ourselves and putting our lives under the leadership and guidance of the Lord. It's not an easy thing with our cross purposes to please ourselves and with our limiting and often crippling desires to please others. But God wants that of us.

At Christmas we're reminded of how Jesus gave up self-desires and people-pleasing to submit to God and to God's Will and Purpose. How was He able to do that? Because He put God first every day. He looked at God, at what God thought more, and less on what others thought. He decided to follow God daily just as Jesus hopes we will daily follow Him (1 Cor 11:1). An old hymn sums up the spirit of this well: "I have decided to follow Jesus—no turning back, no turning back."

We can follow each day in this holiday season and in the New Year as God's disciples, led by the Spirit, or we can walk to please ourselves and walk always worrying about what others think. You need to arrest those thoughts that lead you astray from drawing close to God. Stop and seek after God. Learn what is on His mind for you to do. His way is always the best way. Following His Leading always brings the best results. It's your destiny to advance in wisdom and favor with God. Did you know that? To hear His Voice, to live the life Jesus came and died to give you. Why would you settle for less? When your eyes are on Jesus, your heart tuned to God's mind and God's leading, God gets bigger and bigger in you every day. People start seeing God in your life and it draws them. Jesus said "I will draw all men unto me' (John 12:32). He came to earth, submitted to God, lived, taught, and died so you could carry on that mission as His disciples.

Prayer:
Lord, help us to direct our hearts and minds toward You in this holiday season and new year to come, to seek to know Your mind and Your heart for how we are to live each day, for how we are to walk out our lives, for how we are to do the work You give to each of us.

Scripture of the Day:
"Herein is my Father glorified, that ye bear much fruit; so shall ye be my disciples." - [John 15:8]

The Word for the Day is "Mouth."

Quote for the Day:
"Next time, think before you run your big mouth!" - Appalachian saying

When I was a kid, I was known as a "quiet guy." I was active and played hard, I just didn't say much. As I have come to know God's wisdom, about how the mouth can get you into trouble, I have realized that my quietness might not have been such a disadvantage after all.

The Bible tells us that the words of our mouth can have consequences both good and evil. The main determinant of what we speak is the condition of the heart. We are exhorted in the Word to keep our heart with all diligence, or care, "for out of it are the issues of life" [Prov 4:23]. Jesus taught that a good man out of the good treasure of his heart speaks good, and an evil man out of the evil treasure of his heart speaks evil, 'for out of the abundance of the heart his mouth speaketh' [Luke 6:45].

The wicked are snared and defiled by the wicked words of their mouth [Prov 6:2; Matt 15:11], but the Word gives the righteous wisdom as to how to keep, or guard, his mouth: "He that keepeth his mouth keepeth his life" [Prov 13:3]. Psalm 17:3 says: "I am purposed that my mouth shall not transgress." We must make an intentional, deliberate aim to control our mouth. The Word tells us "The heart of the wise teacheth his mouth, and addeth learning to his lips"[Prov 16:23]. The more we know the wisdom and truth of God's Word, the more the mouth will be instructed to speak aright. We are instructed not to be rash (reckless, impulsive) with our mouth and 'to not let our hearts be hasty to utter any thing (impetuous or wrong) before God' [Eccl 5:2]. "The heart of the righteous studieth (carefully considers) to answer" [Prov 15:28]. When we keep our hearts and mouth in the way of righteousness, we can be assured God hears our prayer to: "Let the words of my mouth, and the meditation of my heart, be acceptable in thy sight, O Lord, my strength, and my redeemer" [Psalm 19:14].

Prayer:
Lord, we will let no corrupt communication proceed out of our mouth, but only that which is good to minister edifying and grace to the hearers [Eph 4:29].

Scripture of the Day:
"A good man out of the good treasure of his heart bringeth forth that which is good; and an evil man out of the evil treasure of his heart bringeth forth that which is evil; for of the abundance of the the heart his mouth speaketh." -
[Luke 6:45]

The Word for the Day is "Cedar."

Quote for the Day:
"The qualities that are present in God's people are similar to those found in cedar trees." – Bruce Howell, pastor

At Christmas I always remember the cedar trees Dad brought home from the woods for us to decorate for the holidays. The fresh smell of the cedar filled the house and the tree looked so pretty after we covered it with lights, ornaments, and silver icicles. I remember once we found a little bird's nest tucked in the boughs of our cedar reminding me of its life in the woods, its ability to shelter birds and other wildlife in its branches.

The Bible often compares us to the cedar that God plants upon a high place. "In the mountain of the height of Israel will I plant it: and it shall bring forth boughs, and bear fruit, and be a goodly cedar: and under it shall dwell all fowl of every wing; in the shadow of the branches thereof shall they dwell" [Ezekial 17:23]. It's a beautiful picture of how God wants us to be planted in Him, to flourish, to bear good fruit in our lives, and to be a help and shelter to others. I didn't realize, until I did a little research, how different the Biblical cedars were from the conical, eastern red cedars we find in Tennessee at Christmas. The Biblical cedars, particularly the famed cedars of Lebanon, were tall, aromatic evergreens with a strong thick trunk prized for its high quality timber. They often grew up to 130 feet tall with trunks up to eight feet in diameter. The giant trees grew in mountainous regions in high altitudes—a mighty tree and highly praised in scripture. The timber was used to construct buildings and boats, and King David used it in building his palace and in planning the temple his son Solomon built later [1 Chronicles 17:1; 2 Chronicles 2:3-8].

Our lives are meant to be 'excellent as the cedars' [Song of Solomon 5:15]. However, there is a caution not to strive for greatness without godliness as the Assyrians—powerful, cruel, and barbaric, with many gods. Ezekial warns 'the ungodly will be brought down despite their greatness' [Ezekial 31:18]. In contrast the cedar planted in the Lord 'whose branches turn toward Him and whose roots thereof are under Him will become goodly and great' [Ezekial 17:6-8].

Prayer:
Lord, may we grow and flourish as the cedars of Lebanon, becoming a beautiful credit to You, always following after Your way.

Scripture of the Day:
"The righteous shall flourish like the palm tree: he shall grow like a cedar in Lebanon." - [Psalm 92:12]

The Word for the Day is "More."

Quote for the Day:
"There is much more of God available than we have ever known or imagined, but we have become so satisfied with where we are and what we have that we don't press in for God's best." - Tommy Tenney

Most people are always wishing for "more" of something—more money, more possessions, more friends, more position and fame, more pleasures, more love, more things. The list could go on and on. There is something in the nature of human beings that makes them look at their lives and always wish for something "more" in some area. In this, we are sometimes a bit greedy. Erich Fromm wrote: "Greed is a bottomless pit which exhausts the person in an endless effort to satisfy the need without ever reaching satisfaction." We seem to always aspire to have more but not to be more.

There seems to be a hunger in the heart for more, but that hunger is a misdirected one. There is one area where we can hunger and seek for more that is always right and good—and that is to hunger and seek for more of God. The things and ways of God, His truth, His knowledge, His will, His wisdom, are more to be desired than anything, and nothing else in this world can compare to it [Psalm 19:7-10; Prov 3:13-18]. God not only has reward for all eternity for those that seek Him and the kingdom of God, but also 'manifold (much) more in this *present* time' [Luke 18:30]. When we walk and please God we abound more and more, and become "more than conquerors through him that loved us" [1Thess 4:1; Rom 8:37].

Today our focus is too much on attaining more of the things of the world than things of the Spirit. We have become satisfied with a much smaller faith, a much weaker relationship with God, a more inferior and less intimate fellowship with God than what is available. As Tenney says, 'we have become satisfied with where we are and what we have and don't even press in for God's best.' God wants to increase us more and more in every area of our life. But it is up to us as individuals to seek more of God: "But seek ye first the kingdom of God, and his righteousness; and all these things shall be added unto you" [Matt 6:33].

Prayer:
Lord, we want to seek You more and more in every way, and increase in You more and more in every way, that we might impact others to seek God more.

Scripture of the Day:
"The Lord shall increase you more and more, you and your children." - [Psalm 115:14]

The Word for the Day is "Longeth."

Quote for the Day:
"God longeth to teach us to know Him and love Him evermore." – Julian of
Norwich

There is something about the holidays that makes our hearts yearn toward home.
The holidays seem to call to us to go back to that place and those people we think
of with the word "home." We love songs like "I'll Be Home for Christmas" and
"There's No Place Like Home For the Holidays." Even if we have no actual home
to travel to, our hearts travel back in time to holidays spent at home in the past,
blessed and happy memories that make us smile. God, too, yearns for us to come
"home" to Him. Our true home, more than a physical place and address, is with
God. The Lord is imbedded in our inward genetics and He is our heavenly Father [Matt 6:9; Eph 4:6]. We are made in His Image, and He calls to us from our
inward being to come to know Him, to come home to Him [Gen 1:27]. If we've
drifted away from the Lord, and aren't close to Him any more, His Spirit still calls
to us, wooing us to come back home to Him again.

We have two homes in the Lord—one for eternity and one for now, here on earth.
Many times our focus gets fixed more on our eternal home, what the old hymn
calls 'the sweet by and by.' It is a glorious home we can look forward to and even
yearn for. Paul said, 'I am torn between the two' as both homes called to him [Phil
1:23]. For now, however, we have promise of a more abundant life here than we
often realize or fully partake of [John 10:10]. First we are promised that when we
come to the Lord, we become His children and heirs of all the blessings of salvation [Heb 1:14]. We become grafted into the vine, heirs to all the blessings of the
covenant God made with His people in the past [Rom 11:17-24]. Jesus also left
us the keys to the Kingdom and said to us, when He went home, that He'd left us
His Power, the Spirit of God, to live a higher life than possible before [Matt 16:19;
John 14:15-21], to walk as He had walked, to inherit the rights and power He paid
for us to have [Luke 10:19]. Truly coming home to the Lord also means coming
into all the blessings and gifts He has left us.

Prayer:
Lord, may we come home to You fully, with an open heart, in this holiday season
and receive all that You have given us and all that You want us to walk in.

Scripture of the Day:
"My soul longeth, yea even fainteth for the courts of the Lord: my heart and my
flesh crieth out for the living God." - [Psalm 84:2]

The Word for the Day is "Consolation."

Quote for the Day:
"I have cried out to the Lord for grace and mercy, and they have covered me completely. I have found the sweetest consolation since I made it my whole purpose to enjoy His marvelous Presence." - Christopher Columbus

Lin and I drove to Blount Memorial Hospital in Maryville today to visit a dear friend of ours whose husband was having heart surgery. She had called us the night before to inform us of the situation and ask us to pray. We stayed with her in the waiting area and encouraged, comforted, and consoled her, mainly by just showing our love for both she and her husband, both dear friends. The surgery went well and we stayed with both for awhile as he recovered. Lin and I were deeply touched as she hugged us and with tears told how much our mere presence had meant to her for comfort, consolation, and faith encouragement. Lin and I were humbled that such a simple thing could mean so much to someone.

The Word in 2 Thessalonians tells us that we have an everlasting consolation in God. The Lord Jesus Christ Himself gives us assured consolation that He will give us comfort, consoling, solace, and reassurance to comfort our hearts and make us feel better after a trial, disappointment, or affliction. How does God impart this consolation to us? The Lord Jesus imparts His comfort by His divine love for us, by His compassion and mercies, and by the fellowship of His Spirit [Phil 2:1-2]. We have a strong and sure consolation in the Lord because we can lay hold on the hope set before us knowing that it is impossible for God to lie; all the promises of God in Jesus are yea and Amen [Heb 6:18; 2 Cor 1:20]. God also imparts His consolation through His Word. We learn the promises of God in scripture and can then rejoice for the consolation they impart [Acts 15:31].

How do we impart consolation to others? Mainly by having the same heart as Jesus toward others and by showing love, compassion, mercy, and the comfort of the Spirit [Phil 2:1-4]. With an humble spirit we can share the comfort of the Spirit, the truth of the scriptures, and our love to give consolation to others.

Prayer:
Lord, help us to show the great love and consolation of Jesus, the truth of His promises, and His comfort by our caring for others.

Scripture of the Day:
"Now the Lord Jesus Christ himself, and God, even our Father, which hath loved us, and hath given us everlasting consolation and good hope through grace, comfort your hearts, and stablish you in every good word and work." -
[2 Thessalonians 2:16-17]

The Word for the Day is "Ponder"

Quote for the day:
"I think we often miss some great opportunities to ponder." – Wade Hughs, Sr.

We all remember the Christmas story when the angel came to Mary and told her she had been chosen to conceive a child, and we know she wondered at it. 'How can this be?' [Luke 1:34] she asked, and later, we read that "Mary kept all these things and pondered them in her heart" [Luke 2:19]. I've often thought on that Scripture and imagined what it must have been like for that young woman to receive a vision—a thing impossible in the natural—that required faith in the supernatural.

"Now faith is the substance of things hoped for, the evidence of things not seen" [Hebrews 11:1]. By faith we can believe and do all things, even hard things. The Word says we need a 'childlike faith' [Matt 18:3]…and as we age, I think we lose a little of that wonder, that simple childlike faith and innocence. At Christmas I think we all see a glimpse again of that wonder—watching the excitement in little children, enjoying their wonder and belief, hearing again the beautiful Christmas story, reading of the angels speaking and singing to men, of the wise men led long distances to the Lord.

Like the sparkle and magic of Christmas, faith will take us places we haven't yet seen or imagined. We get a lot of ideas about things we might like to do or try, things we wish we could accomplish, works and even ministry that pull on our hearts, but when an idea or vision is God's idea then—oh, my—there is true opportunity. It was God's idea, God's calling, that Mary 'pondered in her heart.' It seemed impossible. It seemed incredible. But 'all things are possible with God' [Matthew 19:26].

Mary was no different from you or me, a simple girl, not privileged, less educated than most of us with less material goods. The norms of her day had her life laid out before her, more restricted than for women of today. But she was willing to believe, ready to hear, and open to 'Ponder',…to consider that God could use her for His good and for His glory.

Prayer …
Lord, open our hearts this Christmas season—and in the coming year—to more faith. Give us again a little wonder and a deep hunger for more of You.

Scripture of the day:
"Ponder the path of thy feet, and let all thy ways be established."-[Proverbs 4:26]

The Word for the Day is "Learn."

Quote for the Day:
"I've discovered that when we take time to renew our minds with God's Word, we learn how to think like God thinks, say what God says, and act like He wants us to act." - Joyce Meyer

God is always hoping we will seek to learn more of Him. He wants us to acquire or gain the knowledge of Himself. If we set our hearts to learn, we have the promise of God that He will help us by instructing and teaching us the way we shall go [Psalm 32:8]. But how specifically do we learn of the Lord? The Bible actually gives us a three-step plan for learning more about God [Deut 5:1].

First, we must hear God's truth: "So then faith cometh by hearing, and hearing by the word of God" [Rom 10:17]. It is good to hear any believer or minister that speaks the scripture in truth. But we are warned to take heed how we hear [Luke 8:18]. Hearing the ways of the world and the wicked can be a snare to the soul [Jer 10:2; Prov 20:25]. Any that preach error or corrupt the Word must be avoided [2 Cor 2:17]. It is best to hear God's Word with our own ears by reading the Bible ourselves. It is the inspired Word of God which we can trust to be "profitable for doctrine, for reproof, for correction, for instruction in righteousness" [2 Tim 3:16].

The second step in learning of the Lord is to keep, or hold on to, His Word. We should let the Holy Spirit help teach and guide us into all truth and learning of Jesus [John 16:13]. And then stand fast in that truth and firmly believe the Word: "But continue thou in the things which thou hast learned and hast been assured of, knowing of whom thou hast learned them" [2 Tim 3:14].

The third step of instruction in learning is to not only be a hearer, but also a doer of the Word [James 1:22]. We need to learn of God's precious promises, believe for them, and stand in our rightful authority in Jesus to manifest victory over all the works of the enemy. We should speak and command our mountains (or problems) to be removed! [2 Pet 1:4; Luke 10:19; Mark 11:23].

Prayer:
Lord, we will be hearers, keepers, and doers of God's Word that we might be more and more conformed to the image of Christ Jesus our Lord.

Scripture of the Day:
"Take my yoke upon you, and learn of me; for I am meek and lowly in heart: and ye shall find rest unto your souls." - [Matthew 11:29]

DECEMBER 21   **Lin Stepp**
The Word for the Day is "Star."

Quote for the Day:
"God will use whatever He wants to display His glory. Heavens and stars. History and nations. People and problems." – Max Lucado.

The Star of Bethlehem or the Christmas Star is one of the most beautiful parts of the Christmas story. The Star appeared as a miraculous sign to mark the birth of Jesus and to guide the shepherds and then the wise men to Bethlehem.

Astronomers and scientists still have no clear theory for the star because the star was a supernatural phenomenon to announce Jesus' birth. Prophecies in other countries and in the Bible said a star would come…'I shall see Him, but not now; I shall behold Him, but not nigh; there shall come a Star out of Jacob and a Sceptre shall rise out of Israel' [Numbers 24:17]. Astrologers and wise men had been watching for this star in other countries, knowing it was coming. After the star appeared, the wise men traveled, following the star long distances of well over 700 to 900 miles to Bethlehem, coming from Persia, Arabia, and Sheba—the countries of Iraq, Iran, and Saudi Arabia today. It was a long and dangerous journey and would have taken many months. Even more miraculous, the star was visible by day—as well as by night—and it moved so the wise men, and the small armies traveling with them, could follow it.

Simple shepherds were the first to travel to see Jesus, coming after the angels appeared to announce Jesus' birth. "As the angels were gone away from them into heaven, the shepherds said one to another, "Let us now go even unto Bethlehem and see this thing which is come to pass" [Luke 2:15]. It seems likely that they would have been guided by the star to find the stable in Bethlehem. The wise men soon followed. "And lo, the star, which they saw in the east, went before them, till it came and stood over where the young child was…and when they were come into the house, they saw the young child with Mary his mother, and fell down, and worshipped him: and when they had opened their treasures, they presented unto him gifts; gold, frankincense, and myrrh" [Matthew 2:9-11]. It was the miraculous star that announced Jesus' birth and led both shepherds and wise men to Him. As you look up into the night sky at the stars during the holiday season, imagine the glory of that star and what it might have looked like.

Prayer:
Lord may we never forget all the wonders You create with Your hands.

Scripture of the Day:
"When they saw the star, they rejoiced with exceeding great joy." - [Matthew 2:10]

The Word for the Day is "Prepare."

Quote for the Day:
"Secularism teaches us that we ought to look to this world. Christianity teaches us that the best way to prepare for this world is to be fully prepared for the next."
- Charles Spurgeon

With Christmas just a few days ahead, Lin and I had family and guests coming to visit, and some to stay a few days with us. So the last couple of days we had been working to prepare for our guests. This involved a lot of house cleaning, grocery shopping, and a lot of effort. But it was a good, satisfying feeling to finally have everything clean and ready for company. We wanted our guests to enjoy their visit with us and to feel special.

I think God is pleased when we take the effort to show love and respect for others by preparing for their company. The Bible tells us that we are to prepare for the way of the Lord. John Baptist proclaimed: "Prepare ye the way of the Lord, make his paths straight" [Matt 3:3]. But what does 'prepare the way of the Lord' mean? Several dictionary meanings of the word prepare are: 'to make ready for use or consideration;' 'to make ready or able to deal with something;' 'to put in a proper state of mind.' I think we prepare for the way of the Lord by setting both our heart and mind in a proper state.

Scripture gives us instruction if we want to walk with and fellowship the Lord, or to 'prepare the way of the Lord.' Samuel instructed the people to prepare their hearts by 'returning to the Lord with all their hearts, to put away strange gods, and to serve the Lord only' [1 Samuel 7:3]. We must set our mind that we are going to serve the Lord only, turning away from the mold of this world, and then purify our hearts by repenting and turning from wrong ways. We make His way "straight," clean, clear, uncluttered, when our heart is devoted to Him above all, when we value Him above all else. A guest to your home could not walk 'straight' if the floors were cluttered and filthy and he had to constantly step around stinking garbage. Likewise, we show love, respect, and devotion to the Lord if we invite Him to our heart's home by staying clean and prepared.

Prayer:
Lord, we will prepare Your way to us by keeping our mind fixed on You and our heart pure [Is 26:3, Matt 5:8]. Thank You for Your perfect peace and blessings.

Scripture of the Day:
"For this is he that was spoken of by the prophet Esaias, saying, The voice of one crying in the wilderness, Prepare ye the way of the Lord, make his paths straight."
- [Matthew 3:3]

The Word for the Day is "Room."

Quote for the Day:
"Let us pray, and as we pray, let us make room for Jesus in our hearts."
– D.L. Moody

It seems likely that Mary and Joseph started preparing for their long journey to Bethlemen about this time of year. The travel distance from Nazareth to Bethlehem is 65 miles. If the couple traveled 13 miles a day, the trip would take five days, and with Mary so heavy with child, it probably took more. Then after the long, hard journey and sleeping out-of-doors each night, they arrived in the city to find it packed with other travelers coming in demand to Caesar's taxation decree. Winding through the crowded city streets, Joseph found no place for them to stay at the lodging houses or at the inn. But mercifully, the innkeeper offered them lodging in the stable, seeing Mary was near her delivery time.

Do you think you would you have opened your doors to this tired couple? What if they had been famous or prominent people? We often are more impressed with people of importance. Yet the Word clearly declares "There is no respect of persons with God" nor should there be with us [Romans 2:11]. Perhaps this is the reason God allowed His Son to be born in a humble setting, and that the first to come to see Jesus were shepherds, simple working men[Luke 2:8]. The next were wealthy kings and wise men from afar. Despite their status, they traveled, following the star to the stable, bringing their gifts and kneeling in the dirt before the manger. It's good to remember Jesus welcomes all equally and so should we.

Making room for Jesus doesn't only involve salvation, either. Making room for Him means making time to grow in grace, knowledge, and understanding every day. Jesus came so we could study, learn, and grow in Him, but as Dwight L. Moody said: "So few grow because so few study." We won't make room in our homes, our hearts, our time to grow in the Lord. We won't study and seek to grow deeper in Him every day. We've opened His gift of salvation—like a pretty Christmas gift—admired it, given thanks for it, but then put it on a back shelf. Like in Bethlehem, there is no room for Him in the main, busy part of our lives.

Prayer:
Lord, help us to open our time and hearts to make room for You in the busy inn of our lives, so we can grow in you.

Scripture of the Day:
"Come in, thou blessed of the Lord; wherefore standest thou without? For I have prepared the house, and room for the camels." - [Genesis 24:31].

The Word for the Day is "Birth."

Quote for the Day:
"For millions of people who have lived since, the birth of Jesus made possible not just a new way of understanding life but a new way of living it." - Frederick Buechner

The birth of Jesus is celebrated and remembered at this time of year with many holiday traditions. Churches have Christmas services of congregational and choral praises and celebration. Local events like The Nativity Pageant here in Knoxville are special for the community. And families read and share the Christmas story with children and the adults enjoy family traditions. This is a joyous, happy time of sharing the blessing of the birth of Jesus.

The birth of Jesus was the most important birth in the history of mankind. It was the fulfillment of prophesies of old that God would send a Savior into the world [Isaiah 9:6]. "And the Word was made flesh, and dwelt among us, (and we beheld his glory, the glory as of the only begotten of the Father,) full of grace and truth" [John 1:14]. Jesus lived on earth as a man, experienced life in the flesh of a man, but without sin. Jesus fulfilled His mission at Calvary, reconciling God and man by His sacrifice: "Behold the Lamb of God, which taketh away the sin of the world" [John 1:29]. Through His death, burial, and resurrection, man was given the hope and gift of eternal life.

Because of the birth of Jesus, we can have a new birth, not a flesh birth, but a spiritual birth in Him. Jesus said "Ye must be born again" [John 3:7]. Our spirit is reborn, made alive in Him, and we become a new creature, a new spiritual man that never existed before [2 Cor 5:17]. As a new man in His image, we can share the love of Christ, the ministry and works of Jesus, and the gospel to the world. Other men can then become new creations, born again to everlasting life in Him. So rejoice this Christmas for the birth of Jesus Christ. Rejoice for the new birth we have in Him, and let His Light shine forth from us that all men can be translated out of darkness into His marvelous Light [1 Peter 2:9].

Prayer:
Lord, we celebrate and thank You for the birth of Jesus Christ our Savior and Lord. We thank You for the new birth He gives to us: that we might be born of His Spirit, and that we might be witnesses of His redemption to the world.

Scripture of the Day:
"Now the birth of Jesus Christ was on this wise: When as his mother Mary was espoused to Joseph, before they came together, she was found with child of the Holy Ghost." - [Matthew 1:18]

The Word for the Day is "Wonderful"

Quote for the Day:
"What a wonderful story it is, the Christmas story. Only God could have thought of it." – Norman Vincent Peale

Christmas is a wonderful season and a wonderful day. Most of us can almost hear the words of the song "The Most Wonderful Time of the Year" when we even think about it. And for most of us, Christmas is a glorious time of year—a time for giving, a time for sharing, a time for gathering with friends and family, and a time for celebrating the birth of Jesus.

In thinking about the Christmas story, we often forget to acknowledge that the Lord was a highly creative author in formulating it. He created every aspect of it, even threading anticipation for it far ahead of the actual event. Through God's hand and anointing, and by the Holy Spirit, righteous men of old penned the words and story, with Jesus the main character, the author and finisher of our faith [2 Tim 3:16-17: 2 Pet 1:20-21; Heb 12:2]. And what a wonderful story it is. God could have orchestrated the events of Jesus' birth in any way of His choosing but, as typical for God's miraculous ways, the Christmas story has a plotline full of rich characters, suspense, conflict, memorable settings, with splashes of miracles throughout. It's no wonder, like the old hymn says, that 'we love to tell the story.' Like all the best classic stories of all times, the Christmas story reaches and touches all audiences, all ages, and has endured and been loved for over two thousand years. Whatever God does always lasts and endures, and when God writes a story it lives on forever and His Words don't pass away [Is 40:8; Matt 24:35].

What is our role to be at Christmas? Certainly not the role of Scrooge—stingy, unloving, and ungrateful. At Christmas, we should be an expression of God's love in every way. Dale Evans wrote: "Christmas, my child, is love in action. Every time we love, every time we give, it's Christmas."

Prayer:
Blessed Lord, because You loved us and sent Your Son, we can love with Your love not only at Christmas but everyday. Thank you for that greatest gift of all.

Scripture of the Day:
"For unto us a child is born, unto us a son is given: and the government shall be upon his shoulder: and his name shall be called Wonderful, Counsellor, The mighty God, The everlasting Father, The Prince of Peace." – [Isaiah 9:6]

The Word for the Day is "Greater."

Quote for the Day:
"There is no power in the world today greater than the power of the Holy Spirit, and when the blood of Christ and the Holy Ghost are linked together, we have an energy that nothing can stop." - Kathryn Kuhlman

God is greater than we often realize or know. We can fail to comprehend the excellent and unsearchable greatness of His power and fail to praise Him for His mighty acts [Psalm 66:3, 145:3, 150:2]. Psalm 77:13 asks: "who is so great a God as our God?" God is above all: "For of him, and through him, and to him, are all things: to whom be glory for ever" [Rom 11:36]. I think God would have us come to a greater revelation of His power and might.

As awesome and inconceiveable to realize as it is, God has transferred that greatness to us through Jesus. Man was made in the image of God [Gen 1:26], and through Jesus was restored to that rightful place in Him and even more. We were given a better convenant established upon better promises [Heb 8:6]. Through the blood of Jesus we have obtained an eternal redemption [Heb 9:12]. We have been given the keys of the kingdom of heaven, become sons of God and joint-heirs in Jesus [Matt 16:19; 1 John 3:2; Rom 8:17]. God would have us come to the truth of this and so much more that we are and have in Jesus.

The Lord wants to increase you more and more [Psalm 115:14]. More and more means greater, not less. Knowing who we are in the Lord helps us to walk in all God has provided and made available to us. Why should we walk in less when God has provided a greater power and ability for us, a greater estate, a greater blessing for living and ministry in this world? There are too many to list here, but just a few of the realities of the exceeding greatness of His power to us-ward who believe: we can do all things through Christ who strengthens us; God always causeth us to triumph in Christ; we shall do the works of Jesus and greater works if we believe on Him [Phil 4:13; 2 Cor 2:14; John 14:12]. "Thou shalt increase my greatness, and comfort me on every side" [Psalm 71:21]. Let us show the world a greater God that men might believe and be saved.

Prayer:
Lord, we will increase in You more and more that we might be more equipped to show and minister God's love and power to the world in a greater way.

Scripture of the Day:
"Ye are of God, little children, and have overcome them: because greater is He that is in you, than he that is in the world." - [1 John 4:4]

The Word for the Day is "Frankincense."

Quote of the Day:
"Then they opened their treasure chests and gave Him gifts of gold, frankincense, and myrrh." – Gary Chapman

After Jesus' birth the kings and wise men came bringing gifts. "Now when Jesus was born in Bethlehem of Judaea…behold there came wise men from the east… and when they came into the house, they saw the young child with Mary his mother, and fell down and worshipped him: and when they had opened their treasures, they presented unto him gifts: gold, frankincense, and myrrh" [Matthew 2:1-11]. Most of us wonder a little about these gift choices, but all were standard gifts to honor a king or diety in the ancient world. And all prized.

Frankincense was one of the consecrated incenses described in the Old Testament and used with offerings to God. It is a resin tapped from *Boswalia sacre* trees by slashing the bark and allowing the resin to bleed out and harden. The hardened resin looks kind of like gold rocks. It was used to create a high quality incense and in Exodus is described as a holy anointing oil. 'Take unto thee sweet spices…with pure frankincense…and make a perfume, a confection after the art of the apothecary…pure and holy…and put it…in the tabernacle where I will meet with thee' [Exodus 30:22-38].

Myrrh was less expensive than frankincense but also highly valued as a perfume and anointing oil, often used in burial. It is suggested myrrh represented Jesus' death to come, gold Jesus' kingship, and frankincense Jesus' willingness to become a sacrifice. All were highly valuable gifts brought to Jesus. Some sources have valued the offerings combined at more than a half million dollars, a vast amount in ancient times. In many places in the Word, the praises we offer to God are noted as incense or perfume to God, holy and pure. "Let my prayer be set forth before Thee as incense; and the lifting of my hands as the evening sacrifice" [Psalm 141:2]. "By him therefore let us offer the sacrifice of praise to God continually…giving thanks to His name" [Hebrews 13:15]. Perhaps throughout the Christmas season we can offer our own type of frankincense, as the wise men did, by remembering to praise and thank God for the gift of Jesus.

Prayer:
Lord, may we be wise and offer our gifts of praise to you for all you've done.

Scripture of the Day:
"Saw ye him whom my soul loveth?…[He is] perfumed with myrrh and frankincense." - [Song of Solomon 3:3,6].

The Word for the Day is "Neglect."

Quote for the Day:
"Surely no sharper grief can be inflicted upon the Spirit of God than when we leave His gifts neglected and unappropriated." - Alexander MacLaren

A few days have passed since the Christmas holiday, and with the house quiet again, we reflect upon the special joys of this time. We thank and praise God for the most important thing, the gift of His Son Jesus to the world. We thank God for the warm fellowship with family and friends, the talk, the food, and the opening of gifts! Everyone loves to receive gifts, and to delight others by giving gifts. What makes a gift so special? I think it is the uniqueness of the nature of gifts. A gift is not necessarily earned, but is given out of the motive of love by the giver. A gift does not need payment, the giver has already paid for it—it's free! There are only two responses to a free gift: we can accept the gift, or we can reject it.

Why do men neglect or reject God's free gift of salvation in Jesus? They may not even know that a free gift is being offered to them. We know we are saved by grace through faith [Ephesians 2:8], and we know that faith cannot come without hearing the Word of God [Romans 10:17]. So a man must hear the good news of the gospel to even know the gift of salvation is offered by God. Someone needs to be a "preacher" to share the good news: "How then shall they call on him in whom they have not believed? and how shall they believe in him of whom they have not heard? and how shall they hear without a preacher? And how shall they preach, except they be sent, as it is written, How beautiful are the feet of them that preach the gospel of peace, and bring glad tidings of good things!" [Romans 10:14-15]. Of course the Word can fall on hardened hearts that have not the love of the Truth, and although Light has come into the world, they love darkness (sin) more than Light [John 3:19].

God has given us many gifts according to the Word, and we should study the scriptures to learn all the free gifts that are ours by faith. "Every good gift and every perfect gift is from above" [James 1:17], so let us accept and not neglect all the gifts of God and then share the glad tidings of good things with others.

Prayer:
Lord, help us receive all the gifts of God with grace and thanksgiving; not neglecting, but stirring them up that we might be a spiritual gift and a gifter unto others.

Scripture for the Day:
"How shall we escape, if we neglect so great salvation; which at the first began to be spoken by the Lord, and was confirmed unto us by them that heard it." - [Hebrews 2:3]

The Word for the Day is "Wondrous."

Quote for the Day:
"Grace wondrous grace. By the grace of God I am what I am. Yet not I, but the Grace of God which was with me." – Martyn Lloyd-Jones, Welsh minister

The holiday season is filled with wonder, and even when Christmas is past we still think back on it often. Like the scripture in Job 37:14, 'we should often stand still and consider the wondrous works of God.' We should keep our hearts and eyes open to see the wonder of God around us every day, not just at the holidays. Whatever is beautiful, whatever is good that we see, God made it all. "In the beginning…all things were made by him; and without him was not any thing made that was made" [John 1:1-3].

God can do wondrous things not only in the earth, in nature and all we see, but through His people. "The Bible is full of ordinary people who went to impossible places and did wondrous things simply because they decided to obey God" [Andrew van der Bijl]. Noah was enabled to build an ark because he believed [Gen 6:13-22], Mary was enabled to be the mother of Jesus because she believed [Luke 1:38], and Peter walked on water because he believed he could [Matt 14:28]. So often we can all do more than we might imagine through the Lord. Nothing is really ever impossible to God [Luke 1:37-38].

As you clean up from the holiday season, take down the Christmas tree and the decorations around the house, and put away your gifts, don't let the wonder of the holidays escape you. Keep in your heart the remembrance and blessing of all God did bringing Jesus into the world and the difference that made in who you are and who you can be through Him. Understand your life is wondrous, rare, and precious. Know that your life is a wonder, your salvation a wonder, and what God can do in your life is a wonder, if you will believe. In reality, all that we are belongs to Him; our time and our days are His. If we will give the time to seek God and His Will and be open for Him to use us, we will see the wondrous happen in our lives as God works in and through us.

Prayer:
Lord, help us to always see the wonder Your Hands can bring and to take a leap of faith in this New Year to believe that the wondrous can happen in our lives.

Scripture of the Day:
"Blessed be the Lord God, the God of Israel who only doeth wondrous things, and blessed be his glorious name for ever." - [Psalm 72:18-19]

The Word for the Day is "Adam."

Quote for the Day:
"A sin consciousness identifies with Adam. A righteousness consciousness identifies with Jesus." - Kenneth Copeland

We know that God created man in His own image. And the Lord placed the man in a garden eastward in Eden. God fellowshipped and walked with Adam in the garden, and it was paradise on earth for man. But Adam then messed it all up when he disobeyed the Lord, and sin and death entered the world: "Wherefore, as by one man sin entered into the world, and death by sin; and so death passed upon all men, for that all have sinned" [Rom 5:12]. This is why the quote above equates sin consciousness with the first Adam. But God had a plan to restore man's estate with Him by salvation in His Son, Jesus Christ.

As the old year passes and a new year begins in a few days, God wants us to put off the old man and live in the newness of life we have in the Lord Jesus [Rom 6:4]. We may have hurts or needs from the past, but we can thank God for all the good blessings ahead. God wants us to focus on the new man we are in Jesus and on our benefits and rights in Him. In the New Testament, we're reminded that Jesus, the last Adam, was made a quickening spirit, a life-giving spirit. We need to remind ourselves of this new life we have been given. The free gift of grace unto justification has come by one, Jesus Christ [Rom 5:15-16]. We are made righteous in Christ Jesus and by Him we shall reign in life [Rom 5:17]. Let us dwell on our spiritual reality in Jesus, not the earthy nature of the first Adam, remembering that Jesus came to give us life, and that more abundantly [John 10:10]. Resolve to rule and reign in life with Jesus from this day on.

In Jesus, you have rights and benefits from heaven. We have exceeding great and precious promises that by these we might be partakers of the divine nature, on this earth now [2 Pet 1:4]. Jesus has promised to supply all our needs, and He wishes above all that we prosper and be in health [Phil 4:19; 3 John 2]. Find the promise you need in the Word of God, stand in faith, and receive your triumph in Jesus: "For we are unto God a sweet savour of Christ, in them that are saved, and in them that perish" [2 Cor 2:14-15].

Prayer:
Lord, we thank You that we have been made a new righteous man in Jesus, putting off the old flesh nature and walking in the Spirit that we might glorify You.

Scripture of the Day:
"And so it is written, The first man Adam was made a living soul; the last Adam was made a quickening spirit." - [1 Corinthians 15:45]

The Word for the Day is "Zeal."

Quote for the Day:
" No one can be a good Christian who does not with holy zeal set out to know, delight in, and live by the Word of God." – John R. Rice

I hope if you take one word with you into the New Year to come that it is "zeal." I pray you will be more zealous for a deeper relationship and walk with God, that you will eagerly want to spend more time every day in the Bible, learning about God, His promises, His ways, than ever before. I hope you will zealously seek to know your full purpose in God, to learn to hear His voice and to follow in His leading with all your heart and mind and soul [Matt 22:37]. Passionate, zealous people are world changers and I pray your life will change the world you are in and the people you impact.

C. S. Lewis once wrote: "The only thing Christianity cannot be is moderately important." A mediocre, stagnant, middle-of-the-road, going along faith is almost worse than no faith at all, and God is not pleased with a lukewarm faith. He said clearly: "So then because thou art lukewarm, and neither cold nor hot, I will spue thee out of my mouth" [Rev 3:16]. The first place you go to increase your faith is into the Word of God, not with a chapter or two here or there or by reading a few verses for your Sunday School class, but by spending deep quality, disciplined time in the Word, in God's presence, and in prayer [Col 3:2-17]. What we focus on and study zealously changes us and comes out in our lives.

You should want the 'zeal and passion and knowledge of the Lord to consume you and burn in you like a fire' [Psalm 69:9]. Only the passionate in this world really influence anyone. "Passion gives you an advantage over others, because one person with passion is greater than ninety-nine who have only an interest" [John C. Maxwell]. Passionate people are extraordinary rather than ordinary, zealous versus lukewarm. If you're not excited and zealous in your faith, the problem is not with God, or your church, it's with you. You are responsible to be zealous in your faith and love for God [Rom 12:11]. If you're not on fire for God, re-fire yourself this year. "Your soul is too important to let it die on the vine" [Allen Webster].

Prayer:
Lord, help me to be passionate and zealous in my faith in this coming year and to walk closer to You every day, pleasing You with my life.

Scripture of the Day:
"For I know the forwardness [eagerness] of your mind, for which I boast of you …and your zeal hath provoked [inspired] very many." - [2 Corinthians 9:2]

Books by J.L. and Lin Stepp

The Afternoon Hiker
Discovering Tennessee State Parks
Exploring South Carolina State Parks
Coming next – Visiting North Carolina State Parks
Traveling Georgia State Parks

Books by Lin Stepp

The Smoky Mountain Series

The Foster Girls	*Tell Me About Orchard Hollow*
For Six Good Reasons	*Delia's Place*
Second Hand Rose	*Down by the River*
Makin' Miracles	*Saving Laurel Springs*
Welcome Back	*Daddy's Girl*
Lost Inheritance	*The Interlude*

The Mountain Home Books
Happy Valley
Downsizing
Eight at the Lake
Coming next – Seeking Ayita
Shop on the Corner

Christmas Novella
A Smoky Mountain Gift
In When the Snow Falls

The Edisto Trilogy
Claire at Edisto
Return to Edisto
Edisto Song

The Lighthouse Sisters Series
Light the Way
Coming next –
Lighten My Heart
Light in the Dark
The Light Continues

AUTHOR BIOS

J.L. Author Bio:

J.L. Stepp is the best-selling co-author with his wife Lin Stepp of three regional guidebooks, *The Afternoon Hiker, Discovering Tennessee State Parks*, and *Exploring South Carolina State Parks. The Afternoon Hiker* features 110 Smoky Mountain trails descriptions and over 300 color photos. The guidebook *Discovering Tennessee State Parks*, a 2019 American Book Fest Best Books Award Finalist in Nonfiction: Travel Guides and Essays, offers directions to and descriptions of all 56 of Tennessee's state parks along with over 700 color photos. And the new *Exploring South Carolina State Parks* guide is designed similarly to give descriptions of all South Carolina's parks, accompanied by rich color photos throughout as well. A native East Tennessean, Stepp owns S & S Communications, established in 1990, which published a monthly outdoor magazine called *Tennessee Fishing & Hunting Guide* and handled a UT sports sales line for over thirty years. A graduate of The University of Tennessee, Stepp's background includes over fifty years in sales, marketing, management, and publications. He enjoys a wide variety of outdoor sports, including golf, fishing, and hiking. Due to the popularity of the Tennessee state parks book, Stepp and his wife are currently working on a new regional guidebook of North Carolina state parks.

Lin Author Bio:

Lin Stepp is a native Tennessean, businesswoman and educator. *A New York Times, USA Today, Publishers Weekly*, and Amazon best-selling international author, Lin has twenty published novels, including her twelve beloved Smoky Mountain novels, all set in different Tennessee and North Carolina locations, her three Mountain Home books, a novella in one of Kensington's Christmas anthologies, and four South Carolina coastal novels, including her three Edisto Trilogy books and her first release in the new Lighthouse Sisters series. Lin and her husband J.L. also write regional guidebooks, including a Smoky Mountain hiking guide, and both a TN and a SC state parks guidebook. Stepp's latest 2022 releases are *Eight at the Lake*, set in Dandridge near the Smoky Mountains, and *Light the Way*, set at the SC coast. Lin's title *Claire At Edisto* was the 2019 Best Books Award Winner in Fiction: Romance, sponsored by American Book Fest, her novel *Welcome Back* a finalist in the 2017 Selah Awards. Lin enjoys speaking for events, festivals, libraries, and book clubs, reading, hiking, exploring out of doors, and keeping up with her readers on Facebook, Twitter, and through her monthly blog and newsletter which you will find on her website at: www.linstepp.com